PRAISE FOR LIVING DANGEROUSLY

"Transparently and vulnerably Rabbi Katsof catalogues struggles with a damaging financial obsession. Finding and embracing an integrated balance between career, family, and spirituality lead to important insights in his account. Whether Jewish or Christian, we can benefit from this portrait of the pursuit of being God-oriented in the face of our modern materialistic society."

John Ashcroft,
former US Attorney General

"I have known Irwin Katsof through his original rabbinical life and through our tour together to Israel to celebrate its 50th anniversary, and this book is from his heart and expresses his life's journey as he searches what is important for happiness and fulfillment. It has lessons we can all learn from, take it from me!"

Ken Goldman,
former CFO of Yahoo.com

"In a dog-eat-dog world, which is fueled by insatiably capitalistic appetites, my friend Rabbi Katsof offers some humbling insight on how to discover one's inner peace. In this book, he shares his personal imperfections to help enlighten the reader on the things that hold true value in life beyond the monetary. Rabbi Katsof's 'humility over hubris' approach to unpacking his unique perspectives on how to balance matters of the mind along with matters of the heart is to be enjoyed, studied, and applauded for generations to come."

Omar Epps,
actor, rapper and producer; co-star of the TV dramas House MD
and ER; winner of nine NAACP Image Awards

"With his fourth book, Rabbi Katsof hits a home run. It is a very honest – and entertaining – account of the failures and successes of his fascinating life. In addition, it is full of great business insights and wisdom for living. A meaningful and enjoyable read."

Howard Jonas,
telecom entrepreneur; founder of IDT Corp. and Genie Energy;
author of I'm Not the Boss, I Just Work Here

"Irwin Katsof brings to this compelling memoir his rich experience as a rabbi, his broad knowledge of the business and investment banking world, and his profound struggle to keep a balance between work, family and religion. He draws the reader into his stories with the art of a master story-teller."

Gregory D. Brenneman,
chairman of CCMP Capital; former president and
CEO of Continental Airlines

"In *Living Dangerously*, Irwin Katsof lays bare his soul to reveal a remarkable compassion for humanity, the importance of charity, and the journey we all must take if we are to successfully balance our professional and personal lives. As an Evangelical Christian, I'm one Southern Baptist who has been deeply blessed by this Torah-observant Jew's wisdom and common sense – especially Irwin's reminder that all of us are called upon to do God's will here on earth."

Tom Tradup,
vice-president of Salem Radio Network

"As he moves from materialism to spiritualism, from a self-absorbed human being to a giving one, Rabbi Irwin Katsof captures the very essence of the ever-present conflicts we all face, and does so in the most exposed and touching manner ... A book of life lessons culminating in what we should all cherish most. Truly a captivating memoir which I have thoroughly enjoyed."

Ayelet Torem,
CEO of APMakers Innovative Capital

"Remarkably moving and instructive story of life, business, growth, spirituality and family."

Mario Lopez,
host of the entertainment news magazine shows
Extra *and* Access Hollywood

"An uplifting read for anyone who wants to learn about how to balance work, family and spirituality."

Mark Schulman,
producer and manager of 3 Arts Entertainment

"Any book in which the author dares to reveal the 'good, bad and ugly' of their life experiences is definitely worth reading. This type of honesty, integrity and vulnerability is exactly what the world needs now more than ever. This book contains just that!"

Dr. David Berceli,
founder of Trauma Recovery Services and TRE For All,
author of Shake It Off Naturally

"Irwin Katsof brings to this compelling memoir his rich experience as a rabbi, his broad knowledge of the business and investment banking world, and his profound struggle to keep a balance between work, family and religion. He draws the reader into his stories with the art of a master story-teller."

Ileana Ros-Lehtinen,
former chairwoman of the House Foreign Affairs Committee and
former member of the US House of Representatives (R-Florida)

"Every chapter contains an insight into life, a lesson on relationships, or common-sense wisdom for the aspiring entrepreneur. This book is a worthwhile read for any executive battling away in today's cut-throat, eat-or-be-eaten environment and trying to stay sane in an insane world."

Doron Cohen,
chairman of Dun & Bradstreet Israel and Latin America

"This heartfelt memoir offers insightful lessons for anyone who is struggling to reconcile their professional life with their values."

David M. Schizer,
dean emeritus of Columbia Law School and author of
How to Save the World in Six (Not So Easy) Steps

"*Living Dangerously* is about the author's struggle to balance work, family and community. He demonstrates that striving for riches is meaningless without making enough time for family and giving back through charity and community engagement."

Bob Diener, president of Travel Funders Network, founder of Hotels.com, and author of The Savvy Traveler *and* Biblical Secrets to Business Success

"This book offers valuable insights into life, imparts valuable lessons on building relationships and provides essential wisdom for aspiring entrepreneurs. It is a must-read for executives navigating the competitive and unforgiving modern business landscape while striving to maintain balance in an increasingly chaotic world."

Michael Serruya, managing director of Serruya Private Equity and founder of Yogen Früz

"The stories related in this book are both touching and powerful. They help us realize that within each of us lies the wisdom and truth to ultimately come back to our deepest core. No matter how lost we might each feel at times, this book aptly demonstrates that there is always hope to return to our true self."

Mark Minevich, UN advisor, co-chair of AI for Global Alliance, and president of Going Global Ventures

"I read Rabbi Irwin's book with admiration because of his honesty, bravery and ability to self-reflect without the stops, biases and deflections most people take advantage of. Rabbi Irwin's journey and clear understanding of his and his family's needs, and the price that comes with pursuing his goals – while at the end not losing his soul, no matter the temptations – is a lesson to all of us."

Tsvi Gal, director of tech services at Memorial Sloan Kettering Cancer Center

"This is a very rare business book – honest and from the heart. Unlike most business books by successful entrepreneurs (which glorify the CEO and leave out the pain), this brutally honest book tells about the failures, the stresses, the lost time with family, the heartache and the moral questions involved in starting a new business. It gives a deeply personal account of Irwin's struggles to achieve business success – without destroying his health, his sanity, his family or his soul. We all need to read this."

Richard Steffens,
former Acting Deputy Assistant Secretary for Asia,
US Department of Commerce, and author of
Secrets of a Venture Capitalist

"This is a gem of a book. Very readable and full of wisdom and practical guidance for how to live a meaningful life. I highly recommend it."

Bill Owens,
40th Governor of Colorado and senior fellow at the
University of Denver's Institute for Public Policy Studies

"Living Dangerously is a journey which so many experience in varying degrees. Irwin brings the key to success home: 'Less is More.' Once understood, everything is possible!"

Dr. Peter Kash,
author of the international bestseller Make Your Own Luck

"*Living Dangerously* relates Irwin Katsof's journey from once devout rabbi to entrepreneur at the highest levels of business and the challenges involved in preserving his soul. Having traveled widely with Irwin, I find that his refreshing candor comes as no surprise. This fast-reading book captures his abject failures and dazzling successes, and provides readers with unforgettable lessons in life that transcend Wall Street."

Joe Reeder,
14th Undersecretary of the US Army

"When I need gas, I drive to a service station and fill up my tank. When I need wisdom, I go to Irwin Katsof and fill up my soul. Since we met in 1985, he has always been a beacon of hope and clarity for me. Read his ageless words and he'll do the same for you."

Mark Schiff,
stand-up comedian and author of
Why Not? Lessons on Comedy, Courage, and Chutzpah

"This is the best book ever! It brilliantly provides outstanding insights into the world of business and high finance and offers invaluable advice on how to lead a meaningful and truly fulfilling life! A must-read! You're in the hands of a master!'

Morty Davis,
chairman of D.H. Blair Investment Banking Corp. and author of
Happiness Guaranteed *and* From Knocks to Hot Stocks

"A beautiful read. Insightful. Provocative. Essential reading for every executive trying to balance work and family and soul. I will use it as a guidebook on how to live a fulfilling life."

Yitz Applbaum,
founding partner of MizMaa Ventures

"Anyone who knows Irwin Katsof knows that he achieves anything he sets his mind to. His memoir, *Living Dangerously: My Struggle to Get Rich Without Losing My Soul*, is a testament to that. This book, full of wisdom, reads like a thriller."

Armando Lucas Correa,
journalist and writer, author of the international bestseller
The German Girl

"Irwin has one of the most unique backgrounds of anyone I know, and so I value his insights on life and personal values tremendously."

Eric R. L. Fleiss,
managing director and CEO of Regent Properties Inc.

"*Living Dangerously: My Struggle to Get Rich without Losing My Soul* is a powerful and honest account of Rabbi Irwin Gabriel Katsof's journey to find success and meaning in life. As someone who has experienced the highs and lows of life, I can attest to the importance of this message. Rabbi Katsof's story is a testament to the fact that you can be successful and true to yourself, and that there is hope and salvation for those who feel lost. This book is a must-read for anyone looking to find meaning and joy in life."

Reverend Samuel Rodriguez Jr.,
president of National Hispanic Christian Leadership Conference

LIVING
DANGEROUSLY

My Struggle to Get **Rich**
Without Losing My **Soul**

IRWIN GABRIEL KATSOF

Prepared for press by:
Estie@EDPressSolutions.com

ISBN: 979-1-957-4661546615-6

For information, comments, or questions:
irwin@katsof.com

Distributed by:
BeverlyHousePress.com

Printed in United States of America

This book is dedicated to my family.
It took me a long time to come to the realization
that they are what I most value and cherish in my life:
my beautiful, loyal and smart wife, Judy,
all of my absolutely amazing children –
Batya, Aaron Yosef, Yaakov, Simcha, Bracha,
Sholom, Sara, Ilana –
and their special spouses,
and my twenty-five amazing grandchildren
who never cease to give me pleasure.
I thank God every day for blessing me
with such a special family.

Contents

Introduction:
The Worst of Times,
The Best of Times

JUNE 26, 2008 – THE WORST OF TIMES

As I make cold calls trying to raise $5 million in equity in order to close a $40 million real estate deal in Odessa, I feel a wave of anxiety settle over me. Gloom. Fear. Worry. Darkness. I am sinking into despair. For some reason I don't know what to do at this moment. I should be calling individuals who could invest $50,000 or $100,000 – and I have a list of many – but I need to find the whole $5 million in ten days, and to raise that much from small investors involves making too many calls and soliciting too many people than I can handle at the moment.

The "what ifs" are strangling me. What if this happens ... what if that happens ... what if the deal falls apart at the last minute?

I can't remember when I ever felt like this – sure, I've had anxiety attacks before, but they never immobilized me. This time I just can't function. I lie down and, mercifully, sleep overtakes me. I manage to sleep for two hours only to wake up to that feeling of dread again.

My wife Judy has rarely seen me take an afternoon nap. She's rarely seen me looking depressed and certainly never this depressed. Worried, she asks me, "What's wrong?" but I can barely answer her. Also, I do not want to share with her my fears and worries. She has already put up with too much – my constant absences in pursuit of another deal in some corner of the globe, my neglect of my family even while at home, where I am inevitably chained to my cellphone, firing off texts, setting up meetings, talking about nothing but money. How long before it becomes too much to her and she demands a divorce?

To allay her concerns, I pretend to act normal and go into the kitchen for a snack, where my kids are unwinding after a day in school. But it is difficult for me to interact with others at this moment. I am on the edge of losing balance. Each sentence spoken to me feels like a nail grating on a chalk board. I am ready to erupt, and it takes all my willpower not to. I want to drink myself into oblivion, just so that I will not feel this way, but I am not much of a drinker, and I know that I will feel sick the next day.

Without an outlet, I am at my wits' end. And now the anxiety mushrooms into a full-blown panic attack. I just know something is sure to go wrong, because it inevitably does.

JULY 26, 2023 – THE BEST OF TIMES

When I wake up at 5:30 AM, my instinct is to jump immediately out of bed. There is a strong voice inside of me urging me to start my day as I once used to do. I listen to its barking: "Get up! Get going! You have things to do!" But I have learned to distance myself from such inner voices. I do not need to listen to them, even though they can be quite loud and demanding.

This is a benefit of my mindfulness meditation practice. I simply tell myself that the "old me" would have jumped out of bed and started paddling away on that hamster wheel, but the "new me" needs a little more rest today. There will always be things to do, and I don't doubt that even on my death bed I will be thinking of my to-do list.

At around 6:30 AM I get out of bed and suit up for my morning run. I used to exercise out of a frantic need to look good. Now, at 68, I exercise out of a desire to live a long and healthy life with my cognitive faculties intact and with as much flexibility and strength as possible. And I am no longer compulsive about my exercise regimen; if I am tired, I take it easy that day. But, most of the time, my four-mile morning run leaves me feeling energized and I love that feeling, so that is usually enough incentive to get me going.

As I run, I listen to the birds chirping and feel connected to nature and the beautiful world that God has created. I feel so blessed and so fortunate.

Afterwards, I recite my morning prayers. I am still at a point, after the ten years of frenetic business activities and so many disappointments, where this is one of the harder things for me to do. I find it difficult to get meaning out of these ancient words, but I want to recite them nonetheless.

Then I sit in quiet meditation for a half hour, just watching my thoughts float in and out of my consciousness, continually bringing my focus of attention back to my breath. This, too, is difficult to do. I find myself day-dreaming often and thinking of other things than my breath, but all the research is clear that a regular session of meditation leads to a longer healthier life, so even though it is not that enjoyable while I do it, I know it is good for me. A year ago, I could not have imagined that I would sit even for five minutes like this, let alone for a half hour, just observing my mind and my breath.

I then take a few minutes to write in my journal and count my blessings:

o   I am healthy.
o   I have a beautiful, smart, loyal wife and I love her very much.
o   I have eight wonderful children who give me so much pleasure.

- o I have twenty-five gorgeous grandchildren who constantly amaze me.
- o I have close friends.
- o I have a job that I enjoy.
- o I have a decent income and can pay my bills.
- o I have some savings in the bank for the first time in my life.
- o I am growing and changing and learning about myself.

I am thankful to God for all these blessings, and I am also thankful for the teachings of Rabbi Dr. Jonathan Sacks, the former Chief Rabbi of the British Commonwealth, who passed away recently after a prolific career. I find his writings to be very inspirational and uplifting, and I make a point to study them every day. He connects me to my soul and to the pleasure I take in my Jewish roots and Jewish practice. While I pursued deal after deal, it had been difficult for me to feel connected to Jewish teachings. And in this regard, I was not a good role model for my children; I rarely had Torah insights to share with them at the Shabbat table. But Rabbi Sacks has given me a way back in.

Afterwards, I play my flute for a few minutes. I find it usually connects me to my soul. I play my own compositions which reflect how I feel at that moment. Today, the tune speaks of the joy of being alive.

I then go down to the kitchen and have a cup of coffee with my wife Judy. This is our time to check in. I love sitting and chatting with her, gazing out at our garden, now in full bloom. Then we go out for breakfast. Our daughter Sara, who lives nearby, has introduced us to several funky, counter-culture restaurants, which we really enjoy. We just sit there together and talk – sharing things about the kids, the grandkids, about our lives, about our emotional states.

If it appears that it takes me a long time before I start work in the morning, that is absolutely true. Almost every day I take the first two hours of the morning and use them for me and my physical and spiritual health. Not for work, not to advance in business, but to connect with my inner world, my soul. And to connect with my wife.

Today, another task beckons before the workday will begin. Sara had asked me if I could take her two-year-old toddler, Mia, to nursery school. A year ago, I could not have imagined myself doing anything like that. Today, I consider it one of my greatest pleasures. When I open the door, little Mia leaps up with a huge smile on her face and runs into my arms. I think if I were to die right now, it would be perfectly okay. The utter joy I feel seeing this little person recognize me and run to me is simply beyond words. My heart just opens totally. And the feeling of gratitude to God for this moment overwhelms me.

WHY I WROTE THIS BOOK

This is the story of my worst of times and my best of times. Of how – after working for many years as a fundraiser for a non-profit organization – I embarked on a quest to become rich, so that (as I told myself) I could become a major philanthropist giving away money instead of asking for it. For ten years I lived as a tortured, compulsive, driven human being and woe to anyone who got in my way. That was me at my worst. But then, at my lowest ebb, by the grace of God, I discovered the best of myself.

In these pages, I have elected to be brutally honest, to lay bare my worst self in order to prove to all those who feel the way I once did that there is a way out. There is hope. There is salvation. You can be successful and you can be true to yourself. You can do a good day's work, and still have time to love your family and be present for your children. You can step off the treadmill and not regret it. You can find meaning and joy in life. I know you can, because I did.

The Wall Street Test

After twenty-two years of getting a bi-weekly paycheck working as a rabbi and fundraiser for Jewish education, I decided to strike out on my own – to make money instead of asking for money.

I have to admit that the people I moved among – the people whom I approached as potential donors and who were among the richest people on the planet – influenced me. Everyone was a multi-millionaire, everyone was a self-starter. These people were not heirs or blue bloods. They had made it on brains and guts. I had brains and guts, couldn't I make it just like them?

By the time I decided to go for it – this was in 2004 – I had a $30,000-a-month family overhead (utilities, taxes, insurance, two cars, five kids still at home to feed and clothe, plus three married kids with three grandkids to support in various ways), and I'd need another $15,000-a-month to cover office overhead (rent, equipment, secretary, etc.). Since I had no savings to speak of, I took out a loan against the market-inflated value of my house (the bank called it a home-equity line of credit) for $460,000. I figured I could live for almost a year on that before having to bring in any revenue.

It was a big risk, and it scared me. I was living on the edge but, in many ways, I had always lived on the edge. I am a junkie for excitement and tense situations; it makes me feel alive. (Some grist for a shrink here.) Why did I always have to push the envelope? Why was

I living such a precarious life? Why couldn't I be happy with a regular 9-to-5 job like everyone else? I did not know the answers to these questions.

What I did know was that there was big money to be made out there, and it was the guys on Wall Street who were making it. So that is where I needed to be if I wanted to rake in some of those big bucks.

Of course, I made it very clear to everyone I spoke to – and repeated it to myself – that I hadn't left the public sector to make a million dollars a year, but to be able to *give away* a million dollars a year. Even if I wasn't going to be working full-time on behalf of God, mom, apple pie and Jewish outreach, I still wanted to make a difference in the world. And I was dead serious about wanting to make enough to donate at least one million a year. As proof, I made a commitment to give away 20 percent of my net income. Torah law, which I live by, requires that 10 percent of one's net income be donated to charity, but those who have the means are encouraged to donate up to 20 percent. I intended to be one of those who had the means.

It was funny and kind of cute that suddenly my wife didn't know what I did for a living. Everywhere we went, people who knew I had left my previous employer, Aish HaTorah, would ask Judy: "What is Irwin doing?" And she would sheepishly say, "He is in investments now, but don't ask me what he actually does, because I have no idea." When we would get home she would say to me, "Can you please explain to me again exactly what is it that you do now?" I never did explain it to her, because I wasn't sure myself. I just knew that to make big money I had to be "an investment banker."

I got help from a friend of mine, Michael Vasinkavich, the senior managing director of Rodman & Renshaw, a 53-year-old investment bank which specialized in underwriting the biotech industry. Michael found me a small office near the storage closet in R&R's very posh digs next to Radio City Music Hall. He also gave me some pointers to get me started, and I immediately started in on some deals.

However, he warned me that the first thing I needed to do was to get a "Series 7" certification. To someone working with securities, the "Series 7" is like the driver's license to a teenager – you can't get behind the wheel without it. To get it, you must pass a grueling test. Only then are you allowed to get paid in the securities industry – and I did want to get paid.

I googled "Series 7" and found a whole host of outfits that promised to prepare me for the test. I ordered three different study guides (averaging $200 each). One would have sufficed, but I figured I should get several just in case one was better than the others. I was manic about it. I also ordered CDs with practice questions and DVDs with filmed lecturers, and even registered for a class in Manhattan. I figured the clock was ticking, and every month the home-equity line of credit was getting drawn down.

DEADLY BORING, MIND-NUMBING

I enjoy studying, but when the books, CDs and DVDs arrived and I took a look, I blanched. This was nothing I could sink my teeth into – it was going to be deadly boring at best and mind-numbing at worst. Consider topics such as: "The Securities Act of 1933," "Underwriting Equity Securities," "Issuing Exempt Securities," "Exchange Markets," "Basic Option Positions," "Annuities," etc.

The books recommended sticking to a study schedule and offered several options: a four-week study schedule of 25 hours per week; a five-week study schedule of 20 hours per week; an eight-week study schedule of 15 hours study per week, etc. None of those schedules fit my abilities. Looking at the chapter headings, it seemed to me I needed a 52-week study schedule of 40 hours per week.

Though I am no dummy and like to read, and though I did well in college and yeshiva, *this* was daunting.

At the outset, I tried reading the first two chapters many times over as a way of getting the material into my memory banks. It didn't work. I just couldn't seem to remember any of the details. Worse still, when I read over the "Options" chapter (which covered strategies and product knowledge), I couldn't even figure out what the words meant!

For the past twenty years I had read the *Wall Street Journal* regularly, and I had always enjoyed it. I also enjoyed sitting in the offices of my major donors listening to them talk deals and finance. I always thought I had a good grasp of what they were discussing, but now I felt totally out of my league. This was not going to be easy, to say the least.

After three months (I'm talking February-March-April 2006 here) of making literally no progress, I decided I needed a new strategy. I stopped going to work and committed to studying full time at home. I had to pass this test if I wanted to ever be able to get paid for the deals I already had in the works.

I spent the month of May working on the material from 5 AM to 11 PM. At least I sat at my desk and moved my eyes over the material during those hours. Very little was absorbed. I did make some headway, but it was minimal. I spaced out a lot. I went to the gym often to work off my frustration and to try to refresh my energy. At least my pecs were growing if not my knowledge. (Maybe I could become a trainer for Wall Streeters.)

The study guides came with sample tests; I took a few and averaged anywhere between 55 percent and 72 percent. A 70 percent was a pass, so I figured I wasn't that far off but, at this pace, I was going to run out of money before getting halfway through.

It was now the end of June, and I had abandoned my office at Rodman & Renshaw for a whole two months, so I decided I needed to resume going to work again, but I hired a car service to drive me from my home in Monsey, New York, into Manhattan so as not to waste time. I sat in the back seat with my mini-DVD player, watching classes on "Options" and "Municipal Bonds" as we sped along the Palisades Parkway. I might not yet be an investment banker, but I certainly felt like one in the back seat of a chauffeur-driven black town-car. I could certainly act the part, even if I still could hardly understand the difference between a short call and a long put!

THE TUTOR

At the same time, I decided to hire a private tutor, something my friend Dick Horowitz had recommended six months earlier. He said it was well worth the expense. I wish I had listened to him in the first place. The Talmudic sages in *Ethics of the Fathers* advise: "Who is a wise man? The man who learns from everyone." I needed to learn to listen to the advice of others, rather than thinking I could master all the answers myself. (My wife has been telling me this for years.)

The tutor – a woman used by Goldman, Sachs and Lehman who was billed as the best – charged $1,200 a day. Yikes! But something had to give. Dick had said that even if I spent $15,000-$25,000 on the tutor, it was an expense that was well worth it, especially when weighed against the value of my per hour earning potential. I arranged to meet her at my office at Rodman & Renshaw.

The first day she came she showed me all the short cuts and formulas I had been missing in my quest to master the material by myself. I was feeling jubilant. I could do this!

Now, ordinarily, none of the guys at Rodman & Renshaw ever ventured down my way unless they needed something from the storage closet. But a funny thing happened around the time that the tutor showed up. Suddenly, the guys discovered me. I felt so popular. It seemed like everyone was cheering me on and wishing me good luck in my studies. "Wow," I thought, "what a great bunch of fellows. They must really want me to get this done, so I can be a real investment banker and help them with their deals." I soon discovered the truth.

In my quest to master the material, I had never really looked at the tutor – a tall, statuesque beauty. I had been so focused on the material and so thrilled that she was able to open the previously closed doors of finance to me that I was somewhat oblivious to her sex appeal. Not the guys in the office. When I figured it out, I got ribbed plenty. Wall Street really was a long way from the world of the yeshiva. I had a lot to learn in more ways than one.

I continued to measure my progress by taking practice tests (with instant scoring and explanations) which I found online. For each chapter, I would take four tests, obsessively keeping track of my scores. On the first test for a given chapter, I usually scored below par but, after four tests, I usually clawed my way up to 80 percent.

I could now see that this was doable. And then my tutor suggested I take a *timed* test. The tests I had been taking allowed me to think as long as I wanted, and stop and read the explanation after each answer. But this was not how it would be on test day.

DRESS REHEARSAL

The dress rehearsal was an exact replica of the actual "Series 7" test of 350 questions which had to be completed in six hours. But I figured it would not be such a big deal – so far, I have done over 30 practice tests (albeit of only 150 questions) and was averaging 80 percent. I took my first timed test. Not only didn't I finish it in the allotted six hours, I received a score of only 52 percent.

I was devastated. It was a dark day for me. I couldn't talk to any-one. I saw my tutor the next day and declared myself hopeless. I was ready to give up. She said it was normal and not to be discour-aged. I had printed out the test, and we reviewed the mistakes I had made.

I went back home and over the next two weeks I only took timed practice tests until I learned how to pace myself. A big insight here is to learn to trust your initial judgment. You only have a minute or so for each question. Some of the questions are six to eight sen-tences long with formulas to comprehend as well, so after reading the question, you really only have 15 seconds to decide on the an-swer. The key is to trust that you know the answer and go with your first response. If you begin doubting yourself, you will never finish. After two weeks of doing these tests, I was back up to an average of 85 percent.

During this time, I was totally obsessed. If one of my children came into my room to chat with me, I patiently – and sometimes not so patiently – explained that I couldn't talk right now. My wife Judy got the same treatment, and she felt totally neglected. I was get-ting up at 5 AM and working on these tests until 11 PM, and then I would crawl into bed exhausted.

I didn't like the person I had turned into – one-track, single-mind-ed, one-dimensional: everything I had always found pathetic in the Wall Street types. When I was fundraising, I would sometimes ask my donors, "Are you living to eat or eating to live?" Or, "Do you know anyone who on their death bed had wished they had spent one more day at the office?" Or, "Is this the person you want to be re-membered as?" Now I was no different.

In hindsight, this should have been a huge red flag. It should have caused me to stop, reevaluate my plan and reset my goals. But I was too far gone for that.

When we spent a short vacation at my in-laws' beach house in Groton, Connecticut, everyone went boating while I sat on the porch doing more reading and watching DVDs. It created a great deal of tension in our family. Judy and the children felt completely abandoned, and I wasn't really open to talking about it. Judy tried to make me understand that no matter what I was involved in I couldn't just drop her and the family. This had been her recurrent complaint over our 24 years of marriage. I thought I had licked the problem, but Judy was now petrified that this obsession with the "Series 7" test was just the beginning of worse things to come. Since I wasn't open to hearing what she had to say, she suggested we go into counseling to help us work on this issue. I reluctantly agreed. It did help. I tried to create more balance. But I still kept saying, "Just wait until I pass the test and then we can go back to a normal life." Judy felt the test was no excuse, and if she allowed it to go unchecked, there would always be "something" that came before normal family life.

She was right. (She usually is.) Most men I know are driven to excel in all areas but the relationship with their wives and children. There are exceptions, but I don't know many. I was just much worse than most, and the pressure to pass the test had tapped into my neuroses and my drive to succeed. I couldn't imagine showing up at Rodman & Renshaw the day after the test if I had failed it. They let you take it twice after you flunked, but I just didn't think I could face the embarrassment if I flunked even once.

All this reminded me of the Talmudic maxim: "If only man would be as concerned about what God thinks as he is of his fellow's judgment." If only I could transfer this fear of embarrassment in the eyes of my fellow bankers to a fear of God's opinion of me, I'd be a saint!

JUDGMENT DAY

I woke up the morning of the test rested but tense. My tutor had strongly suggested that I *not* study the night before or the morning of the test. I either knew it by that point, or I didn't. There was really nothing more I could do.

I said my morning prayers and ate some breakfast. The phone rang. It was my daughter Batya calling to wish me good luck. I heard her voice and the gurgles of my granddaughter in the background, and I cracked. The tension and stress from the past months just over-whelmed me. I broke down in sobs. I went quickly to my bedroom, because I didn't want anyone to see me in this state.

And then the parallel hit me: Judgment Day!

This was what it would be like on the day of my death, when I arrived before the Almighty for my judgment. Then, too, there would be *nothing* more to do! I would have either done the right job in my life, or not. I would have either prepared adequately or not. The time of doing and preparing would be finished.

The Talmudic sages in *Ethics of the Fathers* say, "This world is like a corridor to the next world. Prepare yourself in the corridor so you can enter the banquet hall." It was *so* real to me suddenly. I had read those words tens of times and, when doing Jewish outreach, taught many classes about this insight, but it suddenly became as real as the day before me.

Then a calm descended on me. There was nothing else I could do, and I had just been given a phenomenal insight into living.

Judy drove me to the test center. I entered the squat little building. I had to show them my driver's license, be photographed and fingerprinted. This was serious stuff. Apparently in past years, some people had hired other, more qualified individuals to take the test for them. So now they were making sure no one unqualified had a shot at the Wall Street bonus pool.

The test administrators gave me a key to a locker. I had to put all my belongings there, including my cellphone, keys, wallet, pen – everything. I was allowed to take *nothing* but the clothes on my back into the test room. Inside, each person sat in a little cubicle with a computer screen in front of them and two walls partitioning them from the other test-takers, with a camera on the wall eyeing them the whole time. In another room, the administrators monitored the feed from the TV cameras. It felt like a prison with guards watching.

After two hours I had finished the first part of the test, 15 minutes before the mandatory break. My head was swimming. I could hardly focus. I used the last 15 minutes to review a few questions which I wasn't sure of. I then went outside and ate a light lunch which I had brought with me. I shut my eyes for a bit to try to refresh myself and went back in.

After the next two hours I had finished the last 175 questions. I once again reviewed the few questions I wasn't sure of. I kept remembering my tutor's advice: "Go with your first hunch. Don't doubt yourself. Never go back and change your answers as the first response is usually the right one." Still, I couldn't resist going back over the few questions I just wasn't sure of. I had three minutes left to the expiration of the exam. I hit the key that said: "Finish."

Immediately, the screen lit up: "Are you sure?" I hit: "Yes." Again, it asked, "Are you sure?" I hit "Yes" again. Idiot! Yes, I am sure! For the third time, it asked "Are you sure?"

This time I took a deep breath. My hand moved to the "Yes" button, but I didn't push it. I knew that this was *it* – after this, there was no going back. I was shaking. This truly was like Judgment Day. I had either prepared adequately, lived my life properly or I hadn't, but at this point in time there was nothing more I could do to change it. I resolved in my mind to become a great husband and a great father. I would never again ignore my family. I wanted to be remembered as a good and patient person, not as a distracted, driven, insensitive Wall Street type. I hit "Yes."

A small hourglass appeared on the screen and started spinning around. The computer informed me that my score would appear in three minutes. The hourglass continued spinning as I prayed fervently to the Almighty to help me pass. I probably should have done the praying earlier. It was the longest three minutes of my life. And then the following message appeared:

Exam title: General Securities Representative Examination
Exam series: 7
Number correct: 206.
Percent correct: 82 percent.
Passed.
National average: 73 percent
National percentage of candidates passing the exam:
  66 percent

Tears streamed down my face. I had done it. I clenched my fists and let out a silent scream. YES!!!

Others in the room were still taking this test and other tests so I couldn't scream out loud, but the waves of joy and relief washed over me. I had done it! Thank You, God! I was overwhelmed with joy and appreciation. The Almighty had saved me. He had helped me learn this material. It was the most difficult experience I had since I had studied for my rabbinical ordination many years prior.

I walked out of the exam room and into the control room. The attendant printed out my statement telling me what I already knew – that I had passed. I clutched it in my hands, retrieved my belongings from the locker, and walked out of the test building. Judy was waiting in the parking lot. She had a camera focused on the exit door. I saw her, jumped up in the air and clicked my heels and started dancing.

We went back home, where we opened a bottle of champagne and celebrated with my in-laws. At least they celebrated. I was busy on the phone calling my business friends to tell them the good news.

Then Judy reminded me that the test was over, and so now I had to be a good husband again. No more excuses. She was so right. Less than an hour ago I had promised God that I would change my life and not ignore my family again. I couldn't believe I had fallen so quickly. So I sat down with them all, lit up a cigar (sorry, I was a Wall Street wannabe), hoisted a glass of champagne and said a heartfelt "Thank you!" to Judy.

2

Why Did I Do It?

Why did I abandon a life as a rabbi and fundraiser for Jewish education?

Simply put, I was bored. I was no longer challenged by what I was doing.

Back in the two slim years (1998–2000) of the dot-com boom, I had hit it rich. I made $5 million on the stock market. Suddenly I had a taste of what it was like to have money. After 17 years of renting a humble home, I bought a MacMansion worth more than half-a-million dollars, a nice car (for a change), and I gave away a quarter-of-a-million to charity. I loved the feeling it gave me. I had money, I had power, I could help people. There was a sense of feeling God-like, a hint of the feeling Adam must have had in the Garden of Eden.

I ignored the fact that the lifestyle change, which came with having money, actually cost more money. The big house came with a big mortgage and big utility bills, a pool that cost a fortune to maintain and an acre-plus that required upkeep. I didn't really realize how much I was on the hook for until the dot-com bubble burst and I was left with nothing but big bills.

Going back to being a struggling rabbi was really hard. I went through four months of serious depression. It did not help my relationship with God. But having tasted what it was like to be rich, I could not go back. In short, I was burned out in my chosen career, and I was itching to move on.

Now, unlike some religions which make a virtue out of poverty, Judaism doesn't see anything positive about being poor, nor anything negative about being rich. The Torah records that the three patriarchs Abraham, Isaac and Jacob were all wealthy man. In fact, it says that Abraham and his descendants were blessed by God with abundance. This does not mean, however, that Judaism approves of greed or crass pursuit of materialism. The Talmudic sages in *Ethics of the Fathers* say, "Who is wealthy? The one who is satisfied with his portion."

Though I do have to admit that I was not quite satisfied with my portion, I was not greedy. I wanted to give. I wanted to share. I wanted to be a blessing to others – to bless and be blessed with abundance.

AN IMPULSE

One day, while visiting Jerusalem during the Passover vacation, I was talking about my frustration with my job and hopes for the future with a donor, a Yale-educated MD and a brilliant psychologist whose advice carried a lot of weight with me. She said, "You know, there are a lot of ways to serve God. Being a fundraiser isn't the only way. Who says that becoming wealthy and having the means to be charitable isn't as genuine and as precious in God's eyes as being a full-time fundraiser?"

But I had worked for Aish HaTorah as a rabbi and fundraiser for twenty-two years. How could I leave?

She said, "Let's go see the boss right now."

We almost ran over to the Aish headquarters, bounded up the two flights of stairs to the office of the dean, Rabbi Noah Weinberg, knocked on his door and entered without waiting to hear if anyone was inside. But he was there.

Rabbi Weinberg was always larger than life – a bear of a man; with his long white beard and twinkling eyes, he looked like Santa Claus except for the red coat (his was black). He stood up to greet us with a huge grin, as was his way.

She burst out, "Irwin wants to leave Aish. He thinks he can make a lot of money in business. Who is to say it is holier to be a fundraiser than a rich guy giving lots of charity? What do you think?"

Rabbi Weinberg's answer was as warm and accepting as ever. "Well, Irwin has given us more than twenty years. Every soldier is entitled to move on after that amount of time. He has my blessing."

That was it.

He leaned over and kissed my cheek. He said, "The Almighty will bless you. You will be very successful. It is a done deal. It is in the bag!"

I asked him how he could be so sure.

He said, "You are a talented guy and you have given selflessly to the cause all these years when you could have been doing anything you wanted to do. The Almighty is sure to bless you for your efforts. It is in the bag!"

Then the smile left his face. "Just make sure you don't forget why you are doing it. Every night, before you go to bed, I want you to sit on the floor – on the floor, Irwin – and commiserate with the Almighty's plight. Feel His pain at the suffering of His children. Think about it for five minutes while you sit on the floor and ask yourself what you can do to help His children."

He kissed me, blessed me, and said good-bye.

As we were walking out, he said, "Oh, and I want 51 percent of your charitable giving to go to Aish HaTorah."

I agreed. I recognized that I had an unfathomable debt of gratitude to Aish. After all, if it weren't for Aish, I would never be who I am today – a Torah-observant Jew who relates to his Creator, a husband, a father of eight beautiful children, a man with direction. If I had not encountered Aish, my compulsive personality would have taken over – I would probably be on my third marriage with one or two rebellious kids who wouldn't want to know my name. My life would be a mess.

I was just grateful to God that it all turned out the way it did.

MY AISH CONNECTION

I first arrived in Jerusalem on September 1, 1979, three weeks before Rosh Hashana. I had just spent a year back-packing and hitch-hiking through Europe. Along the way, I had lived a month in Barcelona, a month in Rome, and three months in Crete where I had worked as a stone-mason and a shepherd. When I arrived in Israel, I was wearing my previous experiences – literally. My outfit consisted of a sheepskin coat, off-set by shoulder-length hair which was also very bushy and wild on top, and I was calling myself Manoli (a nice Greek name).

Had my good, middle-class Canadian parents seen me, they would have fainted. In fact, I have no idea how they let me do what I did – since without their financial support, I could not have taken the time to travel. If my kids ever told me they wanted to back-pack through Europe, I would have said, "Over my dead body."

Of course, by then, my parents were used to the fact that it was hard to stop me from anything that I set my mind to do.

It seems that I arrived in the world – on March 14, 1955 – with the words "over-achiever" stamped on my forehead. By the time I was twelve, I had placed second world-wide in a B'nai B'rith public speaking contest, I had my own kids' TV talk show called *Tween Set* on CBC, (the Canadian Broadcasting Corporation), and I had starred in commercials for Snickers Chocolate Bars: "It's new! It's got nougat, and it's covered with grrreaaat milk chocolate!!"

My family imbued me with a strong Jewish identity, though in terms of observance of Jewish law, we could most charitably be described as "traditional." For example, while we really didn't keep kosher as Jewish law demands, we didn't mix milk and meat – we even had two sets of dishes, one for milk, one for meat. My parents took this separation very seriously and ingrained in me the idea that mixing milk and meat was foul. I recall the first time I sat down next to a kid in the high-school cafeteria and saw him gulp down a glass of milk with his hamburger. I thought I was going to vomit, and I had to run out. His name is the only name I can still remember from high school, because it was such a traumatic experience for me.

That said, we still ate pork. When we had Chinese take-out, we'd put our Moo Goo Gai Pan on paper plates so as not to contaminate the kosher dishes. We went to an Orthodox synagogue, but only on Rosh Hashana and Yom Kippur, and we drove there in direct viola-tion of Jewish law. For a kid like me – who was born wanting to do everything 150 percent – it was confusion central.

By the time I hit Bar Mitzvah age, I rebelled against the incon-sistency – what my teenage mind perceived as hypocrisy – and as a mark of my rebellion, I enrolled in a Catholic Jesuit institution, Loyola College.

My Jewish friends called it Goyola and none of them would have thought to go there; (they all went to McGill or Sir George Williams University). Not me. I embraced Loyola with my typical overabun-dance of enthusiasm. I even ran for the president of the student body under the slogan "preserving Loyola's identity." What exactly did a Jewish boy like me, who hadn't even met a non-Jew until his last year of high-school, know about preserving the identity of a hundred-year-old Jesuit school? Absolutely nothing. But I won nonetheless.

I still remember the look of horror on my parents' faces when they arrived on campus on graduation day and saw me coming out of church. My mother wanted to know if I did this regularly. I told her an emphatic "no!" In fact, it was the first time I had ever gone. But it was graduation day after all.

The Jesuits didn't know what to do with me. I had aggravated them plenty with my doings while on the university senate and board of governors, but I also helped bring forward several needed reforms. When I graduated, they awarded me the Father Patrick G. Malone Medal for Outstanding Community Involvement. I had that "change the world" drive, even back then. They also offered me a job teaching English at their school in Darjeeling, India. (Maybe they were trying to send me as far away as possible in an effort to discourage me from attending graduate school at Loyola.)

STRANGER IN STRANGE LANDS

Since it was going to take some time and effort to get a work visa for Darjeeling (a closed area at the time), I decided to travel around while waiting. I thought I'd spend a year in Europe, go on to India where I'd work the next two years, and then travel some more on my way home. That was my four-year plan.

After six months, I'd had enough of Europe, but I felt too rootless, too unsettled to go to Asia. Intuitively I knew it would be dangerous for me both spiritually and psychologically. I saw the odd, blank look in the eyes of the people returning from there. They seemed removed from the world. I understood this as a side-effect of exposure to strange cultures and the estrangement from things familiar. In alien places you can never let your guard down; you are wary of trusting anyone, since all your worldly belongings and documents (such as passport, visa, travelers' checks) are always just a pocket away from disappearing.

I was not ready for India, but I was too embarrassed to go home, so I went to Israel, a place which I had visited as a teenager and where

I had felt comfortable. Before leaving Canada, I had picked up some information from the Jewish Federation office in Montreal, including a brochure about Aish HaTorah, describing it as a place where the modern, inquiring mind could explore the wisdom of the Jewish heritage. As a psychology major, I responded to that approach.

When I arrived in Jerusalem, I asked a stranger how to find Aish, and he took me to the Old City. I wasn't used to such kindness – which people routinely show to each other in Israel – after my time of being a stranger in strange lands.

The admissions guy at Aish took a long look at my very wild appearance and thought long and hard about letting me in. But since Rosh Hashana was approaching, he relented. I called my parents to tell them to hold onto their hats – I was in yeshiva! To heap surprise on top of shock, I asked them to please pack up my suit and mail it to me, as I needed to be properly dressed for the High Holidays.

My father was floored, "Send you your suit?! Are you crazy? It will never get there on time. And, for the cost of the postage, you could buy a new one!" My mother was on the other phone saying, "Albert shhh! Who cares how much it costs. Be happy he wants to go to *shul*. We will fly it there ourselves if we have to!"

I got the suit on time and went to my first full Rosh Hashana and Yom Kippur services ever. I recall telling one of the rabbis after Yom Kippur that I felt my soul lifting out of my body as it was being purified. He gave me a disbelieving look.

After the High Holidays, I took care not to jump into anything. Before I made any commitments to the Torah way of life, I wanted to know a great deal more. I spent a lot of time reading about Judaism and Jewish philosophy, as I needed to reconcile what I had previously learned with the Torah worldview. The classes that had the greatest impact on me were taught by Rabbi Weinberg. This guy made sense! I never knew any religious people who made sense before. He pointed out, for example, that a commitment to truth meant there were consequences. If you found truth, you had to change how you lived your life in order to live in accordance with it. Nobody had said that to me before. At the university, "truth" had no particular bearing on how you lived your life; here it did.

I thought long and hard about it. I realized that whatever changes I committed to now were for life. I started slowly but, by the end of the year, I was fully committed to the Torah path.

Three years later I had learned enough to know how to live a moral-ethical, God-centered way of life in accordance with Jewish law. I was ready to put it into action. That meant getting married and starting a family.

JUDY

The decision to get married did not come upon me just like that. Really, what happened was that my roommate and best friend, Nachum Braverman, told me he had started dating. In the yeshiva world that meant, "I will be married in three months' time."

When he said that, a chill went through my body. I wanted to yell at him, "You can't do that! You can't leave me here in this dark and dingy dorm all alone!"

Next thing I knew I was scanning all the single girls that crossed my path.

One evening, I was chatting in the kitchen with Sheryl Meyer, the wife of one of my teachers, Rabbi Tom Meyer, about what I wanted in a wife. It was important to get this straight because, in the Jewish tradition, you are supposed to use your intellect to identify the qualities you want in a potential mate and not allow your emotions to take over. Now, of course, you also want to be physically attracted, but you don't want to fall into the trap of infatuation without first determining that the woman who is the object of your attraction has the qualities you consider essential.

So, I was telling Sheryl that I wanted someone who preferred the life of a wife and mother to that of a career. I wanted someone who was kind, in as much as raising children involves so much self-less giving. I wanted someone for whom it was pre-eminent to have a strong relationship with God and who was committed to Jewish outreach, since this was the direction I was headed in.

I also wanted someone who was emotionally strong, as I figured we both would have to make a lot of sacrifices in our common bat-tle for Jewish survival. I wanted someone who was loyal and would hang in there when the going got tough. A sense of humor was also important to me. And, of course, she had to be someone I was phys-ically attracted to!

I ticked-off my list to Sheryl, who listened carefully. Then she said, "What about my sister? What about Judy?"

At that moment, Judy was sitting in the living room. I knew her well as she was always at her sister's house, and I was always there as well.

Hmm, I thought, she sure does meet all my criteria, and she sure is attractive! So, I said to Sheryl, "Where do we go from here?"

And Sheryl said, "Let me talk to her."

That's how it began.

THE INTERROGATION

The yeshiva was about to adjourn for Passover, and that meant I would be in Israel ten more days before flying to Los Angeles to organize Aish's first fundraising banquet there. If the banquet was suf-ficiently successful, it would allow us to launch a new Aish branch in LA. I did not have much time.

Furthermore, I was one of those idealists who took a lot of what I heard literally, without the moderating influence of maturity or good judgment. It was just one facet of my being a fanatic about life and just generally doing everything to the extreme. I had heard that one was supposed to be systematic about the dating process, so I showed up for my first date with Judy with a list of fifty questions. Things like: What is the most important thing to you in life? What are you prepared to die for? What would you say if I called you Friday afternoon and told you we needed to have ten guests for dinner that evening?

I was very business-like about this, and sweet Judy sat across from me in the LaRomme Hotel lobby, sipping a cup of tea, and patiently putting up with my interrogation. Mike Wallace from *60 Minutes* could not have asked more pointed questions.

But, in the process, something of my intensity – or (God, I hope so) of my charm filtered through – and we had ten dates in ten days. Then I had to leave.

We were both seriously interested in each other but decided we should put it on hold for six weeks until I came back from LA. This was a difficult thing to do for me and even more so for Judy, as she was just left hanging – a tough emotional place to be.

On top of that, after four weeks in LA, I had garnered enough pledges to launch a branch. And the initial backers, Dick Horowitz and Dave Wilstein, offered me the job of heading it up. Though I had no skills or experience of any kind (in leadership or fundraising), I made up for my shortcomings with my youthful enthusiasm. Of course, I accepted.

The only problem was that I had to begin immediately, whereas I was supposed to return to Israel and resume my dating process with Judy.

What to do?

I spent many hours contemplating how I felt about Judy. I consulted my original list and realized how high she had scored on my wife quiz. She was what I was looking for!

I discussed it with both Dick Horowitz and with Rabbi Weinberg. It felt right. She was the one!

Meanwhile, with or without Judy, I had to start the preparations for living in LA. One of the Aish donors called to say he had a lovely two-bedroom apartment available in one of the few rent-controlled apartments in Beverly Hills. He offered it to me for $467 a month, and Dick suggested I take it. I would have been a fool to pass it by – Beverly Hills for less than $500 a month!

When I went to sign the lease, the form required me to fill in the names of the tenants. I wanted to write "Irwin and Judy Katsof" and then it hit me that I was a bit over-confidant. I hadn't even proposed. What if she said no?

I put it down anyway.

Then I got nervous. What if someone decided to check with her? I was very naïve in those days and didn't know how these things worked. I figured I better ask her.

The only problem was that I was in LA, and she was in Jerusalem. I paced the carpet in Dick's office for an hour or more, and finally picked up the phone and dialed the number for the office of Neve Yerushalayim, the college where Judy was a student. They brought her to the phone.

I said "Hi" and told her I had good news and bad news. I couldn't come back as we had expected to resume the dating process. But would she marry me?

She answered in a display of wit, which would serve her well through all the tough times to come, "Is that the good news?"

Then she wanted to know if I was at least down on one knee. Cute!

I quickly kneeled. She said she needed a few minutes to think, and she thought for what seemed an eternity to me, and then said, "Yes!"

In retrospect, she should have taken this as an omen for so much of our marriage – me on the phone, or better yet two land lines and a cell besides!

Six weeks later, we were married at the Holy Land Hotel in Jerusalem and, ten days after that, we moved to Los Angeles to open Aish's third branch in North America.

Fast forward twenty-two years. Now it was over. I collected my last Aish paycheck. As of January 1, 2005, I was self-employed.

3

The Power of Giving

Though I had left a non-profit organization for Wall Street, my life goal remained the same — I still wanted to make a difference in the world. But to meet my stated goal of giving away $1 million a year, I would have to be making $5 million, after taxes.

You could call me audacious.

In my fundraising work, I always had big goals. I constantly told people that everything worth doing had to have a BHAG — a big hairy audacious goal! Well, going off to Wall Street and stating boldly that I planned to give away that kind of money was certainly audacious. Especially since at the time, I had no income and no savings! I was living on borrowed money.

But I figured it would take no more than a year for me to get on my feet. Little did I know.

My mantra since then has become: "Two and a half"! That is, in business everything takes two times as long, costs two times as much, and in the end produces half of what was projected!

At the outset I started two different companies — Global Capital Associates and Global Strategic Ventures. (I thought of calling them "Universal" but that seemed too pompous — "Global" was big enough!)

Global Capital Associates was going to make a fortune connecting Israeli companies with sources of funding, sales and distribution

31

in the US. In Global Strategic Ventures, I had a partner, my good friend Vitaly Pruss from Russia, and together we offered consulting services to Russian clients who wanted to enter the American market.

In retrospect, neither company had the potential to make me $5 million after taxes, but at the time I had a distorted view of reality because the people I mingled with – those I solicited for Aish and recruited to come on my Israel missions – were probably in the top 1 percent of the American population in terms of earnings. On some level, I knew these guys were in the stratosphere and represented the extreme minority even among super-earners, but that didn't faze me since I never imagined that I wouldn't become one of them. I really never entertained any other option.

PIERCING THE HEAVENS

I plunged in and experienced an extremely chaotic nine months. Meanwhile, I was quickly depleting my bank account which held only borrowed money to begin with, so I was only accruing debt.

Then I got some good advice from a close friend, David Bodner, who was raising money to feed the poor of Israel over Passover. He told me that, according to the Talmud, the cries of the poor pierce through the heavens and are heard by the Almighty, and those who answer their cry for help down here on earth get special credit up above.

If I was to succeed, I knew I needed lots of credit, and I figured helping the poor of Israel was a good thing to do. I asked my son Aaron Yosef, better known as A.Y., to speak to the Zilberman family in the Old City of Jerusalem; they run a large yeshiva and also administer a charity fund to help poor families with holiday expenses. He reported that they had a list of some fifty families that desperately needed food for Passover and that $200 per family would be a great help. I donated $10,000 to this cause – the first of my charitable donations as a Wall Streeter.

In return, I asked that the Hebrew names of my family members be written on the food packages. According to Torah law, giving charity – called *tzedakah* in Hebrew from the word *tzedek*, meaning "justice" – is best done anonymously, but I wanted the poor recipients to pray and pierce the heavens specifically on my behalf. I wanted them to be my flag bearers, leading my charge down that very busy highway upon which prayers travel to upper realms.

By Rosh Hashana, I had used up more than $300,000 of the $460,000 I had borrowed from the bank, though I had also made almost $380,000 through various small deals, all of which got swallowed up in my company's start-up costs. But, at the end of the Jewish year, I technically owed 20 percent of my net income to charity or about $75,000.

I called Rabbi Weinberg to whom I had promised the lion's share of my *tzedakah* and discussed the situation with him. I very much wanted to do the right thing. I had made a commitment to give 20 percent to charity, yet I was still living off my credit line. He suggested I donate the $75,000 to Aish HaTorah, and if I ran out of money, then he would consider it a loan and give it back to me.

It was a very, very scary moment when I wrote out that check for $75,000 the day before Rosh Hashana. I also wrote out another $10,000 to help the poor of Jerusalem over the holidays and sent that to the Zilbermans to dispense, with special instructions that I needed the poor to use megaphones, or whatever else they could muster, when it came to storming the heavens on my behalf.

If I were to succeed, I needed a lot of help from above. I wondered how many other people on Wall Street were employing this strategy. If only I could figure out how to get the rights to the toll booth on this highway to upper realms, maybe I could solve my financial problems.

At the same time, I began to wonder if I was an idiot. Maybe this commitment of 20 percent was a little excessive. Perhaps it made more sense to just give 10 percent like everyone else. Why had I had to make such a big thing about this 20 percent. Me and my big mouth. Stupid me.

Self-doubts and second-guessing set in. Could I renege on my promise? No, that would be wrong. After all, the Almighty runs the world, and He decides how much money we all make. I couldn't possibly lose by doing the right thing.

But then, the right thing is to give 10 percent to *tzedakah* not 20 percent – only the wealthy are encouraged to give more than 10 percent, and even they are not required to do so. I was not wealthy by any means – I was in debt!

But then again, the Talmud says that when you give even the minimum amount the Almighty will give it back to you a hundred-fold. It says that this is the only *mitzvah* where you can test God – give it away and you will witness God paying you back. That would imply that the more you give the greater the return.

I had this running dialogue in my head for days.

I went back and forth, first thinking I was doing the right thing and then thinking I was a fool. I lay awake at night, trying to hear the cries of the poor storming the heavens and wondering if next year I would be one of them, waiting for my care package and crying out to the heavens on behalf of my benefactor.

In the end, my believing side – the part of me that trusts in God – won out. I said: "This is the Almighty's will. You can't lose out if you do the right thing."

THE PAY OFF

In retrospect, I see that if success had come too quickly it would not have been healthy for me. I needed to feel a lack; I needed to turn to God and be clear where my help, wealth and sustenance were coming from.

I once wrote (in my book, *How to Get Your Prayers Answered*) that we don't pray to get our needs met – we have needs in order that we pray. That is how we remind ourselves that God exists – that is how we build a relationship with Him. Of course, the Almighty knows what we need. We don't have to tell Him. But we have to verbalize our needs to remind ourselves that we are dependent on God.

Finally, that lesson sank in. (Don't we all teach what we most want to learn?)

Three weeks after Rosh Hashana, the strangest thing happened to me. A business deal – in which I was only tangentially involved – closed. I had been putting my efforts into other matters and really not counting on this to amount to anything. But, out of nowhere, and certainly through none of my doing, the deal went through and I received a commission which was wired into my bank account – $450,000!

If it had happened any closer to Rosh Hashana, they may have had to bring out the defibrillator to revive me. Get this: I had given $85,000 to charity of money I didn't have and received $450,000 back only three weeks later! Any hedge fund manager would pay dearly for such leverage.

The power of giving could not have been demonstrated any more clearly to me. Even though I had been convinced of it before, now I was knocked out, because I saw God's message in this gift. He could have delivered it to me in any number of ways, but He sent it in such a way as to make it obvious that wealth did not come from my efforts.

This is a concept which, in many ways, is very easy to hear yet hard to live with. We have to put in the effort, but we need to know that the result is not due to that effort. We have to try as hard as we can, but we can't be misled into thinking that the outcome is our doing.

Our job in life is to realize that God really does run the world, and He decides how to respond. Yes, we must try – we cannot just loll around expecting miracles. We can't say we want to win the lottery and not ever buy a lottery ticket. Yet, all we need to do is buy one lottery ticket and not hundreds. Don't think it increases your odds to buy hundreds of tickets.

The object is to consciously accept that it is God who runs the world, and all that counts is doing His will, because that's *all* there is anyway. It is that mindset that opens the door to the ultimate success.

In *Ethics of the Fathers*, the Talmudic sages teach that we must make a start and put in the effort, but the end result is always in God's hands. We are responsible for the start-up, so to speak, but He gets it on the stock exchange (or not, as the case may be).

It was amusing to me that the Almighty was taking no chances I would miss the significance of His message. Over the past nine months, I had spent at most 15 hours on this deal out of a total of more than 2,000 work hours, so less than 1 percent of my effort had generated 60 percent of my income!

THE ENEMY WITHIN

The Almighty clearly knew how dense I can be, and how hard it is for me to give up control. That is why He sent me a message which I could not misinterpret. I realized that He is my Father in Heaven – that He loves me and wants to give me everything good. All I had to do was make myself into a vessel to receive His blessings which are always pouring down, but sometimes I was the one blocking the flow with my own crazy ego.

Of course, all this is easy to say, but hard to put into practice. Way back in college – in a psych class at Loyola College – I learned that it is easy to learn new information, but hard to learn new ways of being. We all know the health statistics relating to over-eating and lack of exercise, but how many of us act on this information? We all know obesity is a major killer and leads to heart disease, but how many of us can eliminate trans-fats from our diet or stick to a simple exercise regime on a consistent basis?

The ego is crazy alright!

The Talmud gets this concept across with a great metaphor. It says that when you go to war, you know who the enemy is. He has a different uniform than you, flies a different flag, is poised on the other side of the front lines. You know where to point your weapon.

But the battle of life – the battle for sanity – is far more complex. The enemy is within. He wears no distinct uniform, and he speaks with your own voice. There is no enemy territory; there are no front lines. Everything is blurred. The crazy notions we mistake for truth – our distorted perceptions – are inside us. We identify with them and are one with them. We do not realize that the enemy resides within.

The battle of life is guerrilla warfare at its height.

Now I was in a fighting spirit. I put on my army fatigues and got ready to head off into the jungle. The Almighty had sent me a message and, for once, I got it.

BACK TO BASICS

Part of the fight meant that I needed to apply myself to Torah study on a regular basis. I could not ignore it, just because I was in business.

But I have never found sitting still and learning easy. I am active, a doer, and anything that is passive is hard work for me. I do love learning new ideas, but they have to have a practical application. And, even then, I don't have the patience to sit for very long. That is why studying for the "Series 7" was so difficult for me, and that is also why I left yeshiva after only three years and went to work in Jewish outreach.

Throughout most of the years I was working for Aish HaTorah, I rarely sat down to learn Torah for more than an hour a day, and this despite the urgings of my boss, Rabbi Weinberg, to learn three times as much. There were periods of times when I actually managed a little more (say an hour-and-a-half), but then I would get busy with some fundraising activity and fall off the wagon.

The same with my *minyan* attendance. I knew it was wrong to miss communal prayers, but I justified it by telling myself that my whole day consisted of serving God. Here I was putting in 80 hours a week running the LA branch of Aish HaTorah and raising money to save the Jewish people from assimilation. Everything I did was a *mitzvah!*

But it was just my crazy ego, deluding me into thinking that I was behind enemy lines. Who was I fooling, telling myself that I was trying to save the Jewish people, while ignoring the needs of the Jewish people who were the closest to me – my loved ones, my wife and children?

My ego got me hooked on the glory and the applause, which comes from accomplishments in the external world, not from changing diapers or reading a bedtime story. Of course, back then I denied that this was what was driving me. I was doing holy work, after all. Mauricio Hatchwell Toledano, a philanthropist from Madrid, called me "the Holy Paratrooper!" I loved that image – the gallant me, jumping out of airplanes, parachuting behind enemy lines, leading special forces to save the Jews.

Of course, once I left Aish HaTorah, I could no longer tell myself any of this. And, in many ways, the transition left me feeling empty. What was I doing it for? Okay, I had great ambitions to give loads of money to charity, but the interaction with Torah – through teaching others which I had so much enjoyed, and through which I also learned – was gone.

So, now what?

LESSON LEARNED

The message sent directly by God three weeks after Rosh Hashana really woke me up. It suddenly hit me square between the eyes that the Almighty really does run the world.

There is no direct correlation between the amount of hours I work and the amount of money I earn. God decides what that ratio will be. Of course, there are important variables. Money that I give away is certainly one. My commitment to use my income and my talents to do God's will is another. My sharing the Almighty's pain over the suffering of His children and striving to make the world a better place also matter. But, ultimately, God decides what is good for me or bad for me at any given point in time.

I knew that the Almighty would not open the heavens for me if He thought I would not use His bounty in accordance with His will. It followed then that it was about time I shaped up, beginning with learning Torah on a regular schedule.

Of course, I was not so self-delusional as to think that I would be learning Torah *for* God. I would be doing it for me – to help me grow, to help me live in accordance with God's will, to help me keep in the forefront of my consciousness that there really is nothing but God.

I knew it was good for me; I knew I needed to do it. I knew that Torah study held the keys to ultimate success for me. But carving out time to do it and sticking to the schedule was the mother of all tests for me.

I applied Colin Powell's doctrine of warfare – launch an overwhelming amount of fire-power at the enemy. (I liked the concept and General Powell did speak a very respectable Yiddish after all – I once asked him if he really did speak Yiddish and he answered, "A bissle," which means "A little bit.")

I hired a local rabbi to study with me one-on-one at 6 AM every morning (except Shabbat) at a local academy of Torah study (called Beit Midrash). We would learn an hour each day, and I would be obligated to pay him whether I showed up or not.

This was my bridgehead – my foothold in enemy territory which I used to advance farther. I would get up at 5 AM and try to get there at 5:30 AM to turn the one hour into an hour-and-a-half. Some mornings I succeeded, and some I failed. The major stumbling block was my compulsive need to check my e-mail upon waking. If there were few messages, I made it there by 5:30; if there were many, I was lucky to be there by 6. It was a real struggle.

In the first six months, I lost the battle more often than I won it. But I was slowly expanding my position. King Solomon in the Book of Proverbs says that a sinner falls once and stays down, but a holy man (a tzaddik) falls seven times and gets up each time. I wouldn't call myself a tzaddik, but I certainly was falling down a lot and somehow finding the strength to pull myself up again. I had a set of bruised knees to prove it.

After an inner struggle, I managed to get better at prioritizing which e-mails to answer. I asked if it really made a difference to answer any of them at 5 AM and the answer was always no, but I still couldn't stop myself. I continued to bring my cellphone with me to the *Beit Midrash* and still sneak a peek when it buzzed. But at least I have made some major strides in this battle and was able to increase my study time as a result. I also claimed a beachhead in *minyan* attendance, even though at times I got antsy and left early.

But my major advance came from applying the time-honored adage I still keep trying to learn from *Ethics of the Fathers*: "Who is wise? The one who learns from everyone."

THE STOPWATCH TRICK

On a flight to Barcelona, soaring above the Adriatic aboard a private plane of one of my clients, I learned an amazing lesson.

After an hour of business talk, he excused himself and opened up a Torah book. And then he took out a stopwatch. I couldn't fathom why. I watched him, puzzled, for a few minutes and then took out my own books. Shouldn't I study as well? I am a rabbi after all.

But then I saw him click-off the stopwatch, speak with his wife for a few minutes, click-on the stopwatch and resume studying. I had to know. "Hey, what gives with the stopwatch?"

He clicked-off and explained that he is committed to learning one hour a day. He doesn't always have one uninterrupted hour and so uses the stopwatch to time his learning. If he goes to the bathroom, he clicks-off the stopwatch. If he gets an urgent call, he clicks-off the stopwatch. That way he knows when he has put in an honest hour.

What a great idea! This is what I had to do!

When I got home from Barcelona, I immediately searched online and found simple inexpensive stopwatches, colorful and cute, for $14.95 each. The first day mine arrived, I took it to my morning study session – we start, click-on, then the cellphone buzzes, click-off, check e-mail, click-on, learn a bit, click-off, go the bathroom, click-on, etc. My rabbi/study partner wanted to know what planet I had come back from. Exactly what kind of conference did you attend in Barcelona?

But soon word got around and others in the *Beit Midrash* approached me about this stopwatch idea. I explained what my aim was and offered to get them stopwatches of their own.

The stopwatch helped me with my self-delusion. Often I thought I was getting in an hour-and-a-half of learning, but found that with all the breaks to check e-mails, go to the bathroom, have coffee, chit-chat, and so forth, it was a lot less than that. If I were an attorney and billing my clients for every minute worked, I would have been much more disciplined about my time and not wasting it on extraneous activities and non-revenue generating work. And here I was supposedly doing the will of God. Wow – I was really blowing it!

There is another teaching in *Ethics of the Fathers* that says, "Do God's will as if it were your will, and He will do your will as if it were His will." I have always explained this teaching with the following example:

Imagine it is late evening and there is a blinding blizzard outside – four-foot snow drifts, howling winds and 20 degrees below zero. But it is time to go to the synagogue to pray. Would you venture out? Or would you use the weather as a great excuse to skip communal prayers. I, for one, wouldn't even think twice about staying warm and comfy inside.

Now, imagine the same weather conditions, but there is a call from a business associate. He says that a fantastic business opportunity has come up to make a fast $100,000 but you need to drive into town now. Would you pack a suitcase in case you got stuck and get on your way immediately?

When it comes to our own personal interest and gain, we have zeal that generally isn't there when it comes to doing God's will. Of course, there are exceptional people to whom this does not apply but, in all honesty, I am not one of them. However, I was determined to change that. I wanted to do God's will and hoped that God would help me with my aims.

The stopwatch made me aware of how much time I was wasting on small distractions. And then I remembered a teaching by the holy rabbi known as the Chafetz Chaim.

The Chafetz Chaim said that most people live their lives as if they were writing a postcard. How do you write a postcard? You start out writing in big letters "HAVING A WONDERFUL TIME, THE WEATHER IS GREAT..." But then you realize that you've said hardly anything but you have little room left. So, in miniscule print, you jam in the rest. This is how we use and abuse time most of our lives.

The Torah tells us that Abraham and Sarah, when they were old, "came with their days," meaning – according to the *Zohar*, the chief work of the Kabbalah – that they had used all the days of their lives wisely and effectively, in accordance with God's will. I want to be able to look back at my life and feel that way.

To the people that think I am too neurotic about time – who would urge me to slow down and enjoy the moment – I can also cite Peter Drucker, the management guru, who advised every executive periodically to record everything he does in a day. I have used this technique and was blown away by how much time I wasted.

If the Torah were writing about me instead of Abraham and Sarah, I am afraid it would probably say, "Irwin came with his micro-seconds."

Oh well, one more battle to fight!

4

Of Godfathers and Oligarchs

As part of the way of generating business in my new career, I had contacted many of the wealthy donors whom I had previously solicited for Aish HaTorah, telling them about the opportunities for investment I was now privy to.

Among those I contacted was Vadim Rabinovitch, one of a few Ukrainian Jews who had become very rich privatizing the assets of the Former Soviet Union (FSU). He invited me to come to Kiev to discuss possible joint business ventures. I had never been to Kiev, but I was game. After all, fools rush in where angels fear to tread.

I booked a business class ticket on one of the Ukrainian air carriers – Aerosvit – which after my one and only ride, I renamed Aerospit. I was welcomed aboard a rickety old Russian Ilyushin plane which seemed to be furnished with seats ripped out of a 1940s railroad car. (And that was in business class!) I kept expecting straw to poke at me from the cushions. I had never seen such decrepit equipment on a plane before. I went to the bathroom and found that the mirror was attached to the wall with a band aid. I was totally freaked out. I began to try to think about my Last Will and Testament and feel badly that it wasn't up to date. I said a prayer and took a sleeping pill, thinking this was the only way I would be able to survive the eight-hour ride – if indeed I did survive it. I awoke with a terrible back ache, but at least I was still alive.

From then on, things improved. Vadim had sent his driver to meet me at the airport and arranged for a VIP arrival. This meant that I did not have to stand in line for the passport or customs checks; instead, I was escorted directly from the plane to a waiting van and whisked away to a nearby *dacha* that probably once belonged to a privileged Soviet-era bureaucrat. There, very polite officials processed my papers, almost apologetically inquiring how much foreign currency I was bringing into the Ukraine. After I freshened up at my hotel, I was taken to meet Vadim.

What always struck me about Vadim was his intensity – he was constantly in restless motion, darting back and forth, walking, talking, sitting, standing, seemingly simultaneously. I felt like I was in the presence of a caged animal, a trait perhaps left over from his years of imprisonment in a Soviet gulag for the crime of engaging in private enterprise. (Two of his ever-present bodyguards were non-Jews who befriended him while he was in prison, and now that he was successful, he was repaying that friendship by giving them jobs as his protectors.)

He rarely flashed a smile and, even when he did, it never lasted more than a second; all his mannerisms were like his speech, which was short, clipped, to the point. I have never had a conversation with him lasting longer than thirty seconds. He didn't so much talk with you as at you. He smoked constantly, and when he wasn't smoking, he was munching candy. There was a bowl, always full of candies and elegantly wrapped chocolates on his desk and on the conference table in his office. His office walls were lined with plaques, awards and medals he had received from Ukrainian politicians and Jewish community leaders the world over. Was he over-compensating for the negative articles that also abounded about him?

He was usually quite fashionably dressed but in off-the-rack, high-end stuff, not in custom-made clothes you might expect of somebody in his income bracket. He traveled everywhere in a leased private jet, and he never walked. He always went everywhere at a run. He was a man on a mission, driven, restless, on edge.

SEEING THE SIGHTS

After we chatted for a few minutes in his office, he wanted to show me the sights. As he walked out, suddenly three men appeared out of nowhere. One positioned himself in front of us, the other two behind. These were his bodyguards who accompanied him wherever he went.

Back then, in the early 2000s, bodyguards were not so much a safety need in Ukraine as a status symbol. Ukrainian and Russian businessmen wouldn't take you seriously unless you had the requisite number of bodyguards. I guess if you didn't have them, it meant you were not rich enough to be a target for kidnappers or assassins, and then you were not worth doing business with. Other status symbols were also important – the kind of car you drove, the watch you wore. A Rolls Royce dealership opened up in Kiev and sold out its entire inventory in two weeks. Same thing with a Lamborghini dealership. Western luxury goods were in high demand.

I once heard a joke about the rampant consumption of luxury goods in the FSU in those days:

One Russian rolls up his sleeve and shows his buddy his new Rolex. He boasts that it cost him $15,000. His buddy looks at him, rolls up his sleeve and shows him the exact same watch. "You sucker! I bought the same watch last week, and I paid $25,000 for it!"

As we descended in the ancient elevator, two of the guards came in with us as the third bounded down the stairs – I was not sure if this was a security move or if the elevator could only take so much weight.

We climbed into Vadim's Toyota Landcruiser while the body-guards jumped into two BMWs, one in front, one behind. Vadim started to barrel through traffic at breakneck speed, having switched on a police siren to clear the way. In his broken English, he told me that he is one of ten people in Kiev with this special privilege. I gripped my seat as we zipped down one-way streets going the wrong way. Moments later, he jumped the sidewalk and stopped the car in front of an ornate building – the Brodsky Street Synagogue – with the BMWs blocking off access to the synagogue at opposite ends. I felt like I was in a scene from *Mission Impossible*, and any second Tom Cruise would come rappelling down the front of the building.

We were met at the synagogue by Michael Josefson, Vadim's partner, who was to be the tour guide. He narrated the history of the Brodsky Street Synagogue, which was Kiev's largest prior to World War II when it was completely destroyed by the Nazis. Vadim rebuilt it as a faithful replica of the original.

Entering, I felt as if I'd left *Mission Impossible* and was now on the set of *The Godfather*. Several elderly men and women who were waiting for the soup kitchen to open approached Vadim to kiss and hug him; one kissed him on the hand even. We went to where the scribe was working writing parchments, and he rose to kiss Vadim on both cheeks. They all obviously felt a great deal of gratitude to their benefactor.

After a whirlwind tour of the synagogue, we took off again with the police siren blaring. Ten minutes later, we pulled up abruptly to a big white gate with an armed guard in full battle dress, a Kalash-nikov slung over his shoulder. This was Vadim's home. I was duly impressed – it was a beautiful home, even by American standards. Walking up the stairs ahead of Vadim, I bent down to pet the dog in front of the door. As I was extending my hand, Vadim yelled and grabbed me from behind. He gesticulated wildly, but the point got across even in Ukrainian: "Guard dog! Eats hand! Don't touch!" No American doggie, this pet.

The interior of the home was tastefully and comfortably furnished. It was not ostentatious by any means, except maybe for the indoor swimming pool. We ate a delicious kosher dinner for which we were joined by Rabbi Moshe Reuven Azman, then the chief rabbi of the Ukraine (or, should I say, one of the three men then vying for the title of chief rabbi of the Ukraine), after which Vadim took me back to my hotel, *sans* blaring siren.

THE OLIGARCH

The next morning at 6 AM, I was picked up – in a black Mercedes this time – and taken to the airport for a flight in a private jet to Moscow, where I was to meet with Dr. Patokh Chodiev, the Uzbek oligarch. Chodiev, a Muslim, was another one of a handful of individuals who became immensely rich – and I mean *immensely* – in the privatization of the assets of the former Soviet system in Kazakhstan, hence the title "oligarch." (A simple word like "mogul" would not describe the wealth and power of this person.)

The flight to Moscow was a short one-hour jaunt. We landed and were escorted to another special *dacha* where Chodiev's driver and the ubiquitous bodyguards were waiting for us. I walked over to the BMW-750 and tried to open the door but I could hardly budge it. Though I lifted weights and had a fair amount of upper body strength, I was stymied. I felt like I was moving 200 pounds of solid steel due to the bullet-proof lining.

We drove surrounded by chase cars to his compound outside of Moscow. At the gate were several Kalashnikov-toting soldiers in full battle gear. Except for that, the place looked like something out of

Beverly Hills, at least on the outside. On the inside, it was furnished in the manner of a Kremlin banquet hall with food to match – ten different courses at least, a feast fit for a Russian czar. Vodka flowed continuously, of course. This is a Russian custom – everyone fills their shot glass, one of the guests toasts the host, and bottoms up. Everyone fills their shot glass, someone else toasts the business deal and bottoms up. Everyone fills their shot glass, and another person … (you get the idea).

I can't hold my liquor well, especially not at noon, so I kind of faked it, pretending to drink from the same full glass over and over. I tried to make a meaningful toast, quoting something from *Ethics of the Fathers*. As the only rabbi there, I felt an obligation to bring God into the picture.

Vadim and Patokh wanted to discuss with me the launch of a new organization to be called the Global Foundation for Democracy. Not satisfied with just being rich, Vadim and Patokh decided they wanted to contribute to humanity in some big way. They asked me to arrange for speakers and participants for the big launch of their organization to be held in Geneva later that year.

In the end, after much drinking and not much brainstorming, I felt like I had wasted my time, as nothing got accomplished. But I was wrong. That is just the way things are done in Russia. Whereas Americans cut to the chase, Russians schmooze, drink, schmooze some more. It often seems like business is going nowhere but this is just their pace – they build a relationship before jumping in. Every deal has to be ensconced in a social experience.

We had a successful launch of their organization as planned. For the kick-off, I lined up a number of prestigious participants, including former Vice-President Al Gore, former Prime Minister of Great Britain John Major, former Prime Minister of Canada Kim Campbell, former Prime Minister of Ireland Mary Robinson, and a few other world leaders.

Vadim and Patokh were so pleased with my organizational skills that they summoned me back to Kiev to help them launch another one of their world-enhancing schemes – to be called the World Congress of Muslims, Christians and Jews.

This was really Vadim's idea, and he envisioned it as a quasi-parliament for world religions that would eventually come under the auspices of the United Nations. (And since Kiev is his home, and the idea his, he envisioned it as headquartered in Kiev.)

A LESSON IN DECISION-MAKING

When I passed the scrutiny of Vadim's bodyguards and entered his inner sanctum headquarters, I realized that the meeting would consist of three Jews – Vadim, his partner Michael Josefson, and me. Patokh, the Muslim sponsor of the project, was not present.

His absence was most disconcerting to me as I had flown all this way specifically for him. He was the guy who was going to bankroll this to the tune of $4-5 million, and I had not only confirmed the meeting with him but double-confirmed it with Vadim. Without Patokh, there was no project and I had just wasted 15 hours of flying time.

"Where is Patokh?" I asked.

"The Americans just revoked his visa, and he is scared to fly anywhere," was Vadim's reply.

Well, that made sense. Ever since another oligarch, Michael Khodorkovsky, the former head of Yukos Oil, had been arrested by President Vladimir Putin on a trip to Russia and imprisoned indefinitely, the oligarchs have been very careful where they travel. (Khodorkovsky, incidentally, came to Israel on one of my fundraising missions and gave Aish HaTorah $250,000.)

Patokh had his own reasons to worry. Though his business is in Kazakhstan and he lives in London, he would like to become the next president of Uzbekistan, where he was born and where he also has considerable assets. The current president there is allied with Putin, and the sudden revocation of Patokh's permanent travel visa to the US spelled danger. (Like the song from *Evita* goes: "The dice are rolling, the knives are out, would-be presidents are all about...") His lawyers advised him to stay put.

Vadim assured me that he found out only a few hours ago that Patokh wasn't coming, and he was as upset as I was. "Sure," I said, "but you haven't spent 15 hours flying. All for nothing!"

"Well, maybe not."

"What does that mean?"

Vadim explained to me that he had gone to a lot of trouble to get the backing and endorsement for the new congress from the then president of Ukraine, Viktor Yushchenko. Now that he had the green light, he knew it would not look good if he failed to proceed. He was thinking of maybe making the founding conference more modest and bankrolling it himself. He'd do that quietly, behind the scenes, and maybe Patokh would step in at a later date.

"Wow, that's great!" I said.

"Wait a minute, I haven't decided yet. I have to think about it."

I said, "Look! It is end the of January. The conference date is scheduled for April – that's less than three months away. You need to make a decision yes or no – today! If you don't, it just won't happen. You just won't get any speakers."

He asked me who I had lined up. I told him that, so far, I had tentative commitments from former Prime Minister of Pakistan Benazir Bhutto, former Secretary of State Madeline Albright, former President of France Valerie Giscard d'Estaing, and from actor Michael

Douglas. I had also had a stellar list of American Christian leaders and Muslim leaders from Yemen, Egypt and Saudi Arabia.

He liked the list. It was impressive.

I cautioned him that this was only a preliminary list and that none of these people would come for free. Some would require a speaker's fee and all would require plane fares, hotels and meals. Even if you keep it small – with only 100-150 invited participants and make it a two-day event – it would cost $1.5 million.

He said he could swing that. But he'd have to think about it.

THE MOMENT OF TRUTH

As I mentioned before, Vadim is an intense guy – a very intense guy – and he thinks fast and makes instant decisions. Thus, I was surprised when he said, "I need ten minutes to think." It was so out of character. I had never seen him do anything like that before. But this did involve an expenditure of $1.5 million with no apparent return.

He got up from the round table where we were meeting and started pacing his office. After a few minutes, he came back to the table and said, "We will ask a question."

I looked at him, "What are you talking about? Who are you going to ask?"

He didn't answer me, but pulled a yarmulke from a bookshelf and tossed it in the air. It landed askew on his head. To top it off, it was a little kid's yarmulke – bright blue velvet embroidered with a goofy menorah – the kind that any Jewish kid past the age of three would be too embarrassed to wear. He took a piece of paper and wrote on it in Russian, "Should we do it?"

He then picked up a Bible (a Hebrew-Russian version), opened it randomly and stabbed the page with his finger. He read the verse his finger pointed to – it was from Exodus 23:15, "You shall observe the Festival of Unleavened Bread, seven days shall you eat *matzah*, as I have commanded you, at the appointed time of the month of springtime, for in it you left Egypt; you shall not be seen before Me empty handed."

He slammed the book shut, stood up, looked at me with a whimsical smile on his face, and said, "It is clear! We do it!"

I took the Bible from him and read the verse again. What had I missed? This verse was talking about Passover and *matzah*. How could it be that from this it was clear to him that he should spend $1.5 million on the World Congress of Muslims, Christians and Jews?

I asked him to please explain. He looked at me and barked out: "The verse speaks of *matzah* and I had decided to do this anonymously. Isn't that clear?"

"Not to me."

"I am being humble like *matzah*. *Matzah* represents humility. Bread represents pride – it is puffed up, full of air. I will be humble and do it anonymously, but if later Patokh wants to be the bread, he can be. Also, the verse speaks of springtime, and we decided to do the conference in April."

"Aha..."

"And it speaks about Egypt – in Hebrew *Mitzrayim*, which means 'constrained' or 'narrow.' Doing this conference allows us to leave the constraints of Soviet society and come out into the open by sponsoring a conference for world leaders."

"Oh..."

"And you can't be empty-handed before God. You have to bring a sacrifice. So too here, you have to spend money. You have to invest and God will send it back."

So that's how he read it. We must do the conference. We must do it humbly, modestly, and it will be okay. And then he asked me if I could get the Pope to come. I looked at him and burst out laughing.

He didn't like my response. He said he thought that he could turn this idea into a World Parliament of Religion for the United Nations and that the UN would give us money to build a center for it in Kiev.

I stifled another laugh, but he caught it and said, "There is a Ukrainian expression: 'Sometimes a fool can succeed where smart people fail.' That's because the fool doesn't know how many problems he can have, so he just goes ahead and does it."

I got the message. He was right. We must try. That had always been my motto when I started out on my audacious projects.

As I sat there chastened, pondering what just happened, he disappeared. I noticed then that he had gone off to a room adjoining his office that is his private little synagogue. He was praying. I suddenly realized that he had more presence of mind that I did. The sun was setting, and I had lost track of time. I went to stand beside him and prayed as well.

We finished, hugged good-bye and kissed on each cheek, as the Russians do.

Perhaps there should be a class at the Harvard Business School on this unusual method of making business decisions. Perhaps the hedge fund world could use a whole new strategy? And what about my own deals? Could this be the sure-fire method to my success?

5

In Free-Fall

After I passed my Series 7, I brought one deal to Lehman Brothers, one to Maxim Bank, and several to Rodman & Renshaw. In so doing, I realized that working for others (and just collecting a commission) was not very fulfilling. On a large transaction, they got a standard 6 percent and I had to negotiate for my cut. Since I was just a deal broker and not an institution, I really had very little leverage. As well, I had no input into how my clients and relationships were handled once I turned the deals over to the big boys. (Sometimes not nicely.) Furthermore, I was building nothing and had absolutely no control over the transaction.

I wasn't sure what to do about that exactly; I needed an advisor, a guardian angel, to help me not to fall off the cliff along the rocky road to success.

God sent me that guardian angel in the person of Paul Stein (not his real name).

Back in 1982, Paul had been my very first donor when I started fundraising for Aish in Los Angeles. That first year he gave $100,000 – which would be $320,000 today – and he was my largest donor (as well as the largest single donor in the history of Aish at that time). Over the next few years, he went on to give over $1 million dollars to Aish (or $3 million in today's dollars), and he was equally generous to other Jewish organizations, such as United

Jewish Appeal (UJA) and America-Israel Political Action Committee (AIPAC), as well as becoming one of the largest Democratic Party fundraisers and contributors.

Some guy!

Paul was an attorney, but he became wealthy as a real estate developer. He also opened his own bank and built up to $400 million in assets. Paul's bank did not make home loans nor hand out passbook savings accounts; instead, it went after jumbo (say $100,000) certificates of deposit nationwide. With large sums of money in hand, the bank then lent it to real estate joint ventures. But, ultimately, it failed – like so many S&L's in the late 1980s when the real estate market plummeted, loans went sour, and thrifts were seized by federal regulators.

To add to his distress, when the Democrats lost the 1988 election, and the Republicans again gained power, Paul was one of a handful of powerful Democrats who was targeted by the Bush administration for his importance to the Democratic Party's fundraising machine. This also happened to two other major Aish donors – one in Florida and one in Los Angeles. Minor shortcuts that Paul took in his business were blown out of proportion, and Paul, reeling from the closure of his bank, declared bankruptcy. But to show you what kind of guy Paul was – his lawyer, who had lost $1.5 million in Paul's investments, not only continued to represent him throughout his troubles, but remained his friend.

When it was all said and done, Paul decided that he would never again take a high-profile community position. He lived a simple life doing real estate acquisitions through creative and complex financial structures. He was always an individual extremely concerned about moral and ethical behavior, but I think the personal crisis in his life made him lean over backwards to always be straight with people. Just about anyone who encountered him walked away feeling that he was one of the smartest guys they've ever met. In my opinion, he was a genius. I also admired him for his focus on what truly counts in life.

Paul taught me the meaning of a real business partnership – that it is one step below marriage. He taught me that deals should be done in a way that, at the end, everyone feels good about what happened and can look each other in the eye, give each other a hug, and enjoy each other's company. If that won't be the outcome, don't do the deal. Life is too short for anything else.

GOD'S KINDNESS

It was truly God's kindness to me that, just when I needed him, Paul resurfaced on my horizon.

Right at that time a friend came to me for help who was experiencing some serious legal/financial problems. I remembered that these were the same kind of problems Paul had experienced years ago, and I decided to track him down and ask him for advice.

We spent some time on the phone catching up on the many years that had passed since our last encounter. At my request, Paul agreed to talk with my troubled friend, and he did so readily. So then, I asked him if it would help me as well – if it would be okay for me to call him from time to time for advice. He was very accommodating and agreed to be available for me.

For my first year-and-a-half in business, he acted as an unofficial mentor to me. I would call him regularly, and he would advise me on business issues that I encountered. I was impressed with his level-headedness and his ability to see things clearly. He didn't get distracted by the myriad details involved in any transaction, but separated the chaff from the wheat. He helped me to understand how to best structure deals and all the variations involved in financing. As things progressed in my new business life, I started to call Paul weekly and sometimes daily, and I would copy him on all my e-mails, so he was aware of what I was involved in and could advise me better.

Bottom line – I reached out to him to help a troubled friend, and the Almighty returned that simple effort to me a hundredfold.

Paul advised me that there was no potential in consulting to make serious money, and he advised me to detach myself from that type of pursuit. But it was difficult to unwind the partnership I had formed with Vitaly Pruss in Global Strategic Ventures, and Paul helped me do it in as ethical and as sensitive a way as possible. I could never have done it without him and would not have even realized that this was not the best business model for me, and that there were better alternatives.

Next, Paul advised me to start my own investment bank. Now it might sound like a totally absurd idea that I, Irwin Katsof, after working as a rabbi for twenty years would start an investment bank. But when I did do it, I never thought of it as anything abnormal. (It was just another audacious idea which seemed like the normal course of business.)

In many ways I was just so naïve, not realizing how difficult it truly is and the degree of financial expertise that is needed to do it. I just had the confidence that I would succeed, because whenever I attempted challenging things in the past, all went well for me. In retrospect though, knowing what I know now, it is truly a miracle that so many pieces fell into place and that I managed to make it work.

It helped that I had Paul at my side.

I realized that while I had an excellent roster of contacts, I needed expertise in structuring transactions with them. I asked Paul to become my partner. But he just had no interest in ever being in the limelight again. He resisted my overtures for several months. We eventually reached a compromise – his son David Stein and one of his son's friends Bill Tandy (both lawyers) would become my partners.

They both passed the Series 7 (as well as the Series 63 and 24) with flying colors and only after a week of study. We also took on a fourth partner: Scott Claymore, an attorney from Florida, who had advised Paul for years and whose extensive expertise would come in very handy when structuring specific transactions for investors. (None of the above names are real for reasons that will become clear.)

We called our firm Doheny Global – I was partial to the "Global" as I had used it before. But I could not call our bank "Global Capital" as Citigroup and Deutsche Bank had appropriated that name. I called it Doheny after the family that turned the La Brea Tar Pits in LA into a huge petroleum company.

Paul agreed to act as an unofficial advisor to our firm but, really, he was there as a close friend who loved the intellectual challenge of deal-making and was committed to help me succeed and, at the same time, to help his son succeed.

Paul would spend hours with me each day explaining the complexities of finance. For me, these lessons were intellectually exhausting but very rewarding. He was teaching me what it means to be an investment banker. I could never have gone down this road by myself. I certainly didn't have the expertise to form a bank or to do deals myself, even though I thought I did.

IN BUSINESS

Though I was an investment banker now, I continued to dabble in non-profit activities which still provided a bit of income for me and, if nothing else, made me feel good about myself. It was in that capacity that I went to visit Nir Barkat, the founder of Start-Up Jerusalem, a non-profit organization dedicated to business development in the Holy City.

At that meeting, I explained to Nir that as an investment banker, among other vehicles, I was specializing in SPACs – special purpose acquisition corporations (also known as "blank check IPOs"). Nir knew what I was talking about; he had been very successful in the high-tech world together with his brother Eli. They had originated several startups which made them rich when these private companies went public (via IPOs – initial public offerings) or were acquired by other companies. After that, Nir had decided to dedicate his time to the political sphere in Israel (he was elected mayor of Jerusalem in 2008), while his brother stayed active in business. Nir thought that his brother would be interested in the new business structure that I specialized in, as it allowed successful entrepreneurs with public companies to raise a large pool of capital, giving them 18 months to find a potentially profitable merger.

It is funny how these things work. I went to Nir to discuss a non-profit venture, to do something which certainly helped me but also was of benefit to the people of Jerusalem, and I walked out with a connection to a potential business deal.

This was a pattern that I would begin to see over and over again in my new business life. I would go to talk to someone about one thing and something else – totally unrelated and unexpected – would evolve. It seemed to me that it was God's sense of humor, His way of always reminding me that I was not in control, that no matter what I thought I had planned, He had other ideas.

I spoke to Nir's brother Eli about the benefits of doing a SPAC a few weeks later. He then connected me to a colleague of his, Guy Gamzu. Guy was also a successful businessman who was very interested in this business idea. Several calls later, after discussions with Guy's lawyer and his other business partners, we had the makings of a deal – a $100 million SPAC to be listed on the alternative investment market (AIM), a division of the London Stock Exchange.

I couldn't believe that it had happened so quickly (though it did involve endless telephone conferences between New York and Israel over a two-month period). On a deal of $100 million, the commission for our company, Doheny Global, would be about $6 million. This would need to be split between me and my two partners (and we certainly had expenses to pay), but no matter how you looked at it, it was a sizeable profit for a two-month-old company!

I was ecstatic.

BEING RICH

Judy had always wanted to enlarge our pool since swimming is such an important activity for her. In LA she used to swim every day, just about all year round. In New York the swimming season was much shorter (May to September) and she would swim at least an hour a day.

But I wasn't content just to enlarge the pool. I found a landscape architect and hired him to develop a comprehensive plan for our property. We were fortunate to have more than an acre, and the land was beautiful. But I imagined it even more so – with walking paths and flower gardens and a fish pond, spanned by a wooden bridge. I had a beautiful vision and I wanted someone to design this for me.

We met with several different swimming pool companies, discussing different pool designs: rectangular ones, kidney-shaped, free form, waterfalls, Jacuzzis. I also happen to enjoy nice cars and was thinking of buying a really super car. A friend of my son brought over his family's BMW M5, the fastest car in the BMW line. It is not something you can usually even test drive as it is a special-order item. But I got a chance to try it. It was amazing. It felt like an F16! This was the car I wanted, plus the new pool, plus the new landscaping, plus maybe an addition to our home …

In case you haven't figured it out yet, I was getting carried away with the idea of being RICH.

Oh sure, at the same time Judy and I were also talking about the specific charitable projects we wanted to do. Judy wanted to start a training program for religious teachers as well as a program for kids at risk, and we were trying to figure out who we would donate to, but – truth be told – I was spending an inordinate amount of time thinking about cars, reading about cars in magazines and test driving them as well.

I forgot about the old adage: "Don't count your chickens before they are hatched." As far as I was concerned, there was nothing to worry about, except how to spend the money.

With my partners, I flew to London to meet with the team of Israeli entrepreneurs to discuss the deal. They signed the engagement letter with us, which meant we were off and running. We really did have our first client.

And then the sky fell in!

Three weeks later, they decided not to proceed – for a variety of reasons. The SPAC market had cooled down, which is something which can happen overnight on Wall Street; things get hot and then just as fast they get cold. They had some concerns about our team and our ability to deliver the deal, and so they decided to back out. I was devastated. I don't recall being that depressed before, except perhaps at the deaths of my parents. It was the only thing I had to compare it to.

I was absolutely one hundred percent beside myself. There was nothing I could do to get the deal back on track. I saw my dreams disappear in front of me. I was a failure as an investment banker. And I hadn't even started! I couldn't make phone calls. I couldn't work. I couldn't smile. I was angry at God and at the world. Why had He led me down this path only to pull the rug out from under me?

It took me a couple of weeks before I was prepared to look at myself and to try to figure out the reason why this had happened.

GOOD ADVICE

I called Rabbi Weinberg and discussed it with him. I told him I was angry with God. He told me I was being silly since God is our Father in Heaven and He loves us and only wants our good. I said, "But I was going to give 20 percent to *tzedakah*." He said, "Irwin, face it – that was a bribe." He suggested that when I pray, I tell the Almighty that if I get rich, I will use my resources to figure out how to ease the suffering of His children. He again suggested I take five minutes each evening to sit on the floor (on the floor, mind you) and to feel the Almighty's pain at the plight of His children.

He said to tell the Almighty that the peace of mind I will get from being successful I will put to good use, that I will work hard to make the world a better place, and that I will use my wealth and commensurate power to wake up others to the problems facing the Jewish people.

He said that all this was a way of letting God know my true goals. Or really letting myself know, since God already knows! He felt that my financial success was in the bag, and I had nothing to worry about except for my immortal soul. (There you go – it was a snap!)

Eventually it sank in. I went for some long walks, smoked a few cigars and meditated – that is, tried to connect with what was good about my failure. If God is my Father in Heaven, then why would He allow this to happen? I had always taught my students that if your son asked you for a BMW and you knew he was a reckless driver, would you give it to him? Of course not. You knew he would just hurt himself and you only wanted what was good for him. Would the son understand you were doing this for his good? Of course not! He would be very, very angry with you.

Well, I had to learn my own teachings.

SLIPPERY SLOPE

It became clear to me that I had been a little too involved in the material world – just at the *thought* of being rich. I had spent a little too much time fantasizing about fast cars and fancy swimming pools and waterfalls and ponds and expensive vacations. I have always known that I liked the finer things in life, but I was amazed at how quickly I could slide down that slippery slope.

Judaism teaches that there is nothing wrong with enjoying the physical world as long as you elevate it and not sink into it – as long as you make the mundane holy. There is nothing wrong with enjoying money and enjoying nice things, but you can't get carried away with them and you must use them for good.

There is a story that I love about the Chafetz Chaim. A traveling salesman once came to visit him in Radin and was shocked by the simplicity of his living space: a table, two chairs, a bed, a bookcase. "Where are all your belongings?" the salesman said. The rabbi smiled, "Where are all your belongings?" he asked. The man responded: "But I am only passing through!" And then the Chafetz Chaim said, "So it is with me. I am only passing through."

That is really how we should all view ourselves in this world. There is nothing wrong with possessions as long as we don't get anchored in them, as long as we remember we are just passing through.

I think I had forgotten that, and God knew it.

After the deal fell apart, my prayers became much more real and much more intense. I suddenly realized that I really needed God's help in becoming successful in my new occupation. We see over and over again that the patriarchs and matriarchs had trouble conceiving children. Biblical commentators tell us that they experienced these difficulties so that they would call out to God in prayer. In the act of creation on the third day, God created grass, but it did not sprout until the sixth day when man was created and prayed for rain. It was all there ready to grow, but it needed man's prayers to become a reality.

I still didn't feel great about what had happened, but I could see the benefits at the end of the tunnel. I also realized that I could not hinge everything on one deal alone, and that I had to line up other business prospects.

I applied myself and made no less than thirty phone calls over the next two weeks lining up potential deals. My partners did the same.

In the fairy tale world, you need to kiss ten frogs to get one prince – well, the business world is much the same. It is a very time-consuming process but a necessary one.

If it weren't for this one fiasco, I doubt I would have worked so hard to create potential deals that might come to fruition over the next six months. This also made me realize how much I was dependent on God's help. It was more clear to me than ever that God was running the world. I knew I had to make my prayers more real, not just in a time of crisis, but every day. I just didn't know how to do it yet.

6

In Uman

I didn't want to go, let me make that perfectly clear. I was pushed into it – albeit gently – by my wife Judy who thought that now was the time to honor a promise I had made to my son to go *someday*.

We have been blessed with eight wonderful children, the older of whom have all found their own unique niches in the Jewish world. My son Simcha – who extracted this promise from me – is a brilliant musician whose extemporaneous compositions on the piano can bring tears to your eyes with their power and intensity. He is deeply connected to his soul, which somehow led him onto the unusual path of the Breslov Hassidic sect. We supported him in his choice – as we have the very different choices of his brothers and sister – but *supporting* your child in his journey and *joining* him are two wildly different things.

Twice before Simcha spent Rosh Hashana in Uman, Ukraine, where Breslov Hassidim and a lot of other strange (and normal) people gather every year at the graveside of Rebbe Nachman, the founder of the Breslov sect. He urged me to come with him.

I had heard about the intensity of the Uman experience from various acquaintances who had gone in past years. I had also heard they brought all their own food and water, and that scared me to no end.

Reluctantly, I told Simcha I would go in 2005 and then got too busy with work, so I cancelled. I then told him I would go in 2006 and again got busy negotiating my first big deal as an investment banker, and so I cancelled again. But, when the deal fell through, I no longer had a good excuse not to go. I kept mum, hoping that others had forgotten about it.

My wife didn't. She felt that it was very important that I go in order to show my support of Simcha and his life. She also had noticed how my spirits were flagging of late and thought that this might prove to be a spiritual boost for me.

I had never been away from my family for *any* holiday in all our years of marriage, and it was to my wife's credit that she was willing to spend this Rosh Hashana alone with five of our younger children. And if she was willing to make the sacrifice, why shouldn't I?

I was trapped.

UMAN, HERE I COME

Arriving by taxi at the outskirts of Uman, I could not get into town without paying a $5 bribe to the police. Once inside, I was overwhelmed by the chaos. Non-stop noise, crush of people, crowds, throngs of Jews everywhere!

I saw not only Hassidim but every type of Jew, wearing every type of dress and head-covering. I spotted two Israelis wearing pink tee-shirts and pink yarmulkes. A guy with a ponytail and an earring. Another one with side-locks (*peyos*) down to his waist. One with orange pants, tie-dye hat, orange poncho and silver chain on his neck. Kids running around everywhere (Breslovers believe that as soon as a boy reaches age seven, he should visit Uman). Ukrainian policemen and soldiers patrolling the streets. Loud violin music playing, a guy in a long trench coat carrying a boom box. Music, music everywhere.

The taxi turned a corner and almost plowed into 30 little pup tents like at the bottom of Mt. Everest. Where had I landed? Kathmandu? Woodstock?

This was the middle of the Ukraine, but everyone and everything was totally Jewish – Jewish signs, Jewish music, Jewish booksellers, Jewish yarmulke sellers, Jewish beggars. A few Ukrainians were watching all the goings-on with a kind of dull-eyed look. I know they hate Jews, and such great numbers had to be disconcerting to any anti-Semite.

Simcha, who got there ahead of me, arrived, bringing along a wheel-barrow and a Ukrainian to haul my three food-filled suitcases to our – what shall I call it? – shack. No, that's being generous. It was, in fact, a hovel, pre-1850 construction. Two rooms. A kitchen consisting of a sink by the front door. A bathroom equally posh. The toilet reminded me of that *Seinfeld* episode where George goes to India and says, "I won't use the toilet while I'm here." I wondered how long I could go without using it. No hot water, but who needs to wash at home when you can share the ritual pool (*mikveh*) with a thousand Jews?

I collapsed on the bed, which must have come from a gulag surplus store – old rusty springs, a mattress (if you could call it that) sagging in the middle and at both ends. Oh no, three days here. God save me! I took a sleeping pill and drifted into blessed oblivion.

FEEDING AT THE TROUGH

The next day after morning prayers, Simcha took me for coffee at one of the many guest houses that the Breslov Hassidim have set up to welcome and feed the throngs.

We walked up a steep and narrow staircase and entered a room no larger than 15x15 feet, absolutely jam-packed, elbow-to-elbow. At a glance, it looked like a public restroom. Bolted to the wall was a long, stainless-steel trough – the kind that could just as easily be used for feeding cattle. Suspended above the trough was a long row of faucets, variously labeled: TEA, COFFEE, MILK. You took a thin plastic up, made for cold not hot beverages – hey, who am I to complain? – and filled up on as much coffee as you wanted. I drank one cup to satisfy my caffeine craving, but then my imagination and my phobias went to work: Where was this coffee being made? Where was it flowing *from*? What went through those pipes before? Had they ever been flushed out?

Thankfully, I had anticipated a coffee-withdrawal problem and brought along two cans of Starbucks' double espresso and cream for both days of the holiday. Thus, I was able to leave the feeding troughs for the more unfortunate souls.

I must mention that cakes came with the coffee. All for free. The organizers had really thought of every aspect. I mean how can you possibly provide coffee in the morning to 30,000 caffeine addicts except with feeding troughs that, in other settings, are used to feed cattle? I could only hope that these weren't bought second-hand.

It takes ingenuity to feed so many people, many of whom just arrived here without pre-planning, and (unlike me) without suitcases stuffed with canned tuna and protein bars. I saw one soup kitchen was giving out free sandwiches, but there were so many people wanting them that the kitchen people had to lock the gates and hand out the food through the slots, else they would not have been able to absorb the crush of people trying to push their way inside.

Somebody should have put up a sign to let them know where Simcha lives. This boy has such a big heart. He can't turn anybody away. Our hut ended up sleeping I don't know how many people because I lost count, and dinners intended for a half a dozen were stretched to feed a dozen, then two dozen, and then he just threw the doors open. As I saw the three-suitcases full of food I brought disappearing, I was happy I had my own secret stash. One *tzaddik* per family is enough.

THE INFECTIOUS UMAN SPIRIT

One of the most amazing parts of the experience was observing the interactions among all the different types of Jews present. Nowhere else in the entire Jewish world would you see such respect and good manners among such diverse Jews!

With so many people jammed into a relatively small area, it is inevitable that people would bump into you, elbow you, step on you, or worse. I watched in amazement when this happened and experienced myself the object of the jostling innumerable times. But every time it happened, people stopped and turned to the offended party, smiled broadly and apologized. It was contagious. If you accidentally bumped into someone, you immediately stopped and looked them in the eye and said, "I'm sorry." It became the social norm.

I realized just how easy it would be to make the world a more pleasant place. In New York City, if someone bumps you, they usually ignore you or – if you dare to voice an objection – follow up with an insult.

At one point, Rabbi Elazar Mordechai Kenig was giving a class in the synagogue. People were talking on the balcony, and it was bothering those trying to listen. Someone below shushed those on the balcony, but instead of doing it with a scowl, he did it almost apologetically – with a huge smile and look of love.

Such a difference – the medium truly is the message!

SKINNY DIPPING

Before Rosh Hashana, Simcha suggested we go to purify ourselves (as is the Hassidic custom) in the *mikveh*. Inwardly, I groaned.

I know that it is a tradition to go to the *mikveh* before Rosh Ha-shana, but it is one of those customs that I have never embraced. I am not sure why, but it just never seemed holy to me to jump into a small pool with a bunch of naked men. It just didn't speak to my soul. Of course, I knew coming to Uman that this was going to be something Simcha would ask me to do. I hadn't lost sleep over it, but I had wondered if I could weasel out of it somehow.

But, after a day of navigating the throngs in Uman, an idea that had never appealed to me before had become totally abhorrent. Though math had not been one of my better subjects in school, I could still do some basic calculations in my head: There were 30,000 people in Uman. Let's say just half went to the *mikveh*, that's 15,000. There were 12 hours between sunrise and sunset. That means that about 1,300 men were hopping into the *mikveh* per hour! A soulful experience? Doubtful!

But Simcha anticipated my fears and suggested we go to take the dip in a nearby lake. A great idea. A ten-minute walk through the woods brought us to a beautiful spot hiding a large water-filled can-yon surrounded by high rock walls. A dozen others had gotten there ahead of us, but compared to the square footage-to-body ratio in town, this was nothing.

Simcha warned me that the water was cold, but I was not pre-pared for *how* cold. I jumped in and the chill took my breath away. This water was certainly below 40 degrees Fahrenheit. I tried to remember what I learned in high-school biology about hypother-mia – how long before you lose consciousness? I dunked three times and quickly scampered out, trying to hold the thought that I had just been reborn and was now a new creation, but I was freezing.

I looked over at my fellow skinny-dippers – the weirdest collec-tion of Jews on the planet – and wondered what they were focusing on. Were they also imagining themselves as new creations, without the saber tattoos on their biceps and snakes on their backsides? Was this a spiritual experience for them?

Going back into town, and trying to gauge if my material-self had somehow been altered by that chilling dip, I could not help but notice the holes in the ground next to the village huts. Septic tank holes! Hopefully, air-tight septic tanks, functioning properly. The more I thought about it, the more concerned I became about that canyon. I remembered the engineer who came to our home in Monsey to deal with drainage issues; he had said that water always flows to the lowest point. Wasn't that canyon the lowest point around here? I began to wonder about that layer of stuff on the pond's surface that had seemed like a reflection from the trees. But was it? As I walked, my skin started to burn and itch. Had I just taken my pre-Rosh Hashana cleansing dip in the run-off from the village septic tanks?

I couldn't get this thought out of my head for the rest of the day. (Suddenly, the murky water after a dip from 1,300 Hassidim per hour seemed a lot more attractive.) I thought to e-mail my wife and have her make an immediate appointment with the skin doctor at home. My Rosh Hashana praying started early.

THE ZION

The epicenter of Uman is called the Zion – this is the gravesite of Rebbe Nachman. It is the North Pole and the South Pole in one – the center of all gravitational pulls in the Breslov world.

Try to imagine an area the size of a couple of football fields surrounded by wire mesh fences and covered by corrugated metal. Inside, it is subdivided into a warren of many rooms at the center of which is the grave itself. The grave is protected by a little stone house and surrounded by another fence. Mordechai Ben David, the famous singer who so effectively blends Hassidic and modern music, told me that when he first came here about 20 years ago, this was some peasant's backyard. You paid a couple of dollars to the owner to get close to the grave. How things have changed!

The central room closest to the grave holds about 1,000 people. It is outfitted with wooden benches with book-holders attached. When I was there, it was overflowing with people who were for the most part orderly, though the same could not be said for those trying to access the small space nearest the grave itself. Here in a space meant for ten, about 200 were pushing to get closer to say the prayer known as the "Total Repair" (*HaTikkun HaKlali*).

A good Breslover is required to say the *HaTikkun HaKlali*, which consists of ten psalms arranged in a specific order by the Rebbe. It is believed that the Rebbe had discerned a certain secret to this order and if you say it at his graveside, his prayers and spiritual power will be of significant benefit to you. There are always people saying this in great numbers next to his grave.

The other rooms in the Zion vary in size. It took me a while to figure out how all the rooms were connected and who holds court in which area. I was constantly amazed that literally hundreds of *minyans* were going on simultaneously at all times. On Rosh Hashana this became really chaotic when the blowing of the ram's horn (*shofar*) started. The first *minyan* started praying before 6 AM and so got to the *shofar*-blowing by 11 AM. The last started four hours later and arrived at the *shofar*-blowing by 3 PM. Others blew in between. So basically, there was non-stop *shofar*-blowing all day and thousands of people jammed together continuously crying out to God. Some would sob hysterically during prayers. I was left wondering what sin they had committed or what calamity had befallen them that they should be moved to such gut-wrenching sobs. It shook me to hear them – as if their sobs were echoing through me. (Simcha later told me that this is how Breslovers sob when they realize how far they are from their Father in Heaven. Imagine that?)

On the first day of Rosh Hashana, Simcha (in his white coat and fur hat) and I (a lot less fashionably decked out) prayed in a temporary structure built for 3,700 people (but packing in 7,000). If the Hassidim were not all pleasant, warm and polite, it would be chaos. It was so tight you had to climb atop the backs of the benches to get out. The aisles and doorways and balconies were jammed. A fire hazard if one ever existed. Not to worry, right outside a fire engine (circa 1950) waited with an equally modern ambulance – both on alert!

The town authorities clearly see this place as a disaster waiting to happen; they have condemned the building and demand a letter from the Breslovers every year absolving them of responsibility if it caves in.

Simcha somehow miraculously got us two excellent seats close to the front and near the cantor – for only $250 each (which gives you an idea of the operating budget for the whole event). It was a powerful experience to open Rosh Hashana there, with everyone shouting out *Amen!* in unison.

For the first time the words of the "Master of the World" (*Adon Olam*) hymn jumped out at me and became real. They brought me to tears. I read them over and over as their meaning seeped into me for the first time. I sang them to myself to a tune I remembered from my youth. I begged God for blessings of good health and happiness for all my family and that we would all merit to grow close to Him. I let the sound of the many *shofars* cut through me and I tried to feel that sound shaking me from my slumber. I hoped it would slice through the layers of apathy I had accumulated in the past year which were keeping me from feeling God's presence.

The second day, Simcha and I prayed in one of the many little rooms attached to the Zion. The place was originally constructed as a passageway and you could have put maybe 50 people in there comfortably. On Rosh Hashana it held 300. Everybody was so tightly squeezed in together that you couldn't move your hands up or down. Whatever position you were in, that is how you stayed until they started jumping up and down and dancing, and then you had no choice but to go with the flow.

As we were dancing together holding hands, I was struck by the realization that Simcha's grip was that of a man – that his hand was a man's hand and no longer a little boy's. It was a poignant moment as I realized that my son had truly grown up. It hit home there in Uman.

TASHLICH

There is a Rosh Hashana custom (called *tashlich*) to empty your pockets and shake out breadcrumbs into the water to symbolize the discarding of sins. This meant that the entire gathering had to get to a body of water.

Imagine a large lake surrounded by steep grassy hills and two access roads about ten feet wide. Now imagine 20,000 men jammed together around this place. It started slowly in the late afternoon and the throngs just kept coming and coming until you couldn't move an inch. Wherever you were you stayed. Then the hippies started a long snaking dance-line that moved through the crowd all around the lake. The Hassidim were also dancing and singing. They sang one tune after another after another for two hours. They then started a version of the "wave" that you usually see at sports games. Tens of people on one side of the lake would start yelling at the top of their lungs and then another group would pick it up across the lake and before you knew it all 20,000 people were screaming.

With all the commotion and emotion, it was truly a miracle that no one fell or was pushed into the lake. Clearly, the Ukrainian policemen feared this might happen. They placed a boat with two lifeguards in the middle of the lake with two life-preservers at the ready, just in case. What these guys thought being surrounded by the screaming thousands I don't know. I would have been petrified if I were them.

As a finale, some Israeli punk rockers took off their earrings and tossed them into the lake. This caught on and lots of people were doing it, all the while singing *Na nah, nach, Nachman mei Uman*. It was wild to see. A truly unforgettable sight.

POSTSCRIPT

Earlier during the holiday, Simcha and I had read the *HaTikkun HaKlali* together, and afterwards he told me that, to complete the "repair," I needed to give a small amount of charity.

As I was going to my taxi after the holiday was over, Simcha reminded me that I had still to fulfill this requirement and suggested that I find someone poor and give him a bit of money. I looked around but everyone was rushing and running around. I did not want to delay leaving. Just then someone approached me and asked me for a donation to the Breslov effort in Israel. God had clearly sent this messenger to help me complete my "repair." The guy walked up to me and no one else. Simcha had a big grin on his sweet face under his fur hat. I kissed him good-bye.

The taxi driver was waiting. As we stood in the center of the tumult, with crowds of people rushing by on all sides to get to their buses or taxis, I placed my hands on his forehead and blessed him that he should have a sweet and healthy new year. That he should grow close to God. That he should learn a lot of Torah. That he should continue to get *nachas* from his gorgeous baby son, Nachman, and continue to develop a loving relationship with his wife, Chaya Rachel. I let him know I was proud of him, and that I was happy I had come, and that it had been a special experience for me. We kissed and hugged a few times. I told him I wasn't sure if I would return, but that it had been very meaningful. I likened it to making a good scotch – you have to let it sit for a while and mature before you know its true taste.

This experience needed some maturing to say the least. I had taken a sleeping pill each night to help with the seven-hour time difference, but the night I left I figured I didn't need one. Under normal circumstances I would have been right, but not after Uman.

I lay awake in bed tossing and turning until morning – the sounds, songs, noises and images I had been assaulted with over the previous three days racing through my mind, my fried synapses misfiring.

I had to admit it had been a truly awesome spiritual experience. Though it was a battle to get beyond the difficult living conditions, the sense of the holiday inevitably came through here more powerfully than anyplace else.

At every meal we had at least 15 people in our little hovel, eating at a make-shift table outside under the stars, with the wind whistling through the trees. Simcha's friends and guests sang non-stop the most beautiful melodies and would occasionally get up and dance. Somehow the three suitcases of food I brought was enough to supply more than 75 servings over the Yom Tov. Just one of the many miracles of Uman.

Another miracle: Here it was possible to feel the oneness of the Jewish people – a taste of what it will be like when the Messiah finally comes and unites this fractured nation.

Although at times during Rosh Hashana, I had to fight to find an open channel to talk to God as there were so many distractions, still I had more one-on-one talks with Him than I had had in a long while. I went for several walks where I talked to myself and to God about how I wanted to be different and what I wanted to change in the coming year. And I had a couple of truly inspiring moments in prayer when I could feel the Almighty's warm embrace, and I had the sense that I had shed some hard husks keeping me from being real.

In short: a truly a life-altering Rosh Hashana. I felt like I lived a year in three days. God willing, I would continue to grow and experience the many little miracles of awareness which I was blessed with in Uman.

7

In Business

By the beginning of 2007, I had again whittled my home-equity line of credit down to $130,000, and I knew that – at the rate I was spending money – this gave me perhaps three months of cash flow. But I was not worried. Doheny Global was involved in four specific deals, which we had been noodling along for some months. In investment banking, deals of this size take a while to progress, but I was highly optimistic.

The first two involved Hollywood legend Ted Field and his film company Radar Films.

Ted is heir to the Marshall Field's fortune and for many years had been a fixture on the Forbes 400 list. He also happened to be among the top ten most successful film producers in Hollywood. He was respected as someone who truly understands pop culture, having produced such highly popular fare as *Texas Chainsaw Massacre, Runaway Bride, Jumanji, Mr. Holland's Opus, The Hand that Rocks the Cradle, Three Men and a Baby, Cocktail, Bird on a Wire, Bill and Ted's Excellent Adventure, The Last Samurai* and *Outrageous Fortune*. While none of his films were Oscar winners, most were profitable, and several had hit the box office bonanza, making $500-600 million on an investment of maybe $10 million, while others became cult classics with multiple sequels. With over 50 films in the last ten years to his credit, Ted was considered a solid player with a track record. He was also a proven entrepreneur in that he started his own record label, Interscope Records, and then sold it to Universal Music for over $500 million.

For the first deal, we were trying to raise $10 million in a convertible preferred stock offering to give Ted more funds to buy promising scripts. Because of its relatively small size, we needed to raise the funds from high net-worth individuals rather than from institutions (like hedge funds). This made it quite a difficult task. But we needed to do it for Ted, even though it was small and not our focus, because of the second (major) deal we *wanted* to do for Ted.

The major deal was a $300-500 million SPAC to raise money to buy out an animation company from one of the studios. The problem was if we didn't raise the $10 million for him, Ted probably wouldn't do the SPAC with us. I mean, if we couldn't raise $10 million, why should he have confidence in us to raise $300 million?

A friend of mine, Marvin Igelman, introduced us to Ted. It is quite mind-boggling that Ted was working with us since we were a brand-new bank – he really could work with any investment banker that he so chose – but by some miracle he was working with Doheny Global.

The truth of the matter is that the assignment he had given us was a real challenge. A small raise is much more difficult than a big raise. Paul was quite confident that we could do the SPAC deal, assuming we were able to get help from some established players in the SPAC market – like Sunrise Securities – which we hadn't lined up yet. However, the issues were clear – the player knew what he wanted to acquire, he was a well-known entrepreneur with a proven track record, and it was a liquid investment involving established institutions.

But the $10 million involved a private company, and it was not a liquid investment, even if it was a safe one paying a 9½ percent dividend, which in pre-tax dollars is really a 12 percent return; more-over, when he went public, it could be converted into stock in his company at a discount of the current valuation. Nonetheless, it was too small to bring to institutions and the return wasn't high enough for professional investors, so that left us searching for high net-worth individuals such as doctors and lawyers. But if we didn't succeed, we probably wouldn't get a chance at the big deal.

DOABLE DEALS

The third deal was a $70 million roll-out of a limousine business which involved the high-tech market. It could best be summarized as bringing the technological sophistication of Fedex and the ease of Jet Blue to the limo business on an international level. The principal in it was Alex Mashinsky.

I knew Alex from my days at Aish when he donated $250,000 after his first company, Arbinet, went public. He was a brilliant Russian, who had more than 30 patents to his credit. His new company was more about technology than limousines – it aimed to do what Sabre did for American Airlines and the airline reservation system. At that time, there was no way to book a limo online, get an immediate price quote, make a reservation and get a confirmation. You could do this for hotel rooms, airline tickets, car rentals, but not for a limo service. Alex had invested $12 million of his own money to develop the software, and our job was to help him raise the money he need-ed now in order to buy the limo companies and to start rolling out his business. If he could accomplish this, all the travel websites would want his service as he would be the only one to offer it. The potential for exponential growth made this a very exciting deal.

The fourth deal was also a tech roll-out that came my way through another one of my Aish donors, Chris Kitze. A brilliant en-trepreneur, Chris ran Disney.com, Disney's first Internet effort back in the mid 1990s. He then built a series of websites for Wine.com, the largest online vendor of spirits. He also ran several other major on-line sites. Chris introduced us to a successful web entrepreneur, Brian Nelson, head of Trankos, a very hot online advertising company. His revenues were increasing 50 percent per year! He wanted to raise $50-100 million to buy two or three other companies in the same field, so that he could build a larger company able to survive the coming shake-down in this line of commerce.

Deals two, three and four were all doable deals. Paul had figured out how to structure each one to allow us to raise the money we needed. But a lot of pieces had to fall into place to make it happen.

Since the $10 million deal was the most worrisome to us, I had been putting a special effort into my own prayers asking the Al-mighty: "God, I really need your guidance and help to show me how to find the contacts for the $10 million raise for Ted. If I don't ac-complish this, I won't be able to move forward with the larger deal. God Almighty help please! Teach me, show me, guide me and help me figure it out. If we get the larger deal, we will be able to help your children even more."

This prayer had been on my lips for two or three weeks, when a strange and amazing thing happened.

THE PRAYER CONTRACT

I had been donating considerable money (more than $100,000 over two years) to the fund benefiting the needy of Jerusalem run by the Zilberman family. The Zilbermans are very special people. When you meet them, you feel a sense of holiness about them. You feel that they look at each person as created in the image of God, a reflec-tion of the Almighty, no matter how that person is dressed, or how he talks, or how he relates to religion. In addition to their charitable projects, they also run several unique yeshivas where children learn

Torah through a special system of memorization – a young child is capable of memorizing very much and, by Bar Mitzvah age, the kids know not only the whole Bible but also the Mishna (the index of Jewish law) by heart.

While I was visiting Jerusalem, the patriarch of the family, Rabbi Yehoshua Zilberman, asked to see me. I told him that I had no more money to give at the moment, but he insisted that we meet. He came to my hotel accompanied by Rabbi Aharon Fox, who spoke English and made it easier for us to communicate, as my Hebrew is not that great.

The David Citadel is a very modern hotel – a lot of marble and glass, big open spaces, bright lights – and it was almost comical to see Rabbi Zilberman in his "old world" attire (long black coat, black hat and scraggly long beard) walking through this space, which screamed "new world." Yet there was a sense of spiritual dignity about him that instantly diminished what was earthly around him.

We met in the executive lounge of the hotel – a room filled with newspapers, magazines, and telecommunications devices. Rabbi Zilberman and Rabbi Fox looked more out of place than ever – I mean, these are people who don't have TVs or computers; they don't even read newspapers!

We chatted about my business. Rabbi Zilberman listened carefully. Then he said he wanted my help. There was a building that the yeshiva had been renting which the owner had put up for sale, giving the Zilbermans the first right of refusal. Rabbi Zilberman wanted to know if I was able to buy it for them, or at least could help them buy it.

I asked how much they needed. I could tell a big number was coming.

He said $850,000.

I explained that I was not in a position to help them with anything of that size. I think when poor Israelis come into fancy hotels, they imagine that the people staying there must all be millionaires. So, I made it clear to them that I was not a rich guy, I was just a *rich guy wanna-be*, but I was not there yet by any stretch of the imagination.

Rabbi Zilberman pondered what I said. He then asked if I could figure out a way that they might be able to borrow the funds to buy the building. I gave him some ideas and names of some people who might be willing to help. He thanked me and then said, "Irwin, you and I should be partners."

I chuckled and told him that I was his partner already. I reminded him of how much money had I had given him over the last two years. He said he appreciated that immensely, but he thought it would be a good idea to formalize the structure.

"Formalize the structure?" I asked, "What exactly do you mean by that?"

He asked me how much money I thought I would make this year. I told him I believed that Doheny Global could make $20 million in commissions. He wanted to know if this was possible in the "natural way of the world" or if such a sum would take a "miracle."

"Why do you want to know this?" I asked, puzzled.

He explained to me that he didn't feel it proper to pray for a miracle, but if it was within our reach, then he would storm the heavens to make it happen.

I swallowed hard.

To give him an honest answer, I called Paul who said that based on the deals in progress, it was entirely possible Doheny Global could make $20 million in commissions, and my share of that would be somewhere between $8-10 million.

I conveyed this to Rabbi Zilberman.

THE DEAL

He suggested that we make a deal. He, Rabbi Zilberman, would pray daily for my success, and if by the end of the year I collected $10 million as my share of the Doheny Global profits, I would donate $850,000 to his yeshiva to purchase the building.

Something about this was scaring me. He was really serious! I smiled sheepishly, said it sounded like a good idea, and why don't I think it over and get back to him in a few weeks.

But he wasn't going let me weasel out of it – he said, "Let's draft a contract right now."

I felt a shiver go through my whole body. A light-hearted, somewhat comical conversation over a cup of coffee in a swanky hotel lounge was turning deadly serious. This guy really believed his prayers would have an impact.

I was astonished, but I shouldn't have been. I mean I wrote two books on prayer! (*Powerful Prayers* with Larry King, and *How to Get Your Prayers Answered*.) I believed in prayer, or did I?

Suddenly, it came to me that I didn't *totally* believe in the power of prayer to change events. By witnessing the seriousness with which Rabbi Zilberman took prayer – that he meant business and was prepared to take on this task – I realized how far away I was from his total commitment to the idea.

Sure I prayed regularly, and sure I asked God for help. But was I shocked when I didn't get what I asked for? No. I didn't *really* believe that prayer would make a difference. I mean, I did and I didn't at the same time. Somehow, I had not absorbed my own teachings on a deep enough level.

His astonishing commitment to prayer had made me realize how weak my belief really was. I was shaken. I had not expected the conversation to take such a serious path. I was suddenly transported into a different reality. I felt God's presence in the room. I wanted to run and hide. The pressure to be real was on.

THE DRAFT

I got up a bit shakily, went over to the hostess in the lounge and came back with a pen and few pieces of hotel stationery. And Rabbi Zilberman began to dictate to me the draft of the contract:

Agreement between Irwin Katsof and Rabbi Yehoshua Zilberman:

I, Irwin Katsof, will be doing deals in the next year, and I, Rabbi Zilberman will be a partner in the deals.

For my part, I, Irwin Katsof, will work physically. For my part, I, Rabbi Zilberman, will pray daily for the success of the deals.

I, Irwin Katsof, obligate myself to tell Rabbi Zilberman the exact details of the deals, so that Rabbi Zilberman will know exactly what to pray for.

Further, I, Irwin Katsof, obligate myself, if I realize a net profit of $10 million, to buy the Zilberman yeshiva building for $850,000. If my profit is less than that, my donation will be calculated according to the profit realized.

In exchange for buying the yeshiva building, the spiritual merit accrued by Torah learning of the Zilberman yeshiva's students will forever be owned by Irwin Katsof.

May it be the will of God that we succeed in increasing Torah learning, making it precious so that, according to the words of the verse, "From Zion, the Torah will come and the words of God from Jerusalem." And may the words of the verse come true for Irwin Katsof, "God will bless you from Zion and

you will see the good of Jerusalem your whole life – you, your
children and children of your children and all Israel."
  Signed:
  Irwin Gavriel Yitzchak ben Avraham Katsof
  Yehoshua ben Yitzchak Shlomo Zilberman

I signed the contract, shook hands with Rabbi Zilberman and with Rabbi Fox, gave each one a hug and kiss on both cheeks, walked them to the elevator and rode downstairs with them in silence. I said good-bye to them at the front door and returned to my room.

I felt transformed.

These people truly believed in the power of prayer – this hit me at a very deep level and it kept reverberating within my being.

I was reminded of the story of Moses when he saw the burning bush. The Torah says, "he turned and saw the bush." Biblical commentators ask, "Why did he need to turn? It was right there in front of him." It was because he needed to stop and look at it. He needed to pay attention! We are all like that. We just need to stop and turn to see what is before us all the time, to witness the miracles that God is sending us each and every day.

I began to think about something I had written in my book *How to Get Your Prayers Answered*. The first step to getting your prayers answered is to "pray like you expect results." If you don't pray like you expect results, then you won't really apply yourself. You won't put in the effort to make it sure that your prayers will be heard. I had forgotten this basic truth!

Rabbi Zilberman really expected results. He was going to pray like he expected results. And because of that, he would get results – and as his partner, so would I.

THE RESULTS

One morning, I awoke to two e-mails.

The first was from Uriela Sagiv, my editor, who wrote that she had had lunch with an Aish supporter, a woman lawyer from Las Vegas who had asked her what she was doing. When Uriela mentioned that she had begun editing my new book, the Vegas lawyer exclaimed, "I always thought Irwin was a genius when he was a fundraiser. Is there some way you can help me invest with him?" So Uriela wrote to me, asking that I be in touch with her friend.

The amazing thing was that this was exactly the kind of person I needed to speak to about Ted's $10 million raise – a wealthy individual, with a high net-worth, who was looking for access to unique deals. I thought it was astonishing that the Almighty had sent me a potential investor through such a round-about set of circumstances. Miracle, God's hand, coincidence? Prayers being answered? Rabbi Zilberman at work? You tell me!

The second e-mail was from Zale Newman. Zale lives in Toronto, Canada. I knew that I had met him and spoken to him on the phone, but I couldn't have picked him out of a crowd if you paid me a thousand dollars. He obviously knew me though. He told me that he had set up a financial advisory company and became involved in a possible SPAC with a group of successful Israeli entrepreneurs. He had already raised around $30 million of equity and was looking at various investment banks to complete the deal. He had already set up meetings with two New York banks when suddenly he thought of me. Why me? He said he wanted to work with someone who was honest and had a similar set of world views, and he had heard that I had opened my own shop and was specializing in SPACs. Was I interested?

I told him yes, and that kicked off a feverish series of calls for the rest of the day between us and his partners. Paul spoke to them three times during the day. As always happens, they were blown away by Paul's brilliance and his ability to show them the clear benefits and weaknesses of each possible investment structure. They were considering working with us. Even more important though, Zale mentioned to me that he had raised his $30 million from wealthy private investors for this transaction – another possible lead to help us raise the $10 million for Ted.

Miracle, God's hand, coincidence? Prayers being answered? Rabbi Zilberman at work? You tell me!

One of the critical pieces we needed to do Ted's SPAC of $300 million was expertise from someone who had done several SPACs through AIM (the alternative investment market in London). We were trying to get a lead into Sunrise Bank, which had done over a billion dollars of SPACs and was clearly the innovator and leader in this field. Actually, they were the only bank doing AIM SPACs. We knew of someone who was a principal at Sunrise, but had no introduction to him.

Then, just before the New Year, FedEx delivered a beautiful box of Godiva chocolates, a holiday present from Warren Newfield, who was a very successful entrepreneur in Toronto. I had tried to bring him to Rodman & Renshaw when I was working there, though I did not succeed. I called to thank him and we chatted a bit. He then told me that he had been visiting earlier in the day with Jay Rodin, the managing director at Sunrise, and he suggested that Jay call me.

He didn't really know why he mentioned me – he just thought it would be good for us to meet!

The next day, sure enough, Jay called. As we started to talk, we realized that our paths were completely intertwined and yet we had never met. It turns out he lives in Monsey as do I. Our sons had been in the same grade in school for six years and played on the same hockey team and, in fact, when we talked about it, we realized that we had been standing near each other two days before at the hockey rink, each of us watching his son practice but we didn't know each other! To top it off, we both stayed at the David Citadel Hotel at the same time; not only that, his son was always in our hotel room playing with my son Sholom, but I never knew his last name.

Jay was about to leave Sunrise to set up his own investment bank. He had plenty of experience in AIM SPACs and said he'd love to work with us on our deal with Ted. Amazing! Another missing piece and now I had found the exact fit.

Miracle, God's hand, coincidence? Prayers being answered? Rabbi Zilberman at work? You tell me!

Then Marvin Igelman – who introduced me to Ted Field in the first place – called. He said, "Irwin, I love to talk to you. You're my favorite rabbi!"

I said, "That is so nice of you to say. You made my day. But why?"

He said, "Well, it's pretty simple – you are the only rabbi who actually *makes me money!* All the other rabbis cost me money!"

But he wasn't calling to pay me compliments, he was calling with another of his business connections. Marvin – who always looked a bit disheveled with wind-blown hair and clothes slightly askew – was like a spinning top, one of those toys with crazy colors that blend into each other as they spin, and his connections were amazing.

He was calling to get me together with Jeff Sagansky, the former chairman of Sony Tristar. Jeff was trying to raise a film fund. Wow, maybe we have a film division going here. First Ted Field and now … I was beside myself. So many possibilities! It seemed as if the Almighty was sending me opportunities by the bucketful.

I didn't stop to think that maybe God didn't have all that much interest in Hollywood. And that maybe there was something askew with having a holy Jerusalem rabbi – who had never watched television, who had never been to a movie, and who had no earthly idea what these things were about – praying for me to succeed in raising money for another *Texas Chainsaw Massacre!*

I didn't stop to think about these things because I was single-mindedly fixated on succeeding and, to make things worse, the gold-dust of Hollywood was further obscuring my vision.

8

My Hollywood Dreams

I was no stranger to Hollywood – after all I had spent a good part of my adult life fundraising in LA, and many of the potential donors I solicited were in the movie business. Furthermore, to make something happen among people who were used to that glitz and glamour, I often employed Hollywood techniques.

This went along with the way I set about my job, setting "big hairy audacious goals" – what I called BHAGs – for myself.

For example, the time-honored way to raise money for a charitable organization in America was to stage a fancy dinner at which a famous person was honored. But, because my middle name was BHAG, I couldn't be content with the usual way of doing things, which had gotten hackneyed by then anyway.

How to have jaded people sit up and take notice?

Do something spectacular!

So, in 1994, while fundraising for Aish, I decided to honor Steven Spielberg and have President Bill Clinton present him with the "King David Award" (which had I made up on the spot). It would be an evening to remember and it would raise a lot of money for sure.

The problem with being a salesman is that sometimes you start to believe your own sales pitch, and you start to stretch the truth. It is a slippery slope. I understand completely now why Rabbi Yaakov Weinberg (Rabbi Noah Weinberg's illustrious brother) told me flatly that I could not lie *at all*, even for a good cause. But I was always pushing the outer edge of the envelope and skirting the grey areas. It is not something I am proud of today but, in retrospect, I see how I got caught up in it.

In this case, I sent a message to Spielberg telling him that the Jerusalem Fund (then Aish's fundraising organization of which I was director) *would like* to honor him at a gala dinner at the Century Plaza Hotel in Los Angeles and have President Clinton present him with the King David Award. (The only problem was I didn't have a commitment from President Clinton to do any such thing.)

At the same time, I sent a message to President Clinton through my contacts at the White House, telling him that the Jerusalem Fund *would like* him to present the King David Award to Steven Spielberg at a gala dinner at the Century Plaza Hotel in Los Angeles. (The only problem was that Steven Spielberg had yet to agree.)

It wasn't exactly a lie – it was true that I *would like* for it to happen. And if they both agreed, it would actually *be* true. But, at that moment, I was playing a shell game, which wasn't exactly honest either.

While I awaited their answers, I learned what it means to have nerves of steel. It was six weeks before the event and I didn't have a definitive commitment from either party, but I had to send the invitations to the printers. So I did it, throwing caution to the wind.

And then I read that President Clinton was coming to LA in two days' time and – lo and behold – spending the weekend at Steven Spielberg's mansion. Oh my! What if the subject of the award came up? My schemes would be made obvious to both men!

The sages teach us that if only we were as afraid of God seeing our indiscretions as we are of people seeing them, we would all be angels. God knew all my schemes and I felt mildly guilty about that, yet President Clinton and Steven Spielberg finding out sent sheer terror through me.

The weekend came and went. I kept expecting the Secret Service to show up at my door and arrest me for misrepresenting the President's Office, but it never happened.

The next Monday though, I did get a confirmation from Spielberg that he would accept the award and another from President Clinton that although he couldn't attend, he would tape a special video where he would address the banquet and present the award to Spielberg.

Of course, later at the banquet when I played that videotape, the word "video" never passed my lips – in fact, people mistook it for a live satellite feed. (Another one of my many sins of omission.)

The evening was a huge success. You can imagine the adrenaline rush! I was flying. And an addict was born. What to do next that could be even more grand?

PRESIDENTS AND PRIME MINISTERS

Then I had an even more audacious idea: to honor an American president – in Israel.

I called Larry King of CNN fame and asked him to be the chairman of the first ever Jerusalem Fund mission to Israel. He agreed. We decided that he would approach former President Ronald Reagan and ask him to accept the King David Award, to be presented by then Prime Minister Yitzchak Rabin.

Thus, another shell game was launched, because I was sure that if I could get one, then I could get the other. How could Rabin ever refuse to present an award to President Reagan?

They both said yes!

The mission was scheduled for December 1995 and included a star-studded cast. Though, in the end, President Reagan was not well enough to come – he had been diagnosed with Alzheimer's disease – but his daughter Maureen Reagan accepted the award on his behalf. The mission co-chairs were all business giants: Merv Adelson, vice-chairman of Time Warner, then the largest media company in the world; Ace Greenberg, chairman of Bear Stearns, one of the largest global investment banks and brokerage firms; Les Wexner, chairman of The Limited, a huge retailing and marketing conglomerate which owned Victoria's Secret, Lane Bryant and Abercrombie & Fitch among others; Lester Crown, owner of General Dynamics, Maytag, Hilton Hotels and the Chicago Bulls, to name a few of his vast holdings; and billionaire Mort Zuckerman, publisher of the *US News & World Report* and of the *New York Daily News*.

Participants were no less illustrious: William Shatner of *Star Trek* fame; Oscar-winner Rod Steiger; legendary violinist Isaac Stern; Lowell Milken, one of the richest men in America; and Israeli billionaire Shaul Eisenberg.

The group's agenda in Jerusalem was to be jam-packed with high-level meetings including Israel's top leaders and opinion makers; it was to culminate with a gala dinner in the Chagall Hall of the Knesset where the Prime Minister would present the King David Award (as well as the newly-invented Jerusalem 3000 Awards to various participants).

THE KING AND I

During the planning for that mission, the momentous peace talks took place between Israel and Jordan – which, for the first time since 1948, opened bilateral relations – and the idea came to me to take the group on a ground-breaking trip to Jordan.

I vividly recalled the news of the 1967 war, which featured bitter fighting for Jerusalem between Jordanian and Israeli forces. So, it was quite mind-boggling to me when I picked up the phone in Jerusalem and dialed 962, the country code for Jordan, and called the palace of King Hussein. When the office of royal protocol answered, I boldly requested an audience with the king, explaining that I would be bringing an illustrious group of American business leaders and stars from the world of entertainment.

They were shocked. First of all, they couldn't understand why a rabbi was calling them. Initially, they couldn't even believe I was calling them from Israel and kept asking for clarification in heavily-accented English, which was hard to understand. I remember yelling into the phone, "I am calling you from JERUSALEM!" And they said, "Are you sure?" The international direct dial lines had just been opened between the two countries, and they really couldn't believe they were receiving the call.

By the end of the conversation however, they agreed to host the group, said "thank you for calling," and hung up. There was no follow-up plan, no way to handle the logistics, no point person to call back even.

I saw that this wasn't going to work, so I asked Larry King to intervene. He wrote a letter to King Hussein (who had appeared on his show), and within a week I received a call from the office of royal protocol asking us to start working on the arrangements for the visit. They even invited the group to have lunch with the king and said they would send a royal plane to pick up everybody and bring them to the palace.

I figured I was on a winning streak, so I made another request. Could the group visit Petra while in Jordan? (Petra, a city carved completely into desert rock, is considered one of the Seven Wonders of the World, and for many years young Israelis would sneak across the border, risking their lives, to see it.) Yes, gladly! Could Jordanian helicopters fly the group there? No problem!

I then bit my lip, sucked in my breath and went for my final request. I said, "Oh, by the way, we are serving only kosher food to this group. So, if they are to have lunch with the king, we would need the food to be kosher." They agreed even to this! As it turned out, the bilateral relations treaty was so new that there was not yet *actual* trade between Israel and Jordan. So, they arranged to fly in kosher food from London. That was easier than bringing it in from just across the border.

COGNITIVE DISSONANCE

While studying psych in college, I learned about a condition called cognitive dissonance, the feeling of anxiety that results when one's beliefs and one's actions clash. And I experienced it in real life when we stood on the tarmac at Ben Gurion airport and a Royal Jordanian 757 pulled up. The doors opened and a very proper young man in an exquisitely tailored pin-stripe suit welcomed us aboard in Cambridge-accented English.

Every fiber in my body was telling me, "Don't go! This is the enemy! You'll get yourself killed!" But I bravely climbed up the access staircase. As I surveyed the faces of my fellow passengers, I could see that everyone was also a little disturbed by this experience. The last passenger to board was Israeli billionaire Shaul Eisenberg, whose personal jet was parked right behind us. As he came on board, I asked him "Why are you coming with us? You have your own plane." He said, "I never thought I'd see the day when the king of Jordan would send his own plane to pick up Jews to bring them to Amman. This is too momentous an experience to miss." When we started to taxi for take-off, I saw that his plane was following us and asked him where it was going. He laughed. "It's worth it for me to fly my plane into Jordan to refuel and save $15,000."

The captain's disembodied voice welcomed us, explaining that the ride would take only 15 minutes. It probably would have been simpler to drive over the border, but for sheer drama you couldn't beat flying in the king's plane. We took off, and I noticed that we kept climbing and climbing and climbing. At what point was the plane going to level off? I had flown a fair amount, so I knew something was not right. I looked around and saw the expressions of the other people who were thinking the same thing. We should have made a quick ascent and descent back into Amman. What was going on?

After 10 minutes, the captain's voice explained that all three airports in Amman were fogged in, so we couldn't land. Instead, they were taking us to the desert to land at a military airport. I began to say the *Shema*, the quintessential declaration of monotheism, which Jews are obliged to say when dying. They were about to get rid of us!

We landed in the desert and were told there was a change in plans. We'd spend the day in Petra, then join the king for dinner (instead of lunch). Moments later we heard the loud thump-thump-thump of military helicopters, something straight out of *Apocalypse Now.*

When they landed, once more cognitive dissonance set in. Only months before these helicopters were armed against Israel. The rifle mounts were still there even though the guns themselves were gone. We piled in and sat down on narrow metal benches where the parachutists would normally sit. As they slowly closed the doors, every hair on my body was standing on end.

We visited Petra, and it truly was an amazing experience. We then piled back into the helicopters for the flight to Amman to meet the king.

KING OF GLORY

Arriving at the palace, we got into a discussion whether or not we were obliged to make a blessing when meeting King Hussein. The Talmud mandates such a blessing – "Blessed Are You, Lord our God, King of the Universe, who has given of His glory to human beings" – upon seeing an earthly ruler who has the power of life and death. We decided that we were obliged to say the blessing as King Hussein could certainly execute anyone he chose by fiat.

When we met the king and pronounced the blessing, we were honestly awed. Still, I couldn't help but think that this was simply an earthly experience, giving us a small hint of what it might be like to meet our real King, our Father in Heaven. A *very* small hint. After all, King Hussein was only third in a dynasty artificially created in 1921 by the British when they carved out the country of Jordan from the lands of the Ottoman Empire. (That's when the two sons of the *Sharif* of Mecca, Abdullah and Faisel, became rulers of two new countries that sprang up overnight: Jordan and Iraq.)

The palace was semi-impressive. It was really an overdone mansion sitting in the middle of the largest army base in Amman. This was the only way the king could guarantee his own safety (which gives you an idea of the precariousness of his rule).

They served us dinner of kosher food they had flown in from London, and then the speeches began. In the middle of the king's speech, I realized that the present we meant to give him was sitting on a bus in the palace parking lot. One of the security men led me through a series of back doors and corridors so I could get it. It was a sculpture by one of Israel's most renowned artists, and it was in a box about a foot-square.

In a mad dash, I grabbed the box and started running across the parking lot toward the palace, not thinking how suspicious my actions must appear to onlookers. But then I saw that all around me were Arab snipers furiously communicating by walkie-talkie. Suddenly, it hit me: "Irwin, you are an idiot! They are going to shoot you!"

I stopped, lifted the box way up in front of me for everyone to see and yelled out: "It is a present for the king! A present for the king from the American group visiting the king! It is a statue!!!"

Then I walked very slowly up the steps of the palace, my heart thumping. At any moment a trigger-happy Jordanian soldier could have fired. But they allowed me to enter the palace unscathed. I presented the king with the statue and returned healthy and safe to Jerusalem.

I organized many more missions after that and visited King Hussein many times over the next six years before he died of cancer. People in Jewish charitable affairs were in awe at how we managed to arrange such high-level visits. I had no idea myself. It was not normal at all for the royal protocol office to make the arrangements they made for us, and very few other Jewish groups were able to arrange a palace visit, let alone meals with the king and helicopters to ferry everyone to Petra as well.

THE NEW KING

After King Abdullah took over as monarch, I managed to wrangle an invitation to a private reception given for him in Washington DC. I figured if I was to continue my visits, it would be important for me to establish a relationship with the new king.

I tried my best to impress him. I explained that I was Rabbi Katsof and that I brought many groups to meet with his father. He said "Aha" in a bored tone of voice. I said I had brought Lady Margaret Thatcher to the palace. "Aha." I said I had brought Senators John Kerry, Harry Reid, Orrin Hatch, and even the Speaker of the House, Newt Gingrich. No response other than "Aha." I could see that I was just one of the hundreds he had met today, and that he was never

going to remember me; I figured this was the end of my special relationship with the palace for sure. Finally, I said, "And this summer I
plan to bring Michael Richards, who played Kramer on *Seinfeld*." The
second I said "Seinfeld," he came alive. He excitedly turned to his wife
and said, "Honey, they are bringing Kramer to visit us this summer!"
They exchanged some words in Arabic and big smiles broke out on
their faces. He grabbed my hand and pumped it hard, saying, "Rabbi,
so nice to meet you! *Such* a pleasure! Give me your card please. We
are looking forward to hosting you this summer."

I had been trying to impress him with the illustrious list of politicians I had brought to visit his father. I hadn't realized that I was
dealing with a new generation. Sure, he was impressed with the
Speaker of the House, but he could meet him and others like him
any time. Pop icons were harder to come by.

Prior to our visit that summer, I got another indication that this
was a new regime. I received a call from the office of royal protocol – they had gone online and checked the website of the Jerusalem
Fund and were trying to understand exactly what the connection
was between *Jewish education* and these visits with the king of Jordan. In the many years I had brought groups to King Hussein, no one
had ever checked our website and called with such inquiries. But
King Abdullah was a student of Oxford and was very media savvy.
He had started a whole web department inside the palace and his assistants all knew their way around the Internet. Somehow, I managed
to talk my way out of their questions, sufficient enough at least that
the king agreed to still meet us – or it could be that he just wanted
to meet Kramer!

Unfortunately, Michael Richards cancelled at the last moment.
(This often happens with Hollywood types as their schedules are so
unpredictable.) So, we showed up at the summer palace in Aqaba,
where we met the new king who was wearing chinos and a jersey.

(Such a contrast to his father who always appeared in an impeccably tailored suit.) He gave a short presentation and then answered our questions.

Afterwards, I went over to him and apologized about Kramer. He smiled and said, "Too bad, Rabbi. And here we had been running around the palace greasing all the hinges on the doors, so we could be ready for his entrance!" We laughed and did pantomime impressions of Kramer rushing through the palace doors.

I got the message – a new age of diplomacy was upon us, and in that new world, pop culture was king.

And speaking of pop culture ...

9

Doheny Presents

The fact that Ted Field of Radar Films had hired our bank, Doheny Global, to do a deal was at first quite mind-boggling to me. I mean, as one of the most successful film producers in the history of Hollywood, he could get any investment bank to do this for him – from the likes of Goldman Sachs to Lehman or JP Morgan. It seemed like a minor miracle to me.

As it turned out, this raise was a difficult one – and probably why the big banks did not want to get involved. It required the investor to lock up his money in a private company, which basically meant he couldn't get it out if he needed to, something he could readily do if he made the same-size investment with a public company.

To entice us to do it – even though on a $10 million deal, we would ordinarily only make a $650,000 commission – Ted promised that if we succeeded, he would make us his banker on his next acquisition, which would be a significant purchase of a major studio with a price tag anywhere between $150 million and $500 million.

His CEO Keith Yokomoto said to us, "If you pull this off, I am prepared to have you sit beside me as you negotiate on behalf of billionaire impresario Ted Field for a $500 million deal. I will say to the others at the table: 'This is Doheny Global. They are our bankers.'" He was willing to do this and even to put his promise in writing if we pulled off this smaller and more difficult raise for him.

To get the deal going, we drew up an executive summary and a management overview, each one being approximately twenty pages of prose, charts, financial figures and PowerPoint presentations. At the end of this process, we were off to the races.

Since Doheny Global hadn't done a deal as a company yet, this was important to us. I prayed regularly, asking God to please let us succeed in raising the $10 million. I pleaded with Him to make it happen. I e-mailed Rabbi Zilberman and asked him to ramp up his prayers. If we could only succeed here, it would be amazing. What a way to start a banking career – do a small raise for one of Hollywood's most successful producers and then be given an assignment to help him raise $500 million for the acquisition of a major studio. If we could pull that off, we would have arrived, in true Hollywood style, like a Rocky epic – a come-from-behind kid swoops in to take home the prize. I could already see myself walking down the red carpet at the Academy Awards.

After months of work, we had our presentation ready. I spent several days going through my e-mail list (of some 3,000 names) and sending teaser e-mails to all the wealthy individuals I knew, asking them if they would be interested in the deal. I got a few bites and some moderate interest. But I was nowhere close. I was beginning to get scared. What if I failed?

Suddenly, I saw myself in a B-movie, going direct to video and missing the Academy Awards altogether. Worse yet, I might end up on the cutting room floor. I renewed my prayers and wrote Rabbi Zilberman again.

Then a funny thing happened …

A SAVIOR OUT OF THE BLUE

I received an e-mail from Norton Herrick, chairman of MediaBay, Inc., a very wealthy businessman and a real estate entrepreneur. I had met him through Paul in 1996, and he had donated $100,000 to Aish Ha-Torah.

Why was Norton e-mailing me?

A couple months earlier, I had been in New York for a meeting and stopped at the Ritz Carlton Hotel to relax a bit and catch up on my e-mail. As I was sitting there, enjoying the view of the Statue of Liberty and New York Harbor, I got a call that the location of our mid-town meeting was being changed; the caller, Tzvi Berg, who had a proposition for us in the Ukraine, lived in Brooklyn and was catching a flight to Europe that evening, so he preferred to meet downtown. The Ritz Carlton was as great a place as any, and we agreed to meet here. Paul would be joining us.

After the meeting with Tzvi, Paul and I spent a few more minutes at the Ritz Carlton catching up on other business news and then walked out together. As we were leaving the hotel, a stretch limo pulled up and who got out but Norton Herrick and his wife. We went over, said hello and standing out in the billowing wind coming off the Hudson, we reminisced about our past experiences together some ten years earlier. Of course, I explained to Norton what I was now doing; we exchanged cards and said we would be in touch.

That was that. When I started sending out e-mails for the Radar Films deal, I decided to try him. When I sent him my pitch, he immediately shot back an e-mail asking to see the deal documents and later that *very* afternoon, he e-mailed again me to say his advisors had reviewed them and were ready for a conference call.

Wow!

I got my partners David and Bill, as well as Paul, to be in on the conference call with Norton's advisors. We spent an hour talking through the deal points. At the end of the call, they said this is a great deal; this is right for us. Biting my nails, I suggested that perhaps

Norton would want to invest $4 million. But they said he was interested in the *whole* $10 million!

We adjourned for a few days so we could get them some additional financial information that they had requested, and so that I could catch my breath. I was feeling quite giddy. Could it be that easy?

Then suddenly it hit me — bam! whammo! the lights went off, the fireworks exploded!

How could I be so stupid and not see it? Divine Providence was at work here, and it was simply amazing!

THE ODDS

What were the odds of it all happening in such a perfect sequence?

Here I was leaving the Ritz Carlton (having just ended a meeting that was not originally planned for there) at the exact moment — not one minute earlier or one minute later — as Norton Herrick, whom I had not seen for eight years, pulled up in a stretch limo!

If the meeting with Tzvi had taken place elsewhere as scheduled, or if Norton had been a bit earlier or later, or if we had been a bit earlier or later, we would have never met up. It was quite amazing that God moved all the necessary pieces into place. People often say that it's a small world, but that is not true. It is a big world, but it seems small because God is very good at organizing it.

That week I had been slacking off in my prayers. I had not been praying as fervently or been as disciplined in attending communal prayers. Yet the Almighty in His kindness and generosity sent me quite a gift and a reminder that nothing is too great for Him to accomplish.

God truly does answer prayers. You should pray with that understanding. Nothing is too great for God to do. Pray like you mean it. Put in the effort. And wait for God to do the rest.

I had sent out a lot of e-mails and made a lot of calls, but the way that God sent this one to me was a clear lesson that He runs the show. It was not my doing at all. It came out of nowhere. I always tell people that you should pray for dry land, but you sure as heck should row for the shore. You need to make the effort but you can't forget to include God in your plans. Now if only I could live like that all the time!

Of course, it was not a done deal yet. And I had many an anxious moment, as Paul and David sat in meetings with Keith Yokomoto working out the terms, while Norton kept calling and wondering what all was going on. At various times I was beside myself with anxiety worrying the whole thing would fall through anyway. What if Norton suddenly had issues with the deal?

By the time I left the US for my Passover vacation in Israel with my family, all systems were go. I felt a huge burden lift off my shoulders as we boarded the plane which was jam-packed with other holiday travelers. Unfortunately, we could not get all our seats together. Sholom, then age 13, was in one row by the window. Bracha, then age 16, was in another row in the middle seat but on the opposite side of the plane, and Ilana, then 5, and Sara, then 11, were in the same row as Bracha, but in the middle section of seats. An elderly Hassidic man with a broad smile was sitting beside them in the aisle seat. I was frantically scanning for some opportunity to rearrange seats so that Shalom would not have to be isolated on the opposite side of the plane. I had his window seat to offer, but would the Hassid trade it for his aisle seat? Many people don't like to cross over two people every time they want to stand up or go to the bathroom.

The Hassid saw me standing there and asked me in Hebrew what the problem was. I explained that my son had a window seat but wanted to sit next to his two sisters as he didn't like sitting next to strangers. I asked him if he would consider giving up his aisle seat next to Ilana and Sara and taking Sholom's window seat. He looked at me and said, "I am a seventh-generation descendant of Rebbe Nachman of Breslav. Rebbe Nachman says the whole world is built on kindness. If it will help you and your children, of course I will switch seats." I asked him, "Do you go to Uman at Rosh Hashana? He said, "Of course!" I said, "I went last year." He smiled and gathered up his belongings.

And so Sholom came to sit next to his two sisters, though Bracha was still stuck in the middle seat across the aisle. There were no more Breslev Hassidim waiting to build a world of kindness to get her another seat. Five hours later though, when I went to check on the kids, Bracha's middle seat was empty. I found all my four kids, cuddled together on the three middle seats, limbs slopping over each other, Ilana and Sara holding hands, Bracha scrunched up next to them and Shalom asleep on his food tray. A world of kindness it was. God had blessed Judy and me with children who loved each other and wanted the closeness of little puppies as they slept. It was a far more satisfying pleasure than getting the Ted Field deal. A deeper pleasure such as only love can be. Looking at them I was brought back to the realization of what really counts in life – family, sharing, love, and kindness to strangers that makes the world a truly awesome experience.

All week I had been feeling wound up, tense, a lion on the hunt for the Ted Field deal, but seeing my four kids snuggled with each other and recalling this simple Hassid's words about kindness brought a far deeper awareness of the beauty of the world and of how I wanted to be remembered – as a person who did random acts of kindness, as a person with loving children who wanted to be close to each other, and as a person who helped bring these things to the world. Thank you, God!

PART TWO

Passover ended; weeks passed. I fretted. Finally, finally, finally, Paul called me to say the meeting that would decide it all was about to happen. Norton was in LA and they were going over to sit down with Ted at Radar Films. This was it!

Ted and Norton had gone out for a drink the night before and gotten to know each other. Their new-found chemistry set the tone for the day. Things were looking good.

I called Rabbi Fox, Rabbi Zilberman's right hand man, to tell him that this was "D-Day" – the time was NOW. He said he would pass on the message to Rabbi Zilberman that this was the time to pray. He himself would go to pray at the Western Wall.

In the middle of the day, I got a message from Paul and David that all was going well. And finally, at 8 PM New York time, he called to say that the meeting was finished. It had taken eight hours (!) but the deal was done. The formal signing of the paper would take place in ten days.

We had finally arrived and the hand of God in making it happen was so clear. Paul and I laughed about it. We didn't miss the fact that God was here – caring for us, helping us, and moving all the pieces to make it happen. There was comfort in that. But, in fact, the real truth is that He is doing it ALL the time; we just don't see it, because our egos and distractions stop us from seeing it.

After Paul hung up, I called Keith Yokomoto to congratulate him. I had sent him my books, and he said he read them all in two days and had enjoyed them. I told him I was working on another book about my transition from rabbi to businessman. We then discussed the difficulty of being ethical in business. He concurred that it was a real challenge. He had been brought up in an intellectual home and being a good, moral person was important to him. But it was a struggle, because the rules of engagement worked against you.

He illustrated the point with some funny metaphors; he said, "You might want to be a gentleman, but if you get in the ring with Mike Tyson, you better know how to box. If you go out for a round of golf with Tiger Woods, you better know a wood from a four iron, and if you play basketball with Kobe Bryant, you better know how to dunk. And if you play poker with the pros, you better know how to bluff." He said that business is the same. "If you get in the game with the professionals, you better know how to play or you are going to pay!"

I then called Norton Herrick. "Mazal Tov!" I told him. He sounded as worn out as I was perky. He said he hoped he wouldn't lose on this investment. But he got along great with Ted and was going out to dinner with him that night to celebrate.

We agreed that it was amazing that had his limo arrived 30 seconds sooner or later, this would not be happening. He did not see the hand of God in it the way I did. So I explained to him the way things went down that day and why I attributed it all to God. He had to agree – it was totally amazing.

Then Ted called. He came right out and said to me that he was now moving on to the BIG deal and that Doheny would be his financial advisor. That was very exciting to hear.

Everyone was happy – Paul, David and Bill were all buoyant. Our first deal as a company! Our gateway into the big-time.

I took a hot bath to try and relax and fell asleep at 10:30 PM but awoke again at 2 AM. I just couldn't go back to sleep; I was too excited. I called Israel to find that Rabbi Zilberman had been saying psalms for me at the Western Wall. He and Aaron Fox were very happy. They would now have some schnapps to celebrate – *L'Chaim* to Life!

It is funny that we humans get so much pleasure out of being able to share our joys. I really wanted to call my Mom and Dad. I missed not being able to call them. Instead, I called my brother Barry and my in-laws. They shared my joy. I called Paul again a few times. I sent e-mails to all my friends. Of course, I told Judy and my kids about it. I called Rabbi Weinberg who told me to write up the story and save it, so I would always remember what the Almighty did for me.

Yes, there was someone – the One – to whom I did not need to send an e-mail. He was with me all along. He held my hand; He manipulated time for me. How could I ever forget? How could I ever forget?

AND THEN THERE WERE NONE

Shavuot ("Feast of Weeks") – which comes seven weeks after Passover and which celebrates the giving of the Torah at Mount Sinai – kept me out of e-mail contact for two days. The moment it was over – as any good e-mail addict would do – I turned on my computer to find only 163 messages waiting for me. A slow two days. But one of them jumped out at me: "Radar Deal Falls Apart."

It said that Ted Field was prepared to go to Miami on Thursday to close the deal, but Norton pulled out at the last moment. We had believed that Norton was putting up the $10 million himself but that turned out not to be so. He was in fact syndicating the deal – selling it to others – and taking a "promote," a percentage of the deal for himself in return for bringing in the investors. But the percentage he put on it was too high. When he could not generate enough interest, he backed out.

I was surprised, but I wasn't upset. It seems that a certain trust in God had settled over me on the holiday, for this year I had come to the realization, in a deeper way than before, that the Almighty runs the world and that whatever He wants to happen will happen. It somehow sank into my bones that I had to put in the effort but that the results were out of my control. I decided I would just let go and not worry about it. What will be will be, and that's okay with me.

It was strange that I wasn't shattered. I accepted it with a real peace of mind. I remembered how devastated I had been when our first deal had collapsed last summer. It took me days to be able to work again, but this time it really didn't impact me that much.

I waited until the next day before I called David, Bill and Paul to discuss it with them. Should we try again?

By then we had a lot on our plate. We had been seriously looking into investments in Eastern Europe, and these appeared much more promising. I certainly wanted to try again for Radar Films because I wanted to be Ted's financial advisor for his big acquisition, but was it worth it?

Ultimately we decided against it, and that put an end to my forays into Hollywood.

10

On a Mission

While the Radar Films deal was cooking, boiling over and fizzling out, I was very busy planning my next mission to Israel. These posh, high-profile trips had been a key feature in my fundraising efforts for Aish HaTorah and now continued to be an important networking tool in my business.

While fundraising for Aish, I brought many groups to Israel comprised of America's political and business leaders. Initially, the missions centered on honoring prominent public figures – such as former President Ronald Reagan or former Prime Minister Lady Margaret Thatcher, for example – who were given the King David Award. At the same time, we would also honor our most outstanding mission participants. Some of them were on the Forbes 400 list of the richest people in America, while others were well known for their philanthropy. During their visit in Israel, I would showcase the exceptional work of Aish HaTorah; they would meet our students and staff and spend time with Rabbi Weinberg, a truly inspirational and visionary leader. Only at the end of the trip would I ask them to contribute to our work. Most honorees were so turned on by what they had seen and experienced that they gladly agreed to contribute to the cause.

A few times I asked potential honorees for donations before the mission, but this was a much more difficult solicitation. One year, I went to Barcelona, Madrid, Paris, Frankfurt and London (where I met Lord David Rothschild, not getting a donation though), and finally to Vienna. It was an exhausting five days and I struck out everywhere. I felt I had wasted a lot of money and energy and time. Vienna was the last stop. I was to meet there with the wealthy philanthropist Rudolfine Steindling (Fini for short). The others I had asked for $100,000; as this was my last stop, I decided to go for broke, expecting to get nothing. So, I asked her for $1 million and – unbelievably – she said "yes."

In retrospect, I see God's gift in it. It just shows you that you need to make the effort and trust in God. I had just been to all these meetings, spent all this time, was disappointed each and every time, and then BINGO!

You can just imagine that I was not at my best when I walked into Fini's office. I had basically given up. Everyone else had said, "no." I was depressed and down-trodden. I felt like a failure and was sure she would say "no" too.

And then I met this lovely woman, who said "yes" on the spot, after only a one-hour presentation. This almost never happens in fundraising; people usually take the time to check you out. It was a miracle as far as I was concerned. One hour investment of time and I walked out with a commitment for $1 million. No less than 48-hours later, she had wired us the first half, and six months later the balance. She also came as part of the mission and had a wonderful time.

A REAL LADY

Another woman who really touched my heart during this time was Lady Margaret Thatcher, one of the recipients of the King David Award in recognition of her support for Israel while she was the prime minister of Great Britain.

Why did she care so much for the Jewish people? In answer to that question, she told me a fascinating story:

During World War II, a Jewish family from Eastern Europe had somehow connected with her parents and requested that they temporarily house their daughter in England. The Jewish family could not get out, but they were able to arrange a visa and ticket for their only child. At the time, Lady Thatcher's family was very poor and had barely enough for themselves, but they took in this Jewish girl, who ended up staying with them the entire length of the war and sharing Lady Thatcher's room. Lady Thatcher said that her parents taught her that it was essential to help all people in need, but it was especially important to help the Jewish people, who had been so unfairly persecuted throughout history.

This was someone we very much wanted to honor.

After a year of back-and-forth discussions with her staff and attempting to co-ordinate her schedule with ours, she agreed to accept the King David Award at an elegant dinner at the Carlyle Hotel in New York to be held in March of 1997.

The fundraising idea behind these dinners was to put on a prestigious event to attract the elite financial crowd. There are always hundreds of causes vying for donors' attention; most are worthy causes, deserving of support, so how do you stand out from the crowd? My strategy had always been to offer something special – something that no one else was offering.

The dinner for Margaret Thatcher – and another one like it honoring President Mikhail Gorbachev (for allowing the Jewish refuseniks to leave the Soviet Union) – were just such events. They were limited to one-hundred couples, each paying $10,000 to attend. The affairs were lavish – the one for Lady Thatcher costing $150,000, the one for Gorbachev costing double that. But we ended up netting

$1.8 million for Aish HaTorah after only a six-week investment of time.

How did I pull this off?

I got a commitment from Gorbachev for a specific date – as well as his demand for a $150,000 speakers' fee (this was a shocker, as Lady Thatcher came for free). To make money on the dinner, we needed a co-honoree who would also be a donor. I put the date on hold and cold-called people on the Forbes 400 list. I had learned my lesson not to jump in; if I got someone who would agree to be honored alongside Gorbachev and also make a financial commitment to Aish HaTorah, well and good; if not, I would not go forward.

It worked. I had no idea how popular Gorbachev was. Barbara Walters and Michael Douglas *volunteered* to attend and present the award. It turned out to be a start-studded event with attendees such as mogul Ron Perelman, then New York Mayor Rudy Guiliani, and several other prominent businessmen.

In business and in fundraising, most people hit singles and every so often they get a double. If they are lucky, they hit a triple once in their career. The rare few hit a homerun. The Gorbachev event was the equivalent of a grand slam, bases loaded, bottom of the ninth, last game of the World Series – and it was an awesome win.

A REAL *MENSCH*

But it was through the experience with Lady Thatcher that I learned some fascinating lessons about what it means to be a real *mensch*.

During the course of the evening, everyone wanted to have their picture taken with Lady Thatcher. She knew this would happen and she had her assistant call us before the evening to find out the color of wall coverings in the room, so that her outfit would not clash.

She was popular. All one hundred of the participating couples posed for a picture with her, one couple at a time. After they all filed through, you would think she'd had enough – all those flash-bulbs can be very irritating – but then she requested that we ask the orchestra members if they too wanted their picture taken. I was impressed. I had never seen such graciousness. I have worked with many celebrities and political leaders and some were quite haughty about the whole picture-taking experience. They limited the number of photos or they wouldn't do posed shots, or they insisted that no flash be used. Others were very accommodating, but I have never had anyone suggest additional photos with staff.

After I arranged the photos for the violinist and the harp player, Lady Thatcher suggested that perhaps the chef of the hotel and his staff would also like their picture taken. I was amazed. But also, I was getting a bit concerned – I wasn't sure just how long this was going to continue. I mean, there is a big staff at the Carlyle – we could be doing this all night. Luckily, it stopped after the chef. I was impressed though. She was a real lady, who understood the importance of being good to the little people.

A few months later, she agreed to come on one of our missions to Israel and I witnessed the same behavior. She was accompanied by three Scotland Yard security personnel. She had an armored van and a chase car that followed the van. Her security detail came to Israel three days prior and cased each venue. They explained that for the first dinner – at the Rockefeller Museum in Arab-populated East Jerusalem – everyone would need to be seated and only then would she walk in and proceed to her table. Furthermore, she had to be seated with her back to the wall, while guards stood beside her to stop anyone from approaching her.

Well, I saw why she was known as the "Iron Lady." She had her own plans. She walked into the banquet room, and to the consternation of her Scotland Yard guards, she took the next 20 minutes to circle around each table and shake hands with each and every guest.

People felt so touched by her personal warmth, lack of pompousness and genuine human caring.

Even if my then five-year-old daughter Bracha weren't involved, I still would have been blown away by her behavior. When she came to our table, she stopped and kneeled down to meet Bracha eye-to-eye. She shook her little hand and had a short conversation with her. She asked Bracha her name and her age. It looked as if she was genuinely enjoying herself doing this.

At the dinner at the Knesset, there were many important guests and speakers. Prime Minister Bibi Netanyahu spoke, then Jerusalem Mayor Ehud Olmert spoke, then US Senator Joe Biden (the future president) spoke, and then New Jersey Governor Christine Whitman spoke. Each person as well as all the honorees were introduced, of course. During this time, the dinner participants had been served the salad course only. When it came Lady Thatcher's turn to speak – she was the featured speaker, so she was last – she got up and said only a few words, announcing that she had just ripped up her prepared speech "to ribbons." Then she explained why: "I have never lost an election and this is because I can read a crowd. This crowd is hungry. As a woman and mother, I say 'Serve dinner!'" She sat down to tremendous applause.

Once again, I learned an important lesson about what makes great people truly great. It is their sensitivity to the little people – the people they don't have to care about or be nice to. It is then that you see their true character.

It reminded me of what we know about Moses and King David. Their life's training was to be shepherds; they learned how to care for defenseless lambs before becoming great leaders. The Midrash relates that on one occasion Moses lost a little lamb and he went out looking for her; he found her a long way away from the herd, drinking from a brook. He realized that she was thirsty and she had walked very far on her small legs to find water. So, seeing she was tired, he picked her up and carried her back. This is when God said, "You who tend your sheep with such mercy will be a compassionate leader for My sheep!"

If only I could learn to be that sensitive to others. In my case, sensitivity was more often than not overridden by anxiety, as I tried to put together all the pieces of the puzzle that made for a successful mission.

MISSION CALLS

Eventually the missions evolved into networking sessions between top American business leaders and Israeli start-up companies that had new ideas and new products to offer. Aish HaTorah would take a commission from any investments made. For example, I brought along Len Leader, then president of AOL investments and, as a result, AOL hooked up with two Israeli start-up companies (Gurunet, which became Ask.com; and Dealtime, which became Shopping.com).

As the missions grew in complexity, I partnered with the New Jerusalem Foundation, which raised money for special projects not covered by the city's meager operating budget (building parks, putting on cultural programs, etc.). From the donations Aish received, we would give 10 percent to the New Jerusalem Foundation. This partnership was clearly articulated to all contributors. (I had learned my lesson.) In return, the New Jerusalem Foundation's executive director, Tzvi Raviv, would help arrange top level meetings for the mission – such as those with the prime minister, the defense minister, finance minister, etc. – as well as taking care of other logistics. When I left Aish, this partnership also ended.

But I did not want the missions to stop. I wanted to continue organizing them, though I would no longer be soliciting the participants for donations. I saw a great benefit to such high-pow-ered networking, and I still wanted to connect Israeli companies with sources of funding, sales and distribution in the US.

In 2006, I brought then Attorney General John Ashcroft and for-mer Secretary of Education Tommy Thompson, among others. In 2007, I brought former Envoy to Iraq, Ambassador Paul Bremer, and then Governor of Texas Rick Perry, among others. If nothing else, it was very valuable for my business profile to spend a week with such notable political leaders. But organizing all the high-level meetings was a real challenge.

Every week, I would send out three dozen (!) letters to people I have never met. Then I would follow up each one with a call. At best I would get a disinterested secretary, though usually I got voice mail or some rude assistant. Rarely did I get through to a receptive audi-ence. Nevertheless, I needed to be charming and friendly and give my best pitch on each and every call, letting the voice mail or the secretary or the assistant know how important my business was.

In past years, I have tried to put off this grueling work on my staff, but it has never succeeded. They all got burned out pretty quickly and told me that they would rather do any other job than cold calls. Some even said they'd prefer unemployment to doing this every day.

I knew how it felt. I gave birth to this process, and I knew that I was really the best person to do it.

Although I have organized many successful missions, I still got scared when I launched one, asking myself: "What if this year no one wants to come? Will I fail? Will I need to cancel the trip?"

Each mission consisted of three layers:

1) the US political leaders who didn't require a fee (but I picked up the tab for their airfares, hotels and other expenses)

2) the participants from the business world who paid the cost and made the mission a profitable undertaking (I needed 35 to make it worthwhile)

3) the Israeli political/business leaders who helped make the trip interesting and a high-level experience for those coming from America

The first layer was generally no problem. And when I lined up prestigious people, it made it easier to recruit other participants. But their tab – something like $100,000 for first class tickets, suites in five-star hotels, etc. – scared me to death. Hence, my anxiety about recruiting the second layer.

There are so many pieces that have to fall into place to make it work that it is a frightening venture. And, on top of it all, there is always the specter of Middle East violence that could topple the whole mission – one bus bomb or kidnapping the week before and eight months of work can be destroyed as people instantly panic and cancel.

But I suppose anxiety pushes one to greatness – either that or to a nervous breakdown. It certainly got me out of bed in the morning to sit down in front of the telephone and start dialing numbers.

ONE DOWN, THIRTY TO GO

For the 2007 mission (which I was putting together during the Radar Films fiasco), I was one month into recruitment and, although the first layer was great, I barely had half a dozen for the second layer. (And all of them were returnees.) I needed 30 more, and they had to be fresh faces to make it worthwhile in terms of networking.

Then, out of the blue, I received a call from Henry Nordhoff's office. Henry was the head of Gen-probe, a $2 billion biotech company, which was singled out by President George W. Bush for the National Medal of Technology for their pioneering work in blood-testing of organ donors (for the West Nile Virus, HIV-1 and Hepatitis C) prior to transplantation or transfusion.

I'd had no response to my invitation, but now Henry's secretary was calling, asking if he could bring his wife. I said, "Absolutely!" In fact, I encouraged people to bring their spouses and children as it is such a special experience. She said in that case he would attend.

I was thrilled. I felt such overwhelming gratitude to God. This was the first new paying person to say "yes."

I had made nearly three dozen calls that week alone and all of them said "no." So, I was beginning to get a little discouraged. And then this gift out of the blue.

At least I remembered to stop and look at the bush:

Thank You, God, for Your help!

11

My Silent Partner

During the time that the Radar Deal was in the works, I happened to pass through Jerusalem on two occasions, each time checking-in with my silent partner, Rabbi Zilberman. And each time he insisted on coming over to see me at my hotel, telling me, "Since we are partners, I have to discuss with you our ventures. I am not coming to ask for money."

The first time we met (since our written agreement), he pulled out a little notebook from his pocket and said, "Okay, you can test me now."

"What are you talking about?" I asked.

He smiled: "Ask me about the different deals. I know them all." He turned the pages and read me the notes that he had made on all the e-mails I had sent to Rabbi Fox.

Of course, the Zilberman yeshiva does not have a computer, but Rabbi Fox's parents do, and this is how I was communicating with Rabbi Zilberman – sending messages via the Fox family, which Rabbi Fox translated into Hebrew. Now I saw that everything I had sent was recorded in this little notebook. Rabbi Zilberman had notes on each one of my transactions and had memorized the names of the individuals involved!

He had questions though. He wanted to understand exactly what a SPAC was – what was a special purpose acquisition corporation?

Then he wanted to know what an IPO was: How did an initial public offering work? He wanted to understand what it meant when I said we would do a "preferred convertible" for a company. And what was a "raise"?

A few things he had totally mispronounced. That made me nervous. I wondered if those were the deals that hadn't gone well. Did he pray and God didn't hear him right?

But it was exciting to see just how seriously he was taking this. He really did have notes on all the deals and knew the particulars of the different transactions. He was a good partner. I was happy I had him on my team. I knew for sure that when he prayed for my success, his prayers were detailed and specific – and real.

I renewed my commitment to keep my prayers real too.

TAKING OFF

The next time we met, it was Passover week in 2008. I had rented an apartment in Jerusalem's Old City for the holiday. It was dusk and the muezzins were calling the Muslim faithful to prayer with their loud, mournful cries echoing from loudspeakers all over Jerusalem. You hear this five times daily here. Easter had just ended, but not the accompanying celebrations and, moments later, the bells of a neighboring church started their loud clanging.

Here we were, the three of us on the balcony of our apartment, trying to ignore the cacophony of three religions trying to get God's attention as the sun set over Jerusalem, a holy city to all of them.

Rabbi Zilberman asked me, "How is it going?"

I thought a moment before answering. I didn't want to give him a pat answer, like "we're making progress," because though we were, it hardly described what was happening.

I struggled for a way to get it all across. And then it came to me.

Since I travel so much, I am a bit of an airplane trivia buff. Some people memorize baseball scores, I memorize the facts of jet travel, because the miracle of flight never ceases to amaze me. I seized on a flight metaphor to explain what I was experiencing. I asked Rabbi Zilberman. "Do you know what a 747 is?"

He did.

"Well," I said, "consider that a 747 has six *million* parts, that it is almost 65 feet tall (that's like a six-story building!) and that *each* of its wings covers an area of 5,500 square feet (that's the size of a parking lot for 45 cars!)"

Rabbi Zilberman was staring at me oddly, like he was trying to figure out what I was getting at, while Rabbi Fox looked amused. I went on:

"Consider that it can house more than 450 people with all their baggage, and that fully loaded it weighs almost 1 million pounds! Yet it flies just under the speed of sound! When it starts barreling down the runway, it needs a very, very long runway to get up to the speed it needs for lift off. It requires 8,000 feet to take off (that is 22 football fields back-to-back.) And it takes 40 minutes for it to reach cruising altitude. That is a lot of weight and a lot of inertia and drag to overcome to get airborne. To get that plane in the air is not easy at all. We take it for granted, but it truly is an amazing feat of technology."

By now, they were both totally perplexed. They had no idea what I was talking about.

I said, "Six months ago, Doheny Global was just dreaming about flight. We were like the Wright brothers, trying to put a flying machine into the air. We had no idea that we'd end up building a 747. But that's what we've done. We went from a small investment bank to a holding company in a few months. Not only that, we've made it down that long runway and are now in wheels-up/lift-off mode, but we are still climbing; we haven't reached cruising altitude yet. And we don't see our flight path clearly. We are still testing this machine we've built."

Rabbi Zilberman listened with interest, then smiled and nodded. He got it.

RUNNING ON EMPTY

Speaking of metaphors – a 747 burns one gallon of jet fuel *per second* which then cost $2+ per gallon. I might have built a 747, but could I fill the gas tank?

I got an e-mail from my accountant the other day that I owed $160,000 in taxes due April 15. Paying the taxes would completely deplete my home equity line of credit, or I would have to sell off my one long-standing personal investment (in the Islands restaurant chain) that was yielding a safe 14 percent. Should I let *all* my chips ride on this venture?

I always liked living on the edge, but this was a razor-thin edge. The Almighty sure wanted my prayers. He was helping me get *real*!

I knew the Almighty loved me. I knew He wanted me to succeed. I knew He wanted the best for me, and all these challenges were there just so I wouldn't forget Him and think it was all my doing. But this was really upping the ante, and it was no penny ante game. The stakes were high, and it was a good thing I had a high tolerance for chaos and anxiety!

I was reminded of the twelve-step program of AA I had read about. The crucial first step is realizing your problem is out of your hands and you must give it up to a Higher Authority. You can't do anything about it by yourself – you have to accept that. You need God. You can't do it without Him. Reading that was helpful.

Of course, I am not an alcoholic. I can't even hold more than one glass of wine. But reading that about AA, I realized how important it is for me to trust that it is the Almighty who runs the world, and my worrying won't change the way things turn out.

I needed to relax and accept that it is all in God's hands.

I decided to start selling my Islands restaurant stocks, so that I would have funds available for living and overhead, and for investing in my current deals which – when I succeeded – would yield 30 percent. I mean, if I didn't believe in me, who would?

But it all made me very nervous. I kept lying in bed at night imagining all kinds of "what ifs," because some part of me suspected that God would not let me get rich. Why?

Theoretically, I know God is a loving God. Look at how much He has given me in my life! Whenever I am with my family – with my beautiful wife, children and grandchildren – I cannot help but think what a lucky person I am. Just to look at the smiling face of one of my grandchildren brings me a hit of instant joy. One of their smiles can instantly lift my worries and plunge me into happiness. But I cannot sustain that feeling. When they are not with me, I fret and worry and obsess about all the deals, which in turn makes me feel distant from God and lonely.

I knew that if I had succeeded in business but did not have this family, I would not be happy. Still, I so badly wanted to succeed, and I worried that I would not.

I kept re-reading the passage in Ethics of the Fathers which states: "Giving tithes serves as protection for [one's] wealth." Most people think that if they give away a tenth of their income to charity, they will be poorer for it. But the Jewish approach is quite the opposite. The Talmudic sages say, "Give a tenth so that God can make you rich." Indeed, they say this is the only place where you are allowed to put God to the test. Well, I was doing that. In my first two years in business, I gave away more than 20 percent of my income to charity. Shouldn't I be getting real rich this year?

Sometimes, I believed that it would happen – it *had* to happen. But at other times, a part of me thought that God would leave me high and dry.

This was showing me that I lacked trust in God in a real fundamental way. God had never left me high and dry. He had given me so much that I did not deserve. Why would I think that He would disappoint me now?

I didn't have a good answer to that question, but still I felt a lack of serenity, and a lack of faith that it would all work out like I wanted it to. I realized that it was something I needed to resolve inside of myself. It was a deep-seated issue, and it was definitely hurting me.

ADVICE FROM MY RABBI

I decided to speak with Rabbi Weinberg about my lack of trust in God. I told him that it was draining me, distracting me and sapping my energy.

In response, he suggested that I focus on all that God has given me to date. If I do so, I would have to recognize that it has been an overabundance of good things. He suggested I put that in one box in my head and separate it from the other box which contains my hopes for the future. He said that my worries that God may not grant me all my heart's desires are slopping over and polluting the good box of so many wishes fulfilled.

Rabbi Weinberg said that I needed to remind myself of how much God loves me. What He has given me is far beyond anything I could have ever imagined thirty years ago when I first walked into the halls of Aish HaTorah. Based on all I have received, is there really any reason for me to be worried that God's goodness to me will not continue?

Clearly not.

So what was I supposed to do about this free-floating anxiety that I didn't seem to be able to control?

Stop and have a conversation with God. Say: "Okay God, I know You love me. I know You want to give me everything possible, just like I want to give my children everything. Except You have all the resources of the whole universe at Your disposal, so if You want to help me – which I know You want to do – then why aren't You?"

Rabbi Weinberg said that if I go through that mental process, I will remind myself that God must have a good reason not to give me great wealth right now. (I needed to remember that metaphor about a teenage boy who wants a new sports car but who could harm himself with it, so his father can't give it to him.) Since God knows everything that's in my heart, He knows what I am likely to do with new-found wealth. His withholding comes from love – for He has my best interests at heart. He is telling me "not right now," just like I would have to tell my teenage son that he could not have a new sports car right now simply because he wanted it.

Then Rabbi Weinberg asked me to consider if I was truly ready for success? If my wildest dreams came true, would I forget God in my life? The Talmudic sages tell us that wealth is a greater challenge than poverty. Would I become arrogant? Cruel? Quick to anger? I could see all that happening in some ways, but I did feel up to the challenge. I prayed, "Just give me a chance, God, even if I fail."

However, I had to admit that when I looked honestly at myself, I saw there definitely was a part of me that lacked self-esteem – a part of me that constantly nurtured the thought that unless I became very, very rich, I would never be respected. Now, I knew this was ridiculous. But I was aware that such a belief was bouncing around in my consciousness. Although I knew that I was a good person no matter what I accomplished – and I had already accomplished a great deal – nonetheless, I still had this absurd belief which pulled down my self-esteem.

And also – as long as I was being honest – I had to admit that I really could get very materialistic. I already had a tendency in that direction; I already enjoyed the finer things in life, like five-star hotels and first-class air travel. I made a commitment to limit myself though. Yes, I did want to improve things in my home, but nothing to excess, and I hoped that my pledges to charity would keep me in line.

Furthermore, if I had difficulty keeping my connection to God real, constant and consistent when things were merely good, I had to wonder if I would lose it altogether if I had everything I wanted. If I only prayed with concentration and intention because I wanted something from God, would having everything eliminate that?

I have to confess there were some potential dangers …

THE TEST

No wonder God was putting me to the test.

For one thing, I thought I could quickly sell my safe 14 percent Islands restaurant investment (that I held onto for five years) and realize an instant $450,000. That would give me cash to live on for another ten months. But when I went to sell, it turned out not to be so easy. There was a dispute going on among the partners, the company's last quarter was its worst in 25 years (!) and it became apparent I could not sell it as quickly as I thought.

Meanwhile, I had $50,000 left in the bank – and that was not even my money but an equity loan on my house!

I needed the Israel mission – plus other side deals I was working on apart from Doheny – to bring in $100,000-$200,000 just to take me past the next 3-4 months. And then I would be okay. Otherwise, I would be flying on fumes, and that was scary.

Of course, I knew what I did was wrong. Instead of putting my trust in God, I was putting my trust in cashing-in on my former investment. To trust in your stock portfolio instead of God is idolatry, pure and simple.

This is why He took it away from me. It was an important lesson that I needed to learn. It is the essence of the prayer which Jews recite every day: "You shall serve the Lord, your God, with all your heart and all your soul and with all your possessions ... and He will send you rain in its proper season, and you will gather your grain, your wine and your oil ..."

This is the way life really works, but it is still scary!

THE STRUGGLE WITH BOXES

To calm down my fears, I spent quite a bit of time contemplating Rabbi Weinberg's words to me, turning them over and over like a Rubik's cube, to see which way the colors lined up.

I followed his advice, mentally making a list of the many and varied blessings God has given me: my life, my beautiful loyal wife, my gorgeous children, my amazing grandchildren that make me smile every time I see them, as they remind me of the miracle of their existence. They are something else – not even in the same realm as the rest of life's experiences.

I'd put all that in one box like he told me to. To this, I added the fact that I can see, I can feel, I can think, I can communicate, I am healthy. I have been fortunate in life to develop a relationship with my Creator. I have been fortunate to get involved with Aish HaTorah and to truly make a difference in the world through my activities. There are hundreds of families' lives that have been changed because of my work with Aish LA. My missions to Israel made a difference to that country. All these projects have brought a richness to my life. God has taken care of me in ways that are beyond what I could ever have expected. And, to top it off, I have always somehow found the financial means to do what I wanted to do. Then came 1998 when I benefited from the stock market boom and got used to some of the nicer things in life, although I subsequently lost all my money in the crash. But, even so, I had been able to maintain a good standard of living.

I had so much to be thankful for.

All that went into one special box. Looking inside, I let myself feel the goodness and the blessings. I closed my eyes. I breathed deeply. I felt my shoulders lifting up. I said to myself, "Feel the love! The Almighty has taken care of you all these years. Feel the protection and care."

I knew that God cares. I felt His love like a warm embrace of the summer sun. So why was I still anxious?

THE OTHER BOX

The other box was full of my unrealized hopes, dreams and expectations ... and fears. The fears magnified each time kinks in deals popped up.

The Radar Films deal fizzled; still, there were many more in the pipeline. But it seemed as if each one was experiencing a roadblock. Where had all the green lights gone? Had someone changed the light bulbs overnight to only reds and yellows? Why was this happening?

I wondered if God was pushing me to the wall because I was failing in certain parts of my life. My praying stunk. My concentration in prayer was non-existent. My Torah learning was nearly abandoned. I was not acting like a good husband and father – I was not as attentive or caring, and certainly not as emotionally involved as I should be. My brain space was totally occupied with machinations of business.

I should have been spending more time thinking about how to be a good person, how to get close to God. If I managed to do that, the rest would follow. Though there is nothing wrong with thinking about work strategies, my primary drive should be toward a closer relationship with God.

I tried to see my relationship with God, my Father, in terms of my relationship with my children. I could readily see how each of my children was struggling with some issue or another, and how none was perfect. But I loved each and every one nevertheless. I didn't love my children any less because of their particular foibles. I accepted their weaknesses and love them as a whole package.

Well, am I any better than God? For sure not!

God is my Father in Heaven, and He accepts me as I am with my imperfections, and He still loves me.

So why haven't the flood gates opened?

I know that there are strings between us and God, but we are the ones pulling the strings, not God. He responds to us based on how we relate to Him. If I wanted Him to be involved in my life and to help me, I needed to reach out. That is all He wants. Just like I do with my kids. I want the ones who don't live at home to call regularly, even daily, and to include me in their lives, to want a relationship with me. It gives me such pleasure when they do that, and I want to give them all the help possible.

Well, am I any better than God? For sure not!

My relationship with God, my Father, works exactly the same way. In fact, everything in the physical world is here to teach us about the spiritual world. We have children so that we can better understand God's relationship to us – we are His children; He is our Father in Heaven.

When I looked at it that way, I realized that I needed to start focusing again on improving my relationship with God. That should be my drive all day – not how to get rich. I should try to turn my spiritual life around, but even more importantly to include God in it and not think that He doesn't want to hear from me because I am failing in other areas.

I knew all that, and yet still I had doubts.

I muttered a prayer: "God help me, please. I know You run the show. I know it is all in Your hands. Please help things go more smoothly in my life. Open the floodgates enough to show me You heard my prayer."

A PRAYER ANSWERED

A few hours later, I had a conference call with my partners. Joining us on the line was a very successful biotech entrepreneur who has started tens of companies over the past 20 years. At that time, he was starting a new biotech firm a month. He was working with several banks. He wanted to know if we would help raise funds for his deals. He would have a reverse merger almost every month, and we could "sell as much paper" – that is raise as much investment – as we could manage. Wow!

For a long time, we had been looking for such a deal and, suddenly, it came to us. But it was way better – now we were presented with a deal a month!

Thank You, God!

Minutes later my cell vibrated with more positive news concerning my mission guests. I went down to the lobby, ordered a drink and lit up a cigar. All this seemed to me like a sign from God that I was on the right path. My prayer had been answered.

As I was sitting there, half a dozen more e-mails came in, letters from developers asking for additional information on projects we were considering in the FSU. There was certainly a flurry of activity. I suppose God was giving me fast and sudden positive reinforcement.

The Talmud teaches that you only need to make a small opening for God in order to watch His abundant love pour in. Rabbi Weinberg would paraphrase that by saying, "Give God an opening the size of an eye of a needle and He will drive a truck through it." For a change, I could see the truck coming down the highway.

12

Cooking, Not Baking

One connection leads to another.

My son-in-law Yoni Kayman suggested I talk with his brother Gershon, who is a New York attorney working for a hard-money lender. This lender funds real estate developers, and Gershon often sees doable deals which do not fit into his company's relatively narrow criteria.

I spoke to Paul about this, and he agreed it was worthwhile to learn more. Real estate financing has always been Paul's specialty – he understands what makes or breaks a real estate deal and how to create the right mix of equity, debt and bridge financing to pull it off. This kind of financing is a lot more like cooking than baking. In baking you don't mess with the recipe or your cake turns out like a brick; it needs just so much oil and just the right amount of sugar and flour. But, in cooking, you have a great deal more freedom to add your own spirit and flavor. Real estate finance is similar – it requires the talent of a master chef, who has a sophisticated understanding of the basic ingredients and what you can and can't mix together. Paul was that master chef.

Gershon referred us to Moshe Feller, who told us that he had anticipated a zoning change to go through in Brooklyn, changing the Greenpoint industrial area to residential. He bid on an industrial piece of land, offering $14 million, $3 million higher than the next highest bidder. His gamble paid off when, a month later, the zoning change he expected went through. Overnight the value of his land went from $14 million to $75 million. He pulled out some money to buy another piece of land but needed Doheny to arrange equity financing as well as construction financing for his project. After several meetings and many phone conversations, we had an engagement letter and were working to raise $90 million to build 240 condos with Moshe.

Gershon also referred us to another developer who needed financing to build an office building on Lexington Avenue in Manhattan. We signed with him as well. Each of these projects could produce anywhere from $500,000 to $1.5 million in commissions for us. Raising the money would require a lot of work on our part, but it was an exciting start.

NEW HORIZONS

We realized that there was a market for us to do real estate finance. With my connections and my partners' – and especially Paul's – real estate expertise, we had a niche. We decided to reorganize Doheny Global into a holding company with three different divisions: an investment bank, a real estate branch and a private equity fund.

As we were formulating our holding company, Rabbi Weinberg called me, asking that I get together with Rabbi Efim Svirsky, a Russian rabbi on the staff of Aish Jerusalem. As it turned out, Efim had a student in the Ukraine named Alexander Feldman, who was a member of the Ukrainian Parliament and among the 100 richest men in the country; he was interested in talking to me about deals but it was all very vague.

I was skeptical that it was really worth my effort, so I just put it on my to-do list, but it never got done. A few weeks later Efim called me again and explained further that Alexander Feldman was a successful *real estate* developer. In fact, he owned one of the largest malls in the former Soviet Union, an old Russian-style mall with 26,000 (!) tenants.

Suddenly, I saw the connection. After all, real estate finance was the same the world over. I called Paul and he concurred. I called the managing director of Alexander Feldman's real estate company, who explained that they were looking for assistance in financing an expansion of another large Russian-style mall in Kharkov. We said we would explore the market conditions in the Ukraine and scheduled a trip to Kiev to meet with him.

As Paul, David and I prepared for our trip to Kiev, we called a lot of law firms, leasing agents and real estate developers with experience in the Ukraine. One constant complaint we heard was that the banks there charged very high interest rates for their loans. Everyone asked, "Can you find us construction financing in the US that is less expensive?"

Why were the banks charging such high fees? There had to be a reason.

One of our first meetings in Kiev was with the project management team of Raiffeisen, an Austrian bank with branches in Eastern Europe. We were shocked by the decrepit state of their offices; they told us that they awaited relocation to a swanky new office tower but, meanwhile, had to do business out of this old building which overlooked a trash strewn lot and hanging laundry. They were clearly embarrassed that their offices did not project the right image for such a high-profile bank and kept apologizing about it.

We asked them how their interest rates in Eastern Europe were set and the answer was simple – the going rate, plus 3 percent. The extra 3 percent was to cover the extra risk. After all, there was still considerable instability in the FSU; governments were see-sawing between capitalist models and communist models. Economic freedoms were rolled out then rolled back, public utilities went private and became multi-national enterprises only to be taken back under government control (Yukos Oil for example). This made banks nervous.

Once a country (like Poland or Romania) joined the European Union, there was a sense that it had entered the mainstream but, even then, there were no guarantees. The way the bankers saw it, the extra 3 percent was a small compensation. They also assumed that everyone in the former FSU was corrupt – developers, builders, contractors and government inspectors. As a result of the corruption, they had to accept that they would never really know how much a project cost and what was its real cash flow. They would never know how much rent the building would bring in, as everyone lied on the contracts to avoid taxes. So, for these reasons, they charged an extra 3 percent, which helped to soothe all the uncertainty.

It was comical – and at the same time frightening – how things worked in the Ukraine. For example, they described to us how installation of fire sprinklers was done. In any Western country, the sprinklers are installed before the walls and ceilings are put up; the inspectors come, check the pipes and connections, make sure everything works, then the walls go up. In the Ukraine, the inspector comes after everything is done. Whether or not it all works and is properly connected only becomes clear in the event of a fire. What is the inspector inspecting? Nothing! He just comes to collect his bribe.

(Incidentally, this kind of corruption was highlighted on Ukrainian TV in the sit-com *Servant of the People*, starring Jewish comedian Volodymyr Zelensky, who was subsequently elected the country's president!)

Armed with the information from the bankers, we told the first real estate developer who wanted to do business with us that we would gladly raise the money for his project, but we would have to control the partnership. We would bring in Westerners to do the architecture, the building inspections etc. As there would need to be 100 percent transparency, there would be a short-term loss for him since he would not be able to cut side deals, but in the long run, he would learn how to build a project according to Western standards and would have access to Western capital.

We sat waiting for his response, certain that he would not accept our terms. But lo and behold, he did so and willingly. He saw the long-term benefit. He understood that if he wanted his company to grow and access Western capital – and eventually to be able to go public in the US – he would have to adapt to Western accounting standards and learn Western procedures, and the best way to do that was to work with an experienced Western partner. If that meant giving up control on a project, he was willing to do so.

We met with a total of six developers during our trip. Five were of interest to us and all five agreed to our terms!

WHEN IT RAINS

Around this time, my old partner and friend from Moscow, Vitaly Pruss, suddenly came to mind. I had worked with him for two years, and I knew he was well connected. I called him and told him what was happening. He was excited to hear it and said he also had projects for us. Within days, we were signing an engagement letter with a company that was building a large office tower and hotel in Novosibirsk, Siberia. The office building was already fully leased and several chains were interested in the hotel.

Suddenly we had multiple real estate financing projects – in the US and the FSU.

But that wasn't the end of it. When my Toronto friend Marvin Igelman (who had introduced me to Ted Field) heard about our real estate activities, he said he had a close friend who was doing some interesting real estate development in Canada – we should talk to him. Several phone calls later, we had another project in the pipeline.

It was strange! Suddenly lights were turning green everywhere. Where it had seemed like we had been treading water for months with nothing really moving forward, we were suddenly everyone's golden boy.

I recalled my last visit to Israel when I had met with Rabbi Zilberman and complained to him that we were not progressing. I had said, "You are praying. I am praying. What are we doing wrong?" I had been frustrated and had implied that he was not praying hard enough.

He had looked at me, smiling brightly, and said with total confidence, "Sometimes it just takes a little longer for the prayers to be answered." He seemed so sure. He seemed to know that the prayers would be answered. His attitude calmed me down, while my own confidence was waning. And with good reason. My home equity line of credit was drawn down to the last nub. Meanwhile, I had run up over $100,000 on 0 percent credit card loans which would be coming due in a few months. I was getting seriously nervous.

The more my anxiety grew, the more my concentration in prayer suffered. At a time when I should have been even more focused and determined, I was drifting away. I found it difficult to keep up my previous intensity and depth of feeling. I was also traveling a lot, shuttling back and forth between New York and Kiev. The traveling and resultant jet lag were disrupting my newly-restarted Torah-learning schedule. And just when I got into the swing again, I had to take off on another trip.

I wanted to be rich already!

I think on some level I was angry with God that I had not succeeded and, as a result, I just wasn't applying myself as much. So why did it suddenly start to happen? Why did the deals start to flow?

Maybe it is as Rabbi Zilberman said, "Sometimes it just takes a while." Maybe I was seeing now the results of his intense devotion, or of my fervent prayers months earlier. Or maybe the entire reason was simply God's boundless kindness.

Still, I was thrilled that things were starting to happen, because I don't know how much longer I could have held on. Perhaps that is why God answered my prayers now – He knew I was starting to lose it. I'll never know why, but I will always be immeasurably grateful.

THE UMAN SYNDROME

Arriving in the Ukraine on business, I ate an early dinner at the only kosher restaurant in Kiev, the King David. I had some vegetable soup and beef stew. Nothing to write home about but it was filling at least. I then went back to the hotel where a message awaited me, asking me to join Vadim Rabinovitch and some important local politicos for dinner. I went back downstairs and asked my driver, Sergei from Uman, to take me back to the kosher restaurant. He looked at me strangely since we had just returned from there. Jokingly, I told him that ever since Uman I had developed a nervous condition, a type of post-traumatic stress syndrome – I have to eat constantly as I am never sure if there would be food available. It comes from having 15 extra people show up for every meal. Sergei didn't get the joke.

When I arrived at the King David, the hostess gave me the same strange look as Sergei did. Less than a half hour ago, she had seen me leave. I mumbled something about Uman, and she nodded knowingly though I doubt she understood. Sitting in the corner of the restaurant under a big silk canopy made to resemble a Moroccan tent was Vadim with his wife Leah, as well as the invited guests.

Vadim made the introductions, and we ordered. More stew. I also had some fish and salad and washed it down with a French merlot. For dessert, I packed away a dish of parve ice cream and some cake. I blamed it on the Uman syndrome.

Maybe I was eating so much because the conversation was so boring. Blah, blah, blah.

It wasn't until the end that Vadim said something interesting about the young man who was sitting quietly at our table. This fellow had been ill recently – so ill, in fact, that he was taken to the hospital where his heart stopped beating. They had to apply electric paddles, but there was no response. They did it six times and still nothing happened. The protocol calls for them to give up after six tries if there is no response – so, they pronounced him dead and started to cover him with a sheet. Meanwhile, he was alive, inwardly screaming, "I'm not dead! Don't leave me!" But he wasn't making a sound, and the doctors only saw a corpse. One of them must have sensed something though, because he said, "Let's try one more time." They applied the electric paddles again and this time his heart started beating. They were shocked! One in a million chance!

Vadim added that, after this experience, the young man went to Israel where he visited a Kabbalist. As soon as the Kabbalist saw him, he said, "You have seen the Garden of Eden. You have seen Paradise!"

I was amazed. I looked at the young man. He did have an intense look on his face. I searched for signs of eternal wisdom. Just then Vadim got up and said, "Let's go!" I grabbed my jacket and walked out with him. As the car was pulling away, it hit me – how could I have left this guy and not asked him about what he saw in heaven?!

I returned to the hotel and was bothered by this all night. I had sat with someone who held the secrets to life, and I hadn't asked him to share some of them with me. What a wasted opportunity!

I thought about going back to the restaurant to find him but what would the waitress say coming back for my third dinner in one night? I was too embarrassed. I went to sleep, dreaming about the Garden of Eden.

THE MAN WHO SAW PARADISE

A few days later, I walked into the business-class lounge at the Kiev airport to await my flight and was astonished to see none other than Mr. Garden of Eden himself. I went over to him immediately. He remembered me from the dinner. Without any preliminaries I launched into my burning questions. He was happy to tell his story, but it turned out that things were somewhat more complicated than Vadim's summary.

Yes, he had indeed "died" at the hospital, while the doctors were trying to revive him. He said he couldn't move a limb and couldn't speak, though he was crying out inside that he didn't want to die. As he was telling me this, he gritted his teeth and contorted his face to demonstrate the intensity of his inner ordeal. But no one heard him. At least not in this world.

He said he now knows there is a God. Before that he called himself a *chafifnik* – a guy who didn't take things seriously. Now he is much more driven and focused. (More teeth-gritting and jaw-clenching to illustrate.) He said he now knows without a doubt that this world is just a corridor to the next world.

I remarked that to describe this world, we often say that it is "something from nothing," but the truth is the exact opposite – this world is really "nothing from something." This world is a mirage. We think it is real because it feels real, tastes real, looks real to our physical senses. But it is just molecules traveling at different speeds – all an illusion.

(My wife Judy hates when I talk about the meaninglessness of this world, but this guy agreed with me. This must be some kind of man thing. We like getting lost in the abstractions and the women are more earthbound and practical – they say, "Enough with the philosophy, just treat me nicely and kindly. Oh, and remember to take out the garbage and put the toilet seat down, please.")

He said he came to understand that honor, money, competition – all that is nonsense. Only God matters. He said he knows that God hears prayers, and now he prays like he means it, where before he just mouthed the words.

As he was talking, I was thinking, "God help me be as real as this man, but please spare me a near-death experience; I am not sure I could handle that." Then I had to ask myself how much did I *really* want a life of truth – would I be willing to subject myself to such an experience if it would give me true clarity? I had to admit that I was not sure.

I looked deep into his eyes as he spoke. I was trying to discern if I could see something different. What did the Kabbalist see when he declared that this was a man who had seen the Garden of Eden? He had an intensity about him, but nothing I hadn't seen before.

I pushed him for more details. He told me that the Kabbalist had not declared that he had "seen Paradise," but that he had "been above." And also, that the Kabbalist warned him not to discuss it.

And then the loudspeaker system announced our flight. The moment had passed.

I was a little disappointed. I had wanted to hear more details. I thought it strange that the Almighty had arranged for him to step back into my life but deprived me of the whole story. I felt cheated – I wanted to know more.

For one thing, I wanted more practical answers (my wife would have been proud). How could I know that my life plan – which in the last year has meant leaving the public sector to make a fortune in the private sector and giving lots of money to charity – was the right course? Was I betting right? Would I succeed? Couldn't I get just a *little* more clarity on this issue?

Here I was so close to someone who had the answers. He could so easily resolve the pesky little doubts that creep up every so often in my life, right when it's time to write more big checks to charity or do some other good deed. But I suppose if he had been able to supply me with too many answers, then I wouldn't have to struggle any longer with my own issues and my free will would be gone.

I boarded the plane, but my thoughts wouldn't leave me.

In my mind, I started talking to God, "Okay, God, I get it – You've given me a little hint to keep me moving along on the proper path but not too much to take away the challenge." Wasn't it a bit like teaching kids to walk? What do the parents do with their toddlers? They stand just out of reach and extend out their arms, in order to encourage the kids to walk the distance. The kids wobble, fall, get up and keep moving towards their open arms. Little by little the parents extend the distance, but always they let them fall joyfully into a warm embrace, shouting "Hooray! You did it!"

So, "God, I could use a 'hooray' today. I could use a warm embrace and some encouragement today. How about it? I am tired. Cheer me on, please. Don't extend the distance anymore. Let me fall into your warm hug, because I am not sure I have the energy to stumble and pull myself up again. I know they say that a holy man falls seven times but gets up each time. I am no saint, and I have fallen a hundred times. My knees are bruised, my elbows sore. So do me a favor, please – stay still for a minute and just hug me. How about it, God. Give me a break today. Please?"

And then it happened. Tears started streaming down my cheeks and I felt God's warm embrace. I was overwhelmed with emotion. I had to take a deep breath. People were looking at me: the guy playing blackjack on his in-flight TV; the woman in front of me talking with her little girl; the guy one seat over sipping his martini. I wondered how many of them have any idea that this world is an illusion, or that it is just one big corridor to the next world, or that on this very plane, sitting somewhere behind me is the guy who has been "above" and seen it all.

These little cocktail napkins sure don't last long when wiping up tears.

"Okay, God I get it. Your presence overwhelms me. I feel Your love, Your goodness, Your constant caring, Your guidance. I am ready to move on, bruised knees and all. I will pick myself up, stumble again, and keep moving until one day, I will become the man who goes 'above,' like my father and forefathers before me. Just not yet. I have so much I want to do. Help me God, please help me see You 'below.' Help me know You, help me be a great husband, a great father, a great friend and help me succeed in my business, so I will have the means and ability to make your world a better place."

SPIRITUAL INSIGHTS

My family's roots are in the Ukraine and I feel a strangely unsettling connection to the place. It has gotten so I looked forward to my business trips to Kiev, anticipating what spiritual insight God might send me each time around. After I met the man who'd had the near-death experience, I began to pray for such insights.

On one visit, I had some extra time so I went for a stroll in the street market of old Kiev. It is a place full of surprises. Here you can buy typical Ukrainian souvenirs: witch figurines with big noses perched on straw brooms; chess sets of warriors in the medieval battle dress; *bullovas*, round wooden balls covered with metal studs and mounted on a stick, the fighting tools of Ivan, the Terrible; and here you can also buy all the Nazi memorabilia you've been longing for, including your very own Iron Cross and a full Gestapo uniform.

The first time I visited there, a few different merchants, seeing my yarmulke, approached me with old Jewish books. One was a prayer-book and it was dated 1858 – its yellowed and worn pages cried out to me. I bargained with him and rescued it from his clutches for $10. Another merchant, witnessing the transaction, quickly shoved in front of my face another small-prayer book with a red heart on the cover. This one was just as beaten up but it had a name in front and was dated 1911.

I felt like I needed to rescue these holy relics from this unholy place. I wondered how many tears were shed over these pages. I wondered what happened to their owners and the owners' descendants. Did they die in the pogroms? Were they shot at Babi Yar along with 100,000 other Ukrainian Jews? Were they shipped off to Auschwitz?

What did the owners of these prayer-books ask from God a hundred or even fifty years ago? Nothing more than simple survival, a piece of bread, rescue from the murderous hoodlums who were rampaging through their streets. They cried: "God save me – don't let me die. Protect me from a humiliating and tortuous death."

How petty my prayers for financial success were in comparison! I felt humbled and embarrassed and, at the same time, very thankful for God's blessings in my life.

A LITTLE GIRL'S SECRET

Flying home, I took out the little worn prayer-book with the heart on the cover. It had once been red but it has now faded to a burnt orange. As I examined it, I felt a bump under the cloth and I realized that the heart was hiding a Star of David. I feel sure that it once belonged to a sweet young girl – what motivated her to cover the Star of David with a heart, why did she have to hide it, and who found her out, who took this little book away from her?

Leafing through the little book, I felt my eyes filling up and soon my tears were flowing so hard, I could barely see. My chest felt constrained, tightening in a vise-like grip. I was having trouble breathing through my sobs.

I think the other people in business class must have been freaking out. The woman in the window seat beside me appeared to be shrinking further into the cabin wall, as she tried to distance herself from the sobbing man next to her.

This was the same experience I had after my last journey to Kiev. Also then I started crying on the flight home. Good thing it wasn't the same stewardesses, or the next time they'd be pointing at me – "There goes the crier in 2B" – and greeting me with a box of Kleenex.

I took the prayer-books home and placed them on the bookshelf in my study, immediately behind my chair. They felt special and precious. Somehow, they connected me to a sense of spirituality and other-worldliness. I was really not sure why, but they did. I felt their presence with me, sitting like watchmen atop my shelves – reminding me that life is short and where my true focus should be.

Somehow the trips to the Ukraine were putting me in touch with deep soul stirrings that I didn't know were there. My roots are near Odessa on the Black Sea. My father's parents, my Bubbie and Zeidie, fled there in 1914. I wonder if my soul connects to this land that has been so horrible to the Jews in the past and is pained by treading this soil. Perhaps my soul lived a prior life in the Ukraine, and I am reconnecting with the pain of that existence.

My grandparents immigrated to North America from the Ukraine at the outbreak of World War I, managing to board the last ship sailing across the Black Sea. Or so the story goes. But having heard similar stories from many of my peers, I came to think that there must have been an awful lot of ships that sailed out of Europe on that day, a whole armada at least. Anyway, they came to Canada penniless, and slowly and painfully made a life for themselves.

When they arrived, they were Torah-observant but their beliefs had to adjust to the anti-Semitic environment then dominating Montreal. My grandfather would get a new job on Monday and be fired on Friday, when he told his employer that he couldn't work on Shabbat. This kept up until he was broke and couldn't feed his family. He told me that, one depressing day, he laid down in a park and fell asleep, heart-broken and beyond despair. When he awoke, there was a large snake wrapped around his body about to squeeze the life out of him. Right then and there, he made a bargain with God that if He saved his life, he would do everything necessary to feed his family, even if that meant working on Shabbat.

Now there are no large, man-crushing snakes in the cold climate of Canada, but this was my grandfather's – shall I say, metaphorical? – explanation of why he had to give up the Jewish traditions he was raised with. And, of course, God would never make a bargain with him that would require him to violate God's own law. But it seemed pointless for me to debate the logic of this with him by the time I started to doubt certain parts of his story. What regrets he had in his heart were not my business to unearth.

Obviously, he knew that his decision to abandon the Torah did not save him from the ravages of the Great Depression. Back then he had to walk five miles each way to his job, sometimes in the middle of blinding snowstorms, because he couldn't afford the five cents for the streetcar. This was another part of his story that I had initially doubted, because it was hard for me to believe that someone watched *every* penny. He would also tell me how he worked all day, and then took a second job shoveling snow off the sidewalks at night, and a third job on the weekends. Wow, I thought, could times ever be that tough?

As I was to find out – they sure could be.

13

If It's Tuesday It Must Be …
Bucharest, Vienna, Kiev,
Paris and New York

I left New York's JFK Airport at 11 PM. With the help of a sleeping pill, I was asleep even before lift-off and slept for six hours. I awoke in time for breakfast and the landing in Paris, said morning prayers in the business lounge and caught an afternoon flight for Bucharest, Romania, arriving by 8 PM at my hotel, where I met up with Paul and Bill.

We were there to meet with Dr. Philip Dimitrov, the former Prime Minister of Bulgaria, who, at the time of our meeting, served as a member of the EU parliament and of the Bulgarian national assembly. He had driven in from Sofia to hear our pitch for joining the Doheny Global board. He ate dinner while we talked, answering his many questions about our goals and objectives.

We explained that the Eastern European arm of Doheny Global was looking at real estate development projects with a minimum size of $40 million. We had spent the past month getting to know the Ukrainian real estate market and were now exploring Romania. Next, we planned to tackle Bulgaria.

We explained our operational plan – that when we come into a new market we first meet with the top attorneys and accountants to understand the legal and accounting issues unique to each market; we then meet with real estate consultants (such as DTZ and Colliers International) who explain to us the lay of the land. Real estate is one of those investment areas that is more art than science. A lot of people jump into real estate as it is not that difficult in concept, but it does take a lot of skill in execution. There is always demand, but it just depends on which sector.

For example, at the time of our conversation, there were already five Western-style malls in Bucharest, with eleven more on the drawing board. If we didn't know this, we might get all excited about building a sixth Western-style mall, but by the time we finished, our competitors would have done the same, and we would not be able to get significant tenants. So, malls in Bucharest were a chancy investment, but office buildings were another story.

We explained that after we've met all the professionals, we would take a couple of days and have one of the real estate consultancy firms show us around. We'd get a physical feel for the city, its density and trends. Where is it growing? How fast? What might be needed? What is in development and where? We'd look at sites that have been suggested to us, evaluating such things as: What is close by? What are the access roads like? How far away is the closest competitor and where is the next competitor likely to build? Is the competitor situated next to the main road while this site is a mile away from the highway exit? Are the utilities connected to the site, or is the closest sewage main or electrical connection miles away?

After several days of this type of research, we'd have a feel for the city and its development needs, be they for office space, retail shopping centers, residential housing, or logistics centers to handle all the merchandise being shipped in from abroad. There might be a great demand for residential housing but does enough of the population have the earning power and disposable income to buy if we build it? All these were issues we'd take into account when deciding what project to invest in. Then there was the cost and value of the parcel of the land. This was where local expectations and reality often clashed. You could find a parcel of land that might be good for a condo, but it was only zoned for a four-story building. Oh, but the neighboring piece of land had a 25-story condo on it. So what? The former landowner had to go through a laborious three-year-process to have it rezoned and, to push that through, he had to build the government a new post office on the city edge which cost him $5 million. Once he got the zoning change, he was able to get a very good price for his land, and now the guy next door thinks he can get the same price (minus the zoning change).

Stories like this abounded. Land speculation in Eastern Europe was rampant. Everyone was buying up vacant pieces of land expecting that over the next 3-5 years the value will increase a hundredfold. The problem was that if someone were to come in and build on all the land held by speculators, there just wouldn't be enough people living in Bucharest or Kiev or Sofia to populate these buildings and shopping centers and offices. Sure, there may always be another fool to buy that vacant land from you, but at a certain point in time, the music stops. Someone is left holding the "tulips," as happened in that crazy boom-and-bust in Holland.

Thus, our job was to anticipate the trends, know the current demand, accurately project future demand, and then select the appropriate sites to develop. To do all this, we were working closely with DTZ, one of the most prominent real estate consultancy firms in Europe. Thanks to their advice, we signed on to do a hotel project in Novosibirsk, Siberia, where the best hotel at that moment was a Russian three-star. Our client selected SwissHotel, a solid four-star European banner. One might think: Why not do a five-star Marriot or Ritz Carlton? But DTZ told us that a four-star in that city would do better. We were also planning to build a mall there, after analyzing the average income of the population and their needs and trends. Novosibirsk just happened to be the Silicon Valley of Russia – Oprah Winfrey's website was then being designed there – and the home of Intel, Nokia and Motorola R&D plants.

This is what we explained to Dr. Dimitrov. To be on our board, we would ask him to participate in several telephone conferences a year, entailing perhaps 15 hours of his time and, in addition, we would need him to make some trips to the US and would compensate him for his time. His main job would be to introduce us to potential deal flow in Bulgaria and in other Eastern European countries. We explained that we are not land speculators – we want to develop building projects that would help the country and its economy.

He said that he was very interested in joining our board or perhaps becoming a limited strategic partner, but would wait until his term as leader of the opposition in the Bulgarian national assembly was finished to preclude any appearance of a conflict of interest. He expected that to end in sixty days, and then he hoped to take a teaching position in the US.

After the meeting, I schmoozed with Paul and Bill for a bit and then returned to my hotel room from where I called Judy and spoke briefly with each of the kids. At 1 AM, I took a sleeping pill and dozed off.

The next morning, I had a flight to Kiev through Vienna. Even though Bucharest and Kiev are only an hour apart by air, there are no direct flights between the two countries. So, it ends up being a four-hour plane trip. But convincing Dr. Dimitrov to join us was worth it. By then, we also had interest from Lech Walesa, the Nobel Prize winning former Prime Minister of Poland, as well as Petre Roman, the former Prime Minister of Romania. If they all joined our board, we'd have three of the first post-Communist-era leaders of Eastern Europe, men who understood the needs and developments in their countries better than most. This was a pretty impressive line-up for a new firm, to be sure.

FREQUENT FLYER HANGOVER

To fly to Bucharest, I left JFK Saturday evening arriving via a three-hour layover in Paris Sunday evening Bucharest time, which was noonish New York time. I stayed in Bucharest only twelve hours and saw nothing of the city except for the Marriot. Meanwhile, twenty-six virtual hours had passed.

The next morning, I left Bucharest aiming for Kiev, but I had to fly in the opposite direction, to Vienna, a *one-and-a-half-hour* flight which brought me to my destination only *half an hour* after I started out (because of the time zone change). I then left Vienna and flew *two hours* to Kiev, flying over Bucharest and arriving *three* hours later (again due to time zone change).

Thus, I went through two time zones, covering three-and-a-half hours of flight time to fly only 550 miles. But all the flights were on time, and I lost none of my luggage except some sleep-time and a few brain cells. When I boarded in the morning, I still had the sleeping pill in my system and felt like I was sleep-walking. Good thing I was not flying the plane!

By the time I got home, I had spent 60 hours traveling with 7,000 miles in the air over two-and-a-half days; I had seen five cities, five airports and two hotel rooms. Thank You God for bringing me back safe and sound!

As soon as I got home from my 60-hour travel marathon, I was fielding e-mails from Paul and Bill who stayed behind in Bucharest and were negotiating several deals. When they finished there, they moved on to Kiev. I found it very difficult not to be in the thick of things, stuck reviewing reports 4,500 miles away. This must be how the folks at mission control feel when the Apollo orbits the earth, and they are stuck down on earth reviewing reports from the astronauts.

However, I had a lot of work to do back home to prepare for the Israel mission in June. I also had a family that needed me in the US, whereas Bill was a single guy and Paul's children were all grown and off on their own. Nonetheless, it was difficult to be so distant from the center of the action.

I had become used to knowing everything that was going on with my business, but now there was just too much action for one person to be on top of it all, plus it was happening on a different continent, seven time zones away from New York.

After a hectic week in the Ukraine looking at properties, we found several deals that had strong potential. There was certainly a lot of activity and interest. All these deals would take a lot of time and energy and follow up. It was exciting yet frustrating – there was so much potential, yet it all took so much time. Hearing about it over the phone, I could only feel distant.

SIBERIA

After Ukraine, they all flew to Novosibirsk, Siberia, another four time zones east – and I felt helpless.

The mayor of Novosibirsk, Vladimir Gorodetsky, a forceful personality well-connected to the Putin administration in Moscow, had turned his city into the Silicon Valley of Russia. With a rapidly-growing middle-class and a lot of visitors, the city needed a good hotel and shopping center. That is where we came in.

We entered into discussions with a bank in Novosibirsk, and finally agreed on the terms. Our law firm made an official English-Russian translation of the engagement letter, certifying to its exactitude.

This is critical as a small difference in nuance can give the terms a completely different meaning. A certified translation is a linear translation with the English and Russian carefully matched up line-by-line, which is then bound with a cord and sealed with wax. This ensures that no one can tamper with the official translation that the law firm is certifying to be accurate.

The process had moved quickly – we went in only three months from the first meeting to a signed document. The project was quite large, costing $100 million with an anticipated payback period of 4.7 years. The shopping center development – to be called Sky City – would include a cinema, skating rink, restaurants, supermarkets, etc. It was actually a reconstruction of an old railway station in the city center, a hub fed by both subway and bus lines. Ursa Bank was investing $15 million of its own money and wanted us to bring in another $15 million in equity plus arrange for construction financing. Inasmuch as another shopping center in the city (not as well located) had been 100 percent leased six months before opening, this project had all the signs of success!

My partners arrived in Novosibirsk on Sunday evening. Although this was the high-tech capital of Russia, the local cellphone system left something to be desired, and it was impossible for me to get through to them. Our communication was sporadic at best.

I spent a tense weekend, as this was a big deal for us – and we needed for something to go right after the Radar Films fiasco. We had invested a lot of time and energy and expense in researching this project and flying to and from Novosibirsk. I called Rabbi Fox and asked him to pass the word to Rabbi Zilberman to pray extra hard.

Meanwhile, I felt like the army captain who was back at base camp, while his top combat troops were off on a dangerous mission deep behind enemy lines. Due to the danger, they were enforcing strict radio silence. The captain had not heard from them for 12 hours and had no idea if they had been ambushed and massacred or were still alive and on schedule. Emotionally, it is worse for him, even though physically it was a lot less dangerous to be sitting at the command center.

I was a nervous wreck. I prayed. I tried relaxing and giving it all up to God, but I just couldn't manage. I went to bed Sunday evening, knowing they were just heading off to meetings with the Russians, and that by the time I woke up, it would all be decided. Paul had e-mailed David suggesting that we increase the interest rate as investors would be nervous about loaning money to companies so far away. They'd rightly feel they couldn't monitor the projects from such a distance. I could well understand that!

Knowing the increased rate might throw a monkey-wrench into the final talks, I tossed and turned all night. But, by morning, the news was good. The documents would be signed that night at a celebratory dinner. Both sides were happy and excited.

I felt a big burden lift from my shoulders. A deal! And a big deal at that! Thank you, God!

I walked around all day saying: Thank You, God! Thank You, God! I fired off e-mails to my extended family and friends. There was still a lot of work ahead of us, but we now knew we could make joint ventures in strange lands – in Siberia no less!

WOW! Who would have ever thought? Thank You, God! Thank You, God!

THE NEXT STEP

By August 2007, my partners had moved to Kiev. We realized that if we were to be successful as real estate developers in Eastern Europe, we would have to commit major time and effort. We also realized that the potential returns were enormous, and that this was a worthwhile investment.

First Bill, a single guy with a brilliant Romanian girlfriend named Miriam (a lawyer who is fluent in seven languages) moved to Bucharest. Then David and his new wife Leah relocated to Kiev. And soon Paul, our advisor, and his wife Danielle followed, though Danielle could not stay in Kiev full time due to family demands back in LA.

All the hedge fund and private equity fund managers we spoke with were impressed. They told us that we were probably the only fully American team that had actually relocated to FSU to do development. The best other companies could offer was a Russian staffer with some American know-how.

Furthermore, we were doing things Western style, using Baker & McKenzie for our legal work, Deloitte & Touche for our tax advisory work, Savant International and Ave Arup, the world's largest engineering companies, as our project managers, and contractors bondable in Western Europe.

Because of this, all the banks we approached were interested in doing our construction loans. They were not used to sitting down in meetings with individuals who understood finance and underwriting issues, and since my partners were attorneys, investment bankers, and real estate professionals, they were a treat for the banks to deal with. We were assured funding for up to 70 percent of our costs.

But besides arranging construction loans, we had to raise the 30 percent equity and mezzanine investment capital for our projects. Not to mention we had to do all the due diligence – such as ensuring that the land had proper title, that proper permits were obtained, that accounting and corporate structures were established, that architects were selected and plans drawn up.

It was a huge undertaking and the pressure to keep everything moving forward was extremely intense. My task was to raise all the capital, and I found this more than a trifle overwhelming.

I am naturally self-directed. I obsess until I get the job done. This trait of mine can cause me to cross the line at times and become a bit manic and compulsive. My family has suffered over the years due to my single-minded focus, whether the goal was an Aish HaTorah fundraising banquet or a Larry King book tour.

My one-track mind has led me to neglect the less glamorous but nonetheless important duties and responsibilities of husband and father. As my wife Judy has often reminded me when I pleaded that my obsessions should be excused since I was working on behalf of the Jewish people, "Your family are Jewish people too. You can't neglect them to take care of perfect strangers! God isn't applauding you for emotional neglect while you try to save the world."

This time my behavior was no different, except I did not have a charitable cause to hide behind. The goal of financial success wasn't any kind of excuse.

But I didn't know how else to do it. I tried to juggle all my responsibilities, but the pressures of the huge task ahead of me won out. Besides, I was petrified of failure.

I had to raise $7 million of equity and $16 million of mezzanine debt for our first project – a 500,000-square-foot shopping center in Novosibirsk, Siberia. I became obsessed with the job at hand, and the compulsiveness that was my weakness took over. I dropped my Torah learning altogether, and my attendance at morning prayers started to wane. Judy began to feel that even when I was physically present at home or at dinner, emotionally I was distant. I am not sure if the children sensed the difference, but Judy found it especially painful.

I see in retrospect that she had suffered silently for years from my emotional neglect, while I toiled away "for the Jewish people," and – truth be told – for my own sense of accomplishment and the approval of others. All my motivations – the good and the selfish – were intertwined. I wish I could say that I was a selfless servant of God, working for the greater good, but I think the applause was a far greater motivator.

But now I was not pursuing applause as much as I was trying to ward off failure. It was frightening to think that if I didn't succeed, Doheny Global would fold. We would have invested ten months in Eastern Europe with nothing to show for it.

Even more frightening was the state of my personal finances. I was just about out of money. Although two checks had come in from two deals I had done three months earlier and I was able to refinance my home, I was running scared. Frantic, I arranged a personal loan from some old friends to give myself an additional cushion of three months.

I couldn't stop wondering what I would do if I failed. I spent many hours visualizing worst case scenarios – having what you'd call daytime nightmares. I kept asking myself what would happen if I failed, and how I could survive it?

Oddly enough, imagining the worst helped me to regain a sense of calm. I saw myself having to reduce my living expenses, such us cutting out my trainer, my Israel vacations, and even returning my performance cars back to the showroom. At other times, I imagined declaring bankruptcy and going back to work as a salaried employee at an investment bank.

As I turned over each possible nightmare in my mind, I'd conclude, "I could weather that storm. I would survive if that happened."

I knew that, somehow, I had found the resources to survive to date. The Almighty had helped me through everything up till now, so there was no reason why He wouldn't help me in the future.

This exercise helped me to settle down, to quiet my negative thoughts and to get down to the task at hand of raising the capital we needed to do our deals.

After all, it was only money.

THIRTY DAYS HATH SEPTEMBER

After I had been involved in the equity raise for a month, it became clear that it would not be all that hard. As expected, many institutions and funds were very interested. Of course, an expression of interest was a far cry from a check in the mail, and their decision-process was painfully slow, but at least I found many doors open to me. Likewise, friends and acquaintances were also interested, and I was much heartened by their encouragement and faith in me.

In the process, I learned something fascinating about myself. I became aware of the fact that no matter how well things were going, I was prone to worry about failure, which repeatedly put me into a state of anxiety.

Things were going well, but I'd nevertheless manufacture tension. I had learned to live in this state for so long that it felt like a second skin to me – stress and I are one!

I also discovered that I would drive myself from peace of mind to high anxiety simply by indulging fearful thoughts, which would quickly drive me down the road toward panic.

What I had to learn was that my thoughts were not reality. In order to feel a certain feeling, I first had to indulge a certain thought. Feelings don't arise in a vacuum. If I chose to think anxious thoughts about my work, I would for sure feel anxious. If I chose to indulge positive thoughts, I would feel calm and relaxed.

But since all of this happens quickly on a subconscious level, it was hard for me to catch myself. Even when I was aware of my own role in the vicious cycle, I could still make myself into a nervous wreck even when I was succeeding and should have been feeling great.

A nervous wreck is not much of a husband. A nervous wreck is distant and distracted and pushes himself even harder to work to assuage his fears. A nervous wreck can't think clearly.

I worked on calming myself down by replacing my anxious thoughts with realistic thoughts. "Look at the interest in our projects. Look how well the deals are proceeding," I told myself.

This was all true, yet I had a hard time loading it into my brain which was pre-wired for worry. Feeling anxious was a more comfortable state for me than feeling relaxed and happy. In a sad way, it was quite comical.

I couldn't continue like this. For one thing, my wife would not put up with it – as she clearly let me know one day...

14

The Heart of Me

It all began with an argument over the cellphone – a Blackberry at the time.

I had been traveling a lot – Ukraine, Bulgaria, Romania – and violating rules I had made for myself ... like never being away over a weekend from my family, never leaving on a trip on a Saturday night, which really puts a damper on Shabbat. But I had done that twice in the past month.

I well remember the impact that my father's travel schedule had on my mother and our family. My father represented a several menswear lines – men's hats until they went out of style, men's coats and winter jackets, men's sweaters – and he traveled constantly because his territory was Toronto and Western Ontario while we lived in Montreal. For the bulk of the year, he was gone Sunday through Thursday. We only saw him on weekends. I was worse – my wife didn't always get to see me on weekends.

So, in order to make up for that and to re-open my lines of communication with her, I took Judy out to dinner. As we were going out the door, she suggested I leave my Blackberry at home so there would be no interruptions – we could talk and enjoy each other's company without the phone ringing or the e-mail zinging.

I said, "You are kidding, right?"

No, she was dead serious.

The only time that I was not connected to my Blackberry was when in flight – and that's because I had no other choice. The airline makes you turn it off but, even then, I surreptitiously turned it on as we descended so that the Internet could activate the first moment it is possible to receive a signal. My Blackberry was with me always, even in the bathroom – I put it on the counter while I showered, so I wouldn't miss a call or e-mail. I did leave it in my gym bag while I worked out with my trainer, but every half hour I took a break to check my e-mail, and I had it with me when I walked the treadmill.

Yes, I was an addict!

It was exceedingly difficult for me not to be connected. Once when service went down for 18 hours, I came completely unglued. It was not a pretty sight, I am ashamed to admit.

So when Judy suggested I leave my Blackberry at home – and by the look in her eyes I saw she meant it – I reluctantly agreed. As I unbuckled it from my belt, I felt like a gunslinger being asked to remove his holster in the middle of Dodge City. I felt scared, naked, vulnerable.

Everyone over 50 should get a colonoscopy, but few people I know run to do it, even knowing that it can be life-saving. That was kind of how I felt disconnecting from my Blackberry. I knew it was for my own benefit, but I was not thrilled about it.

Dinner was nice, though I was a bit distracted wondering what e-mails I was missing. Once I said to Judy, "It was a great idea to leave the Blackberry at home. I wish I had it with me, so I could write about how good it feels."

She didn't laugh.

When we got home, I ran to my office and checked my e-mail. There was nothing there that couldn't wait. I was glad I had left it at home. I wondered if once I "made it" in business, I would be able to relax more and unshackle myself, or would I just be even more addicted.

I made a commitment that this summer I would leave the Blackberry at home when we visited my in-laws at their beach house on Sundays.

FAMILY TIES

Okay, I admit it – during the twenty-five years that I worked for Aish HaTorah, my family came second to my job. And this was wrong. God could not have been standing up in heaven, cheering me on as I worked 18 hours a day doing Jewish outreach, when I wasn't doing simple outreach with my own family.

In retrospect, I realize that I was imitating my father, who worked incessantly and, even when he was home, wasn't emotionally present. Of course, most men of his generation were struggling to bring enough money to pay the bills. I well remember what that meant in our family.

Friday morning was the day to pay the bills. My father would sit at his desk in the den and shuffle papers around. He would pile the bills under a little lamp on his desk, and then he would take out his checkbook and start writing checks. I recall it being a tense time in the household. My brothers and I learned to stay out of the way – we'd become invisible on this day, as my father fumed, "What is this bill for? How can we possibly keep this up? Where will the money come from to pay for summer camp for the boys?"

I learned from my father that earning a living was difficult, and one had to be prepared to sacrifice oneself for the sake of staying ahead of the bill collector.

When I started to work for Aish – my first real job after college – I just cloned my father's approach. I had learned about trusting in God, but I had not integrated this concept, so even though I was religious, I was a religious workaholic – and my family suffered as a result.

In the beginning, this was easier for my wife to accept as the cause was good – I was working for the Jewish people. Mine was a higher calling. But over time, as more kids came and more responsibilities were placed on her shoulders alone (I was out saving the Jewish people and not available), she began to mind more and more. Her constant refrain became: "We are Jewish people too."

In any marriage, unresolved resentments tend to build up over years. Judy's resentments came to a boil when I left Aish in 2004. She had made many sacrifices for the cause – for at least it was a meaningful cause which brought purpose to our lives – but now she was through. My long work hours could no longer be shielded under the pretenses of working for a greater good. I was working for one thing alone – me, my success.

Judy wanted me to be present physically for the dinner hour, for the kids' bed-time, for their school events and for *her*. This was difficult for me. Even when I was home, I was distracted and pre-occupied. My busy mind was always running ahead – calculating, planning, worrying. Sitting down to dinner, I wasn't in the here-and-now. It was impossible for me to take pleasure in the simple things – like playing games with my kids or taking walks with my wife.

This was not acceptable to Judy. She wanted more than this from her marriage. She wanted what every wife deserves – the attention of her husband, his caring, his involvement in her life and the life of our family.

This I could not deliver, because I was simply too anxious about succeeding, especially with our personal debt mounting, as each deal I put together foundered. I felt like a failure in every respect.

We got some counseling, but it only made things worse as 25 years of Judy's buried resentments bobbed up to the surface. The tension in the home was palpable.

In response, I just wanted to run away – and this I did. I buried myself in work even more, extended my trips out of town, spent more time at the gym. My wife felt even more abandoned, and I felt even more anxious. Things were spiraling out of control. I was in danger of wrecking my marriage.

Thank God that Judy found the strength to speak out. She told me that the married life we were living was unbearably lonely for her and a bad example for the kids. They would go on to repeat what they were seeing – a loveless marriage with an absent spouse. She said we had to do something about it. She didn't want to live the next 25 years of our marriage this way. To her, being alone was better than being lonely in a marriage.

I visualized what it would be like if my wife left me – I would lose my family, my gorgeous children, everything that was most precious to me. Life would be empty, bereft of any genuine pleasure. I broke down in sobs.

Judy is very loyal. Probably any other woman would have left me years ago. I was lucky that she loved me and wanted to make things work. But I had to make a commitment to make things work also.

THE PRANSKY APPROACH

Several friends of ours had attended the four-day seminars at Pransky and Associates in La Connor, Washington, with great results, and suggested this might help us. Pransky and Associates do not offer counseling, rather they seek to help seminar participants unlock their own resources so they can solve their problems by themselves.

I called Rebbetzin Feige Twersky in Milwaukee, as I had heard she had trained with Pransky. She said the tools taught in the four-day seminar were totally congruent with the Torah approach to life.

I felt we were in a crisis, and I didn't know how long I had to save my marriage – I dropped my work, and we took off for La Connor.

The Pransky understanding of the human psyche recognizes that there are three forces at work: mind, consciousness and thought. The "mind" – Jews would call it the "soul" – is the source of true wisdom, but we access it only when we are willing to let it flow and do not block it with distractions; it is also the source of all true feelings like love, gratitude, contentment, trust, and self-respect. "Consciousness" is the human power to bring thought to life, and "thought" is the ability to create via mental activity.

Our thoughts are like icebergs – most of what we think hovers below the surface of our consciousness. But everything starts with thought – what we think, we immediately feel. Thus, the Pransky approach is to work on quieting the thought whirlwind. The approach is to learn to relax in order to allow positive thoughts flowing from the mind/soul to dominate. This leads to positive feelings rather than ones tainted with bad memories. This begins a positive cycle – the positive feelings lead to more inner peace, which in turn produces more good thoughts and feelings, which in turn opens the flow of the mind's wisdom, because it is now not blocked by anxieties and distractions.

RE-UNION

When we arrived in La Connor, they asked me to turn off my Blackberry for the four days of the seminar. I tried. I couldn't turn it off completely, but I made strides. I gave the Blackberry to Judy as it was too tempting for me. I went one full day without it, and then asked to check my e-mail for a half-hour. After that, I managed to turn it off for two whole days. I felt freed.

My assistant, Maria, put an auto-message on my e-mail system, telling people I would be unavailable for four days. I immediately got concerned e-mails from male friends who have known me for 15 years and who knew I never turned off my e-mail for anything but Shabbat and the Jewish holidays. They all knew me as the fastest draw in replying to messages. They could only think that I was very sick and in the hospital. I explained that I was trying to slow down my obsessive mind, get a new focus on life and work on my marriage. They understood and asked me if I could let them know how it went as they probably needed the same thing. Most men do.

The experience was wonderful for Judy and me, and it brought us to a new level as a couple. It was a very romantic period. We were staying in a quaint little inn in the town of La Connor – population 700, one traffic light. We had nothing to do but work on ourselves and our marriage. We began to communicate again, to get to know each other, to forgive the past. We realized that the mistakes we made came from innocence – neither one of us did anything to hurt the other on purpose.

My wife is a beautiful, smart, funny, loyal woman, who has brought up our eight wonderful children. I saw what a great tragedy it would be if we got divorced. I could get super rich through my real estate development in Eastern Europe, but I would be a failure as a human being.

CHANGE

During the seminar, something very deep inside me clicked. I had a deep awareness, a transformative change in my consciousness that said, "I am going to be different." I asked Judy for forgiveness. It became clear to me how much I had neglected her and hurt her over the years. I truly wanted to change. And I believe I came back from La Connor a changed man.

Going forward, although we have had our ups and downs, I became much more focused and less distracted. My mind settled down, and I've been more present in the family. The first big change – I started taking an hour for family dinner and driving the kids to school (which takes 20 minutes each way). We would stop for hot chocolate at the kosher donut shop, because I wanted to be with them and experience this time together. I'd pick them up from school a few times a week also.

One day, my daughter Sara asked me, "Is everything okay? Why are you spending so much time with us, taking us to school?" It was precious. She felt the difference.

All that made Judy much happier. We worked on having heartfelt, soul-connection talks a few times a week. We didn't just talk about scheduling and family matters, we talked about our feelings and what really counts to us personally. Sometimes, during the week, we'd feel ourselves drifting off and we'd say, "It's time for a soul-connection chat." We now had a language to communicate with each other, and we knew how to reconnect when we drifted away.

As for me, my mind had slowed down, and I was nowhere near as anxious and hysterical as I used to be. I still had a lot of growing to do, but I felt like I was now tapping into the richness of life, into the beauty that this world had to offer.

One night, I had three hours alone as Judy was out for a women's function, and I enjoyed my solitude. On another occasion, I was stuck in a plane, waiting six hours for take-off and I enjoyed the time – I read and listened to Pachelbel, the music that touches my soul. I sat in my seat conducting the orchestra, and even though the stewardess and my seat-mate probably thought I was weird, I felt great. My soul was alive.

I felt like I was a millionaire many times over – in real terms. My wife was happier. I was developing a closer relationship with my younger kids. I was spending more time on the phone talking to my older kids who live in Israel. I no longer felt empty, isolated, worried. I was becoming more human and I was loving it. I knew I had a long way to go, but I was on the right track. I also knew that I was a recovering workaholic and I had to take it day by day, one step at a time.

At heart I am a family man, no matter my drives, dreams and desires. The part of me that is dedicated to family is the strongest part of me – the heart of me. It is a gift I got from my Mom, God rest her soul.

MY MOM

When I left yeshiva in 1982 to start Aish LA, I was two years short of completing the studies for my rabbinical ordination. I certainly didn't need to be a rabbi to be a manager and a fundraiser. But when I learned that my mother's cancer had metastasized, I decided – at Judy's urging – that it was time to finally get ordained (to get *smicha* as it is called), knowing how thrilled my Mom would be.

All those years, while her friends boasted of "my son, the doctor," and "my son, the lawyer," my poor Mom had to bite her lip. If she couldn't have a son who was a doctor or a lawyer, "my son, the rabbi" would be the next best thing. I knew it would mean a lot to her, and it would also help me in my work in LA. Thus, I embarked on an 18-month crash course, studying alone or with a tutor from 5 to 7 every morning, as well as every evening, and making frequent intensive-study trips to Israel.

Finally, I was ordained on November 19, 1992, and my parents flew to Israel for the ceremony.

I noticed then that my mother had trouble with stairs, that she was often short of breath and, at times, seemed to be in pain. I didn't realize just how sick she really was, because she hid it so well. In retrospect, I realize that she was keeping herself alive for the ordination. She had already married off her three sons and had seen grandchildren from them all, and this was the next thing she wanted to see.

After she returned home to Montreal, she quickly disintegrated. I did not know then that she only had nine months left to live.

I was living in LA then. Each morning, I would bundle the four oldest kids (they were ages 6-9 then) and drive them to school. On the way, I'd call my Mom and put her on the speaker phone so all of us could chat with her. They would yell, "Hi Bubbie, we're going to school with Tattie," and invariably fight over who got to speak first. It kept us all connected, even though we were 2,500 miles apart. I also hoped to show my children the respect and love I felt for my parents so that one day, when I became old and infirm, they would also show it to me. I heard it said that your children will treat you in your old age the same way they saw you treat your parents. So, if you ship your parents off to an old age home because they are too much of a burden, you might as well reserve a bed there for yourself too.

THE LOCKED DOOR

Every two weeks, on Thursday evening, I would fly to Montreal and spend Shabbat with my Mom (who was usually in the hospital) then fly back to LA on Sunday evening.

On one of those visits, I was sitting by her bed as she moved in and out of consciousness following an operation which determined that all hope was gone. I held her hand and caressed her forehead. Suddenly, her hand jerked up into the air and started making small circles, round and round. She was working at something, trying to accomplish a task, but I had no idea what. After a while, her hand relaxed and dropped to her side.

She slept. I sat.

Then she awoke and looked up at me. She looked scared and sad. I asked her what happened – what was she trying to do. By then we had made it a habit of talking openly about her approaching death.

She said, "I was trying to open the door. It wouldn't open. I didn't seem to have the right key."

I asked, "What door? To where?"

"The next world. My mother and father were there and my sister also."

She said they told her to come to them, but she could not figure out how to open the door and she was frustrated by this.

I told her it was okay. I held her hand tight and told her that when she was ready, she would figure it out.

I didn't want her to figure it out though. I didn't want to let go of her hand. I was afraid she would reach for the right key this time. Perhaps if I just stayed there, never letting go of her hand, I could hold onto her forever.

My intellectual self knew I could not, but my emotional self simply refused to accept it.

JOY IN THE SNOW

When I made the trip to Montreal, I would often take two of the kids with me.

One trip during the cold weather months stands out especially. I had taken the two oldest boys, AY, then age 8, and Yakov, then age 7. Having been born and raised in LA, my kids had little experience with snow, and they were looking forward to this special treat.

We arrived at the hospital on Thursday night, and we planned to sleep there in order to spend all Shabbat with my Mom. Friday, during the day, the hoped-for snow arrived in abundance, and we watched it out of her seventh-floor window, as it accumulated down below. The boys, bored already by sitting around, were itching to make a snowman.

I suggested they go outside and play below my Mom's window, out in front of the hospital where the main driveway snaked around a large island piled high with snow. Thrilled, they bundled up in their borrowed snowsuits and rushed outside, promising to play in the designated area only.

Meanwhile, I set up a chair by the window for my Mom, so she could watch the kids frolic. They rolled in the snow and made angels with their hands and feet. All the while they kept their eyes on us, waving every few minutes and attempting to throw us a snowball. Invariably it would arc upwards and fall back on one of their heads, provoking much laughter. Then they had a snow ball fight, and when they tired of that, they started making a four-foot-tall snowman. Their snowman was eventually complete, and they added some candies from their pockets for eyes and licorice for its mouth. They were so happy with the final result. They jumped up and down and danced with joy.

Their innocence and playfulness were very touching for me and my Mom to see. We sat there with tears in our eyes – tears of joy, tears of gratitude for God's blessings to us, tears of knowing we would never sit together again, watching my children and her grandchildren frolic in the snow. A bond was created between us in that instant that still binds us today – years after her death, I remember and the tears flow anew. If it was not for her illness, we would never have experienced that moment when we marveled together at the wonder of life captured in the snow.

I feel the pain of her loss now as if it was fresh. Fresh as that falling snow. The pain is as cold and as stark. The pain envelops me in totality now as the snow filled Montreal on that day. Falling nonstop, blanketing everything, bringing me to confront reality:

We are all going to die. We all know it. Yet we seem to need to be close to death to really face that fact. In Judaism, we are taught that only when we come to terms with death can we truly live. Why is this so? Because only death brings with it the awareness of just how special every moment of life is. Without that awareness, we miss so much of life as it whizzes past us – without that awareness we miss the simple joys all around us, infusing each second of existence.

A MOMENT IN TIME

I remember another moment with my Mom. I had rolled her wheelchair onto the balcony of my parents' home. We sat there together and a little blue jay flew by and landed on a tree. My mother, who was then in great pain and in the last days of her life said, "Look at the bird. It is beautiful!"

She smiled, even though pain coursed through her dying body. I truly felt her words. She had become wise. I felt that in that one phrase she had captured the awesomeness of existence. It was a simple phrase but she said it with such conviction that I knew it meant a lot more.

The snow falling, the snowman, the kids in the snow, the bird on the branch. Life. Death. All are one. It is all there is, and it is what we must grasp somehow. If only we weren't so busy with our plans and worries, we would see it all the time. My mother saw it. At the end of her life, she lived with full awareness of those special little moments, and I was lucky enough to share that awareness with her. Her parting gift to me was a richer understanding of what unites us in life – the oneness of God: "Hear O Israel, the Lord is our God, the Lord is One!

And yet, and yet ... I do not understand why the pain at her loss is as fresh today as it was at the time of her death. I think the most painful moment in my life was the first time I said *Kaddish* for her – the prayer of mourning, which is really a song of praise to God.

After the funeral, when I stood up to lead the prayer service, the reality sank in. She was gone. At that moment, I thought I would die from the pain. It just hurt so much. What is that pain? Was it her loss? Was it the realization that I, too, will die? That those kids who were making a snowman will one day be saying *Kaddish* for me? Was it knowing that I cannot sustain that keen awareness and am missing so many moments in my own life?

It was all that and more.

15

Just Around the Corner

By November 2007, the whole team was working diligently to make the Novosibirsk shopping center happen. Drafts had been going back and forth between Bill and Paul in the Ukraine and Scott Claymore, our tax/partnership expert in the US. There were some forty due diligence documents that had to be produced. And it was quite exciting to see it coming together. It felt like success was just around the corner.

The hedge fund, Hudson Bay Capital, tentatively agreed to commit somewhere between $3-5 million. The head of Hudson Bay, Sander Gerber – whom I have known ever since he donated money to Aish ten years prior – was impressed with the team we had assembled to work in the FSU, and he was astonished that they were all living there full time. We had sent his company the final economics so they could properly analyze the deal. We were waiting now to see if they would approve the structure. Until they did so, we couldn't finalize the offering memorandum. But once it happened, I still needed to raise several million more.

Still, my network continued to expand daily. Eli Slomovitz, an international real estate developer, promised to set up meetings for me with representatives of two other funds. Tzvi Berg introduced me to an interested investor who introduced me to another. And good ole Marvin Igelman promised to speak to investors in the Toronto area.

It was strange and wonderful, how investors – or, I should say, *potential* investors – arrived at my door. The network of introductions was an amazing one when I looked at all the coincidences – or was it Divine Providence? – that had to happen to make it all come together.

Life is strange. Exactly what God's plan is I honestly don't know.

ANOTHER DAY, ANOTHER MILLION

At the end of November, I heard that Sander Gerber of Hudson Bay Capital was considering investing $5 million, and that if he did so, he planned to invest another $5 when the Novosibirsk mall was 70 percent leased. This was exciting news.

In less than one month, I had $9 million in soft commitments, but still needed to come up with $3 million more. And I had only two weeks to get that together.

My hopes rested with Saul Stein (not his real name), the head of a real-estate empire worth $2 billion and the largest private landlord in America. I had aroused his interest sufficiently to get him to agree to come on an "investor tour" of the FSU that I was putting together. He was considering investing $3 million.

But then, like a splash of cold water in my face, an e-mail from him popped up on my cellphone:

Irwin: I have decided not to proceed with the visit to Russia. We've met internally and none of us can get over the "*Wall Street Journal* fear" that much of Russia and its affiliated states are run by the mob and that, in effect, something we may own we may not actually end up being the legal owner of, and we find this very fearful. So at this point in time, I can't get our investment committee to agree to invest in any of the former USSR states. Respectfully, Saul

This was a major disappointment. And all the more so because, at the time, I didn't believe this was true. The FSU of 2007 was not the FSU of 1997. I thought it was a totally safe place to invest – in fact, others thought like I did and billions of dollars were being invested there every day by all the major banks and lending institutions. But, in retrospect – with all that has happened with Russia and the Ukraine, and the resulting sanctions by the West – he was proven right and I was proven wrong.

Saul was a potentially important investor – not just because he played with large numbers, but because he was known as "smart money," so others would have followed his lead.

Still, though I was disappointed, his rejection didn't shake me that much or make me hysterical as it would have some months ago. I had more confidence in our ability to do this deal, no matter what. One person in or out wasn't going to make that big a difference to our bottom line.

I liked the calmer space that I had found within myself, and I wouldn't let anyone knock me off center so easily. When I felt myself starting to get anxious, I'd tell myself, "No need for anxiety. It is all in your thoughts. Calm down. You will figure it out. You have done so before, and you can do so again. God will help you. Have no fear."

And God did. Saul Stein changed his mind about the "investor tour." Influenced by Sander Gerber, he decided he wanted to come and see things for himself after all. I would make sure he was wowed.

A GOOD DEED

While I was preoccupied with money, my then 16-year-old daughter Bracha was preoccupied with good deeds. She and eight of her classmates from a Beis Yaakov school in a suburb of New York were spending ten days in Kiev, living in the dorms of an orphanage there and learning what Jewish life is like in modern Ukraine.

I had spoken to her a few times during her visit and knew she was having an eye-opening experience. I told her I would arrange a farewell dinner at the King David restaurant for her and the entire group from New York, as well as the girls from the orphanage. What she didn't know was that I planned to surprise her and attend the dinner.

I showed up at the King David restaurant half an hour early. The main dining room had been re-arranged to create one large horse-shoe table to accommodate the 30 girls (ages 7 through 17) who would be attending. I had selected the whole menu ahead of time and had ordered a three-piece band to play *Shalom Aleichem* when the girls filed in.

I waited for the whole group to arrive and for the band to strike up the music, and while all the girls were standing around giggling, I snuck up behind up Bracha, placed my arms around her shoulders and spun her around. It was one of life's special moments.

Then Bracha brought me around to meet the girls she had be-friended during her stay. They could barely say hello – they were still in awe at being in the restaurant with a three-piece band playing in their honor. Bracha explained to me that, for almost all of the girls present, it was the very first time they had been in a restaurant. The little ones had gotten dressed in their very best clothes and had been waiting in the lobby of the dorm building since 3 PM, more than four hours early. This was a momentous experience for them.

I was struck by the expressions on their faces – all happy – and the contrast in their eyes, which told a different story, hiding haunt-ing memories, deep fears and old traumas. After a few minutes of milling around, enjoying the music and getting introduced to every-one, we took our seats at the horseshoe table.

It felt wonderful to be sponsoring the dinner. What a great feeling to do something nice and kind for someone else! And yes, there was also a sense of power in using my resources to help others.

I could see from the surprised looks on the girls' faces as they sized up the food piled on the table that this was a unique experience for them. For the first course, I had ordered many different kinds of salads – cucumber salad, pickle salad, egg salad, grilled vegetables, and other kinds of appetizers. But the girls filled up as if this was the whole dinner.

And then the cutest thing happened. When they finished, they started to stack the dishes, asking where to bring them. They had never before been in a restaurant and couldn't fathom that someone would clear up after them. The dorm mother explained to them that there were waiters and waitresses to do these chores. They continued clearing dishes and stacking anyway – they just couldn't seem to understand.

Then the waiters came out with the main course. Plates of chicken, beef brisket, baked potatoes, French fries, Russian dumplings, grilled fish.

The girls were amazed, their eyes wide. They had never seen so much food in one place before. It was entertaining just to watch them. Shyly they began spooning the food onto their plates, but as soon as they emptied one plate, they just as quickly refilled it. They weren't used to food – especially meat – in such abundance.

When we finished the main course, the real fun started as desserts were brought out: pastries, chocolate mousse, cream puffs, non-dairy ice-cream. I watched with immense pleasure as one of the little girls impishly pulled the ice cream and a chocolate cake over to her and shoveled goodly portions of both onto her plate with glee. I was happy I could provide such a simple life pleasure to these young girls.

JOY AND SADNESS

But, even through the joy, I could sense the sadness. Some of the faces troubled me. They looked like they had lived a lot more than their few years. Something in their eyes, their fleeting glances at me, the way they clung to each other hinted at their past.

One girl in particular drew my attention. She was a skinny little kid with a hard, closed face. I asked my daughter Bracha what she knew about this girl. I almost wish I hadn't.

When she was three, her mother her died and she was left alone with her father, who didn't really have the skills to bring up a little girl. He quickly remarried and started a new family, and she was shipped off to the orphanage. But a terrible fear of abandonment plagued her. Bracha said that if she left her for a short while her eyes turned sad, she became quiet and pouted. If Bracha told her she would be back in five minutes but returned in ten, she wanted to know, "Why were you late?" She was clingy and demanding of exclusive attention. She had an extraordinary need to be attached to one person, who belonged to her alone.

I asked Bracha about another one of the girls who seemed out of place. She had long blond hair and bright blue eyes, but an angry expression crossed her pretty face. Bracha explained that when she was two years old her family moved away from the Ukraine, leaving her behind. Only occasionally did she hear from her mother by phone. She was another clingy girl who was dealing with abandonment issues.

The other stories were just as sad. Orphaned girls, abandoned girls, abused girls.

Bracha pointed out another girl who ran away and hid when her father came to visit. She told Bracha she was scared of him, and that she liked the dorm because it is quiet and peaceful, whereas at her home everyone was always screaming. Bracha said that once they passed her father's apartment, and the girl shuddered in fear.

As Bracha talked tears came into her eyes, as they did into mine. I think a deeper bond was created between us at this dinner in sharing both the joy of the moment and the pain of these girls' lives. From this experience, Bracha gained a deeper appreciation for our family back home and the blessings God had given us. And so did I. If my grandparents had not left the Ukraine in 1914, it could be my children in this school. We had a lot to be thankful for.

I hugged Bracha good-bye and retreated to my hotel room. I really couldn't handle any more of the intensity of the dinner. I called Judy and told her about how beautiful it was, as well as the haunting stories of these girls' lives. I asked her, half-joking but also half-seriously, if she would consider maybe adopting one of the girls. In her usual straightforward way, Judy answered that I should first work on being home a little more and meeting all the needs of our current family before expanding it. She was 100 percent correct. I had been traveling and absent a lot, and my own kids probably felt, in some ways, like the abandoned girls in the dorm.

But my wife had a wonderful idea. She suggested that we invite a couple of the girls to join us for Passover week in Israel. We chose two girls whose parents did not celebrate the holiday and who had never been to Israel. It turned out great. They had an awesome experience and their presence enriched out family's celebration as well.

I needed my wife to keep me grounded. I was off thinking that I could save every orphan in the Ukraine, and my wife was there to remind me to maybe try spending a little more time doing homework with my own kids first. She always had a way of bringing me back to earth!

INVESTOR TOUR

In the winter of 2007, I took a group of five potential investors to the Ukraine and Moldova (Saul Stein never did come and did not invest); we did not include Siberia in the itinerary as at that time of year it was too cold (not to mention too far).

We flew into Kiev, where I had leased a Yak-40 jet to take us around. Unlike my previous experiences with Yaks, this was a luxurious plane, done up in soft beige leather – eight armchairs and a couch – with a staff of five to ferry us and look after our comfort.

They had attached a camera in the nose of the plane, so we had a pilot's view of take-offs and landings. It was more scary than exciting, especially when the plane seemed to be missing the runway on landing. As it turned out, the camera was mounted off center, creating this optical illusion.

Although only some of my investors were Jewish, I took them out to dinner at the kosher King David restaurant. And I couldn't resist combining a good deed with business – I still had something of the do-gooder left in me – so I invited the girls from the orphanage to join us. We were sitting at a corner table when they walked in so prim and proper, heads held up high – it was a poignant scene. This was only their second visit to a restaurant ever. Of course, they all asked about my daughter Bracha, so I called her on my cellphone. It was worth the $3.50 a minute, as all of them exchanged greetings with her. It gave me an enormous lift to see them so happy, and to hear the surprised pleasure in my daughter's voice.

Everyone who came on the trip was blown away by the opportunities we had under contract and seemed enthused about investing. We also showed them other projects which we hoped to develop in the future – a possible hotel site in central Kiev, and a 165-acre site in Odessa overlooking the Black Sea, where we hoped to build 650 homes, as well as our newest site in the pipeline – a project to build 1,000 condos in Chisinau, Moldova.

But we needed $9 million to make Moldova happen and $30 million to make Odessa happen.

HIGH STAKES

To build up my self-confidence for the grueling task of raising so much money, I kept telling myself that God runs the world, and that God had given me a soul which is tied into universal intelligence. If I could just get out of my obsessive-compulsive, repetitive thinking, and instead allow myself to relax and tap into the universal mind, then the answers would come to me.

Meanwhile, I had been e-mailing my silent partner with the specifics so that he could intensify his prayers on my behalf. The stakes for him were high as well, because if these projects succeeded, I would be paying off the loans he took out to buy the yeshiva building. I calculated that Doheny Global's profit in Novosibirsk would be $15 million, in Moldova $11 million, and in Odessa $60-70 million. While it would take three years to complete these projects and collect the money, there would be a nice payday waiting for us all at the end of that time – if I could only raise what we needed NOW.

I found it hard to contain my impatience. And when I next met with Rabbi Zilberman, I expressed my frustration at how long things were taking. In response, I got an earful from him.

He cited a somewhat archaic passage from the writings of the 18th century Italian Kabbalist, Rabbi Moshe Chaim Luzzatto, better known as Ramchal:

The order arranged by the supreme wisdom [of God] stipulates that for human beings to receive abundance from Him, it is necessary that they should be aroused towards Him [in prayer] and draw close to Him and seek His countenance. And in proportion to their arousal towards Him, so will the abundance be drawn down to them.

Rabbi Zilberman gauged my reaction and then asked, "You wonder about all the people who don't pray and they nevertheless receive, right?"

I shrugged my shoulders.

He smiled, "The answer comes to us in a verse from the Book of Proverbs where it states that sometimes wealth brings harm. When is this? When the wealth arrives without prayer, for then it arrives from 'one who gives grudgingly.'"

Seeing the mystified look on my face, he hastened to clarify. "It is written that you should 'put a knife in your cheek,' rather than eat food given by someone who gives grudgingly. Such nourishment contains no blessing, but only the opposite. But when a person prays, then abundance comes down and it arrives from 'one who gives benevolently.' Then nourishment is full of goodness and blessing."

Rabbi Zilberman urged me to continue with my own prayers. He said that the Ramchal wrote about this issue in his book *The Way of God*. He quoted:

> For behold, the more one becomes entangled in worldly matters, the farther he gets from the supernal light, and he becomes more enveloped in darkness. But, if he first casts his burden upon God by means of prayer and only afterwards begins all his efforts in worldly matters, this rescues him from sinking into physicality and materiality.

I thanked him for his advice, and as he was walking out the door, he made this enigmatic remark, "Don't worry. Our prayers will be answered because I have been sneezing a lot."

I laughed thinking it was a joke, but then he explained that it wasn't. He cited the Talmud: "He who sneezes in his prayer, it is a good sign for him."

It sounded weird to me, but I was grasping at straws – anything to keep up a positive attitude. If Rabbi Zilberman was sneezing in prayers and he didn't have a cold or an allergy, then success must be just around the corner.

But where exactly was that corner?

The answer was – as I found out – not in Siberia.

NOT IN SIBERIA

I had spent four months speaking to potential investors, describing the deal to them, explaining to everyone where Novosibirsk is, why the FSU isn't a scary place to invest, and why they should fork over their hard-earned savings to us, in order to invest in a real estate development deal in the capital of Siberia.

During that time, the value of the US dollar had steadily declined, and as the dollar had gone down, the cost of the project had gone up. As we got closer to closing the deal, we began to get worried about the resultant factor of disappearing profits. We had started out with an estimate of $70 million for construction (all hard and soft costs included), but now were seeing that it would more likely be $80 million. At the same time, the value of our potential leases had also gone up, so we reasoned it could all balance out. But the worst thing was to go into a deal with the costs unknown.

Paul kept telling me that no matter how much work we'd put into a deal and no matter how much time we'd invested, we should never go ahead with it if we stopped thinking it was still a good deal. This was a difficult thing for me to hear, especially after what I had been through to make it happen and wanting to close on it so badly, but I had to acknowledge the wisdom of his advice.

By the first week of December, we had enough capital committed to close, but we decided not to go through with it unless our local partners in Novosibirsk were willing to change the terms to accommodate this BIG unknown – i.e., the cost of the construction. Needless to say, they were not crazy about this.

We were having similar problems with our local partners in Moldova and had begun to wonder if the only way for us to do deals in the FSU was to do them independently and not with partners. It seemed that unless we made it clear to them that we were prepared to walk out, they would never give in on any contract points. We literally had to be prepared to leave the deal to get anything done.

In the meantime, David and Paul went to Odessa for a few days. In Odessa, we had been working to finalize the purchase of 165 acres overlooking the Black Sea. We wanted to sign the sales agreement with a closing projected for the middle of March 2008.

This was the FSU deal that looked the best of all. Not only would we be buying the land outright, independent of local partners, we could expect to make more money on Odessa than on both Novosibirsk and Moldova combined.

When we first started looking for business in the FSU, we were not so fussy about which deals we pursued. We were new and wanted to explore as many deals as possible to get a better feel for what was what and who was who. But after ten months of experience, we were much more savvy. Alas there was a price for all this learning.

As the Novosibirsk and Moldova deals unraveled, I found myself in a strangely calm place emotionally. I had been working so diligently for so long on this, I should have been devastated. But as odd as it may seem, the turn of events did not unhinge me.

Part of the credit for my calm attitude goes to a book entitled *The Garden of Emuna* by Rabbi Shalom Arush of the Breslover Hassidic sect. It had been given to me by my son Simcha (who, as I mentioned, is a Breslover) but I had put it aside. I figured it was one of those hokey Hassidic books that I so dislike. None of the stories ever seem real, and they usually portray their rabbis as totally perfect and perfectly holy which I just can't relate to, and so I had just kind of pushed it off. Judy had read it and was impressed, but it wasn't till another friend said this book had changed her life that I became open to its teaching.

When I read it, I found it was not at all what I had imagined. The book was written in a modern idiom, offered practical advice and was really quite uplifting. Basically, its message was that everything comes from God, and there is a good reason for whatever happens. The message resonated with me and fit well with the approach to thinking I had learned at Pransky. In short, it made a lot of common sense.

I thought about the message of Rabbi Arush's book in relation to what had happened in the FSU. What was the good in it? One answer, I had to admit, was that it would give me time to be with my family and not to be anxious over the next few weeks. I really wasn't sure, but it felt like the right answer.

SUPER BOWL

Since now I had some free time, we decided to take a short mid-winter vacation as a family and visit Judy's parents in Florida, where I would get to enjoy the Super Bowl with Neale, my father-in-law.

I watch only one football game a year: the Super Bowl. Even though I rarely know who is playing, who is the favorite, or much else about the game, I really do look forward to this once-a-year slice of Americana. And though I am a total health-food nut and rarely eat junk food or drink liquor, the morning of the game, I decided I should do it right – I went out and stocked up on potato chips, popcorn, pretzels and beer. It just seemed to me that football and junk food have to go together.

I was in a good mood despite recent events in my business life. I had hunkered down in the living room with my father-in-law and my sons, watching the pre-game shows, boning up on the pre-game stats and getting an early start on the junk food, when the phone rang. My mother-in-law, Barbara, answered from the kitchen. I could hear her muted voice, but I was not paying much attention until I heard her exclaim, "You won't believe it, but my son-in-law is a rabbi! And he is visiting us right now from New York!"

Oh, oh – my alarm bells went off!

IS THERE A RABBI IN THE HOUSE?

A few minutes later, she hung up and came into the living room to explain. An acquaintance from the tennis club, a woman who is a hospice worker, had turned to her for help. It seems that a Jewish patient was dying of Lou Gehrig's disease. All his vital organs were shutting down, and it was only a matter of days, perhaps hours. The hospice worker was trying to help him prepare for the end and fulfill his dying wishes. He had asked her to summon his son, his ex-wife and, of course, a rabbi. Any rabbi willing to come would do.

This being Florida, it shouldn't have been hard to find a rabbi. Or so the hospice worker thought. Except for one thing: Super Bowl Sunday. Apparently, I was not the only rabbi who decided to take the day off and watch the Super Bowl while clogging his arteries with fat-saturated snacks. The only difference, it seemed, between me and all the other Florida rabbis was they had answering machines they could ignore, and I had a real-live mother-in-law answering the telephone ever so cheerfully.

Barbara was very excited by what she considered to be an amazing coincidence. A woman she hardly knew, and who certainly had no idea what her son-in-law did for a living, called her looking for a rabbi to help a dying man on the very day that the son-in-law happened to be visiting! I myself was neither impressed nor amused by the coincidence. I couldn't believe that God had other plans for me that day. I did what any responsible Jew would do with the Super Bowl about to start – I told her to check the yellow pages. There had to be dozens of rabbis listed. If she truly couldn't find anyone else, she could call back.

She called back – no one was answering the phone. I was stuck.

BEST LAID PLANS OF MICE AND MEN

Reluctantly, I had to admit that maybe – just maybe – God had some other plan for me that day than watching TV and stuffing myself with popcorn. Neale, the trooper that he is, offered to drive me over to see the dying man.

I knew nothing about Lou Gehrig's disease, but I was stunned by what I learned. It is a disease of the central nervous system – named for the famous baseball player Lou Gehrig who succumbed to it – which gradually destroys the body while leaving the brain intact. The victim slowly loses the use of his hands, legs, kidneys, bowels, larynx – he cannot write, eat, wash, walk or talk. The process is painfully slow; it takes years as the body shuts down. It is like being buried alive slowly, day by day. But the brain is painfully alert the whole time.

I didn't really know any of this until the hospice worker briefed me, but the information hardly prepared me for what I saw when I walked into the dying man's room. He was propped up in a hospital bed with tubes going in and out of his body, now flowing with blood that his kidneys could no longer cleanse. I greeted him warmly as I walked over to his bedside. He didn't respond. I repeated my hello and then noticed his lips moving, but just barely. His larynx had shut down so all he could do was whisper a word at a time, pausing after each one to muster up the effort for the next. I had to put my ear right up against his mouth in order to make out what he was saying and, even then, it was exceedingly difficult to understand him. I took his hand. There was no reaction – his arms, hands and fingers were lifeless flesh which no longer sensed anything; they lay like atrophied sticks beside his brittle frame. I listened intently as he forced out the words in a hoarse whisper. The rasping sound his breath made cut through my core even deeper than the searing sounds of the *shofar* on Rosh Hashana.

He said, "Rabbi, I ... don't ... go ... to ... *shul* ... but ... I ... want ... you ... to ... know ... that ... I ... am ... a ... good ... man...."

I muttered something comforting in reply. But he wanted to go on.

He said, "I ... was ... a ... used ... car ... salesman ... all ... my ... life ... and ... no ... one ... ever ... sued ... me.... I ... was ... a ... good ... man."

I couldn't think of anything adequate to say. I felt his pain. His aloneness. His fear. I felt how deeply he wanted to be remembered after his death as a good man. Tears were rolling down my cheeks.

His declaration was so poignant. His proof that he was a good man was that – though he engaged in a profession that sometimes does not have the best reputation – no one ever formally accused him of breaking the law. He wanted to make this declaration to a rabbi, as if convincing me would somehow convince God: "Though I never went to *shul*, I was a good man. No one ever sued me."

His ex-wife was there stroking his head. They had reconciled already. Whatever hurt or anger had led to their divorce – all that was forgotten. She was comforting him as tenderly as she could. It was very touching to see.

I wondered if at this moment they wished they had acted differently in the past. Would they have split up if they could do it all over again? His son was waiting in the living room. They had not spoken in years because of an argument no one clearly remembered. I explained to the dying man the importance of making peace, of asking for forgiveness and of forgiving. He understood. I went out to the living room and explained the same thing to his son. I suggested to the son that he go in to see his Dad and set things straight.

I stayed outside with Neale while the son visited with his father. Sometime later, the son called me back in. They had reconciled. All I could think of was what a shame they hadn't done it years earlier. I vowed to myself never to make such a mistake in my life.

THE LAST FAREWELL

I explained the importance of saying *Vidui*, the confession of sins that we recite on Yom Kippur and also prior to death. I recited it with him. More tears – at least mine. It seems that Lou Gehrig's disease inhibits the tear ducts from functioning. I pondered the horror of it – wanting to cry and not being able to, feeling all choked up and not being able to express any emotion.

I explained the importance of saying the *Shema* at the end of life – our effort to get it straight for the last time – that all that counts is God, that God is all there is. The *Shema* – "Hear O Israel, the Lord is our God, the Lord is One" – is the Jewish people's mantra; it is our slogan, our synopsis of what the essence of life is all about.

He looked up at me and I saw the pain in his eyes. I said each word of the *Shema* slowly, one word at a time, and he repeated the words after me, in his hoarse whisper. I thought I saw tears, but they were probably mine. I was crying so hard that everything was wet and blurry.

We finished the *Shema* together. I hugged him. I told him that I loved him and that God loved him, and that he should know that I was completely convinced that he was a good man.

I then said goodbye and left him with his wife and son.

Then Neale and I went back home. I don't remember who won the Super Bowl much less who played. I didn't care.

The hospice worker called the next morning. He had died that night, towards dawn. I was angry with myself – I should have gone back there to be with him at the moment of death. I wished I had thought of going back later.

Might my presence have made the passage to the other world easier for him? Might I have glimpsed the world above in his eyes? Might I have learned another lesson for living from his dying?

I wondered if he remembered or if he had the presence of mind to say the *Shema* at the final moment, if he truly got that one essential, crucial message.

I certainly did.

16
The Lighter Side of Life

On my 52nd birthday, I took all the kids out for dinner, and then we went home where they all gave me their little presents as we dove into a Carvel ice-cream cake.

I remember when 52 seemed ancient – and now I couldn't believe that I was past that number and relentlessly moving on. For the prior ten or so years, I had become a fanatic about what I ate and how much to exercise daily. Medical research says that one's genetics and family medical history are the best indicators of one's own health. This scared me to no end as both my parents died very young, which meant that, statistically, I was on the wrong end of longevity.

To counter my bad genes, I ran on the treadmill five to six days a week and worked out with weights, doing resistance training two days a week and a core training once a week. I'd go for regular semi-annual medical check-ups to monitor my cholesterol (160), my body fat percentage (15½ percent and dropping – it has dropped from 26 percent since I turned 50), and all the other signs of health (or lack of it).

One day a week I'd let myself totally pig out, and I'd eat whatever I felt like eating – usually that meant a lot of junk food like licorice, candy, and cake, but the rest of the week I was very disciplined. I'd eat only whole grains, non-fat dairy products, lean proteins like salmon or tuna steaks, and skinless chicken breasts. I was doing whatever I could to fight the relentless march of time and my poor lineage.

I am fortunate in that – also due to my genes – I happen to look younger than my age. I love asking people how old they think I am. It gives me great pleasure to hear people miss by 10-15 years. Silly, I know. I mean, it is genetics – I did nothing to accomplish that. Judaism teaches that we should value wisdom, which comes with age, and a sign of age is graying hair. Yet I am happy mine is still not gray, and it is still all there.

PILL POPPING

My obsession with staying healthy had led me to engage in considerable pill-popping. I'd take a multi-vitamin daily, a baby aspirin (since medical wisemen then said that this was one of the easiest things you can do to avoid a stroke, now they are not so sure), and two omega-3 marine oil pills (to increase my good cholesterol).

At age 50, my cholesterol was 201 – exactly what traditionally has been considered normal – but when I spoke to several of the top medical practitioners whom I got to meet on my biotech trips to Israel, I was told that, according to more advanced thinking, you should really be closer to 150.

My doctor – one of the top doctors in Manhattan, according to *New York* magazine – prescribed for me 5 milligrams of Crestor a day. Crestor is a statin, one of a class of miracle drugs that lowers cholesterol. Ten days after starting it – and at 5 milligrams, the lowest possible dose one can take – my cholesterol dropped to 150. And I have managed to hold it there ever since.

Probably the most significant thing about my 52nd birthday was my trip to the pharmacy where I went down the aisles looking for something which I never thought I would be buying – "a pill caravan." I had always snickered when I saw people take out these long pill boxes divided into seven compartments for each day of the week, but here I was buying one for me.

The pill caravans come in different sizes. For people who take one or two pills, there are small ones, but because I was taking four pills a day, I needed the largest. To add insult to injury, it also came with bigger lettering on the top, as if the manufacturer assumed that the more pills you take, the dimmer your eyesight is likely to be. I half expected the box to come with a discount coupon for the purchase of a cane or a walker.

Buying the pill caravan affected me more than anything else I did on that day. It felt like an "old person" kind of thing, even though most of the pills I was taking were really for preventive care and not for illness. After all, an ounce of prevention … Still, I was left wondering how much of my pill-popping was appropriate and how much it betrayed my lack of trust in God. I mean if the Almighty wants me to be well, won't I be well? And if I am meant to be sick, will all the miracle pills in the world make a difference?

At the same time, aren't we responsible to take care of the vessel that God has given to us, to the best of our ability? Wasn't I doing just that?

I walked around all day wondering about my pill caravan and what impact its contents had on my health and longevity. How much would my exercise really improve my quality and length of life? Then I began to calculate: Let's say I exercised one hour a day, 300 days a year, and it all took really two hours of time (what with traveling to the gym and showering after) would the amount of time it added to my life really be significantly more than the actual time spent?

I began to worry that I did not spend enough time doing good deeds to merit a long life, especially now that I was no longer working full time for a charitable organization. I had led a very charmed life, and I always attributed that to the fact that I was immersed in doing God's work all day long. But I wasn't doing that anymore. And so now I worried that perhaps I'd lost that grace. If I died tomorrow, would my life be fulfilled? Would I have done enough? What would people say about me at my funeral?

But as I sat there at the kitchen table waiting for the cake, I realized that I had accomplished quite a lot that was truly meaningful. I felt good about that. I looked around at my beautiful children and my beautiful wife as they brought the ice cream cake into the room. I huffed and puffed and blew the candles out. One came back on. Oh well, so much for my strong aerobic capacity.

To heck with all this worry. I dove into the cake and forgot about calories and cholesterol and just enjoyed the moment, the family, the beautiful smiles and the delicious vanilla and chocolate cake with the yummy sprinkles.

THE PODIATRIST

My 52nd birthday and my ruminations on my health brought about a resolve to do something about my aging and aching feet. I have been flat-footed all my life. There is only one kind of shoe I can wear, and that is the Dressports by Rockport. I am able to wear my running shoes when I work out, but aside from that, I am stuck with Dressports.

For some strange reason, I have always procrastinated when it came to getting orthotics even though many people have told me it would help. Then, on a visit to my chiropractor, I noticed that he shared an office with a podiatrist; I mentioned my problem and he referred me to his neighbor. True to form, I cancelled and postponed the appointment three times but, finally, I found myself sitting in his office.

He was a very warm and friendly guy, and we chatted away. He told me that he had treated seven different priests and ministers – all for free – but he never had the privilege of treating a rabbi. Of course, he'd extend the same courtesy to me. As it turned out, it was some courtesy. My health plan did not cover orthotics, and I would need two pairs, each one costing $750.

While I was thrilled to be saving so much money, at the same time I felt uncomfortable. Was I entitled to such a generous offer? Now, I had never told him I had been ordained; the chiropractor must have. But I had also not clarified that I was no longer a practicing rabbi and was now in business.

I left his office somewhat sheepishly and walked out to my car. That day I was driving my wife's spiffy Land Rover, not exactly the car of a struggling public servant. I saw him walk out after me going to an appointment; he got in an old, beat-up Ford.

Driving home, I felt more and more guilty. At the start of my new career, I had read the books by Meir Tamari explaining Jewish law concerning the accumulation of wealth and business practices – *Sins of the Marketplace* and *The Challenge of Wealth* – in order to prepare myself for the ethical gray areas I might encounter. I well remember what he said: "Jewish law forbids the defrauding, deceiving or misleading of people in *all* matters referring to buying and selling."

Was I not misleading the podiatrist? Was I not accruing material gain from the title "rabbi," which I was not entitled to use anymore? But then again, I rationalized, would I not be hurting his feeling by rejecting his gift?

Suddenly, I saw how a simple thing like an extra $1,500 can suddenly confuse one's thinking. Money is dangerous. Suddenly, one plus one doesn't equal two.

I went back to *Sins of the Marketplace* to seek further guidance. Two passages gave me pause:

"If God will be with me and protect me on this path that I am treading and will give me bread to eat and clothes to wear..." (Genesis 28:20) In his oath, the Patriarch Jacob prayed first for protection and only then for food and clothing, expressing the spiritual and religious guidance needed in the search for wealth and material goods. Without such guidance, injustice, dishonesty, fraud and oppression easily become acceptable ways of earning a living and satisfying economic needs and wants. Ever since Adam and Eve were expelled from the Garden of Eden, earning one's daily bread, providing an acceptable standard of living and preserving one's wealth have become as difficult as the miracle needed to split the Red Sea for the Israelites leaving Egypt.

The *yetzer hara* [the evil impulse] for obtaining and retaining material wealth is probably one of the most powerful impulses people have. Still, money is not considered evil in Judaism and, like all the other evil inclinations, can be used positively when controlled and educated by the Torah and its *mitzvot*. Because of its very power, there are more commandments about achieving the education needed to earn "kosher" money (at least 120) than there are, for example, about kosher food.

It was clear to me that I had to let the podiatrist know I was no longer a rabbi, and that it would be my pleasure and the right thing to do to pay for the orthotics. I was amazed though that I had been tempted and did not clearly see the right and *only* response to his offer. It should have been obvious to me to say to him immediately and without any hesitation, "That's nice of you, but although I used to be a practicing rabbi, I am now a regular working guy like everyone else you see."

How could I have rationalized this for even one second?

I had been influenced by the deference shown a rabbi and enticed by the prospect of saving money. I had to remind myself that God runs the world and no one ever comes out ahead by not doing the right thing. I committed to explain to him my actual situation when I returned to pick up the orthotics.

THE RIGHT THING

Finally, after months of waiting, the orthotics arrived. When I went to pick them up, the podiatrist greeted me with a warm smile, "Hello Rabbi! So nice to see you again."

I immediately launched into the little speech that I had been rehearsing all that time. I said, "You know, I feel uncomfortable accepting the orthotics for free. I no longer work as a rabbi. It is nice of you to do this for me, but I think it would be unfair. I am out there just like you, trying to make a living. I am not a public servant, which I assume is the reason why you wanted to do this for me for free in the first place."

He looked at me surprised. He said, "Ah, well, in that case, I will give you the family discount rate. Instead of $750, I'll charge you $250 per pair. How is that?"

I said, "That is very kind of you. Are you sure? I can afford more."

He said, "No, I insist. Besides your health plan will cover the office visits if not the orthotics themselves."

I was happy to have cleared that up. I thanked him profusely, happy to have gotten the orthotics at last. Now, I would finally have some relief from my flat feet.

I took them home and began to wear them as he had instructed me – one hour the first day, two the second, three the third, and so forth. But every day they felt more and more uncomfortable. I couldn't get used to them. My feet were sore and achy – even more than before.

Then a week later I got an envelope from my health insurance. They would not be paying for the office visits after all – these were not covered by my plan. Now, I faced another test. I had to write a check for the cost of the office visits, even though in the end I got nothing except sore feet.

This time I did not hesitate. I was not going to rationalize anything away nor let temptation snare me again. This was a small price to pay for the lesson the Almighty so lovingly taught me through this experience.

Now I was much better prepared to face the challenges that would come my way in business.

And soon enough one did, but before that I had other problems to deal with.

RESTORING CONFIDENCE

For more than a year-and-a-half, Rabbi Zilberman had been praying up a storm for my success, but I've had scant results, with deal after deal petering out. He perceived that things were going awry, and he asked for an explanation.

As Paul was then in Israel, I dispatched him to restore Rabbi Zilberman's confidence in us.

They met in the lobby of the Hilton Hotel in Tel Aviv, where Paul was meeting with some potential investors in our Odessa project. In his inimitable way, Paul focused all his attention on Rabbi Zilberman (as his translator Rabbi Fox later related to me), turning off his cellphone even though the rabbi told him this was not necessary.

Rabbi Zilberman fired off his questions. Why was Doheny changing focus? Why was the earlier direction not a productive one? What was happening?

Paul explained that in the investment business a lot of money is chasing after you, asking to be invested. Even if you do not make good choices for the investor, you can still make a lot of money while the investor loses. He explained the herd psychology which encourages this. People feel a risky investment can be justified because everyone is doing it. He gave the example of the billions of dollars that were invested in inferior mortgages. He said when he first began in business, he observed situations where investors made money, but ended up resentful and angry because of how they had been treated. He called this "winning the battle and losing the war." The real goal, he said, is to build relationships of trust in which the ultimate outcome of a profitable deal is mutual appreciation, harmony and gratitude among all involved.

Then Paul explained why some of our deals went sour. In Novosibirsk, Siberia, the rising labor costs plus the risks of investing in such a distant place made the project less attractive, even though in the end there was still a possibility of profit. To drop it was a very hard decision for Doheny, because we had already spent $300,000-$400,000, plus hundreds of hours of work. But continuing would not properly represent the interests of our investors. He said that this is the type of moral dilemma that takes a lot of strength to confront and pass the test and, in fact, most businessmen fail at it.

Rabbi Zilberman was impressed. He said this was a big revelation to him. Until now he had thought this kind of search for harmony, fairness and mutual appreciation was found only in academies of Torah study. He quoted the Talmud that the test of a real wise man is if he can make personal decisions with the same balance and objectivity which he brings to advising others. He also said that the Talmud has many examples of subtle balancing of the interests of the various parties in a transaction.

Rabbi Zilberman then had many questions about our latest focus in Odessa.

Paul explained that through my contacts, Doheny had investigated numerous properties in the Ukraine and determined that the project overlooking the Black Sea had extraordinary potential. He spoke about the universal attraction of all human beings to a large body of water – perhaps this is because the magnificence of nature unconsciously brings people closer to the Creator, which is what everyone wants. He said that, in most countries, it would take ten years to get permission to build residential units at the seashore, whereas in the Ukraine the government was actually pushing this and insisting the project be built as soon as possible, because they were seeking to prevent erosion. This, too, made the site an extraordinarily good opportunity. He also explained the very delicate and complicated problems of how to deal with the very big potential of the neighboring kilometer of coast, and whether or not to involve the present investors in this additional property.

Rabbi Zilberman was sold. "How can we best focus our prayers?" he asked. In response, Paul told the story of his father's stroke and subsequent coma, how the doctors said the situation was completely hopeless, but after Paul cried out to God, he walked back into the hospital and found his father had regained consciousness. He said he knew absolutely from this personal experience that prayers are heard and answered and, therefore, he very much appreciated Rabbi Zilberman's prayer contract being part of our enterprise.

To this, Rabbi Zilberman responded that whenever Doheny faced a particularly crucial juncture he be immediately informed, so that he could pray for the right decision. Paul heartily agreed.

Paul went on to describe the difficulties of trying to deal with many potential investors, institutions and individuals – what it is like to keep all of them actively interested and, at the same time, not misleading any of them.

Rabbi Zilberman listened with rapt attention. He said his whole view of the situation had altered, and he understood better now what to pray about and that his prayers would be renewed in their intensity.

Could we lose?

17
Odessa

To make the Odessa deal happen, we had been working on three tracks simultaneously, and they were all finally coming to fruition.

One track involved meeting with various large institutions and funds that might bring to the table the $35 million in equity we needed (as well as the bank financing) to purchase the land in Odessa. The second track involved working with the banks that would be willing to finance $35-40 million for us to start building the initial infrastructure. And the third involved raising $5 million of working capital, which would have to come from "friends and family."

After many months of talking and meeting with tens of people, it was finally coming together. And June 12, 2008 was set as the closing date for the transaction. We would buy the land in Odessa and develop it independently.

We had a large European fund, Secure Management, wanting to invest $35 million, but until we had a signed commitment letter it was not a done deal. Needless to say, while I waited for the "due diligence" reports to come through, I experienced some anxious time. I was happy it was all coming together, but I was petrified it would fall apart at the last minute.

We had been working with a French and a Viennese bank, both of which were interested, but then the seller brought in Bank Pivdenny of Odessa. The Ukrainian bank was thrilled with the deal and said they could finalize it in two weeks. This simplified matters considerably and was encouraging as well.

While the banks and funds were Paul's and David's department, the $5 million raise from "friends and family" had been assigned to me.

FRIENDS AND FAMILY

This aspect of the deal meant rounding up investors who would put up $50,000 to $100,000 each. This was no small potatoes as it would provide us with working capital and allow us to option additional pieces of property.

It was a difficult time to be raising money in the US as the economy was beginning to take a nose-dive. That summer, the sub-prime mortgage crisis had turned into a national financial fiasco. Bear Stearns, the giant brokerage firm had gone into bankruptcy and been sold to JP Morgan Chase in a historic fire-sale. There were more foreclosures in the US than at any time since World War II. A siege mentality had set in as gas prices hit $3 a gallon. Food staples – all trucked through the US and tied to gasoline prices – continued to rise. Linens and Things, Blockbuster and many other national chains were going bankrupt. Even Starbucks was in trouble with their stock price halved, as more and more people cut back on driving to get the daily latte. It was a scary time to be asking friends and family to invest in a start-up, an unknown venture in a foreign land that most people still imagined being ruled by thugs and the Russian mafia.

In return for their trust, we offered to "friends and family" that we would guarantee their investment by cross-collateralizing it against all other Doheny projects and by giving them a guarantee of return of principal plus a minimum of 20 percent per annum, plus a bump of 25 percent on the profit over the regular investors. We did this because they were coming into the deal before it actually closed, so they were showing a real vote of confidence in us.

I started by going through my address book and calling everyone I knew. It reminded me of what I heard Babe Ruth once say, which was that you need to swing at the ball to hit a homerun, and in baseball, if you are hitting 300, you are an "all-star." He also said that he happened to have hit the most home runs but also had the record for the most strike outs. In hockey, the all-stars will tell you that you don't score on 100 percent of the slap shots you never take. Zig Ziglar, a famous motivational speaker and author, always says, "Every NO is one NO closer to YES." According to this advice, I was a true all-star who scored a lot of slap shots and hit a lot of homeruns, but also struck out a lot. It was tough slogging away.

It took me a while to get up my momentum, but eventually I started to raise the necessary money. There were many times when I felt rejected and/or frustrated but just kept on trucking. I had no choice as we needed these funds to cover all the costs of doing business and making the deal happen until the banks came through.

I had raised nearly all of the necessary $5 million – all but $300,000. In so doing I learned who my real friends were. Some people gave me a hard time when I went to them and asked them for an investment. Others immediately sent me the money. Paul told me to learn from it, so that when I do become rich and people come to me and ask me for an investment, I will treat them well and speak to them kindly. His advice reminded me of God's command to the Israelites to remember that they had been strangers in a strange land and to always treat strangers well.

This particular raise also gave me great insight into peoples' character; I saw how each one handled my request. Many said, "I am only investing because I trust you. I don't understand the deal, but

I trust you and know that you would not knowingly lead me down the wrong path."

For example, a group of Syrian Jews, whom I did not know well, invested and, before doing so, they made calls to several people to find out more about me. Later, they told me that they uniformly got good feedback on my character. They said that they came to the conclusion that a rabbi would not throw away 25 years of his good name on a bad deal.

This scared me. If the deal were to fail, my name would be ruined and I might as well pack up and move to Tibet, because I could not imagine ever being able to raise money for anything again.

GOOD FAITH DEPOSIT

Then, out of the blue, Bank Pivdenny of Odessa asked us to open an account with them and deposit $2 million dollars as a show of good faith. At that point, we had $1.4 million available, so we needed another $600,000 which would get tied up until the deal went through. I didn't realize it was an obligation until just a few days before the deposit was due. I thought it was something that would be nice if I could do it. On Friday, when I was told it had to be done by the following Wednesday, I freaked. (And I still had to get $300,000 more for the "friends and family" part!)

I called Rabbi Fox and asked him to get a message to Rabbi Zilberman to start praying for us in a very fervent manner. I was scared. I started to bargain with God. I said that if He helped me with this, I would start learning Torah every morning and make an effort to make it to minyan on a more regular basis. I pleaded with God in all my prayers.

I approached several people for a loan, explaining that it really wasn't a loan, but a deposit in Odessa, for a few days – sixty on the outside. There were no strings attached. The deposit would be under my name and when the deal closed, everybody would get their money back. Most of the people I called were a bit incredulous: "You want me to put my money where? In a bank in the Ukraine? You've got to be kidding!"

I tried to explain to them that Ukraine wasn't Zimbabwe – it was a country well on its way to joining the World Trade Organization, and this bank had $2.5 billion in capital and $200 million in assets. It was only a deposit. And my partners and I would sign a guarantee for it.

They wanted to know what the collateral was. What could I say? "Well, hmmm, let me see, my house is completely mortgaged at this point. Anything else I own is pledged as collateral for other loans. You want my kids and grandkids?"

But that actually worked. I called Gershon, the brother of my son-in-law who does hard money loans with real estate developers, and explained that I needed a $1 million loan – which really wasn't a loan, but a deposit in an Odessa bank for sixty days. I said I would sign on it and give his two nieces (my granddaughters) as collateral. He jokingly answered that he had them already. But he agreed to talk to his partner.

I called Rabbi Fox again and asked him to turn up the prayers. I was feeling totally off balance. The next day I got up early to work out in order to dissipate my anxiety. Later that morning Gershon called back to say he would lend us $700,000. Thank God!

Now I was only $200,000 short. I called Rabbi Fox and said the prayers were working but not to let up.

Then I got a call from Dr. Myron Wentz who had already invested $500,000 with "friends and family" – he wanted to double his investment and his financial advisor wanted to put it $100,000 as well. At first, I told him that part was all sewed up, but after talking to Paul, we decided it wouldn't hurt to expand the "friends and family" fund to give us more working capital since the closing was taking longer than we had expected.

It was done. I had more than I needed. The money was in Odessa on Tuesday, 24-hours ahead of the deadline.

THE GOD FACTOR

God obviously wanted to make sure we remembered that it was *Him* doing all this and not *us*. He was sending us lots of obstacles to make sure we remembered that He was running the show. If you read the Bible, you know He had done this many times before.

As an example take the story of Gideon, one of the greats described in the Book of Judges. Gideon had amassed an army of 32,000 men to go up against the Midianites who were harassing the Israelites of his day. This was a small force compared to 135,000 troops amassed by the enemy. However, God told him that he had *too many* soldiers and should send some of them home, because God wanted to make a point:

> "The people that are with you are too numerous for Me to give Midian into their hands, lest Israel glorify themselves above Me, saying, 'My own hand saved me.'"

Gideon asked those who were afraid to fight to leave, and immediately 22,000 packed up. Still too many, said God, advising Gideon to devise a test as to which of the remaining men were worthy of going to battle. As part of the test, the soldiers were taken to the spring – those who knelt down to lap the water "like a dog" were eliminated. Thus, Gideon was left with 300 men. And, though outnumbered 450 to 1, he easily won the battle.

THE BANK FACTOR

After the $2 million was deposited in Odessa, the chairman of Bank Pivdenny called Paul. He wanted to meet with him, as he now saw we were for real. Instead of dealing with a bank officer, we had moved up to the chairman – we were considered a substantial player since we could wire $2 million on a week's notice.

Paul and David went to Odessa and spent the day with the bank chairman, who mentioned that his bank had been trying for years to open a branch in Pennsylvania. When I heard about this, I called Tom Ridge, former Governor of Pennsylvania (and former Secretary for Homeland Security), who said he could help. A former staff member of his had opened several banks and sold two of them; Tom could bring this know-how to Bank Pivdenny and he was due to visit the Ukraine shortly.

Now that we were bringing Tom Ridge to Pivdenny, the bank chairman knew we were connected. Our business bond would be all the stronger, and we needed a strong bond because, as soon as we closed this deal, we planned to start working on an option to buy 33 hectares (about 80 acres) of adjacent land that would give us over a mile of beach front and allow us to build an additional 100 homes. It would be an amazing project.

Besides this, we had other big projects in the hopper. My personal ambition was to build a major company, which in a couple of years could go public on the London Stock Exchange. So, as far as I was concerned, this was just the beginning. It would take three years for us to cash out of this deal – that is, to build and sell the houses – but if God allowed it all to happen according to plan, my own personal profit on this first deal would be $15 million plus. I would not become a mogul yet, but definitely a millionaire.

IN DEBT AGAIN

Meanwhile, I was in debt as usual.

I knew that once we closed, we would get reimbursed for our costs plus we'd receive a closing fee of $3 million dollars and a monthly management fee of $325,000. But until then ...

I only had enough money to close out May 2008, but I did not know where June was coming from. I had reduced my monthly nut to around $20,000 for my family, but my share of our company expenses was another $15,000. I was down to $21,000 in my personal bank account and down to around the same amount on my business line of credit. If I had not blocked this out of my consciousness, I would have freaked.

I knew that if the deal was delayed any longer, I would have to scurry to figure out how to make it through the coming months. To reassure me, Paul told me that he had seen this over and over again in his life – God had brought him right to the edge of the cliff and then swooped in to save the day. Well, God certainly was doing that with me. This was a real test of my faith. I just wanted – sooo badly – to close this deal already and move on to something else.

I could not but help being nervous about the dwindling funds. As they say in the Air Force, I was flying on fumes!

I made it through May, but as the word "June" appeared on the calendar, I found myself struggling to control my anxiety. It was hard for me to believe that everything was finally coming to fruition. It had been such a long, long haul. But everything seemed to be in place – at least for the land sale – which was due to happen in two weeks' time.

HIGH ANXIETY

Secure Management was in for $35 million. The Bank Pivdenny of Odessa had okayed an $8 million loan. Bank Piraeus of Greece was offering a loan of $38 million for the construction of infrastructure – though that offer was new on our horizon, and Paul and David had yet to meet with them to work out the terms.

Halfway across the globe from the action, I woke up at 5 AM as usual and stumbled downstairs to my office to check my e-mail. Due to the time difference, I knew a lot of mail had probably come in overnight.

I started scanning the headers to see what was urgent, and a message from Paul leapt in front of my eyes. It was headed: "Signing Off." My heart dropped into my stomach and my pulse stopped. Signing off? What happened to the deal? Why was it off? How could this be? In an instant, I imagined myself bankrupt and poor, my children in rags. I nearly doubled over from the pain in my stomach. With trembling hands, I clicked on the e-mail.

Paul's message said: "My cellphone is dying on me. The battery is used up. I'm signing off for two hours while I let it recharge."

I took a deep breath as my heart started to pump again. Thank God, the closing wasn't off. I think I must have been having nightmares about the deal not closing, and so when I came downstairs, only partly awake with my subconscious mind still turned on, I was primed to misread the words "signing off."

Later that day, I told Paul that he almost gave me a heart attack. He laughed and asked, "Why?" I told him how my reading of his innocent comment made my life flash before my eyes – I had gone into emergency mode in a fraction of a second. I immediately imagined myself unable to face anyone I knew and fleeing the country in shame.

ANOTHER $5 MILLION

We decided then and there that we would take an additional $5 million in equity, in addition to the $5 million we already had in place and Secure Management's $35 million. It would be a very safe investment for anyone, since Secure Management had visited the Odessa site many times and hired a stellar team of reviewers. (These included: DLA Piper to review the Baker McKenzie's legal due diligence; Baker Tilly to review the Deloitte's financial/tax due diligence; DTZ to review the Knight Frank's market and feasibility study and to value the project; and Thomas & Addison to review Ave Arup's and Bovis Lend Lease's technical, cost and engineering due diligence.)

Could this be any more secure?

I thought not. And I made that the start of my basic pitch to the investors, which began: "An important European fund, Secure Management, has signed a commitment letter to invest $35 million. The European Bank for Reconstruction and Development is one of the members of this fund and has signed off on the investment. Closing is imminent…"

With that pitch, I started to make calls again to raise this additional $5 million in equity we wanted. I spent half a day making over two dozen calls and sending out as many e-mails to the people I thought most likely to invest. After that, I sat at my desk and looked at my computer screen and said, "What next?"

Again, I began to feel a wave of anxiety settle over me. Gloom. Fear. Worry. Darkness. I felt like I was sinking into despair. I am so used to moving ahead all the time, but for some reason I didn't know what to do at that moment. I felt like I just couldn't start calling individuals who could invest $50,000 or $100,000. I needed to find the whole $5 million in ten days, and making that many calls to that many people was beyond me. The "what ifs" were strangling me:

What if this happened ... what if that happened ... what if the deal fell apart at the last minute? I can't remember when I ever felt like this – sure I've had anxiety attacks before, but they never immobilized me. This time, I just couldn't function. I laid down and, mercifully, sleep overtook me. I slept for two hours only to wake up to that same feeling of dread, of darkness and gloom again.

Judy had never seen me take an afternoon nap. She had never seen me looking this depressed. Worried, she asked me "What's wrong?" but I could barely answer her. I also did not want to share with her my fears and worries. I turned on the TV and watched for a while. Then, I went back to sleep again.

Next morning, thank God, there were no frightening e-mails. To allay another bout of the "black dog" as Winston Churchill used to call his spells of depression, I went to work out with my trainer. This time my anxiety got expelled in exercise, and I managed to lift more weight than I ever lifted before.

I came home, sat down at my computer and pondered who else I could call. Where else could I find $5 million?

GLUM

Just then I got an e-mail from Jonathan Rosner, the vice-president of business development at Gmul, a large Israeli company active in real estate in Eastern Europe. Gmul had been very interested in our deal, but they wanted to be the sole investor and to run the show. So, we passed on them. But now, Jonathan was saying that they were interested in a partial investment. I called him immediately. He said they would invest $5 million but, in exchange, they wanted to be in on all the important decisions involving the project.

We agreed to that condition and, for a moment, I breathed a sigh of relief. But the anxiety went away for a few hours only. Then it was back again. Stronger than ever. This time I was in panic-attack mode. What if something went wrong?

It was difficult for me to focus on anything. I felt my patience running short with my kids. I was on the edge of losing balance again. Each sentence spoken to me by a family member felt like a nail grating on a chalk board. I was ready to erupt, and it took all my willpower not to. I wanted to drink myself into oblivion, just so that I would not feel this way. But I am not much of a drinker, and I knew that I would feel sick the next day. Without an outlet, I was at my wits' end.

A few days later, I awoke in the morning and went straight to my computer. There was another e-mail from Paul. The subject was "Glum." What's wrong now?

Then I realized that it was a typo. Paul had meant to write Gmul. I laughed at myself – I didn't freak out as when I saw "Signing Off" the week before.

Gmul was in and then, just as fast, they were out. First, they said that they would invest – "fait accompli" were Jonathan's words to us. Then, we were told they had changed their mind. Our $5 million was just too small potatoes.

I continued to plow on. So much of my day was spent sending e-mails and calling and waiting for replies. I have come to respect very much those people who return calls and e-mails in a timely fashion. It bothers me when people don't have the courtesy to even send a brief reply saying they aren't interested or are too busy to talk now, or to have a secretary call back and say something on their behalf. I've made it my policy to reply to everyone, as a courtesy and as a gesture to say, "You count. You are a human being with feelings."

Many times, I've had to reject overtures. I've had to say, "This is not for me, as my focus is exclusively real estate in Eastern Europe, and I am sorry I can't meet or get involved in your project, but I wish you good luck." It seems to me this is the decent and proper thing to do. In some ways e-mail communication has become very impersonal, and people don't seem to realize that there is a human being with real feelings on the other end of the ether space.

RADIO SILENCE

With the seven-hour time difference to Ukraine, I have often felt myself getting anxious as the day marched on, and I would wonder what was going on with the deal. Was everything still on track? Have we encountered any issues? Will we be able to close on time, or will there be obstacles?

I remember watching a movie about one of the Apollo spacecraft flights. There was a period when the spacecraft was on the back side of the moon and all communication with it was lost for a period of hours. All the people at mission control sat at their desks in suspense. They watched the hand of their atomic clocks counting down the seconds, minutes, hours until they could re-establish communication with the spaceship. They sat whispering among themselves: Is everything okay? Will we hear from them ever again? What if something went wrong on the other side, and the ship was destroyed? As the moment approached when they would be able to re-establish radio contact, you could see the tension on everyone's face. Then the clock struck, and there was a crackle over the radio and the spaceship commander's voice came over the loudspeaker saying, "Mission Control, this is Commander Buzz Aldrin from Apollo 11. We are rounding the back side of the moon. We are reporting in. All systems are working and functional, and all members of the space team are in good health although a little tired." Hearing that, everyone in mission control broke out in wild cheers, with joy and relief.

That is how I felt at the end of the day, usually around 4 or 5 PM when I could check in with my partners in Ukraine and find out what happened today.

My first question always was: "Is everything okay?" And then: "Did anything happen today to jeopardize the deal? Are we alright?"

They always had some issue to report. The biggest came when Secure Management informed us that they would not be able to complete all the paperwork by the specified date which, by then, had been pushed off from June 12 to June 20 to June 30. This presented quite a problem because if we did not complete the deal by June 30, it could be technically called off by the seller.

Paul said that a formal offer of $38 million from Bank Piraeus of Greece was imminent, and we could take $25 million of that and put it in escrow to re-assure the seller until Secure Management finished the paperwork. But what if we couldn't complete this bank loan in time?

I didn't want to ask Paul, "What if?" He was my Buzz Aldrin. He was taking us to the surface of the moon, and I had to trust his steering ability. All of Doheny was now in a hurtle through space, and I could do nothing but wait.

Every day there was radio silence, when I would go to sleep, only to wake up the next morning at 5 AM to check the day's e-mails, and then wait through another day of radio silence. Day after day after day until the closing.

Then I would take a vacation but, for now, I could not rest until the deal was done.

As the hot and humid July days passed one after another with the deal still not closed – and the date pushed off till mid-August – I found myself calling every rabbi I could think of, asking them all to pray for me.

The delays were fraying my nerves beyond the point of endurance. I was soooo way out on a limb, personally owing over $1.5 million. If it didn't close, I had absolutely no idea what I would do.

18

Audi Blues

In mid-summer, I drove to Manhattan for a meeting with Paul and David, who were passing through on their way back to the Ukraine after a week's R&R in Los Angeles.

It just happened to be the 17th of *Tammuz*, a fast day on the Jewish calendar, marking the date when the walls of Jerusalem were breached by Nebuchadnezzar, the king of Babylon, prior to the destruction of the Temple and the exile of the Jews. I was feeling anxious, upset, distracted and worried – and on top of it all, I was fasting and, as a caffeine fiend, sorely missed my morning hit of java.

But we had to discuss the current status of the Odessa deal. In short, we were all worried about the closing, which had been pushed off for far too long, and which was totally dependent on Secure Management.

I had been taking stock of my life and the status of our company, and it was not a pretty sight. I had come to the conclusion that if we didn't close Odessa, we would be out of business, and I would be ruined financially. I am not really sure why, but for some reason this had not been crystal clear to me before. I had been living with the false optimism common to many entrepreneurs. It's a drug-like high – this belief that the next deal is just over the horizon – which causes one to live, just like an addict, from one fix to the next. But just like an addict eventually crashes when the drug's effects leave his body and no more is to be had, I was crashing as I looked at the status of my finances.

I owed close to $1 million on my first and second mortgages. I owed $250,000 on my credit cards (though I couldn't be sure this was the total because I was afraid to really tally it up). American Express had frozen my card at a debt of $168,000. I had borrowed money from many friends, and at this point everyone I knew had invested in my venture. If the deal didn't close, I would have no one left to go to for future deals and my credibility would be destroyed, crushed, obliterated, smashed into as many pieces as the Berlin Wall and, just like it, never to be resurrected again. I had no idea what kind of a job I would ever get but, worse than that, I would have disappointed – dare I say, betrayed – so many people who trusted in me. Doheny would have no more operating capital to arrange any other deal, and I would have really nowhere else to turn to get a loan to support my family.

The absolute bleakness of the situation was driving me to despair and humbling me. I had to talk to Paul and David about this – they had to see what a really serious predicament we were in.

EYE OF THE STORM

It was an overcast day, with huge dark clouds threatening rain. Sprinkles started on the Palisades Parkway and just as suddenly disappeared. Or did they? Maybe it was my imagination. I could no longer be sure of anything. I had been living in the eye of the storm to such a degree that I could no longer tell what was actual reality and what was my imagination's view of reality.

By the grace of God, I reached the Renaissance Hotel, where Paul, David and I met in the lobby and talked for two hours. They had come to the same conclusion as I did – no matter what, we had to close Odessa. No more postponements were possible. They agreed that we had made some mistakes along the way and could have structured the deal better which would have made it more likely to close. We had talked about bringing in Bovis Lend Lease, one of the world's largest construction firms, as a partner – a move which would have made the deal more attractive – but, somehow, we got distracted by all the demands on our time, being in a foreign country, and the pressures of setting up a new business. We hadn't kept our eye on the ball, because we were juggling loans and short-term cash crunches, rather than focusing on long-term planning.

But we were not losing hope. Secure Management was bringing one of their main investors to Odessa to look at the project. If this investor liked the deal, it made it much more likely that they would be able to close. Why was this necessary at the eleventh hour? Because one of their main investors had run into financial difficulty due to the worsening real estate market worldwide and the credit crunch which was now spreading into Europe, and he was no longer able to meet his commitment to fund their portion and thus they needed a new investor.

Meanwhile, the seller was getting antsy, and since the contractual deadline had passed, there was always the worrisome possibility that someone else could show up with an all-cash offer, and he would sell it to that someone.

We all agreed that we had no option but to close. Even if it meant we had to give up some of our profit, we just had to close the deal. The alternative was not tenable.

STARK REALITY

Driving back home after the meeting, thinking over what we said to each other – the stark reality that we finally faced up to – I felt broken and humbled. I knew that God was bringing me to my knees.

I thought about my life. I missed working for a cause. I really didn't think I could handle the pressure of trying to get rich anymore. This was agony. Why had I started down this road in the first place?

Just the week before, Judy and I had visited our 14-year-old Sholom at summer camp. There we met his teachers, all middle-aged guys who were hanging around the bonfire, roasting hotdogs and marshmallows, and singing camp songs. I hadn't done that since I had been a teenager. They were very warm, sincere, friendly and happy people. I wondered what it would have been like to have taken such a career path – working as a teacher during the school year and spending the summer at camp. It seemed like such a tranquil life – so easy, no pressure. Why was I so driven to make it big? Could I have been happy living a simple life like that?

I came home and talked to Judy about it. Judy said she would have preferred it. Our life used to be very simple, she reminded me. But in the past few years something had changed, as my goals veered away from helping the Jewish people to wanting to be a super-successful businessman.

I asked myself, "What is it God is trying to teach me? Why is it so difficult to close this deal?" God obviously had a lesson He wanted me to learn, and I was not learning it.

I thought of the little kid in class who wants to attract the attention of his friend and he takes the ink cartridge out of his BIC pen and rolls up a piece of paper and spits it through the tube. When he doesn't get any kind of reaction, he sends out a second spit-ball. When that doesn't work, he throws an eraser. When the friend still doesn't respond, he whacks him on the head with his ruler.

I figured God was trying to get my attention, and since the first spit-ball hadn't worked, He was escalating the intensity. I thought about that for a while. One thing that came to mind was that I have been living way over my means. My personal overhead was enormous, consisting of my mortgage payments ($5,200), my car leases ($3,300), and my kids' school tuition ($4,000). Add to that car insurance, health insurance, life insurance, support of my grown children, property taxes, school taxes, house maintenance, clothes, food, gas, doctor and dentist. And you get $30,000. Even if the deal closed the way I wanted it to close with Secure Management – and Doheny got $325,000 a month project management fee – I personally would only bring home $30,000 a month of that, which meant that I'd be ahead by exactly zero. I would still be living on the edge.

I spoke to Judy about this and said I really wanted to cut back on our overhead. I just couldn't take living in such a vulnerable state any longer. We were just too exposed. We had to figure out ways to cut back.

BELT TIGHTENING

Judy was totally supportive. She had been brought up with nothing and had clipped coupons until a few years ago. She was a simple down-to-earth person. She immediately volunteered to give up her once-a-week personal trainer; it was only $400 a month, but she felt it was a luxury she could do without. I tried to talk her out of it because I had a trainer three times a week but, in the end, she cut out hers and I cut out mine.

Then, we took a look where the other money went. Every month, I sent $2,800 to my married kids in Israel plus I paid their and their spouses' cellphone bills. For two of them, I was not the primary means of support, this money was just a bit of extra cushion. For Simcha, who learned Torah full time and had no means of income, this was what he and his family lived on.

I called each one of them. I explained that things were super tight, and we were living way above my means. They were totally understanding, yet I felt like a failure. Helping my kids made me feel valuable and needed as a dad, and even though there is nothing wrong with married kids supporting themselves and it is even expected, I felt awful. Part of my self-worth came from being able to help my children. Judy said it was a good thing, as it was helping them mature and grow, especially Simcha as he would now have to learn to support himself, but I felt guilty that I had let them down.

My guilt got worse when I received a letter from my son-in-law Yoni thanking me for all the support I had given them over the years and how much he appreciated it. I felt lousy, but I had just cut out $42,000 a year.

Then I asked my son Yakov, my 22-year-old who still lives at home, to come into my office for a talk. I explained the situation to him as well. He totally understood. He had been following the ups and downs of Odessa and had been to the Ukraine with me. He was trying to be an entrepreneur himself, and I had helped him a lot over the past three years. I plowed over $60,000 into his online business. I gave him a monthly allowance, and he had the use of my credit cards when he needed them. I also paid his health insurance and car insurance, but he had made a few real estate deals of his own in the past year and had taken over his credit card debt and his car payments. The total for him was $25,000 a year. I explained that I would do it for another two months, but then he was on his own. I felt not as guilty, as this was probably helping him more than hurting him – being more independent would get him more focused and disciplined.

We looked at our car leases. Judy's lease on her Land Rover was up in June. It cost us $9,000 a year plus $2,400 for insurance. We decided to keep it four months past the lease-end because we would need the car when Batya and family came to visit, but then we'd turn it in. We also agreed that I should get rid of my Audi S8 and drive the Mini Cooper, which was a fun little convertible we had gotten Judy for her birthday two years ago.

THE MALE FANTASY

The Audi was going to be tough for me to give up, as I loved driving it so much. It was a limited-edition model with a 450 HP v10 Lamborghini engine, and it sounded like an F-16 when it accelerated; I had never seen another one like it around. New it cost $110,000, but I leased it for $2,000 plus insurance plus gas. By getting rid of it, I'd be saving $30,000 a year. Still...

Getting rid of the car was not just a financial issue, but a psychological issue. It seemed to me, as I thought about it, that it was bad for my male psyche, and perhaps this was one of God's lessons to me. I wanted to be seen as a rich and successful man, even though I really wasn't one yet! But driving an exclusive, high-performance car like the Audi S8 made me feel that way. At least once a week, when I pulled into a parking lot, the car jockeys who know cars, would say to me, "Wow, that is some car! I will leave it right up front here where it belongs!" It made me feel important. Silly, but it did. I think God knew that this was unhealthy for me and wanted me to get beyond this kind of self-deception. He wanted me to be real.

I recalled reading in the *Garden of Emuna* that everything that happens to us – good or bad – happens for a reason and out of God's love, and there is a lesson to be learned in it all. I realized I needed to do some soul-searching and figure out why God was making it so difficult for me to close this deal. One reason I could now see was that I was living above my means – I wasn't being responsible. I do believe that was an important lesson for me to learn. Also, I was caught up with wanting to be seen as rich and important. On a deeper level, I realized I spent most of my waking hours thinking about money. This clearly was not what I was meant to be doing in this world. For sure, God wanted me to be more of a spiritual being, one who cares about how to get close to Him and how to live a Godly life in this world.

I realized that I had totally lost focus on this. Living above my means meant I was preoccupied with money and expenses all the time rather than with things that mattered. Owning the Audi S8 just brought me deeper into the vortex of materialism and status-seeking. The Audi had to go.

The lease would not be up for another twenty months, but Yakov found a website that helps you find someone to take over your lease. So, I listed my Audi on this website, offering a $6,000 incentive. I couldn't believe I was doing it, but I did. Now, it was out of my hands. Now, it was up to God. I figured that if I could get rid of the Audi and drive the Mini Cooper, I would save $40,000 over the period of the lease alone. It was worth it to offer an incentive, when I added the insurance, gas and upkeep I would save, not to mention my soul.

The remaining cuts were small. I decided to cut my disability insurance which was costing me $5,000 a year. What would that do for me if I was disabled? It certainly wouldn't save my house from going into foreclosure; it would hardly put food on the table. I cut the Culligan water ($2,500 a year), the gardener ($4,800 a year), the snow removal ($750). I could cut the grass and shovel the snow myself. By the time I was through, the changes in budget had topped $100,000, and if someone took over the Audi lease, it would be $150,000 in yearly savings. Wow – I was beginning to feel good about all this.

SPIRITUAL MAKE-OVER

Next, I decided I needed to improve my daily prayers, slow down and make the time count, to think about God more. I started doing this and felt better. I had not learned Torah at all in five months, so I decided to try again. That morning at 7 AM, after prayers, I opened *Ethics of the Fathers*. And I still knew it by heart after 25 years when I first had learned it in yeshiva. I spent a half hour on it and then opened up *Garden of Emuna*. I spent an hour learning, and my soul felt re-connected.

I didn't want God to feel He had to bring out the baseball bat to whack me. The BIC pen and spit-balls were doing the job. I had gotten the message.

I called Paul and David in Odessa and discussed all this with them. I asked them to think about God's possible messages to them before they went to sleep tonight. They also understood this and looked at the world the same way.

SURPRISING RESPONSE

The next day Paul called me from Odessa. He said that another fund, White River (not their real name), had agreed to invest $5 million, and they would also deposit $10 million into a Ukraine bank account for us, for which we would pay them 1 point and 12 percent interest per annum. The funds would only stay there until closing – not more than five weeks – but it would help reassure the seller. And, most importantly, if Secure Management didn't close, White River was prepared to step in provided we paid their due diligence costs. This was the last alternative and the least preferred, but it gave us security that we could close even if Secure Management pooped out on us. We had two weeks to act on that offer.

In the three days since I'd met with Paul and David, I had gone from total despair to peace of mind, knowing we could close the deal. It was a little freaky, and I was almost embarrassed to attribute it to my self-transformation.

After I had been brought to my knees, I got the message and made a few small changes. It was so totally clear to me that it was all in God's hands – my complete and utter financial ruin, or my success. The lesson was crystal clear. And once I got it, the reward came only two days later.

I felt like the alcoholic who awakes from a month-long drinking binge and sees reality. I looked around me and said, "Life is beautiful, life is precious."

Of course, I still had issues to work through. Why did I want so badly to be rich? Why was it so important to me to be seen as successful? But I had cast aside some of my personal demons and got my life in a little better order by cutting down my overhead and shedding some of the trappings. It had been a difficult experience to go through, but I felt better for it. I felt closer to my kids, I felt closer to God in my prayers, and I was learning Torah again. And yet it seemed beyond awesome that God would respond so quickly to such a small effort on my behalf.

Rabbi Weinberg always told me that God is our Father in Heaven. He loves us, and just like I would do everything I could for my kids if I saw they were trying, God is no different. It was such an important lesson back then in yeshiva, and now I had learned it all over again.

BRING ME BACK

The *Amidah* – the silent standing prayer which Jews traditionally say three times a day – is composed of 19 blessings. Each blessing has two parts: the petition and the conclusion. In between, you can add your personal request in order to personalize the prayer and make it more real.

Being real has always been important to me. I always wanted to know that I was living the truth and not wasting my life. At times, I have been afraid that I might fail at this. I'd often look at people's faces when I was in a crowd, and I'd see so much pain and fatigue. Henry David Thoreau said, "Most men lead lives of quiet desperation." When I looked around me, I'd see so many eyes that said, "I have given up."

This worried me a lot. Will I give up too? Will I stop trying to change? At what point will I be tempted to say that it just isn't worth it anymore?

There was a photo in a psychology textbook that had a great impact on me when I was in college. The top half showed a bunch of babies smiling and gurgling, and the bottom half showed a group of people in a subway – all somber faced, without life or enthusiasm or joy. The caption underneath said: "What happened?"

The thought scared me. I didn't want to be like that. One of the tools I have used to make sure was the *Amidah*.

The fifth blessing states, "Bring us back, our Father, to Your Torah, and bring us close, our King, to Your work, and influence us to return to You completely. Blessed are You, Lord, who wants us to return."

For many years, I would stop before the concluding sentence and ask God, "Please bring me back to You. Wake me up, even if You have to shake me up. But if you have to shake me up, please be gentle. Don't break any bones or send me any bad diseases like cancer. But do wake me up. I don't want to waste my life. Get me back to reality!"

More recently, I had omitted the "even if You have to shake me up." I was too frightened of the consequences. I was not sure of what the Almighty might need to do to shake me up. I felt like I had drifted away. I didn't think of God as often as I had in the past. I felt distant – like an estranged child. I no longer had the courage to say even cautiously, "Wake me up even if You have to shake me up."

When did I stop saying it? When did it happen?

Now I no longer felt the connection I once had. I heard it said once that if you don't work on your connection with God every day, the distance widens. Even one day of not trying makes you two days removed.

Funny how these pithy sayings suddenly became real to me. I knew that God was my Father in Heaven and that He loved me and only wanted what was good for me. I knew this was true, but I did not feel it right then.

When I recited the *Amidah*, I recited it with deep emotion. I felt the words. I knew they were true and I wanted – in the deepest core of my being – to be close to God. But I still couldn't bring myself to add my little petition for a shake up, even if that was what it took.

TORONTO

Fortunately – although I hate it – I travel a lot. And when I do, I inevitably come across a real cross-section of human behavior which always teaches me. The in-your-face lessons are often God's way of responding to my unspoken prayers.

On this particular occasion, I was on my way to Toronto to meet with some potential investors. In order to board at Newark Airport, I went through the automatic check-in. The line for security was lengthy and snaked its way through the terminal. As I stood there, I asked myself, "How do I bring God into the picture here? How do I elevate this day of mundane tasks – waking early, rushing through prayers, driving to the airport, waiting in line?"

As I pondered this question, I watched as a middle-aged, portly man, with a big belly protruding over his Bermuda shorts, got angry at someone who seemed to be cutting in line ahead of him. Why did it matter so much to him? Why had he allowed this perceived slight to steal his calm, drive up his blood pressure and blow his cool? Where did it get him yelling at strangers with a whole crowd watching?

I wondered if there will be a line to stand in at the end of our days. When we all expire and go back to where we came from, will there be a long line where we need to go through a security check?

Will we need to take off our shoes to get into heaven? Will some people have to stand in another line for secondary screening? Will there be people there screaming and getting irate at those who cut in front of them? Or perhaps, we will all be too worried about upsetting God and not getting through heaven's door.

Wouldn't we all be so much better off if we took that view down here also?

Finally I got through security, with my laptop, shoes, cellphone, wallet and my little baggie holding two ounces of special contact lens solution. These are the precious belongings I have to get onto the plane. What do we get to take with us to the next world?

This world is just an antechamber, a passageway to the next world, say the sages in *Ethics of the Fathers*: "This world is like a corridor to the next world. Prepare yourself in the corridor so you can enter the banquet hall." Down here, I needed so many little accoutrements – tools of this world which I always made sure I take with me on any trip, like my cellphone charger, my laptop charger, my passport – but what are the comparables that I will need to take on that final journey to get me into the banquet hall? I'm not sure. I'm not even sure about the next world.

As a rabbi, it used to be my job to tell people with absolute clarity, "Of course there is heaven, of course there is justice in the next world!" And I meant it too. But now it's not always clear to me, and I wonder about it just like the next guy.

After security, I went hunting for a Starbucks. I found one, down the terminal: not too long a line with a friendly woman behind the counter, asking everyone how they were doing as she served up the coffee. She seemed genuine, friendly. Strange how small exchanges like that, delivered with a warm smile, bring humanity to the tedium of slogging through an airport. When she gave me my latte, she wished me a good day. I just knew she'll get into the banquet hall!

A while ago I had the thought that my goal in life should be to bring a little humanity and holiness to each and every encounter, to treat each person as special. This woman was a good role model.

I got onto the Continental Airlines commuter to Toronto. It was a short flight, but very uncomfortable in a small prop plane. I landed, saying a silent prayer that God would help me be successful in my meeting. "Okay God, please bring me closer to You and please – if You see fit – bring me success. And help me figure out how to bring some holiness and meaning to this day. Amen."

GPS

In Toronto, I rented an Avis car, making sure I got one with a GPS device. When they were first introduced, I thought that they were absolutely amazing. Thanks to stationary satellites that the Pentagon has made available to the general public, we can get driving directions in real time. The satellites track your car and tell you where to turn to arrive at your destination. These satellites are what allows the military to launch a Tomahawk missile from a submarine, send it 2,000 miles through space, and detonate it through a window of a terrorist's home anywhere on the planet. Smart stuff. The technology is absolutely awesome.

I don't remember how we used to get around pre-GPS. I would have been totally lost, navigating the streets of Toronto without it.

Leaving the airport, the GPS's pleasant female voice asked me if I wanted to go to an address in Ontario, and when I answered "yes," it asked me for a zip code. Then the voice began narrating, "Drive two miles until 401 East." Before any turn, it warned me it was coming up, and then when it was time to turn, it would command emphatically, "Turn now!" If I missed a turn, it would say "Recalculating," and start giving me a new set of directions from the point of my mistake.

I just loved the way it led me around. I began to think how great it would be if we had such direct feedback in life. Say I bought a car that was too expensive for my budget (hypothetically an Audi S8). A voice would come on and say, "Wrong move. Recalculating your budget. Go back. Return." Or if I was rushing through my morning prayers, it would say, "Slow down. Think of God now!"

Now I know that the Torah is supposed to be my book of instructions. But, somehow, I haven't downloaded it into my every move yet. And I don't hear the warnings as loud and clear as I should. I also know that everything that happens has a reason, and all I have to do is ask God and I will find the message intended for me. But, in my muddled life, the messages don't seem as clear as the GPS. It certainly would be a lot easier if they were. Of course, then my free will would be severely compromised, and God doesn't want automatons. But it certainly would be a lot easier for people like me, who sincerely want to do the right thing but get lost on the road a lot.

BACK SPASM

In the first week of August, I had two meetings in Manhattan: one with my good friend Vitaly Pruss, just to catch up, and another with a group of hotel developers who were setting up small boutique hotels in Croatia and Bulgaria. The head of the Ukraine-USA Business Council, Morgan Williams, had suggested to this group that they contact me. And when they did, of course I agreed to meet with them. I learned a long time ago that you have to work on business development constantly. You never know what will lead to what and who will lead you to whom.

For example, while I was in Toronto, my son Yakov took my Audi to someone he met through a friend of his, a guy who said he might be interested in buying it. At Yakov's urgings I called him, but it turned out he would only pay a seriously discounted rate – $1,200 per month rather than the $2,000 a month I am paying. I suppose desperate sellers would prefer to lose $800 dollars a month rather than $2,000, but I was not there yet. Nonetheless, I chatted with him and found out that he is a real estate developer, and when I told him what I do, he was very interested. I e-mailed him information on our project and set up a meeting. Perhaps he could be an investor.

This is just one example of what has happened many times. What seems like a dead end turns out to be an amazing lead.

Getting ready to drive into Manhattan, I suggested to Judy that she come into the city with me. She took along Bracha, so that mother and daughter could spend the day bonding, shopping in the Village or Soho while I worked. We agreed to meet for dinner at the end of the day. This is something we have talked about doing more often, but rarely got around to – devoting special bonding time to each child. And yet it is so important to make deposits into their emotional bank account, so that when you need to make a withdrawal, there is something there to draw out.

We all piled into the Audi and happily drove into Manhattan. And then my cellphone rang. It was someone named Karim who wanted the Audi. My stomach immediately tightened. Secretly, I had hoped that it wouldn't really have to happen.

We discussed details about the car and how to proceed. In the midst of the conversation, it developed that this guy was in investments and security. I told him about our Odessa deal. He was fascinated. He said he represented the Governor of Dubai for some of his investments. I told him that our architects have three very prominent projects in Dubai. He was familiar with the hotels they had designed there. He asked me to e-mail him information about the Audi, but also about the Odessa deal and about our company. I promised to do so when I got home.

Overhearing the conversation, Judy started to laugh. She suggested that I just leave the Audi up on the website as a draw to get rich investors. Anyone who is a prospect to lease a $100,000 car is obviously also a prospect to invest in a real estate deal in Ukraine. I had to agree. But then again, it doesn't necessarily mean they are rich – I wasn't when I leased the Audi. For sure they are dreamers with big egos.

I turned to Judy and reviewed with her our new financial plan. We were letting go of the Land Rover and the Audi with their astronomical leases and keeping only the Mini Cooper. "Are you sure it makes financial sense to let go of the Audi?" I asked, "I mean, we'll have to buy another car for me then. How about, I drive the Mini Cooper and you drive the Audi. Then we don't need a new car."

Judy just laughed, thinking I was kidding. But I was serious.

I couldn't believe that I was going to lose that car. As the prospect of giving it up became real, the import of it to my sense of self-respect and self-esteem became more and more evident. I knew that I had bought into the Madison Avenue hype that a powerful V10 450 horsepower beast means you are somebody, you are rich, you are successful. I also knew that it was all an illusion, but I was truly bothered at the thought of giving up the car. I always thought I was a deeper person than this. But this was so superficial. What had become of me?

GOD'S MESSENGERS

The next morning, I went to the Wesley Hills Plaza, a small kosher shopping center a few blocks from my home in Monsey. As I pulled into the parking lot, a kid in his late teens, in jeans and tee-shirt gave me a thumbs up. My heart sank. Soon, I'll be driving an ordinary car and nobody will even give it a second look.

I began to wonder if I really should get rid of it. Perhaps the economics didn't really make sense...

I looked around, but the kid had disappeared. He had looked so out of place in this parking lot, in the first place; this is a middle-class neighborhood, and he certainly wasn't dressed like he belonged. Was my mind playing tricks on me? Was this really Elijah the Prophet in one of his many disguises on a mission from God to test my commitment to change?

I did my shopping and then went to the gas station to fill up – $98 dollars later, I was convinced once again it was time to get rid of this car that needed premium gas at $4.79 a gallon.

But then two guys got out of a pick-up truck and walked over to me. They were agog, "Wow! What a car! Beautiful!" (More of God's messengers?) They began asking questions about the engine and horsepower and speed. I told them, "For $2,000 a month, it's yours." They laughed. They probably didn't even make $2,000 a month.

I drove off, feeling even more conflicted than before. When I got home, I sat down at my desk and started re-working the numbers. In the middle of computing frenzy, with results not looking any better than before, I got up to get a cup of coffee and screamed in pain. My lower back went into a wild spasm. It hurt so bad I thought I would collapse. I doubled over and clutched my chair and desk; I couldn't straighten up.

I hobbled to the kitchen in agony. Judy came running over. Yakov grabbed one arm. Together they assisted me – more like carried me – to the den and helped me lie down. I had to do it in stages, half over, half down, jabs of pain ricocheting through my body with each movement. My lower back was locked. Every effort to straighten left me gasping for breath. I finally made it to a prone position on the floor and shut my eyes – the room was spinning and I thought I was going to faint from the pain.

I felt humbled, scared and totally dependent. What had happened to me? It had been at least twelve years since I had such a bout with my back. I was petrified. I called Dr. Rosenthal, my chiropractor. I had not seen him very often, because, as an avid exerciser, I rarely experienced any problems. Once in a while, an adjustment was in order, but nothing like this. He said to come over immediately.

I could hardly get off the floor without help, and I certainly couldn't drive. The pain took my breath away. Yakov had to drive me to the chiropractor, who said the muscles in my lower back were jammed. I knew that myself. He did some work – massage, ultrasound – and applied some form of electric stimulation. But I was still in excruciating pain. I got home with difficulty and retreated to a prone position on the floor. The pain was unbearable.

Next, I called Dr. Tendler, our family doctor, and asked him for a muscle relaxant. He said he needed to see me to prescribe it. By this time whatever the chiropractor had done kicked in and I was feeling a little better, and so I was able to drive myself to his office. Truth be told, it was the discomfort of being so vulnerable that *forced* me to drive myself. What is it about the male macho psyche that makes it so difficult for us to depend on others? There is definitely something to it, as so many comedians make fun of men refusing to ask for directions. We would prefer to go forty-five minutes out of our way than to admit we need advice on what route to take.

Dr. Tendler saw I was in pain, asked me some questions and prescribed Valium (which he warned would space me out) as well as a muscle relaxant called Skelaxin, which would relax my muscles without the psychological effect. I dropped off the prescriptions at the pharmacy. They wouldn't be ready for some time so I drove home and took to the floor again.

What was happening to me? Everything that I relied on to make my life meaningful – okay, pseudo meaningful – was being removed.

Seems like God had now resorted to a baseball bat to get his message across.

With my financial security gone, with my Audi going, the only point of pride I had left was my physique, which I worked so hard to keep in shape. But in the last few months I had put on weight, so much that I couldn't button my "slim fit" shirts anymore. And now my back!

Even with the medication, I spent two days flat on the floor.

Karim, the guy interested in the Audi called back from Los Angeles. He said that he wanted to pursue the purchase, and – what was even more startling – he said he had met with the representatives of the Governor of Dubai, and they were interested in our Odessa deal. As luck would have it, Paul and David were on vacation in Malibu, since Eastern Europe really slows down in the summer. I e-mailed them about a possible meeting.

Meanwhile, I was still in pain. God had really hit me this time. And yet while He had humbled me to the core, in His great kindness, He was also sending me hope: a possible financial savior through the very mechanism of painful growth. Karim could not only take away my beloved Audi, but also invest in Odessa and save my financial skin.

I took another Valium, even if it did space me out. All this was too heavy to hold in my head.

A few days later, I could walk normally around, though my back was still tender. I crunched the numbers again and, after a talk with Judy, decided to give up the Mini Cooper as well. We would coordinate our schedules so that we could do with one moderately-priced car instead of two. That would save us $10,000 a year. This way, when the deal did close, we would be a lean mean fighting machine, and our overhead would be very low.

I felt a lot lighter, even if a bit bruised. I was beginning to like it.

But that's not how it was to be. And, for sure, I don't know the mind of God. A few days later, Karim decided against the Audi. I was stuck with it.

The lease on the Land Rover was up one month ago, and we had been keeping it on lease extension. I called the dealer and was told that if I returned it today, they wouldn't charge me for the extra days past the lease end.

I asked Judy's opinion and she said, "Let's do it!" We quickly emptied out the car of our belongings – the EZ pass, CDs, umbrellas, books which the kids had read on trips and left under the seat – and drove it to the dealership. We'd be saving $750 a month on the lease, plus insurance and gas. It felt good to be on the road to savings.

WHAT THE BLIND SEE

On the road again, standing in line at another airport, I got another insight from God.

I saw a long-line of obviously blind teenagers making their way to a check-in counter. I watched them intently and was amazed.

In Jewish morning prayers, there is a series of blessings that are meant to help us mortals appreciate God's gifts to us, but it is a struggle to make them real day after day. We thank God for giving us strength, for giving us sight, for giving us clothes and all other basic needs.

When I come to the blessing that thanks God for "giving sight to the blind," I try to imagine how difficult life would be if I couldn't see. All the things I now take for granted I wouldn't be able to do! I wouldn't be able to hop into my car and drive the kids to get ice-cream. Life would be a lot more complex. I usually linger on this blessing for a few seconds as it is easy to make it real. It has been a good tool for me for a long time.

Thus, it was with additional interest that I observed this group of blind teenagers walking in. Some had seeing-eye dogs and others were led by guides, while still others were feeling their way with white canes. They were traveling to New York? What kind of an experience would a blind person have touring Manhattan?

I was pondering this thought when I observed that others in the group were deaf and some of the leaders were signing to them. Oh, my goodness! The Almighty had sent me a real strong message here – a group of blind and deaf teenagers to remind me how precious was my ability to see and hear!

I then saw something else which jolted me. One of the group leaders was signing to one of the teens, but he wasn't doing it the normal way – he was tracing the letters on the palm of the blind girl's hand. I watched and then it hit me – this young girl was not only deaf, but she was also blind. She couldn't see the signs. She had to feel them drawn on her palm. It was mind-boggling to me.

Here I get frustrated when the Almighty challenges me with a delayed flight or a sore shoulder from weight-lifting (my own fault). Imagine the challenges this young woman must put up with every second of every day. Nowadays, when I come to the morning blessings each day, I draw up this experience from memory and linger on it. I let it sink into my bones and try to feel deep appreciation for God's bountiful kindness to me.

Still, I couldn't help wondering how she would feel when she said these morning blessings. I suppose she'd be thankful she was alive. I admired her courage. I wished I had gone over to her and talked to her somehow. I wondered what she was looking forward to in visiting the Big Apple. What would that experience be like for someone living in darkness and silence? When I walk through the streets of Manhattan, I often think of her and it helps me feel appreciation for the simple things in life.

And then I remembered the words to *Amazing Grace*. I didn't know (until I googled it later) that it was written by John Newton, a slaver-trader who saw the error of his ways, converted to Christianity and later became blind! This is the first stanza:

Amazing Grace – how sweet the sound.

That saved a wretch like me.

I once was lost, but now am found;

Was blind, but now I see.

19

Being Human

In August 2008, the newspapers were full of stock market troubles. (Remember the movie *The Big Short* and the story of how the sub-prime mortgage bubble burst?)

The US mortgage market hit bottom, sending shock waves throughout the world. But market woes were actually good for us, as people with money to invest were looking for better places to put it, while the US stock market crashed and burned. I had a place for it – the Former Soviet Union (FSU).

I was under a lot of pressure (not the least of which was the un-bearable delays in the closing of Odessa), and in the midst of it all, I got an unusual invitation from John Ashcroft.

John has led a celebrated life as a civil servant of the United States – as the Governor of Missouri (1985-1993), then as US Senator (1995-2001) and then as US Attorney General (2001-2005). In 2006, I invited him on one of my missions to Israel, and during our tour of the Holy Land I truly enjoyed his wit and easy-going manner and was impressed with his sincerity and his brand of spirituality.

During the trip, I mentioned my love of cars and speed, and he invited me to spend a day on his Virginia farm, where he had cut dirt-bike paths through the woods in order to speed around while doing little damage to himself or the environment. It took me eighteen months to take him up on his offer, because I am so work-oriented that taking a day off mid-week to play filled me with guilt.

But one day he called, and he said something which no one had ever said to me before. He said, "Come visit my farm. I just want to be your friend. I like you. Whether we do business together or not is not important. I want to be your friend."

This touched me. Thinking about it, I felt it was an important thing to be able to say to others: "I want to be your friend." I have since said that to a few people whom I have met and liked. It feels good to say it. And I think it is especially important in our goal-oriented and competitive world.

So, I decided to visit his farm to hang out with him, ride his dirt bike and just "be." It seemed strange to a workaholic like me, who doesn't know how to "be," but I was game to try it (for a day anyway).

Of course, I scheduled a day of meetings in DC the day before. Somehow this made me feel less guilty about spending the next day playing with John.

CITY SLICKER

I slept over at a Washington, DC hotel and early the next morning drove to meet John in Arlington, Virginia. The appointment was for 9 AM, and he was standing on the balcony of his townhouse waiting for me as I pulled up at 9:03. When I got out of the car, John saw that I was wearing dress pants, and fearing that I would get them dirty, went into the house to search for some casual clothes for me to wear. Oh my, silly me, I didn't think of bringing more appropriate clothes for a day on the farm. Such a city slicker I was – always in work mode.

We climbed into his SUV and headed out to the parkway for the 90-minute drive to the Ashcroft farm in the Virginia countryside. He pointed to the cooler on the back seat and informed me that it was full of everything he could find in his pantry with an OU symbol signifying it was kosher. I had explained that to him a week ago when he asked what we could eat together. He said that when he scavenged though his pantry, he was surprised how much kosher food he had – tuna, crackers, canned fruit-cup, and even his bottled water had the OU symbol. I said that I had no idea why they put an OU on water, as *all* water is kosher but, nonetheless, it was included in his treasure trove of kosher food.

John had grown up in the Missouri Ozarks, where his father had been a minister. He considers himself a devout Christian yet he had a *mezuzah* on his front door. The *mezuzah* – a small scroll with a Torah quotation inserted in a narrow box and attached to the door-post – is the quintessential sign of a Jewish home. Why put up a *mezuzah* if you are Christian? John answered that when he learned that the purpose of the *mezuzah* was to help you think about God every time you passed through a door, he decided it was a good idea. "Anything that helps you bring God into your life on a more regular basis is a good thing," he said. He reminded me to think of the *mezuzah* in that way. Of course, I knew that this was its purpose, but I had let myself forget it.

We talked all the whole way up to the farm about the political climate, and time passed by quickly, as we left the DC environs and entered the gently rolling hills of the Virginia countryside. But there was still a part of me saying, "What the heck are you doing?"

JUST "BEING"

Several times during the drive, John said, "feel free to make any calls or take any e-mails." But I felt it would be rude to do so, and I wanted to let go and just "be." So, I didn't respond to several vibrations indicating incoming messages on my cellphone but eventually succumbed – how could I not? – and did a quick check. After an hour, we turned off the main highway and started down a two-lane road that twisted and turned past farms and woods.

John told me that he knew he had to have a piece of the Virginia countryside when he became US Attorney General and realized he wouldn't be getting back to his Missouri farm very often. His wife agreed, as long as he wouldn't build a house on the property. He could have the land and enjoy the nature, but no more homes.

"Hmm," I thought to myself, "no more homes, but what about bathrooms?" I didn't say anything – still, I wondered what was in store for me.

After much searching, John said he found 150 acres that included a rolling pasture, a forest and even a river, relatively close to DC. As we turned onto a dirt path – no grand entrance, no sign, not even a mailbox – John said, "Welcome to my farm!"

He led me toward the barn, which was a large rectangular structure with three walls and an open front, housing a tractor for clearing the pathways, two small mowers for cutting grass and four dirt bikes. John said that he had built the barn himself. I was amazed. I could never imagine taking the time, or for that matter, having the know-how or even the inclination to build such a structure. On the wall were two barbed-wire sculptures – a Statue of Liberty and a grizzly bear – both made by John. He explained that he did barbed-wire sculpture as a hobby.

I thought, "I don't have any hobbies. Who has time for hobbies? How did the Attorney General of the United States have time to build a barn, mow the grass, ride a dirt bike and also make barbed wire sculptures?" I always thought I was good at managing my time, but I was beginning to wonder if I really was such a hotshot.

John pointed out a little shed next to the barn, which he had also built. "The facilities," he said, using the polite term for "outhouse." Hmm, this was going to be interesting. Good thing I had relieved myself earlier in the day. Better not drink too much of that kosher water. I never was one for outhouses.

SOUND OF SILENCE

The silence around us was stunning. Just the wind rustling the leaves on the trees. We walked along a short path that wound its way through the forest and, after a while, my ears picked up the sound of running water – the river. We came to another clearing where a small wooden cabin stood. From a tool shed adjoining it, John took out a large American flag and mounted it on a stand, just like old-time Virginia settlers used to do. We went inside. The one-room cabin was furnished with a small plastic table, a few plastic chairs and a kerosene heater. It was cold and John took it outside to light it, as kerosene gives off a strong smell when first lit. A few minutes later, he brought it inside, and it started to warm up the cabin quickly.

Outside, John pointed out to me an unusual decoration to the cabin – a cow's skull wearing a baseball cap. He had found the skull on the property and also the cap. When he lifted the cap, he discovered a litter of baby mice looking up at him in surprise. Clearly the cap had been turned into a home for a mouse family. It was the cutest thing, and children visiting that year had enjoyed watching them grow up. When they abandoned the cap for better quarters, he hung it up as a memento. Near the cap, John pointed out the holes in the woodwork made by some woodpeckers; it looked to me like they had pecked away at the cap as well.

We took a walk toward the river, gingerly ducking under an electrified fence put up to keep the grazing cattle away from the river as their dung is a strong water pollutant. Along the way, John showed me the carcass of a poor little deer. The bones were all that was left of it after the vultures had done picking it over. They'd had quite a feast.

At the river bank, John pointed out several trees felled by beavers. These trees were once mighty timbers, and if I didn't know better, I would have said that a lumberjack had been at work with an exacting chain-saw. The lower trunks, some of them 4-6 inches in diameter, were neatly sawed on a diagonal from three sides, causing the whole tree to fall. I bent down to look at the cuts the beavers had made, and they were smooth and clean. It was hard to believe that they were not made by a human being and a 25-horsepower 150-tooth chainsaw. The cuts were so exact and so deep. John said he never ceased to be amazed by the beavers' work, even though he had seen it hundreds of times.

He brought me over to the river's edge to look at the dam that the beavers had constructed. They had built it on a diagonal, aiming at a small island, and then back across, further downstream. Though some of the dam had since washed away, when it was new it had spanned 60-feet in length. The dam was intended to slow down the water and create a habitat safe from predators for the beaver clan.

We wondered aloud at the awesomeness of nature and God's wondrous creations. How was it that the beavers knew how to do this? And even more impressive, how was it that they all worked together so well? Amazing teamwork was required to build that dam. (We hadn't seen such co-operation in Congress in generations, probably not since the Founding Fathers.) Who among the beavers decided to go on a diagonal across the river to the closest island, 30-feet away and then to double back to the other side? How did they communicate with each other about the direction, the angle, the location? How did they divide the workload and organize the subdivision of labor? Human engineers would have difficulty coming to the same unanimous conclusion and then following through in tandem.

I was amazed that here we were, the former US Attorney General and me, trampling through the woods in the middle of a perfectly good, potentially productive workday, looking in wonder at a beaver dam. I felt guilty again, and I thought, "This is fascinating, but shouldn't I be answering some e-mails?" I found I was engaged in a constant battle with myself – feeling guilty yet wanting to enjoy myself, relax and just "be"!

BORN TO BE WILD

We wended our way through the woods, listening to the wind and the sounds of the river. Back at the barn, we got onto the dirt bikes, and John showed me how to work mine. First of all, he pointed out the "kill" button. "If you get into trouble, just hit this button and the engine shuts down," he told me, adding that no one had ever been hurt on a dirt bike in all the years he had brought people out to ride. Then he showed me how it worked.

He put my bike into first so I could drive around the clearing and get used to it before we headed off for the wooded paths. That was a good move as I forgot how to shift as soon as I got on. I felt like an idiot until he showed me what to do again. I tried it once more and almost did a wheelie and flipped over when I released the clutch too fast. So much for my dreams of riding a Harley one day. It took some trial and error, but I finally got it right. It was fun biking around the clearing. It also felt relatively safe as there was nothing to hit.

John waved to me to follow him into the woods along a pathway that was about five feet wide and framed by dense vegetation. At first, the curves in the path were gentle, and I was really having fun. I forgot my preoccupations and began to relax. We went up hills and down hills picking up speed, and I switched from first into second and even once into third. Then ... whoops! I turned a bend and found myself heading straight for a tree. I fell backwards and the bike ended up in the bushes.

John, who was looking out for me the whole time, stopped to make sure I was okay. He told me I was doing great and not to worry about that little accident. It happened to everyone, and I was doing a great job. We went on until we came to a spot that seemed too steep for the bike to climb. We dismounted and walked up the mountain from where we could see the river below. The view was stunning. We stood there admiring God's handiwork – the river wending its way down below, totally surrounded by a dense forest.

John pointed out a persimmon tree near us that was laden with fruit. He picked some and gave one to me. A wild persimmon? "Yuck," I thought. It looked all shriveled up and not too appetizing. John said that you can't eat them earlier in the season as they were too tart, but at this time they were sweet. Politely, I agreed to taste it. I said the *Shecheyanu* blessing – "Blessed are You, Lord, the King of the Universe, who kept us alive and sustained us and brought us to this season" – and explained that this was a prayer Jews said when tasting something for the first time in a given year. And I haven't had a wild persimmon yet this year. Then, I took a bite. Sweet, yes it was, but somehow it just wasn't my taste. Seeing my lack of thrill, John suggested I eat a wild pear next to clean my palate.

This was getting to be like wine tasting. Isn't that when you clean your palate with cold sorbet? (Or was that after the fish course?) I wasn't too sure but it certainly wasn't what I expected out in the Virginia woods – a lesson in the etiquette of eating wild fruit.

BEAR COUNTRY

We got back on our bikes and continued to make our way through the woods. I was quite comfortable now and even picked up speed a bit. It was fun indeed!

John stopped to point out that the heap of dung in the middle of the path had been left there by a bear. Oh my! Bear country! Yikes! I hoped that all that I would encounter would be fecal matter and not a large furry mother and her cubs. Then we came across another heap of bear dung. This one was certainly busy eating berries, John said.

We headed back to the little cabin for some lunch. The kerosene heater had warmed the place nicely, and it was very comforting to come inside. I surveyed the decorations on the walls for which his wife found no place in the Ashcroft home. For example, there was the flack-jacket that a close friend had sent John when he was going through the Senate confirmation hearings. Being a staunch conservative who was pro-life, against stem-cell research, a believer in God and prayer, he had gotten a lot of flack from liberal Democrats. Hence the flack-jacket – a cute present.

Also hanging on the wall was a four-foot fake fish stuffed into a net. He had used the net to hang different knick-knacks, including earrings and a necklace, in a playful game with his wife Janet. Beside my chair was a slightly warped and crooked birch ladder, which went up to the loft above the sitting area. The loft was used for sleeping the few times John and his wife stayed overnight. He had made the ladder himself, which impressed me again. It was rudimentary but, nonetheless, it worked. More than I could say for anything I had ever made with my hands. I mean, I wait for my father-in-law to visit so he can change the light bulbs.

We took the food out of the cooler and started to prepare our lunch. John took a pot, put it on top of the kerosene heater and boiled water for us. This truly was a minimalist way of life. The water boiled after five minutes, and I added it to a cup of instant soup. John then made his soup, and I broke open a package of tuna, which we would eat together. John asked me if I usually said a blessing before eating, and he invited me to say it, and I did – both in English and Hebrew. John then sang his own blessing.

Behind me on the wall was a small musical instrument. I asked him about it, and he said it was a ukulele. It was one of the first instruments that he had learned to play, and it was his favorite. I handed it to him, and he started to play a song I hadn't heard since summer camp, "Home on the Range." Then he played and sang "America the Beautiful."

In the US Senate, John had been known as a singer and member of an informal group of tenors that entertained the senators on special occasions. He said he had learned in life that singing brings people together, because that's when the soul comes through. I explained how important music was when the Temple stood in Jerusalem and how Jews always sing during Shabbat meals.

We finished our lunch and got back on the dirt bikes. I felt like a pro by this time and kick-started my own bike. I was ready to hit the open road! We reached a huge tree where John said he'd love to build a tree-house. Indeed, the tree was ideal for it as its branches were thick, firm and spread out like big embracing arms. We joked about how this could be the perfect getaway from the cabin when life there got too hectic. A getaway from the getaway.

GETTING ANTSY

After biking for another hour, I started getting antsy as we still had more than an hour's drive back to his Arlington home, where I would get into my car for a five-hour ride back to Monsey. Finally, at 3 PM we went back to the cabin, turned off the kerosene heater, took down the flag and headed back to the barn, where we put away the bikes. And we started for home.

We were just off the property when John remembered that one of his staffers loved the small wild pears that grew there. We found some of the pear trees, but the only pears visible were quite high up on the branches – at least 20 feet high. "They are too high," I said in my impatience to get going home. "No one would accomplish anything in life if all he saw were problems," John countered. "This is an opportunity, not a problem." (Meanwhile, I was beginning to think we would never get out of there.)

John jumped out of the car and found a huge broken branch. We lifted up the branch and reached up into the canopy of the trees and knocked down a bunch of pears. Then we scurried around picking up the fallen pears, brought them back into the car, and we were off with our trove of presents, and oh yes – all of our garbage from lunch piled into the back of the car with the cooler and leftover kosher food.

I turned on my cellphone and, after a few minutes, it picked up a signal and started humming. I read my messages, but there was nothing urgent. I really didn't miss anything while out for the day.

Back at the Ashcroft home, I went inside to use the regular "facilities," and John sat down to the baby grand piano in his living room. The music wafted into the bathroom. At first, I thought it was the stereo playing through a speaker system; it wasn't until I returned that I realized it was him. What a talented guy!

A HUMAN DAY

We walked outside. I gave him a hug good-bye and said, "Well, we sang together, we biked together, we ate together, and we prayed together. We covered all the bases. A human day. Thank you!"

I got in my car and started off on the long drive home. My mind wandered as I wended my way through rush-hour traffic out of DC. It felt good to spend a day just being, not trying to accomplish. I was impressed with how diverse John's interests were. In comparison, I was very one-dimensional. I called Judy and told her about the day and my thoughts. She suggested maybe I should try to do something personal on Sundays, instead of just working all day. She liked the fact that I was questioning my way of life.

I realized it was important to develop other interests. To take the time to experience the natural world, look at a beaver dam and a felled tree, ride a dirt bike, walk in the woods, even try to build something with my own hands, although I doubted that I was ready to try anything like that just yet. It was time to get back to the simple pleasures in life, especially in this tough economic environment when a lot of the things that used to provide distraction and pseudo-pleasure – such as shopping and vacationing in fancy places – was just not an option anymore.

I felt somewhat whole and complete in a strange way. The experiences of the day had left me feeling more at peace and – if I dare say it – more fulfilled. There was something uplifting about connecting to other human beings in a non-work setting. Just sitting and talking and exchanging ideas with no gain in mind.

I cranked up the music in the car and pondered my life as I drove home. Five hours later, I pulled into my driveway and ran into the house. I went into Sara's and Ilana's rooms and gave them a big hug hello. I am a rich man with such beautiful children. I hugged and kissed Judy also.

And, later in the week, I snuggled into bed with Judy and the kids, ate popcorn and watched a video. A first for me. And on Sunday I took the day off and spent it with the kids.

Maybe a day in the Virginia woods had left its imprint. Now, was I ready to build a barn?

20

Georgia and Me

On August 7, 2008, Russian troops invaded two regions in the Caucasus – South Ossetia and Abkhazia – which had been recognized by the international community as being part of Georgia, but which had asserted their independence. The brief war went on for one intense week during which the Russian troops soundly routed the inferior Georgian military, pushing it out of the region.

Even after the conflict ended though, the Russians seemed intent on teaching the Georgians a lesson and took their time withdrawing from Georgian territory. They seemed intent on keeping forces in place around the Black Sea port of Poti and the city of Gori, splitting the country in two.

When the conflict first broke out, I felt a real sinking feeling in my stomach. How would this affect our Black Sea project in Odessa? Would Bank Piraeus and/or Secure Management back out? I awoke early every morning of the conflict and read all the news about Georgia that I could find – from the *BBC*, *Bloomberg*, *Washington Post*, *New York Times*, *Al Jazeera*, *Ukraine News* and others. I was trying to get a feel for the extent of the conflict, and on how it would impact the other states and satellites of the FSU.

As I came to understand, both Georgia and the Ukraine had wanted to join NATO and had been petitioning to get accepted, but Russia was very much against this happening. Many editorials said that the Georgia invasion was Putin's way of flexing his muscles and sending a warning against such a move to both Georgia and the Ukraine. But they would not be intimidated so easily.

Two days after the conflict started, then Ukraine president Viktor Yushchenko plus leaders of other former Russian satellites including Poland, the Czech Republic, Latvia and Estonia flew into Tbilisi, the capital of Georgia, to stand side-by-side with then Georgia's President Mikheil Saakashvili, expressing their solidarity with him.

I was petrified that this would shake world credit markets and investor confidence. Since 1991, détente had been in place between the US and Russia, and democracy, independence and free markets were booming in FSU states. So why – just when I had decided to stake my financial future on investing and building a company in the Ukraine, the largest former Soviet vassal – the Cold War between Russia and the US had to break out of its long slumber and reassert itself upon the world scene.

Neither Moody's nor Standard and Poor's (which rate the debt of companies and countries) downgraded Ukraine's debt from the B- which it had recently been elevated to. They had already taken the country and its political risk into account in their rating. This was a relief.

But then the increasing tit-for-tat between the US and Russia started to escalate. In response to Russian actions, the US announced the establishment of a missile defense system in Poland, which Russia immediately called a clear provocation. Then both powers started moving their armadas to the Black Sea. Could it get any worse? Why was God doing this to me?

The whole drama was made even more intense for me because of my friendship with Lasha Zhvania. Lasha was a dashing Georgian politician who had served as Georgia's Ambassador to Israel and as Member of the Georgian Parliament. He was immensely likable – young, American-educated, fluent in English, dynamic and idealistic.

Earlier in the summer Lasha had urged me to come to Georgia to explore business opportunities in his country. I wasn't sure how much potential there was, but with Georgia's MP inviting me and offering to introduce me to the business leaders there, it seemed like a good opportunity to explore. I spent some time with my contacts at Deloitte discussing Georgia. They sent me a due diligence report they had prepared on the country which I read thoroughly. I had just made a commitment to accept Lasha's invitation when the hostilities broke out.

That was that. It would be impossible for any private equity to invest in Georgia with Russian troops still a threatening presence there. The news reports, even three weeks later, were filled with tales of looting by various militias, and pictures of burned-out villages abounded.

HEART-BREAKING NEWS

I had kept in touch with Lasha from the onset of the conflict. Some of his e-mails broke my heart. He wrote:

"In my childhood, *Tisha B'Av* was associated with visiting cemeteries of my grandmother and uncle, who are buried in the region where currently Russian artillery bombs civilians and Georgian defense forces ... To the extended meaning of *Tisha B'Av* for the Georgian Jewish Community was added [more sorrow] Saturday night, as most of Gori's small Jewish community had to flee to Tbilisi along with their Georgian brothers, who are being slaughtered in Russian bombing attacks and artillery barrages."

Then he wrote that Tbilisi, Georgia's capital, was bombed on August 12: "We are under Russian occupation, but also it's hard to win the international media war."

"How can I help?" I wrote back, and he answered with an impassioned plea, begging me to bring business leaders who would show the world that Georgia should not be written off.

I felt he was reaching out, and it was important to respond to a friend and a fellow Jew in need. After all, if in 1914 my grandparents had not gotten on a boat out of a Black Sea port and fled to the US, I could very well be in his shoes today.

I spoke to Judy about the trip. Travel is not a popular topic in the Katsof home, as Judy does not like it when I travel. Truth be told, neither do I – I hate being away from my family and my routine, but travel I must. We took a look at our family schedule. The kids were starting school and Bracha was leaving for a seminary in Israel; it was important for me to take her to the airport and send her off on this exciting new chapter in her life, so the earliest I could go would be the second week in September.

I called my travel agent and booked a ticket for September 7 – one month to the day since Russia had invaded Georgia. I then called Lasha and told him that I would be arriving as quickly as my schedule would permit. Though it was not possible that any private equity would invest in Georgia at this time, the US government had pledged $1 billion dollars in reconstruction funds. It occurred to me that this was worth looking into.

I called my friend Ambassador Paul Bremer, who had been the first US envoy to Iraq after the fall of Saddam Hussein. I asked for his guidance as to how it might be possible to get involved in Georgia's reconstruction effort. I figured if I was going, I should try to understand this process. Paul connected me with a colleague, Robert Kelley, who had been very involved in such efforts in Iraq. Robert had built five US embassies in Arab countries but even more relevant was his effort to build the first hotel in post-Saddam Hussein Iraq (with pre-fabricated materials). His advice could be very helpful as over 120,000 refugees were fleeing from the war-torn areas and now living in tents in Tbilisi. He knew his way around the US State Department and the Import-Export Bank of the US, and he knew how to access funds, which was never an easy thing. Even when Congress promised to allocate funds, it often took a long time to see real money.

Armed with that information, I set off for the war zone.

ON THE ROAD AGAIN

I felt a bit nervous but I was also excited. I was booked to fly to Tbilisi on Ukrainian Airlines as there were no direct flights to Georgia from New York. I thought: "Is this a little stupid? What if Russia decides to send a message to Ukraine by shooting down a Ukrainian airplane?" After all, in one of the most famous incidents in airline history, Russia did shoot down Korean Airlines flight 007, killing some 270 passengers. That was back on September 1, 1983, and Russia (then the Soviet Union) argued that the airplane had entered its airspace as a direct provocation by the US to test Soviet military response. Wasn't the current situation ripe for another incident of this kind?

Maybe I should fly Air France. Oh, but then President Sarkozy mediated the peace agreement between Georgia and Russia and was seen siding with the US. Russia has not been too happy with him either. Perhaps I should fly the good ol' neutral Swiss Air.

I had never flown into a conflict zone. This was the closest I had come to war, except for 9/11. Even though my trip was two weeks away, I could feel the tension and excitement in my belly.

As the trip neared, I got more and more nervous. The US was delivering aid by war ship, Georgian diplomats were packing their bags in Moscow, (following a break-down in diplomatic relations), and the South Ossetians were complaining about Georgian spy drones, one of which they claimed to have shot down.

And then it was time to go and, nervous or not, I was on my way. My family couldn't understand it, so I told my kids that I secretly worked for the Mossad. I think they believed me. How could a mere rabbi-cum-businessman be jetting around the world meeting presidents and prime ministers?

As I was leaving, I received an e-mail from my friend Richard Steffens, the commercial attaché to the US Embassy in Kiev and the person responsible for helping American businessmen broker deals in the Ukraine, saying he would also be in Tbilisi that week. He had already forwarded to us a possible new deal with Ukraine's Department of Defense as he believed in our abilities, so this was great news. I asked him if he could set up a meeting for me with his counterpart in Georgia as well as with the US Ambassador. He agreed.

I felt excited and energized. My fears of a repeat of Korean Air flight 007 disaster faded, and I was excitedly looking forward to my trip to Georgia.

The last time I had been in Tbilisi was in February 1982 when I was still single and studying at Aish HaTorah. I went as part of the "Save Soviet Jews" movement to Georgia, Armenia and Azerbaijan to meet with refuseniks. That trip, twenty-six years ago, had radicalized me. It was one of the most impactful experiences of my life, and it turned me into an activist. Seeing Jews who were prepared to give up their freedom and even their lives for the right to emigrate to Israel and study Hebrew was my first experience with people who genuinely put a cause above everything else. There is real power in being so dedicated. It is truly uplifting and inspiring.

It is hard to imagine now that such a world existed once – when it was against the law to study any religion, or to practice any religion, or to show any religious feeling in public. Since religion was the "opiate of the masses," all of these were grounds for possible imprisonment in the USSR. On top of that, for Jews there was an additional crime – the outspoken desire to immigrate to Israel. Since all petitions to leave the Soviet Worker's Paradise were routinely refused, these people were called "refuseniks" in the West; in the USSR they were called "enemies of the state."

Anatoly (Natan) Sharansky was one of the more famous refuseniks who was imprisoned and later freed in a prisoner exchange; he wrote a book about it, *Fear No Evil*. But there were tens of thousands of others. When they tried to apply for an exit visa, they (and sometimes their entire families) were fired from their jobs, but it was against the law not to work, so once without a job they were labeled "social parasites" and even "criminals." In this Catch-22 situation, these poor people had to figure out a way to stay out of jail, feed their families, and still push forward with their appeals to immigrate to the Promised Land.

During this time, there was an underground movement in the USSR focused on Jewish education. Classes were taught in Torah, Jewish literature and the Hebrew language throughout the country, especially in large cities where Jews lived – Moscow and Leningrad – and also in more remote places since the refuseniks were often exiled to farthest corners of the Soviet Union, like, for example, Tbilisi. Tbilisi turned out to be better for Jews because the native Georgians hated Russians more than they hated Jews. If your enemy is also my enemy, then we must be friends, or at least allies of sorts. Thus, Tbilisi turned into a Jewish haven and a hotspot of Jewish learning.

Meanwhile, in the US and Israel, groups sprung up to assist them – "Help Free Soviet Jews" was one, another was "Student Struggle for Soviet Jewry." And this is how the plight of Soviet Jews came to my attention. In 1981, my brother introduced me to a friend of his who ran a Canadian chapter of one of these groups; they organized trips for people who were willing to go into the USSR and clandestinely aid the refuseniks. My brother's friend explained to me the dire plight of these people – that they desperately needed various medicines not readily available to them, and that they craved Jewish religious articles which were not only unavailable but forbidden. The challenge of such an adventure excited me and, furthermore, I'd be making a making a meaningful contribution to a worthy and important cause.

In those days, it was not so easy for Americans to travel to Communist countries. You couldn't just buy a plane ticket and fly over to Moscow. You had to apply for a visa two months in advance; you had to travel as part of an organized tour package which included all your hotels, tours and meals; you were not allowed to wander off by yourself. But a person who had the guts could pretend to go on an organized tour and, once inside, could sneak away and meet with the refuseniks.

I spoke about it to one of my teachers, Rabbi Tom Meyer (who would later become my brother-in law), and he agreed to go with me. We planned our trip for March (not quite realizing the length or severity of the Russian winter), but the tours were wide-open then. We selected one that hit all the hot spots of Soviet Jewry – Moscow, Leningrad, Baku (in Azerbaijan), Yerevan (in Armenia) and, of course, Tbilisi (in Georgia).

SPY TRAINING

We had to undergo training as what we would be doing would be quite illegal, and we needed to be savvy about it and not put the refuseniks in any danger. We were briefed to expect an interrogation and a careful search at the Moscow airport, so we couldn't carry a list of refuseniks' names with us. We had to memorize them, as well as their addresses and telephone numbers. This was easier said than done as all the names were strange sounding and almost impossible to pronounce: Abuladze, Matcharadze, Giaouris, Gogiberidze, Sharashide, Abdushelishvilli, Hachkhiani.... To help us remember, it was suggested we write the names in code in our address books. For example, if the person's name was Ektarina Gogiberidze, we would write Aunt Esther in one place and Uncle Gogib in another place as a mnemonic device and split the phone number and address between the two. A border guard would have to look very carefully and take quite a while to figure all that out.

The week of preparation was quite intense, but it did little to prepare us for the intensity of the actual trip. Once in the USSR, it was all for real, not a spy game.

We would spend the entire day on the bus with the tour group, and then – once everyone retired to their rooms – we would sneak out of the hotel and go find our contacts. The Intourist guide was immediately suspicious of Tom and me, because for one thing we didn't eat any of the food we were served (since it wasn't kosher). I vividly recall sitting on the tour bus when she walked up to me as I munched on some Pringle's potato chips which I had brought with me from America. "Are these matzahs you are eating?" she sneered. With an innocent smile, I answered, "Why no, it's a snack food. Want some?" She gave me a withering look, turned and walked away in disgust.

When the group went into the famed Hermitage Museum in Leningrad for a three-hour visit, Tom and I decided to slip away, figuring we could re-connect with them at the tail-end of the tour. Our contact had told us to meet him at the top of the stairs of one of the subway stations. "How will we recognize you?" I asked. His response was "Don't worry. You'll know me."

We took the subway to the appointed station and then the escalator up to the lobby. The subways had been built as bomb shelters and easily descended 10-15 stories beneath the earth. They were jam-packed, being the chief mode of transportation, as very few people in Soviet Russia had cars. One distinct thing about the place that I immediately noticed – nobody smiled, ever. Life was difficult, the government was repressive, living conditions were abysmal, and there was no hope for any kind of improvement. Nothing much to smile about. True, in an existential sense, they had life and should have been thankful for that, but the culture had taught them not to show emotion and certainly never in public.

After an interminable ascent, we arrived at the street level and scanned the crowd. In a sea of gloom and resignation, I spotted a beaming set of eyes, alive and focused. I walked confidently to him and said, "Hello Demitrus. A pleasure to meet you." He said, "I told you that you would recognize me." And then he explained, "Being a refusenik gives my life purpose. Being persecuted wakes one up. Yearning to be free, to emigrate, has awakened my soul. I was sleeping before and looked like everyone else until I discovered my roots."

We spent the next two hours talking to him, answering his questions about Judaism's understanding of the body and soul, life and death. He was thirsty for knowledge. When it was time for us to go back, he escorted us back to the museum and we snuck back in, but not early enough – the suspicions of our guide had been aroused. All the guides had experience with Jewish tourists visiting refuseniks, and she obviously knew what we were up to. She warned us not to leave the group again.

SABOTAGE PLOT

The next day we took a flight to Tbilisi. Here we had been given the names of two former scientists – the Goldshtein brothers. They had moved to Georgia of their own volition, as it was a little better for the Jews there. Both were brilliant research scientists with high-level jobs in Russia before they had applied to emigrate to Israel; then they were fired and stripped of all prestige. The only jobs they could find were as street cleaners.

We found their apartment in a darkened street and went up the narrow staircase to their home. Finding the place was no easy task as few streets had signs and even fewer apartments had addresses, and most street-lights were not functioning. Somehow we did it.

We were invited into their tiny but neat one-room apartment. Over tea, they pulled out a tattered Mickey Mouse writing board. It was the kind with a piece of clear plastic over a black background; you wrote on the plastic and the writing appeared, then you lifted it up with a ripping noise, and it was gone. It was a child's toy, but here in Tbilisi it was essential to their survival. They wrote: "police outside in street" (rip) "listening to everything" (rip) "top secret" (rip) "we work with the underground here" (rip) "they know we are the only ones who get visitors" (rip) "they asked us to get a message to the West" (rip) "they plan to blow up the radio tower."

Yikes!

He drew a crude picture of a radio tower, erased it and they continued, "they are afraid if they do it, they will get caught and shipped to the gulag" (rip) "they asked us to get this out to the US Congress, so if they disappear people will ask about them" (rip) "this is the only way to ensure safety" (rips) "less Jews disappear because groups in the US clamor about them."

And then he drew another picture of the tower and wrote "Boom, boom."

Yikes!

I felt like I was dreaming. I couldn't believe I was in a middle of a sabotage plot.

Forgetting I wasn't supposed to talk out loud, I said, "But, of course, we will help," and got soundly shushed.

We committed to memory the names and details using the Mickey Mouse board and promised to transmit this message to their friends in US Congress. Then they started to talk out loud as if to snub whoever was listening: "Tell us about the Wailing Wall." They couldn't get enough information about Israel.

When we got back to the hotel, we were afraid to speak. We wrote messages to each other back and forth, knowing the rooms were bugged. Two hours into this, the door suddenly opened and an old lady walked in; when she saw us, she rushed out. The KGB must have thought we snuck out not hearing any noises on their mikes, so they sent in the key lady to check. In those days in the USSR, every floor of every hotel had a key lady. She sat by the elevator and gave you your key, and when you were leaving you had to give her your key back. With labor cheap, this was a way of keeping the elderly busy. Also, it helped the KGB to keep track of your comings and goings, so they could search the room when they wanted.

BUSTED

After this, they were onto us and we were followed everywhere, so we didn't accomplish much in Baku and Yerevan, though we still had our adventures.

In one instance we went to teach an evening Torah class to a youth group, and we got lost trying to find the apartment. When we finally did, we found the people waiting but not with the usual happy anticipation we had come to expect from the refuseniks. Afterwards, we were told that shortly before our arrival, the police busted in and took down everyone's identity card number. This was very bad for them as there would be repercussions – their parents might get fired from their jobs, or they themselves might get expelled from the university. It was horrible. It forced people to pit their idealism and thirst for knowledge against the job security of their loved ones. A tough moral call for anyone.

On another occasion, we visited with a family living under the most dismal conditions I had ever witnessed. It was a one-room apartment, up a dark and dank staircase with crumbling masonry. This family had been attending clandestine classes in Judaism, and they had many questions. The father asked me to show him my *tzitzit* – the knotted strings religious Jews wear on their four-cornered garments (usually under their clothes). He had read about them but had never seen them, and he thought perhaps he could make some for himself, so he could wear them secretly. This way he could be thumbing his nose at the Soviets, and they'd never know. I was heartbroken to hear his plea, and I also knew that making the special knots is not so easy. I went into the bathroom, removed the pair I was wearing and gave them to him as a present. He hugged me, and he put them on as tears of joy streamed down his face.

Finally, our tour was over. As we were about to board the plane home at the Moscow airport we were subjected to a final inspection. Stupidly, I had made notes of the trip and stuck them inside the pages of TIME Magazine. What now? I watched horrified as the official took each book I had, opened it and fanned it to see if anything would fall out. I watched him advance toward the TIME, certain that when he found my notes, I would be sent to prison. I knew that I was doomed. And then with just the one magazine left, he stopped. He told me to put everything back in my bag. God had saved me.

Ten hours later I landed in Montreal, where my father picked me up. "So how was it?" he asked. "Shh," I said, "Not here. Wait till we are in the car." Two weeks in the USSR had instilled such a fear in me of constantly being spied upon that I was too afraid to talk in Canada!

I now understood how a lifetime under such a regime could seriously twist people psyches. Ultimately everyone only trusted one person – a spouse or best friend – but could never talk honestly to others.

That trip made me decide to dedicate my life to Jewish education. It revolutionized me in many ways. It was a peak life experience on par with getting married, seeing my first child be born, my first grandchild. It affected me deeply. I would never forget it.

21

Help Our People Know

That refusenik trip led indirectly to one of my biggest ops as a fund-raiser – a program I launched called "Help Our People Know." (The title was a play on the famous demand Moses made of Pharaoh, "Let my people go.") As part of this program, I sought to raise public awareness about the plight of Soviet Jews – who had been so totally deprived of their Jewish heritage by the anti-religion policies of the USSR – and to raise money for various educational projects to remedy the situation.

When I did it, I was young and naïve. I had just been given the job of heading up Aish LA in the heart of Hollywood, which was a very alluring place. It was a good thing my wife was level-headed and didn't fall for the glitz – thanks to her I stayed on course (mostly).

At that time, my chief tactic for raising money was making a lot of cold calls. I adopted this tactic because I didn't know how else to do it.

In sales or fundraising work cold calls are what separates the men from the boys. Calling people who don't know you – and who generally don't want to know you – is a tough thing to do, and it takes ten calls to get one appointment, and ten appointments to get one supporter.

I would scan the *Los Angeles Times*, the *Hollywood Reporter* and other film industry journals for names of wealthy and powerful Jews, then I would do some research on them and try to find out how to reach them. This was before the Internet, before Google, before Wikipedia, and it was not so easy. Once I had something to go on, I would call them and ask for a meeting.

In 1992, I placed a cold call to the office of Lou Rudolph. I knew that he had been executive vice-president at ABC under the legendary Barry Diller. Barry and Lou had originated the concept of the TV Movie of the Week and had produced hugely successful mini-series like *Rich Man, Poor Man* and *Roots*. When Lou left ABC, he became executive producer at Fries Entertainment, an independent TV-movie production house. That's where I called him and – lo and behold – he agreed to see me.

I was blown away when I walked into his posh Hollywood office – with floor to ceiling windows overlooking the Hollywood hills and the famous HOLLYWOOD sign. I made my usual pitch, offering to send a rabbi to his office once a week with whom he could discuss one-on-one all of life's issues from the Torah perspective – in short, I offered him an understanding, knowledgeable guide to "everything you ever wanted to know about Judaism but were afraid to ask." To my surprise, he took me up on it.

Over time, I had offered the opportunity of Torah study to hundreds of business executives and many took me up on it. They all learned a lot about their heritage, which increased their Jewish pride. A smaller number made changes in their lives as a result of their studies, deciding to keep kosher and observe Shabbat. But Lou was unique in the changes he made. After only two years, he left Hollywood and started living the life of an observant Jew; he even started using his Yiddish name Leibel. He told me that he realized he no longer wanted to produce silly pablum for the masses; instead, he wanted to put his considerable creative talents to changing the Jewish world for the better.

For a teenager or young adult such a dramatic change in life is impressive, but for someone to leave a career track that so many aspire to – now that was truly sensational.

For me, the timing was fortuitous as I was also ready to move on – by then, I had been running Aish's LA branch for some twelve years. Together, Lou and I created an organization called the Jerusalem Fund, which would become the international fundraising arm of Aish HaTorah and would break new ground in innovative outreach programs.

For the office of the new organization, I rented a cute bungalow on Doheny Boulevard near Pico, in West LA. We had it appointed to resemble the little bungalows that many Hollywood producers used on the back lots of major studios. This was great for me as now I felt like I had "made it" – at least in terms of my new digs. I was imitating the Hollywood world around me.

We had the trappings in place. Now, what to do for our first program? Our motto was: "You never get a second chance to make a first impression!" So, we figured it had to be something big!

SOMETHING BIG

That something big turned out to be "Help Our People Know."

The issue for Russian Jews was no longer freedom to immigrate but lack of adequate education about their heritage. Additionally, Westerners needed to be made aware of the old hatreds – which, in czarist times, had made the Jews the scapegoats for all that was wrong with imperial Russia – resurfacing in the former Soviet republics.

Lou and I came up with the idea of doing a satellite broadcast whose goal would be to educate the international Jewish community about this issue and to raise funds for a new Aish HaTorah Russian outreach program.

Today, multi-site satellite hook-ups are something we take for granted. Back then, this technology was still in its infancy. And, certainly, from an end-user point of view, no Jewish organization had ever tried to do such a thing involving even a few cities, let alone a few continents. It was truly an audacious goal – and, in retrospect, an absurd venture.

With a tentative commitment from Natan Sharansky, former "Prisoner of Zion," to appear on the program, I crisscrossed America, recruiting people to host a gathering of 20-30 people in their homes. I explained that, out on their lawn, we would park a satellite dish – then the size of a large pizza – and those gathered would be able to view a live program about Soviet Jewry being simultaneously beamed around the world. Most people had never heard of such a thing and were blown away by the idea. But the technology without a real program just wasn't exciting enough. Some people signed up, but most of those I approached just promised to think about it or said "no" outright.

It was during this time that I first became a frequent flyer. I was living in airplanes trying to recruit people for this satellite broadcast – my dream. But I suppose the idea of Rabbi Irwin Katsof as the on-air host just wasn't much of an attraction. A little disappointing to me – the wanna-be Hollywood rabbi. Billy Crystal I wasn't – this was becoming clear to me!

GOD'S HELP

We started working on this in November of 1994 and, after three months, were still nowhere close. Lou sat down to brainstorm with me and asked the pointed question, "Who do we need to get on board to make this happen?"

Our wish-list was audacious: Larry King, then famed CNN broadcaster; Sumner Redstone, head of Viacom (the company which owned Paramount Studios); and Jeffrey Katzenberg, then head of Disney. We reasoned that if we had such luminaries heading our venture, people would take us seriously and sign up.

Lou suggested I tape their pictures over my desk and come in each morning and stare at them, thinking what I was going to do that day to make this happen. He taught me the importance of truly big goals and of single-mindedly focusing on them – what I always called BHAGs (big hairy audacious goals). Before this, I would never have thought of going after the wealthiest or the most powerful players around. It was the first in many important lessons that Lou taught me.

I took his advice seriously. I found their pictures, taped them over my desk, and did a lot of staring.

One day, while Lou and I were sitting in our little bungalow wondering what we were going to do to make this program fly (and also how to pay our mounting travel costs and other expenses), a friend of Lou's unexpectedly stopped by for a visit. She told us that she had just been to a beauty parlor at the Beverly Wilshire Hotel, one of the ritziest spots in Beverly Hills, and she had bumped into Larry King there. He was also getting his hair done. She was quite an attractive woman and so Larry, who was then single, spent a while chatting with her. She knew how much Lou cared about this project and the degree to which we were struggling with it and so, in the course of the conversation with Larry, she mentioned that a friend of hers was putting together an international satellite broadcast about Russian Jews.

It just so happens that Larry King's real name was Leibel Zeiger and his grandparents were from Minsk, so when she asked if he would like to meet the rabbi in charge, he said "yes." We nearly fell off our chairs when she told us that.

I asked her to call Larry back immediately and set up a time for us to see him. He said to come over right now! Oh my!!!

We jumped into a car and sped to the Beverly Wilshire Hotel. We were going up the elevator when Lou suddenly said, "Hey Irwin, what are we going to ask him?" I said, "Let's go for broke and ask him to be our on-air host and to approach Redstone and Katzenberg to be our honorary chairmen."

Lou added, "And to get a studio for the satellite broadcast!" Why not?

And then Lou said, "Stop! Before we go in there, we need to say a prayer; we need to ask God's help with this venture."

We stopped the elevator and said a prayer. Now I think how crazy it all was. Here we were – a rabbi and a Hollywood producer praying in the elevator of the Beverly Wilshire Hotel, which is owned by the Sultan of Brunei, asking God to help us on behalf of Russian Jews. But if truth be known, God was helping us all along! We were just too blind to see it. What are the chances of the right person sitting next to Larry in a beauty parlor, of all places? We couldn't lose!

We got off the elevator and knocked on Larry's door. To this day I still vividly recall Larry's beaming face. "Rabbi!" he bellowed, "How are you? I heard all about your satellite broadcast to help Russian Jews. What can I do to help? Would you like me to host it for you?"

I was flabbergasted. I hadn't even asked! Was he a mind-reader? Or was God pulling the strings?

"Great!" I barely stammered out.

"What else do you need rabbi?" Larry has a short attention span and he does not waste any time.

I managed to ask him for help with Katzenberg and Redstone. He picked up the phone. Ten minutes later we were out the door. We had Katzenberg and Redstone as co-chairs of the event and a Paramount set for our satellite broadcast. The whirlwind had begun!

THE WHIRLWIND

Within the space of a month, Vice President Al Gore signed up and also agreed to be on the show; then we got US Senators Patrick Moynihan and Bob Dole, and Steven Spielberg and then Jerusalem Mayor Ehud Olmert.

I called back the many potential hosts who had declined on my first try and explained the illustrious line-up. We quickly got 150 hosts on four continents in ten countries signed up to receive the broadcast, plus airtime on Time-Warner cable in New York and Florida.

It was coming together but, in truth, we were suddenly too successful.

I quickly learned why more businesses fail from too much success rather than from failure. We weren't able to handle it. We did not have the infrastructure to input all the names of the hosts and the thousands of participants in each city, to print personalized invitations and solicitation packages necessary for them all, to arrange the technical support for 150 satellite dishes in so many far-flung places. Plus, we now had four different broadcasts planned to accommodate the various time zones. And we had to write a script for a 90-minute program, complete with film clips on the history of Russian Jewry, and set up a follow-up system to handle pledges. We could not deal with it all!

Our systems started to melt down. Literally. Our data processing packages were inadequate, our computers were crashing, and our printers were burning out. I had to hire computer technicians to literally sit in our office 24 hours a day. I hired secretaries and data-entry people to work around the clock. I added fifteen (!) more phone lines.

Tempers flared often as systems crashed and burned, and we were falling behind deadlines in churning out instruction sheets and answering hosts' telephone calls, questions and needs. Secretaries were leaving in tears on a daily basis. (The staff would actually take bets on how long it would take for each new data-entry person to start crying. The office manager – who had a tough, Hollywood-style of relating to people – became known as "Bosszilla.") I was supposed to be a rabbi with good interpersonal skills, a model to others but, instead, I was overwhelmed by the cyclone of human relations failures and technological breakdowns, which were fueling more human aggravation and crises.

It was absolute chaos.

As satellite day approached, we dropped from 150 locations to 100, because we simply couldn't manage the influx of requests and process the paperwork needed for the satellite dish installations. We disappointed many prospective volunteers. Nonetheless, the broadcast itself went off without a hitch, and thanks to Lou, it was a world-class production. It had strong emotional impact and included a powerful monologue by Larry King about the history of Russian Jewry, interviews with dignitaries around the world and up-close and personal interviews with Aish students in Moscow and other Russian cities.

I was Larry's co-host and for one day I got a taste of what it might feel like to be a star. I had my own dressing room, a make-up artist and an assistant director who followed me around all day. Wherever I went, he was never far behind me. We were doing four broadcasts, and we would come on and off the air in between different video segments, so this person was constantly reminding me, "ten minutes to air-time Rabbi Katsof ... five minutes to air-time Rabbi Katsof ... two minutes to air-time Rabbi Katsof..." and making sure I was standing on that little masking tape "x" on the stage. Then the lights would go on and the studio audience would clap.

For one day I had this kind of attention, and it went straight to my head.

They say that one of the emperors of Rome had a slave walk behind his chariot, periodically reminding him, "You are but dust." Luckily for me, I had a wife and a lot of dirty diapers at home to do the same thing for me.

I also had grounding in the Jewish tradition, which makes provisions to help a man with his ego. In the days of Jewish monarchy, the king had to write a small Torah scroll which he had to carry with him at all times in order to remind him that there was a God above him. Even today, a Jewish man wears a *yarmulke* or *kippah*, for the same reason. The *tefillin*, the phylacteries which we put on daily, are also supposed to be a tool to remind us how small we really are and how big God really is.

FALLOUT

In terms of educating people, the broadcast was a big success.

In terms of fundraising, it was a disaster. We received $1 million in donations, but the project had cost us $1.1 million. The many unknowns of the new technology, the huge dimensions of the project – the fact that we had to drop 30 percent of the sites at the last moment and we lacked the proper infrastructure to collect on many pledges – cost us another million in lost donations.

In short, we blew it and we hurt Aish's Russian program as – after such a high-profile program – its donors figured it didn't need money. This is *not* how fundraising normally works, and this did not happen in our other ventures. What can I say, except that it was a huge mistake.

Additionally, there was a lot of collateral damage in terms of hurt feelings.

Rabbi Weinberg flew to LA immediately after the broadcast to meet with me. He was upset by all the reported incidents of *chillul Hashem* (the desecration of God's name that results when a religious person does not behave in a Torah way). The word had gotten out that several secretaries left in tears and that there had been a lot of yelling, screaming and hot tempers, not once or twice but on a regular basis. The buck stopped at my door, because I had failed to put a stop to the madness.

Rabbi Weinberg stressed that we were in the business of *kiddush Hashem* – everything we did had to be a sanctification of God's name. He wanted employees of Aish HaTorah to leave a day of work and say, "Wow, these folks are so kind and considerate," and not "These folks are monsters." A mark of a good man is how he treats those people he doesn't have to be nice to – it's not such a stretch to be nice to your boss or father-in-law, but do you treat your secretary or your cleaning lady with respect?

It was a tense meeting for me. Rabbi Weinberg made it clear that if this type of behavior ever happened again, he would close down the Jerusalem Fund. He was proud of our risk-taking and ability to think big, to care enough about our Russian Jewish brethren to want to help, but the bottom line was that Aish HaTorah was in the business of *kiddush Hashem* – anything other than that was simply not permissible.

This was a very important lesson for me to learn. It has stayed with me to this day. I don't always succeed, but at least I know the standard that I must strive to live up to.

22

Into a War Zone

I was remembering all that as I checked in for my flight for Tbilisi and got ready for a new adventure. I wondered what impact it would have on me, so many years later. A whole lifetime had passed, during which I had gone from a student to a rabbi to a wanna-be business titan. Here I was returning to the scene of the crime. Life is a circle even when we don't want it to be.

As the airplane started to approach Georgia, I quickly looked up our route in the passenger information guide. Sure enough, it was as I feared. The approach was over Russia and the Caucasus Mountains. I looked out the window and realized that the scattered villages I saw were in Ossetia, the very place where the battles had been fought. From up above, the land was brown with very little green.

The pilot slowed the engines and seemed to stall in mid-air as if he couldn't decide if he really wanted to land here or not. The outskirts of Tbilisi came into view from 2,000 feet. The place looked poor and tired. Finally, we touched down, the engines screaming as if they resisted coming to rest here. As we taxied in, I noticed only a handful of Ukrainian and Georgian planes. No American or German planes, which I'd seen in Kiev. No one was here! Was I nuts?

Lasha was waiting for me at the end of the jetway, beaming. He walked me through passport control and airport security. I noticed as I whizzed by that there were very few people in this airport – nobody was coming, and nobody was going anywhere.

Same thing at my five-star hotel. Everything was very quiet. I had a scant hour to shower and change before the meetings began.

First up, Ekterina Sharashidze, Minister of Economic Development. I learned that the Georgian government wanted to define Georgia as part of Europe so it could join NATO, but geographically it really is in Asia as the dividing line has always been the Caucasus mountain range, which puts Georgia in the south along with Turkey, Armenia and Azerbaijan.

Ekterina Sharashidze – a beautiful woman, vivacious, charming, and of course brilliant, a graduate of Penn and Harvard – spent an hour briefing me on the economic trends, GDP, amount of foreign direct investment, all accompanied with colorful graphs and diagrams and comparative statistics. She sounded more like an activist out to change the world than a career politician. This was because she was part of the new blood that came in with the Rose Revolution that re-defined the Georgian government. She was of a totally different breed.

She asked me if I would organize a business breakfast for President Saakashvili when he visited New York in two weeks for the UN General Assembly. She would like him to meet with leaders in investment banking and private equity. I agreed to do so.

After a kosher dinner cooked by the local rabbi's wife, I was left to ponder the situation as Lasha ran back to his duties – President Sarkozy of France had just landed, bringing peace treaty news after a meeting he'd had with Russian President Medvedev in Moscow.

I found the people I was surrounded by extremely energizing. They all had a fire in their belly, wanting to make a difference in helping their country. It was catchy. I was inspired by them, but I did not yet know how I could help them. I asked my US contacts for information about US aid, prefab housing for displaced persons, hydro projects, etc. I wanted to have something intelligent to say before meeting with President Saakashvili the next night. I reviewed the material, wrote up some notes, took an Ambien, and fell into a fitful sleep dreaming of Russian tanks shelling the Marriot Hotel in Tbilisi where I was staying.

The next day brought a whirlwind of meetings with bankers and government officials. Finally, it was time for dinner – or at least so I thought – at the Israeli Embassy.

Entering a section of Tbilisi where all the ambassadors live, we stopped in front of a three-story house with an Israeli flag flying outside. A clone of the Shabak guards that you see outside the Israeli Knesset greeted me at the entrance – he was tall, strong, no nonsense. Then the ambassador from Israel, Yitzhak Gerber, and his wife came out.

Also invited to dinner that night were three Israeli Knesset members who had come to lend emotional support to the Georgian government. With them were some Israeli businessmen who had invested in Georgia, and Alan Shneider, chairman of B'nai B'rith Israel. Alan told me he was there to look into relief efforts by an Israeli organization he supports called Israeli Flying Aid. He had spent the past day with them in Gori, which had been bombed and occupied by the Russians. He suggested I visit Gori to see first-hand what the Israelis were doing there. This sounded exciting – I said I would.

We stood around talking and it was getting on 9 PM, but dinner was nowhere in sight. I was seriously hungry and I feared I wouldn't see the food before I had to leave for a late-night meeting with President Saakashvili. Finally, we sat down. It was impressive – with all the plates and cutlery engraved with the emblem of Israel: a menorah framed by olive branches. But the plates stayed empty because first we had to have toasts. Finally, little dishes of salads appeared – shredded carrots, cucumbers, eggplant. I scooped up as much as I could get because, at this rate, I knew I'd never see the main course.

Sure enough, when I had hardly swallowed, Lasha said it was time to get going.

A MAN FOR ALL SEASONS

Speeding through Tbilisi, we arrived at the President's office, which seemed to me to have only minimal security. The anteroom was decorated with framed newspaper articles about the Rose Revolution which had brought Saakashvili to power, including a *Fortune* magazine cover-story touting Georgia as a great place to do business. Several assistants came in to say hello to Lasha – I could tell he was well loved and respected here. Everyone was perky even though it was 10:30 PM. But it was early by Georgian work standards, where people labor until 3 and 4 AM. This was the reason for 10 PM dinners!

After a twenty-minute wait, the phone on the secretary's desk finally rang and we were motioned to enter. Lasha stood up and buttoned his sports jacket. Hmm. I did the same. As we walked in, the President came bounding toward us. At 6'5" he was a handsome man of athletic build who exuded great vitality. He welcomed me warmly, energetically pumping my hand.

I noticed on his desk the largest and latest Apple monitor – a sleek, impressive piece of design. I couldn't help but think: "This guy is really with it. He knows what hums in the West. This is no dowdy politician."

Without much ado, he launched into a presentation about the war. He made clear his feelings for President George W. Bush, expressing his gratitude to the US for standing by Georgia. Both Vice-President Dick Cheney and then Senator Joe Biden had visited. Other luminaries of the time – Senator John McCain, Senator Barack Obama and Governor Sarah Palin – had expressed their concern and support.

The Georgian President was not a man who holds back – not when expressing his gratitude for the US, nor when expressing his anger at Putin and the Russians. He told me that the scariest time of the war was when the Russians were advancing on Tbilisi, intending to surround the government buildings and force a regime change – that is, to overthrow the government. He and his ministers talked about how to fortify their building and barricade themselves in. But the Russians backed down in the end. The advancing tanks stopped 20 kilometers from the Tbilisi city line. He told me that he believes they stopped because of the pressure applied by the US (as well as other governments), and because he and his people did not cave in. The Russians were hoping that the Georgians would flee, but their military advance had the opposite effect – it galvanized the nation. On the advice of Senator McCain, a call went out to have the Tbilisi citizens make a human chain, stand shoulder-to-shoulder to show solidarity, and this is what they did.

The President had a glow relating this story and his energy was unflagging. Yet, when I looked carefully at his face, I saw that the past month had taken its toll – and his day was not yet half done. I had been told he had worked through the previous night with President Sarkozy of France. After me, he had a meeting with the German Foreign Minister. Amid such a lot of feverish activity, I felt privileged that he gave me his time.

We spoke briefly about meetings I would set up for him in New York, in two weeks' time. Then we shook hands and I headed out. The German Foreign Minister was already waiting.

Accompanied by Lasha, I walked out into the cool Georgian night. It was raining. The square was dark except for a lighted mural on the wall. I returned to my hotel, energized by my experiences. I called home, spoke with Judy and called it a day.

After two more days of non-stop meetings (including with people at the US embassy here), I dispatched a report to Paul and David spelling out the points of attraction:

o It had become a major priority to shore up the Georgian economy and not let the country be taken over by Russia, and to that end various US government agencies – such as USAID, Millennium Challenge Corporation and OPIC (Overseas Private Investment Corporation) – were on board along with their budgets. Together, they had allocated almost $1.5 billion for that purpose.

o In addition, EBRD (European Bank for Reconstruction and Development) had $250 million to spend in Georgia and was very much interested in developing clean energy.

o Georgia wanted to pursue hydro power as it could export some of the extra electricity, realizing as much as $4 billion annually in income. No wonder this was a priority for them.

We decided the opportunities in Georgia were worth a follow-up visit from the rest of the team. There appeared to be good reasons to invest here, and the best time was now when so few other companies were willing to visit and explore investing. But wasn't it Rothschild who said, "When the bullets start flying, it's time to start investing."

Done with business I set off for Gori to see the damage and the good works.

GAL IN GORI

Within a ten-minute ride out of Tbilisi, I found myself looking at gently rolling landscape, little villages dotting the countryside, forsaken churches on hilltops – and the spot in the road where the Russian tanks stopped. That's how close they had come to the capital and the President's office where I sat a few hours earlier.

Arriving in Gori (Stalin's birthplace), I found the town square dominated by a half-a-dozen huge eighteen-wheeler Red Cross trucks and a huge Stalin statue (what else) put up to honor a man responsible for killing more people than Hitler.

From there I called Gal Lusky, the Israeli woman I had come here to meet – the founder of Israeli Flying Aid, who was spearheading the effort to aid the refugees that had flocked to Gori. She said she would come to the square to meet me. While I waited, I took in the sights. A scrawny boy with scruffy hair, dressed in a dirty tank top, pants and sandals approached me begging. He was missing his two front teeth and those on the sides were bronze capped; his face was weather-beaten like that of an old man. He was relentless in his efforts, but my taxi driver said not to give to him. I was torn but since I had no small bills in my wallet, I gave him nothing. Seconds later a peasant woman approached and also asked for money. The driver said that she was speaking Russian; she was not Georgian, so probably a Russian refugee. When I said no, she swore at me and walked off disgusted.

PETITE DYNAMITE

Then out of nowhere popped out a smiling petite dynamo – Gal Lusky – beaming from ear to ear. Though small in stature (and I couldn't help but contrast her against the giant Stalin in whose shadow she stood), she exuded the electric vitality of a person driven by her mission. She had a wiry athlete's body from all the years of living on the edge, and her dark brown eyes and olive skin betrayed her Moroccan background. She was wearing khakis and a t-shirt that said "Israeli Flying Aid." The color was the blue of the Israeli flag with a big Star of David framed by outstretched wings – a Jewish angel.

She told me that she had just come from a tense meeting with UN representatives. They were upset that the refugees didn't want to eat their food. They gave them 300 grams a day of bland white pasta, while Gal who bought food in the local market gave them meat, green vegetables and mashed potatoes. Hmmm, tough choice. Bland pasta on the one hand, meat and potatoes on the other. Duh! Not sure why the UN folks couldn't figure this one out. Furthermore, they were importing their pasta, while Gal was buying her food locally. Guess who was more cost-efficient with their donors' money? Duh!

She explained that she supplied 6,000 meals daily to the refugees from the war with Russia. These were all people who fled from South Ossetia and Abkhazia and were now homeless.

I was full of questions: Who are you? What do you do? How long have you been here?

She told me to follow her to her base. Five minutes later we came to a parking lot where a dozen elderly Georgians were milling around the tables. Gal told me they were not refugees but remnants of the Jewish community of Gori who were too old or too poor to go someplace else. Even though her primary mission was to help refugees, she couldn't abandon these poor Jews, so she was feeding them also.

We went up three stairs into what appeared to be an old, dilapidated warehouse of some sort where we were greeted by a banner-size logo of Israeli Flying Aid – the winged Star of David. A stranger site in Stalin's birthplace I could not imagine.

The rest of Gal's team of eight Israelis and a few locals were there. They took me into the warehouse where five big stainless steel soup pots were set up on propane stoves – lunch was cooking. The Israelis were easy to pick out – they all wore the tell-tale t-shirt. There were also two Georgian babushkas dressed in black. No expressions crossed their faces; their eyes were distant, unfocused. They moved from pot to table as if they were machines. (Gal told me that the Russians had killed their husbands and sons in front of them. She was employing them out of compassion.) There were also young Georgian girls who were cutting tomatoes or peeling potatoes.

Gal told me her Israeli team was made up of volunteers, but she hired the locals to help out. Israeli rock music was playing from someone's Ipod hooked up to a set of speakers. The scene seemed surreal to me.

Responding to the look of confusion and disbelief on my face, Gal ran off and came back moments later with a map. She sat down at a long wood table, spread it out and began to explain.

NO MAN'S LAND

The Russians had occupied a swath of land a few kilometers wide in Georgian territory, just south of South Ossetia and Abkhazia. This was a buffer zone set up to allegedly "protect" South Ossetia. Most of the Georgian villages north of it had been destroyed – looted and burned. There were several thousand Georgians, mostly elderly or children who couldn't flee in the face of the advancing Russian army. And now they were stuck in that hostile territory. She told me that last night she had convinced the Russians guarding the buffer zone – after a five-hour conversation (!) – to let her cross the Russian lines into occupied Ossetia to deliver another 1,000 dry meals to people who, for all intents and purposes, were imprisoned there. As proof, she reached into a hip pocket of her khakis and showed me a Russian paratrooper pin that the soldiers guarding the buffer zone gave her.

On the map Gal showed me the route she took, and the villages she went to. Next to each one she had marked the number of people left behind – 200 here, 50 there, 126 here. She told me that the villages were for the most part destroyed. The survivors she met told her that the Russians had taken hardened prisoners – murderers, rapists, thieves – from a prison in neighboring Chechnya and brought them by bus to South Ossetia, then let them out in the Georgian villages to do as they pleased, which was exactly what they did.

I was incredulous. "Do you mean to tell me you sweet-talked your way past Russian lines into this lawless buffer zone to deliver food to victims?" I asked her. Smiling, she nodded, admitting that it was a risk. She could have been killed or jailed, but then she would have died making a difference. I looked at her and said, "You are certifiably nuts. But I respect your courage."

Out of a little velvet pouch, she produced a MacBook Air, explaining that it was a donation. She turned it on and launched into a PowerPoint presentation about her Israeli Flying Aid organization. It turned out that this trip to Gori was only her latest venture. (I should have known!)

She had been to Sri Lanka after the tsunami. There the government wouldn't allow any aid to the villages where there were rebels, Muslim extremists who had been involved in the murderous suicide bomb blasts in Bali. Nonetheless, Gal was undeterred. Not all the villagers were rebels, and even so they were people in need after a disaster.

She showed me slides of her in Kashmir, after a horrendous earthquake which killed thousands. More slides of her in Eritrea, Chechnya, Sudan, Burma, Indonesia, Rwanda. In several pictures she was wearing Muslim garb in order to be sensitive to local customs. But then she proudly showed me that her team was wearing their Israeli Flying Aid t-shirts under their Muslim robes. She wanted everyone to know that Jews were doing this.

The list of her activities of the past five years covered every tragedy the world had experienced. It was a travelogue of horror and pain, natural disasters and war, human tragedy and despair. Many of these countries were difficult to get into even in peaceful times, if for some unexplained reason you wanted to go there. But she went there immediately upon news of a disaster. Sometimes she had to hire smugglers to take her across the border illegally to reach the victims.

Her craziest venture (in my opinion) was when she sneaked via Turkey through the Kurdish area into Iraq. I mean, this was an area US Special Forces would avoid!

MIXED FEELINGS

I had mixed feelings about her efforts, as she had at times helped some pretty bad dudes, but I couldn't help but admire her verve, guts and determination. And she was a true embodiment of a *kiddush Hashem* – with her deeds, she sanctified God's name and demonstrated what it means for Jews to be "a light unto the nations."

She had scores of other missions on her slides, including Hurricane Katrina. She said her group was the only non-government group that FEMA worked with. They had her enter homes to look for bodies, as they themselves weren't allowed to go in if the home was locked and no one answered their knock.

She said a few groups – like the Jewish Agency, B'nai B'rith and the American Jewish Committee – helped her with funding. But it was not enough. This effort in Georgia would cost her $55,000 dollars. She said she had sold her home last year to support her work.

As I said, this lady was certifiable crazy. Her efforts crossed the line from idealism to sheer lunacy. And yet, I only had feelings of respect for her.

Easier to appreciate were her heroic efforts during the Israel-Lebanon war in the summer of 2006. Besides helping the victims of the relentless Hezbollah bombing, she also helped provide for the Israeli troops in ways the government couldn't – whether it was handing out additional goggles, bandages or hot meals. But, she said, her main focus was always the victims. She didn't care what side they were on. They were victims – period – be it of a natural disaster (hurricane, flood or famine) or of man-made disaster (war). She called herself "the Commando of Souls." She said that her non-partisan work had even attracted the attention of the Arab *Al Jazeera* TV network, which did a documentary about her. She said her niche is to figure out quickly the victims' needs and to provide it all in one fell swoop, while being sensitive to local customs.

Often large bureaucratic organizations lack this sensitivity. She said that North Face Inc. (the makers of outdoor clothing) sent five tons of beautiful down winter coats to Kashmir via Oxfam for earthquake victims. But the local mullah forced the villagers to burn the coats, because they were sent by infidels who, he said, wanted to bribe them to convert and it was better they die from the cold than wear the coats. Fanaticism at its worst but real-politic nonetheless. Gal used her money to buy coats made by locals and gave them away for free.

She told me about a machine that a religious Jew invented which she used in areas where there was no drinkable water. It supplied 1,000 liters of water per day by taking it out of the moisture in the air. Awesome!

She was quite a mixed bag. I could see where liberal Jewish groups would love her efforts and where other more conservative groups might say, "Why help our enemies?" But her argument made sense. Aren't we all created in God's image? Are these not innocent victims? Isn't it a Godly thing to do to show compassion to those less fortunate?

I felt torn. I admired her but felt conflicted about assisting people in countries that were enemies of Israel and America. Also, doesn't charity begin at home? Still, we *are* responsible for seeing the whole world as ours. Why do we have to judge and evaluate all charitable efforts from the narrow confines of our worldviews? Are we not supposed to make the whole world a better place?

My inner thoughts and mental struggles were drowning out her PowerPoint presentation. Truth be told, I was jealous of her conviction and selflessness and courage. I was here in Georgia trying to make a deal, sleeping at the five-star Marriot in Tbilisi, flying business class. I was comfortable while she was on the front lines doing something meaningful.

How did she have the guts to risk her life to be smuggled into such dangerous areas?

Instead of explaining herself, she told me she had to get going as the most dangerous time was dusk. That's when the adults in the refugee camps started drinking and became violent. There were often fights, rapes and random brutality. She would take all the children out of the camp for two hours and show them movies on a big outdoor screen. By the time she brought them back, the worst offenders would have fallen asleep and it would be safer for the kids.

I felt tremendous admiration for her efforts. I felt a real tug of war within me as we walked out of the warehouse. I told her I would help her set up a non-profit group in the US and help her raise money. She was very thankful.

As we said good-bye, we were standing next to a foot-wide jagged hole in the pavement. A mortar had landed there three weeks ago, seriously injuring an Israeli journalist who was covering the conflict.

I couldn't help but think that I was standing at a turning point – both physical and psychological. Here, the Caucasus Mountains define no-man's-land. It's not Europe and it's not Asia. I felt as if

I had been thrown into my own no-man's-land, as if I too was caught between two continents.

Where would this conflict between Russia and Georgia lead? How would it continue to affect the relationship between Russia and the US? How would it affect my deal in Odessa and my wanting to do business here in Georgia?

On a personal level, what was I to do with all these feelings that were bubbling to the surface within me? How could I combine the world of business and the desire to make a difference? What would make my life the most meaningful?

There must be a reason the Almighty had sent me to Georgia and to Gori to meet Gal and the Israeli Flying Aid.

Returning to Tbilisi, I closed my eyes on the way home. It was easier than watching my driver weave back and forth across the highway, risking his life and my life for nothing. My questions would have to wait. I checked out of the Tbilisi Marriot and headed for the airport. I had a flight to catch home and a family waiting to see me.

WHAT NEXT?

It had been an energizing trip. I felt much as I did twenty-six years ago when I came here for the first time to meet with refuseniks and lend support to them. I always remembered it as one of the most galvanizing, most meaningful times in my life. There is nothing like the excitement of doing something that counts, for a higher goal. I felt then an inner shift deep in my core. And now I felt it again.

It was as if the tectonic plates of my existence were grinding against each other again. My worldview was in a state of flux. When that happens below the crust of the earth, the pent-up energy miles under the surface pushes up and the earth explodes upwards from the unrelenting pressure. This is how the mountain ranges we see today were created. Of course, that took many centuries but, at other times, the changes can instant and dramatic – a volcano erupting for instance, or an earthquake splitting the earth, collapsing houses and highways.

And isn't everything in the physical world a microcosm of our personal world? Is it not there to teach us about life?

Changes within us require the force of the tectonic plates of our deep unconscious to push up against each other, at first below the surface of our awareness, until there erupts a volcano in our day-to-day life. One day a rabbi, the next a businessman. How long had that percolated below surface before it burst upward? And what new shift was occurring within me now?

23

The Hallowed 1 Percent

Before the economy fell into the toilet in 2008, approximately 3 percent of the American population earned more than $200,000 a year, and only 1 percent earned more than $500,000.

Let that sink in for a moment.

In reverse, this means that 97 percent of the American population earned less than $200,000. (In fact, 66 percent made less than $50,000 a year.) And only a miniscule sliver of the American people were the high earners.

When I looked at it that way, it was truly a miracle that in 2005, my first year in business, I earned $677,000, and in 2006, I earned $1.2 million. Out of the box, I was in the top 1 percent of American wage earners! Pretty breathtaking, though I didn't appreciate it then.

In 2007, I experienced a hard landing, earning only about $200,000, but I was still pulling in more than 97 percent of the American people. Then 2008 brought a crash-and-burn – as the Odessa deal failed (more about that shortly) – and it's a miracle I walked away from the wreckage. I earned less than $25,000, my mission to Israel lost $10,000, and I had to put $150,000 more into my business than I took out. Then the economy convulsed and started sliding into a deep recession. Consumer debt sky-rocketed. Every day brought news of more individuals defaulting on personal debt and banks collapsing.

My banks, together with thousands of other banks in the nation, tightened consumer credit. My home equity line was cancelled. Three credit card companies recalled unused, zero-balance cards which I had been saving for a rainy day. I tried to use an AmEx card in Judy's name that hadn't been used in five years only to discover that, as a preventive measure, the credit limit had dropped from $30,000 to $2,700 because I had too much other outstanding debt. Just like that more than $23,000 of available credit disappeared.

My friends all reported similar experiences. The banks were pulling available credit everywhere, even from people with good credit ratings. I had to employ emergency evasive maneuvers to survive. This was battlefield triage time. I had to stanch the bleeding fast and just do everything I could to simply save the patient.

I had been able to get through 2007 because I had some savings from 2006 which had been a great year. In 2007, thinking it couldn't get worse, I spent my savings and went into debt. By 2008 I had used up all my home equity line and had started to accumulate close to $300,000 in credit-card debt. I cut my personal family overhead by about $100,000 a year, laid off my personal staff, closed my office, and even cut things like two extra phone lines at home.

For the first time since 1982 (!) I did not have even one secretary working for me. Typically, I had a whole staff, including one assistant whose sole job was to organize my travel and meetings calendar. I've always worked at a very intense pace and keeping my schedule straight was a full-time job for anyone. Then, suddenly, I was alone. It hit me hard to realize that I had no support staff for the first time in literally a lifetime.

I had not bought a new suit in three years, and just when I couldn't afford one, I found that some of my jackets were fraying. What still looked good from my wardrobe didn't fit me anymore because I had gained 25 pounds. The weight gain came from tension, of course, and from totally dropping my exercise regimen. Why? I couldn't afford the trainer or the gym.

DIFFICULT TIMES

But I took solace from the fact that everyone around me was experiencing difficult times. Very few people were not feeling the effect of falling home equity, tightening credit lines and reduced consumer spending. The rumors abounded of Wall Street bankers looking for loans to cover their mortgages.

Even Lev Leviev, the Russian oligarch, was not spared. He had been the main donor to a large network of Russian schools that were now facing a serious crisis as he withdrew his support. Last I heard, they didn't even have money to buy the kids food or milk.

Sheldon Adelson, one of the richest men in the world, had the value of his wealth drop from $38 billion to $1 billion or less. He had been a major philanthropist and the largest donor to Operation Birthright, a program sending college students to Israel. He, too, had to withdraw his support as he tried to keep his empire from collapsing.

Every day there was a new hard-luck story.

In retrospect, I had squandered my two years of plenty, when my earnings had been in the top 1 percent of all US citizens. (So much for learning from the Bible story of Joseph, who advised the Pharaoh to save in the years of feast for the years of famine.) I had invested $270,000 of my earnings in deals and lost $120,000 of that when an electronically-traded funds company, launched by a close friend, went bankrupt. I gave $300,000 to charity, paid a lot of taxes, leased an Audi S8, went to Israel four times with the whole family at a cost of $30,000-$40,000 a pop. These trips were meaningful and pleasurable for all, but way above my pay-grade. It was now time to adjust my life-style and live within my means.

I remember my friend Dick Horowitz telling me that only a miniscule portion of businessmen actually became successful. Somehow, I didn't pay attention to his warning. My vision of life was skewed because, as a fund-raiser, I only dealt with the super-wealthy, those firmly in the top 1 percent, people capable of giving donations of $100,000 or more. And I had wanted to be part of that 1 percent stratosphere.

I also remember Dick telling me that those who made it into that hallowed group had got there the hard way, many of them having lost money before they ever made it to the top. I could confirm that, as I had seen it happen to the people whom I knew but, naively, I believed it wouldn't happen to me. I also saw the human collateral damage that went with the single-minded chase after money – the divorces, the estranged children, the unhappy lives in general.

God gave me the prize I thought I desired in 2005 and 2006, but it almost cost me my marriage, and it certainly distanced me from the really important pleasures and experiences in life. Since then, God has been teaching me about what really counts in life – how to get pleasure from the simple things that don't require earning more than $500,000 a year. Sure, I needed to pay the bills, and I missed not being able to afford to visit Israel, but I was beginning to clarify what is really important and just how I wanted to live my life.

END OF THE GOLD RUSH

I bumped into Tzvi Berg in Tbilisi at the end of 2008. When I first met him years ago eating alone at the King David restaurant in Kiev, we had been two strangers in a strange land eating dinner alone and moved to share our personal pursuit-of-riches stories. We were both exploiting the opportunities of Eastern Europe, part of the modern gold rush.

Last I heard, Tzvi was working on a toll-road project in Romania – it was a huge deal with huge problems, but the kind of dream that inspires many a bounty hunter and many a legend. The first thing he said to me when he saw me more recently was: "No more dreams!" He filled me in on his latest venture, which was much safer. "Now I import food and clothes from Israel by the container, and I sell it in Georgia. It's simple barter. Import-export of goods. I bring it through the Poti port, and then I sell it all to one guy who distributes it. No headaches. I make less, that's for sure, but it's simple. For a change, I like things simple."

Then I bumped into my friend Bill (not his real name), who had been running a hedge fund he started a few years ago. He built it from nothing to nearly $700 million. He had been expecting to make $10 million this year, but instead he was looking at closing up. He fired his all of his employees, and actually took in two boarders into his house to help make ends meet. He said he and his wife are cutting back everywhere. They used to get two ice cream cones (one each) now they buy one and share it. That's how closely they watch everything they spend!

And what was even more anxiety provoking is that no one knew how much worse it was going to get. Could the government stem the tide by pumping huge sums into the marketplace? No economist could be sure. It reminded me of what a friend of mine once said: "The one redeeming thing about economists is that they make astrologists look respectable."

There was one thing that we could be sure of – the world had changed. God had brought us capitalists back to our senses, and through His love was trying to get us back in touch with what really makes life worth living. Personally, I no longer felt possessed by the need to succeed. I could be happy with less. I tried to focus on the more that I do have.

I remember once asking Rabbi Weinberg, "What do I need to do, so God will grant me success?" When I asked that question, I was already successful but, of course, I considered what I had peanuts and wanted more.

He looked at me and said, "Don't be so obsessed about succeeding in business. Ask God to help you get close to Him."

"But I want to get rich," I protested.

He grabbed me by the collar and passionately declared, "It's meaningless Irwin! It's nonsense. It evaporates. Being close to God is all that counts."

I heard him, but I paid no attention. It took me three more years, a world recession and going to the brink of bankruptcy to finally get it.

Now, I still wanted to get rich, but I didn't want to sacrifice the rest of my life to get there. I wanted to be close to God and to live an ethical life. I knew that money wasn't what would make my life pleasurable or meaningful, and it wasn't what I wanted to be remembered for.

It hit home when I read an interview with the editor of the London *Daily Telegraph*. He was asked why his newspaper rarely featured obituaries of corporate titans, preferring to focus on generals, scientists, authors, athletes and the like. He answered, "Because a life spent grubbing money isn't worth writing about."

A DIFFERENT TRACK

Little by little, I set about changing the direction of my life. And as I did so, I remembered my grandmother.

My grandmother, who had lived through the Great Depression, never threw anything out. She had the wildest collection of plastic containers, stashed in every corner of her kitchen, because every container was recycled. She watered down the milk in order to make it go farther. She put away pickles and tomatoes for the winter, and she saved stamps – the "pinkie stamps" from the Steinberg's grocery chain which earned you some small kitchen appliance when you collected enough. She would go to the other side of Montreal to get extra stamps and she collected books upon books of stamps to give away as wedding presents.

All that had seemed quaint to me – until I found myself engaging in similar behavior. I no longer brought my clothes to the dry cleaner's every week. Okay, so my pants got a little creased, so my shirts got laundered at home and were not as pressed-looking, so what? I walked around the house turning off unnecessary lights; I kept the thermostat at 67 degrees and put on an extra sweater. I even stopped going to Starbucks. The thought of spending $4 on a latte just wasn't palatable any longer. I wasn't the only one who felt that way. I read that Starbucks was closing some 600 stores and firing thousands of employees because their revenue had dropped by 75 percent in one year.

For the first time in my life, I was watching pennies – literally. I found myself hesitating when buying anything. For example, I really did need a new sports jacket and new dress pants, but I decided they would have to wait. Even my supermarket purchases were pared down. At the beginning of the summer (when things still looked good), I would buy steaks and lamb chops for the Sunday barbeque. By the end of the summer, I was buying hotdogs.

At first it was a jolt to the system, and I was a little depressed by it, but slowly it started to feel good. I was living within my means. It lessened the pressure on me as my spending dropped. It felt good. But, strangely, just at that time, things started to pick up in business. After many missteps, closed doors and blocked roads, suddenly new highly profitable avenues were opening up for us.

It reminded me of what the founder of logotherapy, Viktor Frankel, wrote in the introduction to his classic *Man's Search for Meaning*:

> Don't aim at success – the more you aim at it and make it a target, the more you are going to miss it. For success, like happiness, cannot be pursued; it must ensue, and it only does so as the unintended side-effect of one's personal dedication to a cause greater than oneself or as the by-product of one's surrender to a person other than oneself.
>
> Happiness must happen, and the same holds for success: you have to let it happen by not caring about it. I want you to listen to what your conscience commands you to do and go on to carry it out to the best of your knowledge. Then you will live to see that in the long run – in the long run, I say! – success will follow you precisely because you had forgotten to think about it.

And this is exactly what happened to me. When I started to think in terms of helping somebody, suddenly success appeared at my door.

ONE DOOR CLOSES, ANOTHER DOOR OPENS

Three months after my trip to Georgia in the aftermath of the Russian invasion, Doheny Global Group signed an agreement with Georgia's Ministry of Energy to develop 100 megawatts of hydro-electricity via half a dozen run-of-river plants; this project was especially attractive because of the possibility to sell excess power to Turkey, where there is a tremendous shortage of energy and where a new transmission link to Georgia was being built.

We had scoped out the multi-national engineering firms specializing in hydro and decided to go with the Swiss-based Stucky Ltd., which had 80 years of experience in this field, having pioneered the double-curvature-arch river dams.

The feasibility studies were expected to take about 6-9 months to complete, construction another 1-2 years, with the timeline from signature to power-online in the range of 2-3 years, depending on complexity.

Pretty amazing!

In setting up the Georgia hydro project, I learned that there were a lot of opportunities in alternative energy projects throughout Central and Eastern Europe as well as throughout Asia. Anyone who could put such a project together in Pakistan, India, Nepal or just about anywhere in the FSU would have a good chance of obtaining generous government backing from one of the many multi-lateral agencies such as the European Bank for Reconstruction and Development, the World Bank, the Asian Development Bank and others. I decided to look into the feasibility of doing a project in Pakistan.

A couple years prior, when I had set up the first World Congress of Christians, Jews and Muslims for Vadim and Patokh in Kiev, I'd met former Prime Minister Benazir Bhutto. She had been invited as one of the guest speakers for the two-day conference. I had spent a lot of time talking with her and had been very impressed with her energy, honesty and charm. I felt like we had bonded in a unique way, and we had promised to stay in touch after it ended. Tragically, she was assassinated one month after our meeting. Her husband, Asif Ali Zardari, rumored to be the richest man in Pakistan, later became the country's president. I still had contact with family advisors, and I set up a meeting with President Zardari in New York to discuss an energy project in Pakistan. It went well, and we drafted a memorandum of understanding. Pakistan's Ambassador to the US, Husain Haggani, was sure that OPIC (Overseas Private Investment Corp.) would provide the necessary funds upon request from his country, stating that this was a top economic priority.

Besides Pakistan, other venues also looked appealing. For example, the EBRD (European Bank for Reconstruction and Development) was providing significant benefits for development in the Balkan countries, particularly Bosnia, where they had just completed the construction of a new electric grid tied into the Western European grid. Thus, Doheny could build a hydro plant in Bosnia, insure it against political risk with OPIC, finance it with EBRD and sell excess electricity to Germany at four times the tariff in Eastern Europe.

In the Ukraine, there were some 1,500 small hydro plants (originally set up to fuel individual villages) which had gone out of commission due to poor maintenance over the past 25 years. There existed the possibility of getting these back online relatively inexpensively, and at a potentially decent profit.

Also in the Ukraine, and elsewhere in Central and Eastern Europe, there was money to be made by capturing energy wasted when natural gas under high pressure made the transition from the Russian pipeline to city gates. All that was required was the installation of turbo expanders which have been around for many years in Great Britain and Germany but, for some reason, this technology had not been exploited elsewhere in the world. This left an opening for us.

Worldwide, there was a need for developing advanced energy storage technologies (such as ultra-capacitors), next generation bio-fuels (such as produced by hydrocarbon-emitting bacteria), and developing green energy from existing biomass (such as woodchips and other wood waste material).

Finally, in the good old US of A, there were plenty of opportunities, especially in developing small hydro as well as biomass facilities to produce electricity. There were many old paper mills which were going out of business, due to the decreasing demand for paper. As more and more people opted to access their news via the Internet, many of the country's newspapers were closing down or scaling down, and this was affecting the business of pulp and paper. But what was a door closing for the paper mills was a potential door opening for Doheny. Significant government funding was available for developing this type of clean energy.

Now, if I had stopped to think back then, I might have asked: "Even if it is clean energy, is it really good for the environment? Aren't you still chopping down forests, for God's sake?!" But just like I closed my eyes to the fact that I had a holy rabbi praying for the success of the producer of the *Texas Chainsaw Massacre*, I closed my eyes to such contradictions here.

Instead, I focused on the positive side of the equation – that renewable energy could be an exciting new income-producing field for Doheny, just when the economic situation made investment in real estate impossible.

To kick-start us in the right direction, I approached a few of my political friends, people whom I have known for years, and spoke to them about becoming my partners in this new Doheny Global Group venture. Their presence as our limited strategic partners would give us significant prestige on the international scene, especially in dealing with the many multi-lateral agencies such as the World Bank, the EBRD, USAID, etc., and the whole alphabet soup of other international agencies. Some important folks agreed:

- o General Wesley Clark (former Supreme Allied Commander of NATO)
- o Christine Whitman (former Commissioner of the Environmental Protection Agency and former Governor of New Jersey)
- o Tom Ridge (former secretary of Homeland Security and former Governor of Pennsylvania)
- o Jose Aznar (former President of Spain)
- o Philip Dimitrov (former Prime Minister of Bulgaria)

- o Mykhailo B. Reznik (former Ukrainian Ambassador to the United States)
- o Joe Reeder (former Under-Secretary of the Army under President Clinton and currently the head of government relations in DC at the then-largest law firm in the US, Greenberg Traurig)

HINDSIGHT

We suddenly had the credible beginnings of a real energy company. And God's hand was now quite obvious in the events of the past two years. At the time, when my anxiety was riding so high, I should have just put my simple trust in Him. Instead, I allowed myself to be caught in the maelstrom of events, buffeted by the seemingly random forces that were bouncing me from side-to-side like a tin can in a windstorm. I had felt out of control, resentful and angry.

Now I saw that every door which closed was a blessing from above. It was not apparent then, but in retrospect it was crystal clear.

When we first started out in business and formed the Doheny Group, we decided we would start a hedge fund with a plan to short the real estate market. In the end, we decided not to do that because the fund manager we found wanted too much of the fund ownership to make it worthwhile for us. All this cost us around $150,000, and we were frustrated and upset when that door closed on us. In retrospect, it is probably a good thing it didn't happen, as the country's hedge funds came under siege and thousands of them went out of business because of the sub-prime mortgage debacle and the global economic meltdown. We might have succeeded if we had shorted the real estate equity market, but then again, who knows?

Our next venture was to buy a small investment bank. This cost us probably another $100,000, not to mention the personal cost to me of spending seven months of my life studying to pass the Series

7. We worked on several potential deals until I stumbled onto the opportunities in Eastern European real estate. We then spent three months checking out Siberia, Moldova and the Ukraine and talking to lawyers, accountants and real estate consultants. We decided to go for it. I was upset that we didn't continue with the investment bank but, in retrospect, it was a good thing that we didn't do that for, once again, with the market meltdown, even the investment banking titans had collapsed. The world's largest investment bank, Citigroup, needed a government bail-out; Lehman Brothers, one of the nation's top five banks, went bankrupt; and Bear Stearns, another of the world's largest banks, got sold at fire-sale prices. Tens of thousands of Bear Stearns and Lehman employees lost their jobs in the blood bath. Hundreds of little banks, comparable to what we would have been, had all gone out of business, or were teetering on the brink of the abyss as there was simply little if any business to be had. If we had put all our efforts into this, we would probably have gone out of business too.

We worked for nine months on the shopping mall in Novosibirsk and 30 days before closing, when the cost estimate from our Russian partner jumped from $70 million to $90 million, we decided to back out of the deal, even though we had spent close to $300,000 on legal and financial due diligence, trips to Novosibirsk, etc. Naturally, I was devastated. Yet, once again, it was a good thing. If we had been involved in the deal, we would have been in great trouble one year after the closing when the bottom fell out of the Russian real estate market. We had planned on having a forward sale (which made the whole project feasible), but many of those types of contracts were broken by the buyers when the bottom fell out of the real estate market in 2008, even though there were significant penalties involved. Simply put, tenants would not have had the money to pay their rent. Banks would have pulled lines of credit. We would have been left with a partly-finished mall, with tenants backing out of pre-signed leases. It really was all for the good.

We had the same experience with our deal in Moldova, where we decided after nine months of work not to proceed. Once again, if we had proceeded, we would have had another troubled property on our hands.

That door closed, and Ukrainian real estate opened. I went through many agonizing months waiting for the Odessa deal to be signed. I was frustrated and aggravated that it didn't close. If we had closed though, with the global meltdown, we would have been sitting on a $38 million bank loan, having to make interest and principal payments and no sales on the horizon. We would have been over-leveraged and looking at losing *all* our investment! In retrospect, it was a real blessing that we did not close that deal.

THE GEORGIA DOOR

The meltdown in the world economy and the global real estate market forced us to look elsewhere and that led me to Georgia, where my partners quickly followed me to explore opportunities in renewable energy, and we brought together a prestigious group of limited strategic partners and lots of doable and profitable projects.

One door closed and another, even better one, opened.

The Book of Exodus quotes God telling Moses: "No person can see Me and live." When Moses persists in asking to know God, God answers, "You will see My back, but My face cannot be seen." The meaning of this verse is clearer to me now than ever before. We cannot often see God's presence in the events when we are in the thick of things, but in hindsight, when we look back and see what occurred, His role is suddenly all too clear.

I remember hearing a story from a friend, Sam Levinson, who on 9/11 was supposed to be on one of the planes that was hijacked, but missed the flight and then got stuck in traffic trying to get to his office at the World Trade Center. He was angry and frustrated. But if he had made the plane or arrived at his office on time, he would have died. So, too, with me. When things were going wrong, I couldn't see anything positive about it. I couldn't see God's intervention but, in hindsight, I could see His kindness to me – it was all for the good.

The Hebrew word for "world" is *olam* shares its root with the word *ne'elam*, which also means "hidden." What's the connection? In this world there is a lot of confusion between good and evil, and good is often concealed. It is clear to me now though that everything that happened – as painful as it was at the time – was all for the good. I also think that the fact that I've had to struggle has been good for my character. If it had all come to me too easily, I believe I would have become arrogant. The difficulties have taught me that no matter how much effort I put into things, it is all in God's hands.

What else have I learned? That I was wasteful with my money. I had no business leasing a $110,000 car. I had one of the most expensive cars in my county, and I certainly have never had the net worth to afford it. And then I got stuck with it because my lease with Chase Finance would not allow someone else to assume the lease. Anyone interested in the car – if I could find such a person, God knows I've tried – would have to take out a brand-new 36-month lease. This made no sense to people as they might as well get a brand-new car. This was a mistake I wouldn't make again. Meanwhile, I had cut over $250,000 from my annual overhead and learned to live a much more sensible and frugal lifestyle. I managed to pay off (half, not all) of my credit card debt and even got my American Express card back. This happened by a fluke. Here again God was very kind. This is what happened:

In December my wife went off to Israel to see the kids and grandkids, whom she missed terribly. We cashed in some of our frequent-miles points and got her a free ticket and, in a sign of the times, she stayed with our daughter Batya, rather than at a hotel. She was gone for four days, when on a Friday morning, I opened the door to the basement and was shocked to discover our belongings floating around in half-a-foot of water. There had been a few days of truly torrential rains and, as it turned out, the waters had overwhelmed the storm drains and backed up into our basement. It was a shocking site. The carpet was totally soaked and anything standing on the floor was ruined. It took a specialist in flood abatement some eight hours to get the water out of the basement and another ten days of hot air blowers, fans and dehumidifiers to dry it out. The insurance company paid us $85,000 for the damage. This is because five years prior – when I wasn't counting pennies – we had invested over $100,000 to redo that basement. My wife wanted the below-ground space to feel like the rest of the house in terms of décor and ambiance, so that our guests – and we had lots of them – would not feel sub-human staying there. After the insurance paid off the water damage, we used $10,000 of that money to replace the carpets and make some other small repairs, but decided to use the rest to pay down my American Express credit card debt. What a relief!

NEW FOCUS

After all those experiences, I was no longer focused on just getting rich. The struggles of the past two years of deals that didn't close and today's financial crisis taught me this. I learned that there are a lot more important things in life – like friends, like family, like being close to God. All that matters so much more than becoming a millionaire.

Did I still want to be wealthy? Sure. But I learned that the chase for money wouldn't make my life rich. Being truly rich is enjoying meaningful moments with people I love and care about. Snuggling up in bed with my wife and my girls and watching a movie while we eat popcorn is a lot more special than closing a deal.

All this was reaffirmed to me by a visit to a house of mourning – an experience that God, in His great mercy, clearly felt I needed to have.

The husband of one of Batya's friends had passed away, and Judy and I went over to comfort the mourners at her request, though we did not know the family. The Jewish sages initiated this custom in ancient times, understanding that those who lose a loved one need a shoulder to cry on and those who come to lend that shoulder need a reminder of the fragility of life.

Well, it worked on me. There were other moments during that visit that I will never forget, because they drove home lessons I needed to learn.

When the young widow spoke about how great her deceased husband was with his small children – how they were the center of his life, how he played with them constantly, seemingly never tiring of their simple games – the guilt rolled in.

I don't play with my little kids enough. On weekend afternoons, which should be my prime opportunity, I slink off to take a nap while the kids play by themselves or with Judy. I start off every week telling myself that this one will be different – this weekend I will hang out with the kids – but my weary body wins the battle and exhaustion wipes out my resolve. During the week, I am torn between work and kids, and work always wins out.

My kids notice, of course. They chide me constantly that I have missed each birthday at least once because of my business trips. I can just imagine what they will say when they sit *shiva* for me: "Dad never played with us. He missed all our birthdays because he was working too hard."

Maybe this is why it was so uncomfortable for me to visit that house of mourning. All my weaknesses came rising to the surface to confront me. The demons I have been running from suddenly surfaced in all their ugliness.

During the hour we were there, when I walked down the hall in search of a bathroom, I saw the deceased man's brother hugging the children. He was holding to them ever so tightly as if trying to replace the love and hugs they were already missing from their father. It was such a special moment. I could sense the strength of the feelings being transmitted in those hugs, and I wondered if – from somewhere in the spiritual beyond – the father was channeling his love through his brother.

Right then and there, I told myself to hug each one of my kids when I got home. I'm generally a pretty good hugger, but just yesterday Sara came to ask me for a hug, and then she wanted to discuss her homework, but I was too preoccupied with my work to take the time to do more than hug her. I resolved to remedy that.

Another moment that spoke to me was when the young man's Torah study partners talked about his commitment to learning – how he always pushed himself to get up in the morning, how he was always ready to learn a little bit more. Will anyone say that about me after I'm gone? I know the answer to that one. For sure not. The last serious study partner I had, I left behind in Israel twenty-five years before. Since then, I have been dabbling in my Torah studies, but I have not had the serious commitment to learning like that young man.

I miss it. I also miss not being involved in my community the way I used to be when I lived in LA. There I had a lot of friends and contacts whose lives I was able to touch and who touched me in a meaningful way. In New York, I hardly knew anybody; I had so few friends. How many people would come to my funeral? I doubt that the people I am making business deals with would show up. Why should they? Of what value would I be to them dead?

Since I have left the non-profit world, I have felt a void in my life. In that house of mourning, I resolved to fill it with meaningful stuff, to make a difference again, to leave an imprint when I am gone, so that my life would have counted for something.

I know that I went there to comfort the mourners, but the visit turned out to be a look in the mirror – and the picture was not pretty. Was I overly guilt ridden? Well, wouldn't you be if you were me?

As I was sitting there, my chair – one of many delivered by a special non-profit organization that brings chairs and prayer books to the houses of mourning – suddenly collapsed under me. The screws holding it together let go, and it broke apart. It was as if the weight of the thousands of people who had sat in this chair became suddenly too much for it to bear, and it collapsed either from all that pain or from the added burden of my guilt. I knew right then and there that God was sending me a sign: "Wake up before you collapse!"

Thank you, God – I think I got it.

LESSON LEARNED

The next morning, I turned a new leaf. Instead of letting my girls take the bus to school, I decided I would drive them myself. "My work can wait," I told myself. I woke them up with kisses and hugs, and I rolled out the family convertible to make this a really fun ride.

The day was warm and sunny. I put on a music tape and let it blast out as I drove down the street with three of my most precious belongings sitting in the car with me. They were laughing as we drove with the top down on a beautiful spring day singing together to the music, waving our hands over the top of the car. We stopped for hot chocolate and bagels on the way, and by the time we arrived at the school, I felt so good to be enjoying the simple things of life.

I let them out, kissed and hugged them and sent them on the way to class, hoping that they would remember this day. Life is a series of moments. Nothing more, nothing less. That day, inspired by the experience of the house of mourning, I tried to create a moment they would remember. It made my life a little bit more meaningful. I hope they will talk about it when I am gone.

And just in case they don't, I am writing this book – to explain myself. So that they know that for some of the years when I was not there for them, I was working hard to help other people. I hope it will matter to them that their father started Aish LA and initiated programs like "20-Something," which brought thousands of young Jews drifting away on the sea of assimilation back home to port; that he raised awareness through "Help Our People Know," about the plight of Russian Jews who for so many years had been denied knowledge of their roots; and that he spread Torah values throughout America with "Words Can Heal." That program – along with my two books on prayer, *Powerful Prayers* and *How to Get Your Prayers Answered* – was my proudest accomplishment. I want them to know about that.

24

Words Can Heal

"Words Can Hurt, Words Can Heal" was the brain-child of Chaim Feld, an Aish rabbi from Cleveland, Ohio. Chaim had come up with a concept for a campaign to expose people to the Torah view of *lashon hara*. Literally meaning "evil speech" in Hebrew, *lashon hara* is shorthand for a whole series of ethical laws which prohibit gossip and slander, specifying how we are allowed to speak about others, under what conditions we can ever say anything negative, and the degree to which we must just generally watch what we say. One can easily imagine how much nicer the world would be if even a small portion of these laws were followed.

It was a worthy project and, in early 2001, Rabbi Weinberg asked me to help Chaim enhance, expand and package the program so that it would have the large-scale appeal of my other programs.

To me, words like "enhance," "expand" and "large-scale" are like a red flag to a bull. They get my juices flowing and I go into over-achiever attack mode. I don't know if this particular neurosis is described in the disorder manual of the American Psychiatric Association but, if it is, I could be the poster boy for it. If I take on a project, I obsess and obsess until I figure how I can make it the biggest and the best. My drive to succeed takes over, to the detriment of everything else. I don't know how to do it half-way. This obsession with total success is almost a curse. I'd love the peace of mind that comes with settling for less.

I immediately began to see the full range of possibilities. I wanted to turn it into a program that would speak to all of America and not just the Jewish world. I envisioned it as a national movement, with a media campaign, a book, celebrity spokespeople, and a board of prominent leaders that would get this issue noticed. Up to this point, I had been fundraising for Jewish education so I was limited in what I could accomplish, but now I had a vehicle with universal appeal.

As this would take me out of normal Aish fundraising mode, I formed an independent non-profit organization for the project and hired some top-shelf consultants, including David Suissa, who had started a boutique advertising firm in LA which he had built up into one of the pre-eminent ad agencies in the nation. He had won many awards and was brilliant as well as very dedicated, having single-handedly published the magazine *Olam* as a Sunday newspaper insert. He agreed to work with the team I had put together in creating a media campaign.

Though Chaim had wanted the title to be "Words Can Hurt, Words Can Heal," through many discussions with David and his people, it got boiled down to "Words Can Heal." The feeling was that less is more. Don't complicate the message and keep it positive. Everyone liked it.

While exploring who would make the right spokesperson for the campaign, I contacted Goldie Hawn. I had never met Goldie but had a relationship with her via e-mail and telephone as I had repeatedly tried to interest her in coming on one of my Israel missions. She had always been friendly and receptive, but we could never work it out. When I e-mailed her about "Words Can Heal," she agreed to meet – it was right up her alley.

It was an important lesson. You need to figure out what people care about and use that to get them involved. Goldie is a sensitive, caring human being, and the message of "Words Can Heal" truly appealed to her in a way that a mission to Israel, featuring politicians and businessmen, did not.

She invited me to her Pacific Palisades home and I arrived at the appointed time. At the front door, I was met by her housekeeper who was just leaving. She said Goldie had told her to expect me and that I should come in and wait. Goldie and her partner, Kurt Russell, were flying back from Las Vegas and were a little late due to strong head winds. Meanwhile, I should make myself comfortable. With that she took off, leaving me alone in Goldie's house.

It was unbelievable, and it sure was exciting. I went into the living room and sat down on the oversized sofa, but after a while I got antsy and started to walk around. Seconds later I was joined by a big friendly Saint Bernard who sniffed me up and down, then having clearly decided I was harmless let me be. I called Judy to tell her what I was doing, "Can you guess where I am? I am walking around Goldie Hawn's kitchen!" I felt like such a voyeur. I know Hollywood is just hype and what really counts in life is being a good person, but nonetheless this was fun. I loved every second of it. Silly I know, but I was having a great time. With Judy still on the phone, I described the various public rooms downstairs – the kitchen, the den, the backyard, etc. Of course, I didn't go upstairs where the bedrooms must have been – that would have been an invasion of privacy and betrayal of the trust I had been granted.

Fifteen minutes later Goldie and Kurt showed up. Goldie kicked off her sandals and sat cross-legged across from me, while I gave her the whole pitch for "Words Can Heal." She loved it and agreed to become one of our board members as well as the spokesperson for the program. We were off to the races.

As a rabbi, I don't have any physical contact with women, except for my wife and immediate family – no hugs, kisses on the cheek, not even handshakes. But Goldie took me by surprise as we were saying good-bye. Suddenly she wrapped her arms around me in a hug and kissed me on a cheek. I was mesmerized and couldn't move. I mean this was Goldie Hawn! I am normally fairly good at keeping people at a distance, but Goldie caught me totally off guard.

After I left, I quickly called Judy and told her what happened, adding that I will never wash that cheek again. Wow – what a way to get started.

THE LAUNCH

WCH – as we began to call the project – just clicked. One thing led to another to another and the whole program took on a momentum unlike anything I had ever experienced before. David Suissa's staff, together with Michelle Chandler, our PR person, developed a complete campaign including billboards, newspaper ads, slogans, radio commercials, even a 30-second TV commercial. The TV commercial would have cost over a $1 million to produce, but David convinced the crew that worked on other campaigns for him to do it for free, so the whole shoot cost us only $10,000 in expenses. It was a powerful and moving collage of one-word statements from people of many different nationalities all saying a different word in the "Words Can Heal" pledge:

I pledge to think more about the words I use.

I will try to replace words that hurt with words that encourage, engage and enrich.

I will try to see how gossip hurts people, including myself, and work to eliminate it from my life.

I will not become discouraged when I am unable to choose words perfectly, because making the world a better place is hard work.

And I am helping to do that, one word at a time.

I went to see Len Leader, former President of AOL Investments, who had been a supporter of Aish. He loved the concept and agreed to give us $300,000 to launch WCH in the Washington, DC area with a complete media campaign which would include a 30-second commercial on CNN seven times a day. We got Jerry Stiller, who played George Costanza's loud-mouth father on *Seinfeld*, to do radio commercials for us and also tape a message to members of Congress.

Soon, we had resolutions in the House and Senate (thanks to Congresswoman Ileana Ros-Lehtinen and Senator Harry Reid) calling for a national "Words Can Heal" day. They both passed of course.

We were really picking up steam. We approached the National Press Club with the idea of doing a lunch program with me and Goldie. It turned out to be the best-attended lunch they'd had that year, except for the one with King Abdullah of Jordan. C-SPAN and PBS showed the unedited broadcast on over 3,000 stations nationwide. Goldie spoke beautifully for a half-hour about the importance of kinder speech and teaching it to our children.

After that, I went to see Pete Coors, whose company was based in Colorado, where twelve students and a teacher were killed and many others injured in the Columbine High School shootings. He committed $250,000 to develop a complete curriculum that could be used in schools nationwide, including a 30-minute rap production to teach the WCH message to high-schoolers. It was powerful and spoke the language of inner-city kids.

Meanwhile, I recruited a national board of directors for the project, which included everyone from Newt Gingrich on the right to Alan Dershowitz on the left and represented all religions.

Executive suites across the country were suddenly open to me: KB Homes, Applebees Restaurants, McDonalds, Guardian Life Insurance, All State Insurance, CNN, Schwab, Bristol Meyers, Eli Lilly, Bristol Meyers Squibb, Kraft Foods, Sears, and on and on. CEOs and company chairmen were welcoming me and I was zipping across America in a whirlwind of meetings.

In the end very few of the large corporations came through, and I learned another very valuable lesson. I was coming in at the top level through my networking, often meeting with top brass. They would give me an enthusiastic response then pass the idea down the line to the head of marketing or public relations or corporate sponsorships. These people quite often resented that it was coming from "on top" and would put up a lot of passive resistance, or let it sit in committee forever. Eventually, I saw that there was just so much dead wood in corporate America that it was difficult to get anything done that way. I had heard this said before but never truly understood it. Most people don't want to take a risk on something new. They prefer to do things the way they have done them for years rather than take a chance on something new. Since WCH was new, in its infancy, most large corporate relations departments passed – Peter Coors was an exception as well as a few other corporate leaders who took on the responsibility and made sure their subordinates followed through.

To raise the money that was not coming in from corporate America, I decided to hold two fund-raising banquets, one featuring Goldie Hawn and Susan Sarandon, and another featuring New York Mayor Rudy Giuliani. This time it was not hard finding honorees and donors from the Forbes 400 list. The degree of interest was amazing. We raised over $1 million from the two dinners.

One of the first people I approached to be the banquet honoree and to make a significant contribution was Richard Driehaus, the hedge fund manager of $3 billion plus. When I went to meet him in his offices – in a historic and exquisitely restored building in Chicago – he seemed surprised that we wanted to honor him. He carefully checked out my credentials and said he'd let me know. Three months and many calls from me later, I had heard nothing from him. Then a month before the banquet, he called to say he would participate and donate $250,000 as well.

I found it interesting that the first person I approached came through. It was as if God was saying, "You really don't need to work so hard. Just pay some attention to Me. If only you ask for My assistance, I will answer." But I was so caught up in the chase that I forgot to pray for help. In retrospect, I see that God sent me what I was looking for early on, but since I wasn't including Him in my life, He let me stumble around all by myself. As I have often said, there are definitely strings between us and God, but it is not God who is pulling the strings, it is us.

(Although Driehaus agreed to participate, when he and company president Roger Geurin arrived for the dinner at the St. Regis Hotel in New York, they were a bit worried that perhaps this was all a big scam and no one would be there. It had seemed like such an outlandish proposal – come to a gala dinner with Susan Sarandon and Goldie Hawn – and Geurin, the quintessential skeptic, wasn't sure it was all going to happen until, of course, it did.)

MEDIA BLITZ

Meanwhile, we commissioned a national poll to see what the American people thought about the issue. The poll found that that 80 percent of Americans believe that verbal slander is a problem in the workplace and 71 percent think that people talk behind their backs.

The results of the poll turned a soft news story about another non-profit do-gooder effort into a hard news story about righting a societal wrong. We mailed the poll results as well as information about the campaign launch to thousands of media outlets nation-wide, knowing that we would create a stir. Just how big I had no way of knowing, but I found out in a dramatic way.

We were just finishing dinner, and my ten-year old daughter went to answer the ringing phone. She came to announce that it was someone from CBS asking if this was the home of Rabbi Irwin Katsof of WCH. I figured it was a friend playing a practical joke. I took the phone half-expecting someone to start laughing on the other end. Instead, I heard a young woman's very polite and official voice, "I am calling from *Good Morning America* on behalf of the host Bryant Gumbel. We received a press release, and I am trying to track down Rabbi Katsof. We have made several calls over the past few hours. No one answered at the office. We weren't really sure where you lived so we have been combing different phone books in California and New York. Is this the right person?"

I said, "Yes."

"Then great. Bryant Gumbel would like to interview you tomorrow morning between 8:04 AM and 8:09 AM Can you get to the studio by 7 AM for make-up?"

Of course, I said, "Yes."

I was ecstatic! I immediately called Michelle Chandler, our PR person, and we rehearsed all kinds of possible questions and answers for hours. Michelle told me that in the allotted 4-5 minutes, all that counted were sound-bites. I had to know my message and shape it to fit whatever questions I was asked. I could not let myself go off into uncharted territory, no matter what curves I was thrown. My message was that a poll has shown negative speech was a national problem. We had a broad coalition and a great program. I rehearsed over and over.

That night I tossed and turned, unable to sleep, rehearsing my responses to all of Gumbel's possible questions. Although I had been on national TV before when Larry King and I did our book tour, this time I was flying solo and it was the morning news hour, the most watched TV slot of the day. It was big stuff. In the morning, I could have dispensed with my usual caffeine fix as the nervous energy coursing through my veins was probably equal to three cappuccino double shots.

I was ready! My answers to any possible questions were reverberating in my brain. I knew them cold. I've heard that in combat training, they drill you to the point where you no longer have to think about your response, it's pure reflex; if you need to take the time to think, you are dead. This works for pilots in dogfights and infantry in hand-to-hand combat and trench warfare, and it also works for interviewees facing Bryant Gumbel, then one of the most experienced on-air hosts. I was ready for combat.

I had a local car service take me into the city as I was too jittery and distracted to drive, and besides I wanted to continue reviewing my notes. I arrived in plenty of time. I was greeted by a friendly receptionist and brought to the waiting room. She offered me tea or coffee – like I needed more caffeine – and also fruit and water. In the room was a TV monitor so I could watch the progress of the shows.

Shortly, I heard them announce that "after our next commercial break we will be hearing from a rabbi who has launched a national campaign to eradicate gossip and slander." I was escorted onto the sound stage as strains of a Dove soap commercial played in the background. It was super cold on the set. I think they keep it that way to balance the heat from the stage lights. They sat me down in a comfy armchair and attached a miniature mike to my lapel, then strung the wires through my shirt.

Seconds later, Bryant Gumbel was facing me and greeting me coolly, as he rifled through the sheaves of paper in his hands. This was one of half-a-dozen interviews he would do that day and one of thousands he routinely does a year. Nothing out of the ordinary for him. And then – yikes! – the floor director was crouching in front of the camera and counting down, using his pointing fingers for emphasis – "ten, nine, eight …three, two, one, you are live!"

"Good morning again, this is Bryant Gumbel with Rabbi Irwin Katsof. The new 'Words Can Heal' movement announced today a national poll claiming that over 80 percent of the American people believe they are talked about behind their back at work and that over 70 percent of the American people believe that verbal slander and abuse is an issue in their lives. Rabbi, do you really think you can do something about this? Come on now, this has been going on for ages. It started with Adam and Eve and the snake. What's the big deal anyway?"

What did he have for breakfast? He had come out swinging. But my training kicked in and my reflexes took over. I smiled and took a deep breath.

"Bryant, thank you for having me here today to talk about 'Words Can Heal.'" (Big smile.) "Our national survey indeed showed this is an issue the American people are deeply bothered about and that it is important to them. Yes, we believe we have tools to help deal with this issue."

"What kind of tools, rabbi?"

"We are launching a national media blitz today complete with billboards, TV and radio ads and a 'Words Can Heal Pledge' which we encourage people to take by going to our website. We also have a beautiful 30-second TV commercial on this subject."

"Talking about the commercial, let's give our viewers a chance to be the first ones to see it."

The TV commercial rolled. All 30 seconds at 8:03 AM on national TV. That alone was worth about $500,000 of paid ad time. What a break!

"Rabbi, we only have a minute. But do you really think you can make a difference?"

"Yes, Bryant, we do ... One word at a time, one child at a time, one classroom at a time, we can make a difference. It might take a generation, but all good things that are important take time, and we see from the feedback we have received already that this is a task worth working on."

"Well, thank you, rabbi for your time and good luck!"

Phew! It was over, and I was exuberant. Michelle was waiting in the ante room, and we jumped for joy.

From then on, it was one show after another. Altogether, we were on over ninety TV news shows in the next thirty days and scored over 160 different mentions in magazines and newspapers nationwide – some were mere snippets and some were full articles. Most were positive and a few negative.

On the negative side, we got nailed because Mort Zuckerman, the CEO of *US News and World Report* who also owns the *New York Daily News* was on our board. The *Daily News* has more than a few gossip columns. When its competitor *The New York Post* got wind of this, they ran a box on its editorial page ridiculing an anti-gossip campaign with the publisher of the big gossip rag on its board. Mort called me, furious, especially so because he had never actually agreed to be on the board!

I had sent him a letter asking if I could add his name to the effort and, when I had not heard back, I assumed it was okay. Big mistake! We took his name off post-haste, and I had to apologize profusely.

On the positive side, Goldie Hawn and Susan Sarandon got on *Oprah* to publicize their new movie and managed to talk about WCH for a good five minutes. They showed the book cover and gave the WCH pledge. It was a homerun!

We rolled out the first school curriculum in Colorado. The feedback from students, teachers, and parents was excellent. We were getting thousands of hits on our website as people were downloading the pledge and signing up for our weekly newsletter with handy tips for speaking with greater kindness.

Meanwhile, I approached Steven Goldsmith, a senior domestic policy advisor to then President George W. Bush. Steven had been on one of my missions to Israel and he agreed that WCH would fit well with the president's agenda; he set up a meeting for me with Alicia Clark, who worked in the policy department. From then on, every three weeks or so, I would get a strange call from someone on the President's staff. The person would say that he or she had been referred to me by Alicia Clark and would invite me to DC for a meeting. This went on for three months during which I had five different meetings with five different staffers. I never really understood who they were, but if they wanted to meet me to discuss WCH, then who was I to say no? They were all very smart and well read; they clearly understood campaigns and social movements and were evaluating my plan. I had a feeling I was being judged and graded.

(Of course, each time I went to the White House, I'd wander around and call Judy. "You wouldn't believe where I'm standing now!")

Finally, I got the word from Alicia Clark telling me that the policy, politics and strategy departments – all those people who had met with me – had all signed off on WCH and had suggested to Karl Rove, the President's chief of staff, that it become part of his campaign to make America a better society. This meant being a part of a Rose Garden presentation of a series of national non-profit social programs.

As part of the planning for that presentation, I got a call to meet with policy advisor John Bridgeland (Steven Goldsmith's replacement). The date set for the meeting was Monday morning, September 11, 2001 (yes, that's right!) and I flew in Sunday night so I could be fresh, ready and on time. He had been vague on the time – it could be as early as 8:30 AM or as late as 11:00 AM, but he would page me when I should come over.

I was sitting less than a mile from the White House waiting, when I got his page at 8:45 AM. I immediately returned the call but there was no answer at the White House. I checked and re-checked the number and kept calling, not understanding why the White House switchboard was not answering.

Then I happened to glance at the TV which was on but with the sound off. And I realized that the call would never come, as the world changed in a blink of an eye. The World Trade Center was under attack. Moments later I heard a boom in the background – the third plane slamming into the Pentagon (though I did not know it then).

I looked out my window and saw thousands of people streaming down the street. Everyone on Capitol Hill had been told to go home and so there was a mass exodus. I quickly packed up and went downstairs to my waiting car. I asked the driver to take me to ABC news, where I had an interview scheduled, but he refused to take me there as he said it was next to the Israeli Embassy, and he was afraid that might be the next target. Realizing that my interview was probably cancelled as well, I said, "Well then take me to the airport. I might as well fly home." But the airport was closed and so was the train station. I managed to get to the Thrifty Car Rental place moments ahead of the throngs of people who did not want to be stuck in DC like me. Due to the thousands of people fleeing Capitol Hill, it took me three hours just to get out of town in my rented car, but eventually I hit the highway for home. Cellphones weren't working but my e-mail still was, so I was able to let Judy know I was okay and on my way back.

I never did hear from the White House and the Rose Garden presentation never happened, as the Bush administration's domestic agenda got hijacked (so to speak) by events. For the WCH program, it meant that we had to pull back since the nation had other things on its mind. We had been fortunate that we managed to accomplish what we did before 9/11.

By mid-November though, we were able to continue. In many ways our campaign's message was even more salient in terms of healing some of the rifts among the different ethnic/racial/political groups in America. We continued rolling out our educational program complete with teachers' lesson plans, curriculums for different age groups, accompanying posters for the classrooms – all done in very hip, modern images and bright colors, illustrating the WCH message. Every school that participated got a complete package including corollary material. We also launched a character development program for schools and after-school programs.

The response was terrific, and famous people volunteered to get involved, among them Arnold Schwarzenegger, Maria Shriver, Henry Winkler, and Rob Reiner. Miss Texas wanted to make this the centerpiece of her activism program. (I think eradicating world hunger and working for world peace was getting a little stale.) She attended our LA and Chicago events and came to the Rudy Giuliani banquet complete with her little tiara; apparently, she is required by pageant rules to wear it at all official functions and photo ops. It added some glamour and maybe even helped me get some donors. I mean, Rudy Giuliani or Miss Texas: Who would you rather have your picture taken with?

All in all, the WCH program was a big success, and it opened more doors for me than anything I'd done before. I had gotten an important message out to America.

That's what I want my kids to remember about me and obliterate any feelings of parental neglect they may harbor. I want them to know that I always tried hard – okay, too hard – and that even though there were a few years when I went astray trying to get rich, in the end I got back on track. I went back to doing what I had done all my adult life – devoting myself to a cause for the greater good. And in the early 2000s, the greater good meant clean energy.

25

Saving the Third World

In my new incarnation as a clean-energy czar, I met the President of Pakistan, Asif Ali Zardari, in his suite at a Manhattan hotel. He was in New York to address the opening of the UN General Assembly. In the meeting with us was Riaz Lalligee, a close confidant of the President who handled the Bhutto-Zardari family's business ventures and who would be our partner in the deal. At one point the President called in Husain Haggani, the Pakistani Ambassador to the US, and said point blank to him, "This deal is a priority. Do everything you need to do to assist Doheny. Let's get this done."

The project involved generating electricity from rapeseed, which is generally grown to produce soaps and oils. It burns very well, has no negative carbon dioxide effects and is plentiful in Pakistan. The President said this deal was so important he was prepared to allocate 90 percent of Pakistan's rapeseed harvest to this deal.

In my naïveté, I figured this was a slam dunk and had already started counting our profits. We immediately drafted the terms of a joint venture agreement between Doheny and Riaz's group but, after we shipped it off, a week went by without a response. When two weeks went by, I sent an urgent text: "WE NEED TO TALK!"

That got a response from Riaz, who apologized for not being in touch sooner. He said he had been traveling in China with the President. He would get to it immediately. But another week went by. I sent another urgent text. This time his response said, "Call me on my London cell." Now that was puzzling.

When we finally did speak, Riaz said that there were several items in the draft agreement that he really didn't like. His key concern was that we had suggested in the terms of governance that in the initial stages Doheny would handle all the bookkeeping and the disbursement of funds, and then, as the projects started and outside money started to flow, we would bring in a third party (such as a Deloitte or Price Waterhouse Coopers) to handle the accounting. Riaz was not thrilled about this. He saw no need for an outside firm and certainly didn't want any disbursements handled by Doheny.

This objection raised red flags. There is a little piece of US legislation called the Foreign Corrupt Practices Act. It is a detailed law that prohibits US corporations or citizens from bribing a foreign company to get a deal. It outlines a whole host of acts which are illegal such as paying middlemen as supposed consultants. Many individuals and executives of US corporations have been indicted, convicted and sent to prison – and been heavily fined to boot – for participating in bribery in foreign countries. All the partners at Doheny were very firm that we would not participate in any illegal acts. No deal was worth going to prison for, no matter how much money was involved.

The problem I began to foresee in dealing with the Pakistanis was this was how business was done there and, indeed, in most parts of the world. For example, Riaz insisted in bringing in a consultant who would arrange for the purchase of the land. He wanted to be involved in arranging the purchase of the equipment and had a sophisticated scheme in mind for how the equipment seller and the builder would contribute equity which could eventually disappear. We gently tried to explain to him that we could not structure the transaction this way, but every time we tried to rewrite the governing documents to keep things legal, he kept returning to the same theme.

We went back to the drawing board and tried to rewrite the agreement yet again and come up with a legal structure that Riaz and his group could live with. We e-mailed a new set of documents to him, but the same scenario was repeated. No reply for a week. This time no reply to urgent texts. This was an exceptionally frustrating way of trying to do business. On top of it, when we did speak, there was always a suggestion of a structure that we couldn't accept.

To make it even more complex, if I called Riaz in Pakistan, he would say in a hushed tone, "I can't talk now. Call me in London next week." Or he would talk as if in code. He would say things like, "You know our friend that we talked about..." Or, "You know the boss man" (referring to the President) "... well, I am traveling with him next week ... he likes this and thinks it is good." He would never say the President's name on the phone nor refer to any deal specifics. The apparent assumption was that someone was listening in on the conversation.

When I would reach him in London, he'd be clearer but never really straight forward. He would insist on a personal meeting in London or Dubai. He was always positive and excited about the deal, but the pattern would repeat itself – no answers to e-mails, texts, etc. It was like a script from the movie *Groundhog Day* – basically the same bad day over and over.

After four months of this repetitive routine, Paul, David and I discussed the situation and decided that it just wasn't worth our time and effort any longer. By now, there were a lot of other opportunities on the horizon, and it made more sense to pursue those.

I sent Riaz an e-mail suggesting we have a talk about the status of the deal and, true to form, never heard back from him. Only this time, I didn't follow up. And, predictably, nothing happened.

NEPAL

Though Pakistan did not work out, I was not discouraged in my quest to bring clean energy to the Third World.

Meanwhile, the US seemed to be teetering on the brink of another Great Depression. The economists and pundits were no longer wondering if there will be a recession, for it had arrived and was only getting worse. Citibank was trading at under $5 as was AIG and Bank of America. Some 600,000 Americans were losing their jobs every month, and the unemployment rate was inching toward 10 percent.

Stories abounded of top bankers being laid off. Foreclosures were at a record high. People I knew had closed down their hedge funds, stopped going out to eat at restaurants, moved back in with their parents. This was worse than anything we could recall in our lifetimes.

Leaving all that behind, I got on a Virgin America to London, connecting to Air India bound for New Delhi and from there connecting to India Air for Kathmandu, the capital of Nepal.

I had been giddy planning this trip, because I had wanted to visit Nepal ever since 1978 when I embarked on my four-year trip around-the-world and, after a year in Europe, ended up in Israel where Aish HaTorah changed my life. Needless to say, I never made it to Asia. Back then, I was a spiritual thrill-seeker, yearning for a connection to my soul – and I found it in Jerusalem.

I had never looked back and never regretted that I had missed imbibing spirituality at the feet of the gurus in India and Nepal. But, nevertheless, I did want to see those mystical places. So when, in March of 2009, I heard from the Infraventures Division of the World Bank that they were looking for a hydro deal in Nepal, I jumped at the chance. And a day after my 54th birthday, I found myself embarking on a trip to Kathmandu – not as a spiritual seeker but as an energy developer.

Why was the World Bank so hot for Nepal?

Well, with the Himalayas – the world's highest mountain range – passing through and with eight of the world's fourteen highest peaks situated in Nepal, there is a lot of melting snow and falling rain, producing 144,000 megawatts of hydro power potential. Meanwhile, Nepal had a serious energy shortage. In Kathmandu, electricity was on only six hours a day – the other eighteen hours were called "load shedding" – better known as "blackout." Outside of the capital, the situation was even worse. Furthermore, Nepal borders India which also had a severe energy shortage.

For Westerners, these kinds of conditions are hard to comprehend. Sometimes in a bad storm the lines may go down and we lose power for a few hours but, anything more than that, we freak out. Power shortages are rare events in our daily lives, while in Nepal they are as regular as sunrise.

Within two weeks after hearing of the possibilities from the World Bank, I had networked my way into the US State Department office in Kathmandu (through my US Department of Commerce contacts in the Ukraine – what can I say: it's a small world). They were thrilled that a US company would come to explore business in Nepal and said there was very little business interest here. (I would soon learn why.)

I spent several hours on the phone with them and exchanged heaps of e-mails. By the end of two weeks, they set up quite an interesting schedule for me. I would meet the presidents of the three largest banks in Nepal; these banks could potentially finance any deal we do there. I would also meet the president of the Nepal Electric Authority, as well as representatives of the companies responsible for the country's largest hydro projects. I would also meet several smaller hydro developers who might want to do a joint venture with us. And, of course, representatives of the World Bank, USAID and the Asian Development Bank.

It was a very intense, jam-packed schedule with close to forty meetings in four days. That is a lot of meetings!

WELCOME TO KATHMANDU

I'll spare you the details. Let's just fast forward.

Kathmandu turned out to be everything I did not expect. Rather than a blissful haven for truth-seekers, a spiritual oasis of Asia, I found it to be over-crowded, noisy and totally unpleasant. It was not what I imagined the hippies of the 1970s flocking to. But a lot has changed since then.

Imagine being confined to a games arcade – 25x25 feet – filled with five times the number of people it should legally hold, and all the machines are ringing and pinging simultaneously while everyone is clamoring for a place in line. That scene defines Kathmandu for me.

My wife once remarked, after we had spent a day at Disneyland, that if she had to work at a ride like "It's a Small World" or "Pirates of the Caribbean" – and listen to the same tune playing over and over all day long – she would go insane. I agreed. Well, Kathmandu made Disneyland seem like a monastery in comparison.

The streets were filled with hundreds of scooters and motorcycles, all zig-zagging past each other or careening on collision paths. The streets were mostly one lane with two-way traffic. The congestion was unlike anything I had ever seen, except maybe in Manhattan at times of grid-lock. But what made it worse than Manhattan was the quantity of motorcycles on the road and the fact that they didn't seem to follow any discernible traffic laws. At any one time, there would be fifteen motorcycles swarming around my taxi from every angle. The drivers wore helmets (this appeared to be the law) but not the passengers, and almost every scooter and motorcycle had at least one or two passengers. I'd often see a man driving, a girl in the back, sitting side-saddle to accommodate her skirt, and a baby on the handlebars. How can that ever be legal? And by what logic would the law require the driver to wear a helmet (because it is dangerous) but not a baby? And who in their sane mind would put a baby on the handlebars (law or no law)?

Hanging over the city was a grey cloud of pollution. It was so bad that many pedestrians and motorcycle drivers wore cloth masks to cover their noses and mouths. I should have followed their example. By the third day, my throat was stinging from the foul air, and I was sucking down cough drops.

I was wound pretty tight after my transfer in New Delhi, where I had arrived on a non-stop from London. Part of my trip was on India Air and part on Air India (not the same airline), and I was required to collect my luggage from one to check it onto the other. But I was a transit traveler, and I did not have a visa to enter India, which caused me no end of problems collecting and re-checking my luggage. I tried to explain to five different customs officials (all nervous after a series of terrorist attacks in Mumbai and being extra cautious) that I had to get my suitcases, but to no avail. They kept telling me to go sit in the corner and just wait for someone to come get me. "No one knows I am here," I insisted. "I came in on India Air and am flying out on Air India. How will they even know that I am sitting in the corner waiting for them and, if they do, then how the heck will they ever find my luggage?" No one had a comeback to that one, but they were not willing to let me go either.

I had visions of someone in New Delhi walking around town eating my protein bars and vacuum-packed tuna, while I spent the next week in the transit lounge dying slowly of hunger. I kept thinking of my daughter Batya who, when her children misbehave, sends them to a corner of the room for a "time out." I had been put in the corner too.

Lo and behold, after thirty minutes of punishment in the corner, someone showed up asking if I was Irwin Katsof. "Yessiree Bob, that is me," I perked up. "Can I leave the corner now?" He looked at me like I was weird and asked me to come along. He took me to another transit lounge and parked me in another corner for twenty minutes. "My flight is boarding now!" I fretted. But he assured me that I would make it in plenty of time and my luggage would get on it too.

As it turned out, the flight was nearly an hour late – I don't know if it was waiting for me and my stuff, or just on Asia time – but, when I arrived in Kathmandu, my bags were there waiting for me. The arrivals lounge felt more like an inner-city bus station, dimly lit by barely-functioning fluorescent lights. As I learned, the airport authorities don't replace light bulbs when they burn out since there are only six hours of power a day anyway, and they need to save money when the electricity is functioning.

As I walked out of the terminal, I got a whiff of smog, dust, dirt, diesel exhaust, all attacking my nose, while my ears were assaulted by unrelenting noise of thousands of people yelling for taxis, yelling for their relatives, yelling for arrivals to come here, go there. Among the sea of signs, I saw one for my hotel, the Yak and Yetti. Its representative, a grizzled elderly man led me to a thirty-year-old (at least) mini-bus and loaded up my luggage. We headed for my first encounter with Kathmandu's traffic purgatory.

Where were all the beautiful vistas I had expected? Where were the Himalayas? Not here. At least not on this side of the smog.

On the way to the hotel, I thought my life was about to end some five times but, at last, I made it. At the hotel, everyone was unfailingly polite. Repeatedly, I was greeted in the traditional Nepalese way with intricate hand gestures, a bow and *Nemaste*, which means

"I bow to the Divine within you." And I began to fall in love with the gentility of the Nepalese people. With such congestion, such over-crowding, you'd think people would be at each other's throats, but they are not; instead, they are incredibly courteous to each other. If they were New Yorkers, they'd be punching and shooting by now.

GETTING THE PICTURE

Over the next three days of whirlwind meetings – each one requiring a twenty-minute battle through the streets – I asked a lot of questions about the country, the infrastructure, the electric grid, the tariff being paid for hydro power, the difficulties of getting a project done, the possibility of getting a long-term power purchase agreement, etc.

At the end of three days, I had a list of upsides and downsides to doing business in Nepal. Bottom line, it was not the best place to do business. Why not? Let me count the ways:

o To begin with, the government was weak, inept and corrupt. A crisis could erupt at any time, and strikes and work stoppages happened with regularity.

o The Nepalese Electrical Authority was bankrupt. The tariff was low and not likely to be increased any time soon. Even if it were, people paid their bills in Nepalese rupees (in other words, not in real money). And you couldn't sell power to India.

o Transmission lines were not stable, and there were no plans to improve them anytime soon.

o People were stealing from the grid left and right, and illegal hook-ups were the norm.

o Violence, theft and sabotage on the construction sites required the developer to hire a virtual army for protection.

o Owners of licenses have unrealistic expectations and often wanted 10-15 percent equity for their license. Meanwhile, the interest rate was 10-11 percent.

On the upside – yes there was an upside – there were 144,000 megawatts of potential. There were people who would invest in equity, and the Nepalese Electrical Authority (despite its problems) has always paid its bills. The US Department of Commerce would go to the moon to attract investment here. Any profit would be tax-free for ten years, and there were other great tax breaks as well. All businessmen here were Western-educated, had multiple graduate degrees, spoke English well and were smart, well-informed and a pleasure to deal with.

But there were better places in the world to do hydropower without the downside.

Of course, it was good that I came and found all this out first-hand. And I saw that no one I spoke to had all the pieces of the puzzle. Everyone seemed to have a small corner of the pie but not the whole pie. At the end of three days of meetings, I felt like I was probably one of the better-informed people on the state of Nepal hydro and its prospects. I had asked a lot of questions and did a lot of fact-checking until I put the jigsaw puzzle together.

I felt good about my experience. In three days, I had moved from total ignorance to being pretty well informed. I felt like a real businessman. I had taken in a lot of data, sifted out fact from fiction, organized it, dissected it, prioritized it, summarized each meeting and e-mailed my partners and then made a final summary of the situation with a suggested plan of action, which everyone agreed upon.

Now it was time to experience the real Nepal. I had learned that the Nepal I had imagined when I was young did exist, but it existed outside of the Kathmandu Valley, some 30 kilometers into the countryside. I arranged a tour with Itrek the next day.

THE REAL NEPAL

With my Itrek guide, Shree, a bright young head of the company (who I later discovered was Nepal's gymnastic champion in the late 1990s), I headed to Bhaktapur, 30 kilometers from Kathmandu as the crow flies, but not by Nepalese roads. Since there really are no good roads connecting these two cities, we traveled by cow path, on which we were joined by real-live cows as well as yaks and motorcycles. Off the road, we saw local farmers tilling their fields and others carrying huge and heavy loads on their heads.

After some 45 minutes on a dirt path, we finally reached Bhaktapur. The third largest town in the Kathmandu Valley and once upon a time (in the 15th century) the capital of Nepal, Bhaktapur is known as a cultural treasure trove. Many tourists visit Bhaktapur yearly to get a sense of the indigenous lifestyle here and to see the majestic view of the Himalayas. And I was going to be one of them.

I had told Shree I wanted to get as far away as possible from the hectic urban pace and density of Kathmandu, while traveling no more than an hour out of town. I was not disappointed. Old Bhaktapur is a walled city where cars are not permitted. It is full of temples, pagodas, palaces and ancient monuments, some dating back 500 years. We meandered up and down narrow alleyways and found a fascinating new site at every turn.

I loved it all – the history, the people, the simple, slow-paced way of life.

I turned a corner and found a woman soaping up her hair from a big pot of water. This was the first time I encountered this, but not the last. It became a common site throughout the next two days of hiking and trekking. In most places outside of Kathmandu, there is no indoor plumbing; water is available at public faucets, but it flows only at certain unpredictable times. Thus, people wait for the water to be turned on, never knowing when that may be, and when it happens, they quickly run to fill up their water jugs and immediately use the water for their needs because it can be turned off at any time.

I came upon people taking showers, brushing their teeth, washing their hair, their clothes, their pots and pans with water from wells by the side of the paths where we were hiking on or in the alleyways of the towns. They didn't seem embarrassed about it, though normally they behaved and dressed very modestly. In fact, tourists were advised not to wear shorts, short skirts, or bare their shoulders in deference to local sensibilities.

After three hours of wandering the alleyways of Bhaktapur and buying a lot of local souvenirs for my family, we headed out. It had been a wonderful experience. My best memory was visiting a little shop (no bigger than a toilet on a Boeing 747) selling hats and sweaters. In the corner I saw a ladder going to an upper floor and heard stomping from above. I asked what was upstairs. The shop-keeper invited me up, where I found his sister sewing on an old-fashioned, foot-pumped sewing machine; she was making the goods he sold down below. Her workroom doubled as the family's bedroom and, in the corner, stood another ladder. In response to my inquiries, they took me to the third floor, to the family's kitchen outfitted with a wood-burning stove.

I learned that this was a typical Nepalese country house. The bottom floor is usually either a shop or stable, the middle floor the bedroom, the upper floor the kitchen. Electricity is non-existent (Kathmandu where they have power for all of six hours a day is an exception), so women work by the door or window, their faces weather-beaten, their teeth rotten or gone, yet their facial expressions warm and soft.

We spent the night in Nagarkot, a favorite tourist destination due to its spectacular views of the whole Langtang Himalayan mountain range. We stayed at the "Country Inn," which was listed as a three-star resort. My room was a 5x10-foot space but the small-ness was more than compensated for by the floor-to-ceiling window overlooking the valley. The bed was a wooden pallet, the bathroom a toilet-and-shower-in-one, literally (you sit on the toilet to take a shower which is positioned right overhead). Normally, I would never stay in such a place but I found its simplicity charming.

I called Judy and the girls using Skype. I uploaded the photos I took earlier in the day and relived every moment with them. I told them that there was something about the simplicity of the lives of the people I saw that touched me deeply. Perhaps it was the primi-tive way they lived – with an average income of $400 a year. Perhaps it was their gentle smiling faces, despite the fact that their lives were so tough. (Nepal has one of the highest infant mortality rates in the world and life-expectancy for adults is only 55 years!) Perhaps it was the image that I came to have of them as conquered and yet un-bowed. I responded to these people with – and this is the only word that comes to mind – reverence.

A HIKE IN THE HIMALAYAS

The next morning, I woke up while it was still dark and met up with Shree's cousin who would be my guide for this part of the trip. We would hike through the mountains from Ngarkot through Bena-pi and Nala to Dhulikhel. I don't know what I was thinking when I agreed to this 13-kilometer hike (which is about triple the longest distance I've ever walked and that was on level ground and not at elevations of 2,000 meters).

The hike took me five hours, and it was well worth it, though it was painful. By the last leg of the journey, I could hardly put my foot down without experiencing excruciating pain from a multitude of blisters on the soles and heels of both my feet. My leg muscles were burning and I was visibly limping.

When we were a short way from our end destination, the sky clouded over, lightning lit up the mid-day sky and we were pelted by a freak rain-storm that lasted only minutes. It occurred to me that my camera and Ipod were probably the most conductive objects on the mountain and could well attract the lightning. In my mind flashed a newspaper headline: ENERGY DEVELOPER ELECTROCUT-ED IN FREAK STORM. I wanted to get off the mountain as soon as possible but, though our destination was near, I could hardly walk anymore. In the end, the car was able to drive a bit up the road and pick us up.

I must have also gotten dehydrated because when we got into the car in Dhulikhel, I drank a two-liter bottle of water and still didn't need to urinate.

Yet I left uplifted and exhilarated. For five hours, we had followed a pathway through the mountains and had not met another tourist. We had passed by the front doors of many homes, stopped to chat and to watch the adults working, the kids playing, the animals grazing. In one field where they made bricks, I saw two young girls, perhaps eight or nine years old, carrying loads of clay on their backs easily weighing 30 pounds, with bands around their foreheads to stabilize the loads. It broke my heart to see them work so hard. I stopped to take their picture. They smiled and posed for me holding their heavy loads. My heart melted. I gave them some rupees.

That experience was one of many that I found poignant and inspirational. Simply put, the people I had met along the way had touched my soul – especially the little children. They would suddenly appear along the road, their faces always dirty and noses always running. Yet they had innocent smiles and their eyes shone with genuine warmth. I fell in love with several of them. I usually gave them a few rupees although they rarely asked me for anything. I wondered what their futures held. Would they even make it to adulthood, as one of every seven Nepalese children dies at a young age. Their impish grins, runny noses, dirty faces, ragged clothes – all cut right into my heart. I wanted to do something to help them. They had so little financially, yet seemed so much more content than my kids. I could hear my son asking me for a fancier cellphone and my daughter wondering if she could upgrade hers.

Our Western goals are so out of whack; it seems like we are on an ever-ascending escalator to greater and greater material acquisition, though this has never brought us true happiness. This is not to say that the Nepalese have found true happiness in their poverty, and I am sure they would change places with us in a heartbeat. But it seemed to me that, overall, they are more content with their lot. Their strivings are few – a good meal, a pair of shoes. Their attitude brought into sharp contrast my and my family's current financial situation.

While I loved my life in the US and felt proud of my country – our standard of living, our health care, our values – nevertheless, I envied the Nepalese their simplicity. I felt alive among them in a way I didn't feel at home. Why? I could not answer that question.

As soon as I got onto the plane for home, I was planning a return. I wanted to take another hike in the mountains, perhaps with some of my friends, this time around the Annapurna Range and the Mount Everest base camp. When I got home, I went and bought hiking boots and resolved to train in Rockland County where there are mountain hiking trails. I even went to a mountaineering store to check out the equipment.

I decided this hiking would become a new hobby of mine, a way to express myself. That and photography.

While in Nepal, I took over a thousand pictures. I enjoyed this immensely. I would get right in people's faces to get their eyes, their souls, their expressions. Several times I just plopped myself down on the street in the market to grab the right expression. It gave me great pleasure. Perhaps this was part of my maturing process, finding new ways to express myself ...

26

Looking Good, Feeling Good

By April 2009, after all our investigations into alternative energy – hydro and biomass – we had pretty much decided that:

We would do a hydro project in Georgia (166 megawatts of hydro-electricity via five run-of-river plants) and in the Ukraine (rehabilitating old existing hydro plants that had fallen into disuse).

We wouldn't be doing a rapeseed project in Pakistan because we simply could not come to an agreement that would accord with the US Foreign Corrupt Practices Act. Not to mention that, according to the CIA, the Pakistani government could fall any day.

We wouldn't be doing a hydro project in Nepal because the government there was weak, inept and corrupt. Any construction site required an army to protect it; if not, all the supplies would be immediately stolen. Transmission lines were not stable, and people were stealing from the grid left and right, illegal hook-ups being the norm. To top it off, you couldn't sell excess electricity to India.

We wouldn't be doing a hydro project in Bosnia because of all the political infighting in the Balkans. We did a due diligence trip there for three days only to learn that the people in Serbia and Bosnia and Herzegovina all still hated each other, and thus it was almost impossible to get anything done, even though EBRD would have loved to fund some projects there.

We wouldn't be doing a hydro project in the US, even though the field of small hydro (where our partner Stucky shone) was wide open. Upon further investigation, we saw that there was just too much government regulation and, because of this, few (if any) hydro plants had been built in recent years. The environmental laws were just too stringent, and it took too long to work through the permit process. I spent time tracking down lawyers involved in hydro power in the US and realized it wasn't worth the effort.

BIOMASS

However, it was during that investigation that we discovered that producing clean energy from biomass was indeed a huge opportunity here in the US. Biomass is the name given to renewable energy sources: wood, farm products, manure, landfills and food waste. We were in particular attracted to biomass from wood chips. We found a consultant specializing in biomass, Mid-South Engineering of Arkansas. They were expert engineers in their field, in a similar way that Stucky was an expert engineer in hydro.

Why was biomass from wood chips so attractive?

At the time, there were many paper mills closing in the US due to foreign competition, rising fuel costs and plunging demand in the paperless economy of the digital age. In terms of developing a biomass energy plant, this happened to be good for us. You need several things when developing an electricity generating plant, and first and foremost is a dependable source of fuel; you need to be able to sign a long-term contract for this fuel with a stable price and guaranteed delivery. And this you could do with wood producers.

It is important also that the fuel is close to the power plant or it becomes cost-prohibitive to transport it. In terms of a paper mill, it usually sits close to the source of wood, or on a river which can be used to deliver the wood easily and cheaply. The mill to chop the wood is usually on-site and has all the permits in place.

Furthermore, communities with closed paper mills would embrace us, as we would be bringing back jobs to their area. In many ways it was a perfect storm as the US government was pushing more renewable energy sources, while the demand for pulp and paper was decreasing.

The new $787 billion American Recovery and Reinvestment Act (ARRA), the stimulus plan that then President Barack Obama had signed into law on February 17, 2009, provided very attractive financing packages for biomass energy, giving as much as 30 percent in a capital grant once the plant was operational – meaning that you got back 30 percent of the cost of the equipment once you started the plant. This meant excellent financing possibilities.

THE NEXT GOAL

We now have to identify which paper mills to focus on. And this is where Mark Culpepper of Mid-South Engineering came in. Mark had several projects to show us, but two in particular looked good – closed down paper mills and power projects where the fuel supply could be available on a long-term basis since the paper mills were built close to the source of lumber. All we would need to do would be to add on the electricity-generating component.

Mark connected us with people in Greece where, we had previously found out, similar tax incentives existed, and there was a good possibility of doing a similar project on the Greece-Bulgaria border.

Paul and David immersed themselves in this area and became experts in understanding the development of biomass power-generating plants. It amazed me how they could absorb so much new information. In three weeks, they had taught themselves pretty much all that one could possibly know about the industry, both from the technical perspective and from the financing perspective. I was trying to merely grasp the basics to be able to explain the deal to others. I went on Google to see what I could find. I typed in biomass and stimulus plan, and a front-page article from the *Biomass Magazine* popped up, which gave a great explanation of the new tax code and why this was such a good opportunity for us.

According to Paul, the opportunity to become super-rich by developing clean energy from biomass was greater than anything we had undertaken since 2005.

Paul and David and I had a long talk on Sunday. Paul reminded me how, when I left Aish, I said that what I hoped to be able to do was to give away as much money as I raised for Jewish education each year. In my best fundraising year that was $2 million, but it usually hovered between $500,000 and $1 million.

Once I struck out on my own, I gave $250,000 to charity in 2005 and a bit more than that in 2006. But my giving had dropped precipitously in 2007-2009 as my income fell away. Well, Paul said that, as far as he was concerned, I was closer than ever before to actually being able to make that dream come true through the opportunities that biomass presented.

This was exciting news, but I had been disappointed so many times in the past four years that I was hesitant to let myself get too excited about the possibilities.

David felt that we had a very small window of opportunity before many other energy entrepreneurs put all the pieces together and realized what a treasure-trove existed in the closing of old paper mills when combined together with the new tax incentives of the Obama legislation. We needed to move fast.

We still kept Georgia hydro moving forward and fired off an e-mail to Stucky to clarify some points in their pre-feasibility study, but any trip to Tbilisi to finalize the letter of credit with the

Georgian energy ministry would need to wait until we got the US deals closed. I awoke excited and full of anticipation. Maybe I had learned my lessons about wealth, and God was actually going to let it happen at last.

MY SILENT PARTNER WEIGHS IN

Of course, I had to tell my silent partner that all his prayers were finally paying off, and I did when I came to Israel for my annual Passover vacation.

In a sign of the times, I brought the family on free tickets that we were able to get through frequent-flier miles because of the many El Al trips we had taken over the years, and we rented an apartment at a fraction of the cost of a hotel. On the plane over, I recognized several people from Monsey, and they were also staying in rented apartments rather than in hotels due to tough economic times. In fact, the hotels were functioning at only 50 percent capacity, and taxi drivers all reported that tourism was down significantly.

As soon as I arrived, Rabbi Zilberman wanted to see me. And of course, he asked me how the hydro project in Georgia was going and how long it would be until we would start construction. I explained to him that we were just finishing the pre-feasibility report, then we'd be arranging the line of credit with the bank, and only then we'd arrange the financing. So, actual construction was somewhat down the line.

He was particularly intrigued by the world situation – as he read no newspapers, nor accessed the Internet – and he sought to understand how we could work in Georgia with the existing tension. I explained that, in our case, the tension was actually good – as long as it stayed in the cold stage and didn't break out into war, of course. The fact that Georgia was threatened actually made it more important for the West to fund energy projects there, as well as in the Ukraine, in order to help these countries attain energy independence from Russia.

He found this fascinating and made a note of it. He asked what was happening in Pakistan. I realized it had been a long time since I had given him an update, as we had abandoned Pakistan a few months before. I explained to him the different projects we were working on, particularly the exciting prospects for biomass in the US. I said that if someone had told us a year ago that we would be exploring alternative energy venues, I would have told him it would be more likely that we would be exploring farming on the surface of the moon. It is strange the way God's hand leads you. Paul, David and I had been talking to a staffer at the Department of Energy in DC to understand the different provisions in the new legislation when she happened to mention a 30 percent grant for a project's capital cost.

We said, "What?! Tell us more."

After we did additional research, we realized what a bonanza this was for biomass projects, which quickly became our number one priority, and even closing Georgia went onto the back burner for ninety days. We also networked through our US Department of Commerce contacts and found out that Greece had similar grants of 30-40 percent of a biomass project's capital costs. And so, we began exploring biomass in Greece as well as in Bulgaria, Romania and Latvia, all of which had similar incentive provisions (some better than others), making such projects highly attractive.

But the US was our top priority right now. It was only a matter of time until everyone figured out what we knew about the tax incentives, and we wanted to get a running head-start.

And, finally, we were exploring the development of ultra-capacitors, a new type of battery which can be used with renewable energy such as wind and solar energy storage but, more importantly, can be of tremendous use in the harnessing of energy in hybrid cars.

(The stimulus plan has allotted $2 billion for these types of innovations.) We had been contacted by a Ukrainian businessman who was involved in a company that actually had some of the best technology in ultra-capacitors worldwide, and he was interested in having Doheny invest in his company. We initiated discussions with him to see if it was indeed possible to bring this technology to the US and elsewhere.

PERSONAL PROGRESS

Rabbi Zilberman was fascinated to hear about our progress. He said that he was praying three times a day for us. He listened intently for two hours as I explained all our different business lines. At the end, he paused, thought for a while and then said, "When we met last met a year ago, you seemed very tense." (This was when Odessa was pending and mired in delays.) "Now you seem very calm. What has changed?"

I explained how I had cut my cost of living significantly. In the process, I realized that having a lot of money to spend wasn't what made me happy, that I was working on getting pleasure out of the basics in life. I had been brought to my knees by God, brought as low as I think I could have handled. I was happy that I had not been tested any further – by having to declare bankruptcy or by losing my house to foreclosure. I felt like I had given it all up to God and accepted that whatever would be, would be; it was not in my control, and I could live with that. As a result, I felt happier than I had been in years and more content with my lot. I knew that if I had become rich earlier, I probably would have become arrogant and doubted that I would have kept my values straight, so what had happened really was for the best.

I still felt like I was lacking sufficient meaning in my life. I wished I had a charitable project that I could throw myself into. I envied those who were dedicated to a cause that was bigger than them. While in Israel, I had met some old friends who were passionate about non-profit projects they had started, and all I could think was: "I envy you. I wish I had that in my life. You are lucky to have that, and you have no idea how special it is." Still, I felt more content now than I did a year earlier.

Rabbi Zilberman said that it showed. He told me he thought that the fact that we were still alive in business while the world economy was in shambles *and* that we had so many deals in the pipeline was an amazing accomplishment and a sign from God. When everyone else was failing, it is quite something that we were growing and progressing.

When he finally left, I felt enriched by the meeting. He always left me feeling better, and I believed he was a special and holy individual. It was good to have him as my partner. I still hoped to get rich one day, but not for the status or to be able to buy nice things as much as being able to help him with his school. That would bring the meaning to my life that I felt I was lacking.

When I got home, I went to my file cabinet and pulled out the original contract we had written together on October 15, 2006. Wow, that was three years before! I read through it again. My part was to work physically – and boy oh boy, had I done that – while Rabbi Zilberman's part was to pray daily for my success. I was obligated to give him specific details of what deals needed praying for. But it was the last paragraph of the contract that jumped out at me. It said, *"God will bless you from Zion and you will see the good of Jerusalem your whole life – you, your children and children of your children and all Israel."*

No matter what has happened financially, I felt that I had already been blessed, especially after spending Passover with my eight beautiful children and now seven grandchildren. I felt like my cup was really running over and the blessings were overabundant.

Strangely, at a time when I cared so much less about getting rich, Paul told me that my chances were higher than ever. He said he thought that, between the Georgia hydro projects and the US biomass projects, I had the chance to fulfill the dream I had back in January 2005 when I left Aish HaTorah and went into business. It actually could really happen now, and I could make enough money to become a philanthropist able to make a difference in the world through my charitable giving.

It has been a long road, and that would certainly be a nice thing if it did happen. With Rabbi Zilberman praying for me every day, I should have had no doubts.

27
Doing the Right Thing

The process of personal growth, of personality change, continues to amaze me. The dynamic forces at work within me, within all of us, that push, shove, and yank us in different directions humble the greatest psychologists. There are fifty-two divisions in the American Psychological Society, and each one has many subdivisions, and each one proposes to explain the complex phenomena of the human personality. Only an arrogant fool could claim to know exactly how this all works. In fact, if he did, I would send him to a shrink!

It is as if there is some kind of magnet within us – or is it without us? – a force field of energy which pulls us in various directions at times, and when it is at work within me, it never fails to surprise me.

On one spring morning, I had two meetings in Manhattan. The first was with Daniel Zeta (not his real name), one of my "friends and family" investors. I met him for lunch in the Garment District where he works. His wife had recently been diagnosed with breast cancer and she'd had a double mastectomy; she was just starting reconstructive surgery. When we sat down to eat, I asked him how she was doing. I wasn't just making small talk; I was really concerned, having had a mother who died from cancer, though I didn't tell him that.

When I asked him about his wife, I reached into my holster and – I have no idea where the urge came from – I turned off my cellphone. Now, in my case, this is comparable to a deep-sea diver turning off his oxygen tank. I might miss an e-mail! I might miss an important message from an investor and a deal could collapse, God forbid!

But something welled up inside me which said, "Turn the blasted thing off and just be here now!" That was a message that influenced me deeply when I was a kid reading the 1971 bestseller *Be Here Now* by Richard Albert (aka Baba Ram Dass), who taught that everyone is a manifestation of God and that every moment is of infinite significance.

Because I did that, I enjoyed the lunch and felt more present. As I left the restaurant, and I started walking down the street, I turned on my cell to see what messages I had missed. Nothing earth-shattering. I walked and typed my answers, using my peripheral vision to make sure I didn't walk into anyone. A silly thing to do, but something I see all the time on the streets of Manhattan now. It's better than driving and texting though, something which has become all too common. A few e-mails required my action, but nothing was earth-shattering.

I went to my next meeting – with my good friend Vitaly Pruss. Again, I turned off my cellphone. We spent a good hour together, even though he continuously checked his own cell every time it beeped. The next day, I got an e-mail from him:

> *Irwin – it was good seeing you yesterday. I noticed you didn't pull out your cell even ONCE while talking to me (which I can't say about myself). Is this a new thing you are doing? If yes – it is great.*

I answered him that I had made a conscious decision to do this. He wrote me back:

> *I definitely noticed and appreciated it. Great thing to do! You know I love you. But one of the things I remember about you is that as soon as the Blackberry got invented, it took away your presence*

and got you very distracted. At least from me. I remember you
checking it every single time we met. I hated it. I hate it in myself.
Great, great, great development. Please keep it up.

This was wonderful encouragement.

Though I've known for a long time that I was addicted to the cell, it became more apparent to me while in Nepal, where I had no service for a week and I experienced pseudo-vibrations. It was as if I was hallucinating. It reminded me of what they say about people who lose a limb and then still "feel" sensation in it. That's exactly what happened in Nepal when I felt my cellphone vibrating even when it was impossible!

COMING UNGLUED

After that, something inside me decided that it was time to become unglued from the tyranny of the cell – in those days, the Blackberry.

When I returned home, I came to the dinner table and left it in my study. I turned it off earlier in the evening, even if it meant missing incoming calls or e-mails. I decided that I would no longer check it, or read or reply to any e-mails while I was driving. I knew this was something I shouldn't be doing anyway and wanted to stop a long time ago.

Again, when I took a break for lunch, I left my Blackberry in my study so that I could relax for a few minutes and not be constantly off balance. I still had a long way to go to unleash myself from the torment of this unrelenting slave-driver and ruthless master, but in small baby steps – halting, stumbling, falling, pulling myself back up – I began to detach.

When a baby starts to walk, no matter how much he stumbles and falls, nothing can stop him. It is just a matter of time before he is walking. The process is irreversible. I could see the same thing happening to me.

I felt myself relaxing and becoming more centered and at peace with myself. This allowed for some small openings inside my consciousness, and a greater sense of God's presence began to creep into my day. It felt good!

I had decided to trust in God more. And I could see the light at the end of the tunnel – the biomass deals were coming together, financial ruin was no longer imminent, my spending was under control, and I was living within my means again. I was not sure where my new power came from, but somehow, someway, this time I had the strength to implement previous insights.

For sure, I'd had this awareness before. For sure, Judy had pointed out to me many times that the incessant checking of the Blackberry was compulsive and unhealthy. Instead of living in the here and now, I was always under the spell of this small device. I lacked the strength of character to stop myself from checking it constantly.

And now, at last, I was winning this battle. Undoubtedly, I will fall again and have to pull myself up again. Like King Solomon says in Proverbs, "A righteous man falls seven times but rises again."

The body and the soul are in a constant struggle for who is going to rule our being. Usually, the body wins out because the body is screaming at us in surround-sound, and the soul is this little voice, whispering in the corner, "Hello … don't forget about me, please."

Perhaps this time, my soul was winning out. I actually envisioned myself on board a large ocean-liner, running over to the railing and tossing my cellphone overboard into the churning sea. I wasn't prepared to go that far in real life, but I liked the image and held onto it as I went to dinner and left my cell sitting on my desk, all alone in the dark.

THE BODY'S WEAPON

When I discussed this with my friend Dr. Fred Mermelstein, who is a research scientist, he told me that an addiction to the cellphone uses the body's own weapon – a neuro-chemical called serotonin. This, in his words, is how it works:

"The successes we can have in the workplace can be enormously satisfying and the many accretive little steps (such as answering e-mails) make us feel better and even excited as we sense we are getting closer to achieving our goals. Each success and feeling of accomplishment that comes with each e-mail drives up the levels of serotonin in our brain. (This is the same neuro-chemical that makes us feel good in other aspects of life, and which is also triggered repeatedly in addictions to sex, gambling, chocolate, drugs etc.) The self-satisfaction that we feel causes the serotonin in our brains to rise, and we come to crave it on a continuous basis. When this becomes incapacitating and when we start to hurt those we love, we need to do something to control it. The strength to do so may come through faith in God. Interestingly, strong faith and the positive feelings that come with such devotion may also stimulate serotonin levels to rise."

When I heard this, I said, "Fred, you are telling me our brains secrete this drug, this serotonin into our system when we do something we perceive as pleasurable. Is that right?" He confirmed it.

"So," I said, "if I am so busy and distracted that I don't get the pleasure available from *real* experiences – such as hugging my children or my wife – then I start to look for it in the instant pleasure of the Blackberry, or, God forbid, things like gambling, drugs, porn, etc.?" And, again, he agreed.

"That reinforces what I am feeling! When I slow down and really connect with my beautiful family or with God, I feel great. The more I can access this simple, real stuff, the less I need the fake stuff like the Blackberry or speeding in my Audi to get a rush of serotonin."

"Hmmm," he said, "Irwin, you're on to something."

SPEAKING OF THE BODY

Because the previous year had been an exceptionally difficult one, I'd neglected my body as well as my soul.

Emotionally my life had been in turmoil, completely unbalanced, out of whack. I had been like a tempest-tossed ship; I felt like my very soul was being torn asunder, ripped from its roots and thrown into the detritus of life. This was because the prospect of a financial collapse frightened me more than anything. It wasn't just about not being able to pay the bills; it meant giving up a dream – the dream of making it, the dream of becoming a philanthropist, the dream of being a giver rather than a taker.

As a result of all the stress, I'd lost all my discipline of healthy living. I had always prided myself on being fit and in shape. But unable to withstand the pressure, I ate more and more, and I gained twenty-five pounds – that means I gained several inches around my waist and went up four suit sizes. I had to bring all my suits to the tailor repeatedly, until there was no more material to let out. The Vietnamese tailor in my hometown looked at me with her big mournful eyes and said, "No more material here." She said it in a whisper as if she, too, was embarrassed by how fat I got. I was forced to go to Syms to buy new suits – a doubly humiliating experience as I hadn't bought a suit at a discount store in thirty years. But now I had to pinch pennies and shop with normal citizens, the denizens of urban America, the bargain hunters.

Two summers before, when he participated in my Israeli mission, Rick Perry, then the Governor of Texas, had given me a beautiful Texas Ranger belt-buckle as a present. It was the last night of the mission when he presented it to me in a wood and glass box, and I was quite touched by the fact that he had thought of schlepping this gift all over Israel during the week of the mission. The oversized belt-buckle featured – very prominently I might add – the Texas symbol, the lone star in gold and silver tones. When he gave it to me, the Governor said, tongue-in-cheek, "Oh, by the way, this lovely item was made by one of our more loyal state employees when he wasn't making license plates." So I guess it wasn't real silver if it was made in prison. I still loved it.

The only problem was that there was no actual belt attached to it. But David Nance, one of the mission folks said, "I'll take care of it for you." He took it back to Austin and, sure enough, three weeks later a gorgeous, genuine black alligator belt showed up at my door by FedEx. I wore it with pride, though only on special occasions because it was so huge.

When we started exploring renewable energy deals in America, I called Governor Perry and set up a meeting in Austin. I got up early to catch the 7 AM flight and, as I was getting dressed, I figured this would be a perfect day to wear my Texas belt and buckle. For sure he would want to see me wearing his present.

I put it on – or I should say, I tried to put it on. I stood in the bathroom in shock, because I couldn't even get one end of the belt to meet the other end. There was simply no way – minus donning a male girdle, which I had read about and seriously contemplated buying – that I could instantly remove the extra inches that I had added to my waistline.

I couldn't believe this! I was so looking forward to wearing the belt. I knew the Governor would ask about it, but I pre-empted him and told him I was going to wear his belt today, but when I went to put it on, it wouldn't fit anymore. I was pretty embarrassed about this and explained how I had put on the extra pounds, not that he couldn't see it for himself.

Naturally, we then launched into a discussion of the importance of fitness. Indeed, the Governor wore a pedometer on his belt so he could measure how many steps he walked each day. All his staff members also wore these pedometers.

Hearing him talk, I made a decision to get back in shape.

I flew home and discussed it with Judy. She had recently been introduced to the gym at the Jewish Community Center in our neighborhood. I decided to check it out. They had a deal where they waived the new member charge, so I felt I was keeping to our family austerity plan. But even if I couldn't afford a private trainer any longer, there was no excuse for me to become an aging, overweight businessman. I used to be a treadmill fanatic but, in the past few years, I have found it causes too much stress on my spine. I ended up with a sore neck after using it, so I chose to work out on the elliptical trainer instead.

I approach all things methodically and like to measure my progress. So, I kept track of my calorie burn. After a few weeks, I was up to 60-90 minutes of exercise a day. As soon as I came home every morning, I would write it down on a chart: Sunday – 800 calories, 80 minutes, 5.17 miles; Monday – 750 calories, 70 minutes, 4.72 miles, and so on. Losing weight is a pretty mathematically simple exercise. One pound equals 3,500 calories. Burn more than you consume (or consume less than you burn) and you start to lose weight.

Keeping track made me feel good, and I could see my progress. I would also weigh myself each morning when I first woke up. After a month, I had worked up to burning around 4,000 calories a week and, after two months I was down 10 pounds. I felt great. My old clothes began to fit again.

It was time for the big test. I took my pride-and-joy out of a dark corner of my closet; I had left it there so I wouldn't be confronted with my human frailty on a daily basis. Slowly, I put on my Texas belt. Not only did it make it round my waist, but it buckled! The Alamo still stood. I felt like a proud Texas Ranger!

I decided to wear it all the time, as my regular belt tore and then got lost somehow, and I hadn't bought a new one. Maybe a part of me just didn't want to go out and buy a new one. Or maybe, I just didn't know how to do anything in moderation. If I was going to watch my pennies, I was not going to spend money on a new belt. Anyway, putting on my Texas belt gave me more pleasure than stepping on the scale. It was a little audacious to wear in New York, but what the heck? I could be audacious – I'd been to hell and back and lived to tell about it!

RENEWAL

Through my many painful experiences, I have learned that doing business is not easy. If it was easy, everyone would be rich. The reason everyone is not rich is that doing business requires a lot of intelligence, skill, patience and perseverance, and (last but by no means least) a lot of God's grace. No matter how smart you are, I am convinced that the Almighty has to assist you, or it simply isn't going to happen.

In May 2009, Paul and David went to Little Rock, Arkansas, to meet with Mid-South Engineering, a firm specializing in biomass. They spent two days looking at possible biomass projects that Mid-South had identified for us. From their previous research they knew that to make any biomass project doable, we needed three key things, or it was simply a non-starter:

o a long-term, stable supply of wood chips to be used as a fuel source o a long-term bankable purchase agreement for any electricity we would generate from said wood chips; we could be developing a lot of electric power, but if we didn't have anyone (financially strong and stable) who wanted to buy it, we would never get the bank financing for our project

o a proper contract for the engineering, procurement and construction (EPC) part – that is, for converting a paper mill into a biomass energy plant

At the end of sixteen tiring hours of driving around, they zeroed in on three particular projects that we would have to take the next two months to examine, in order to work out the due-diligence details. That meant that even if everything looked good, it wouldn't be until the first quarter of 2010 (nine long months away) before we would be able to even close the deal!

After that, it would take nine to eighteen months before the plant became operational, and the money started dribbling in.

See what I mean?

POTENTIAL PROJECTS

The first potential project was in Mississippi. Here a 50-megawatt plant could be developed in an area with a huge pine stock (in excess of 2.5 million tons per year), which could provide all the necessary fuel. The local county had already paid for a 60-acre site to be cleared. The county had also issued $10 million in bonds to provide funds for the infrastructure, of which $2 million was still available. In addition, the State of Mississippi would provide $10 million of grant money to the county for further development of the project.

At first glance, this looked very exciting. It certainly had the long-term source of wood, and the county was already invested in the construction, so this made it more likely that it would happen.

While we would still need to negotiate for a long-term power purchase agreement, there was a lot of potential there.

There were also two sites in Missouri. Each of these sites could generate 30 megawatts of electricity. There was also significant hardwood stock to provide the fuel for these power plants. We still needed to figure out all the other elements, but it seemed promising. (Yeah, okay, we would be cutting down a LOT of trees, but it was green energy, right?)

Simultaneously, we were exploring Greece to identify several sites for biomass power plants there. Greece was attractive because it had a lot of government incentives for the development of biomass. And while many developers were chasing deals in wind and solar power, biomass had not attracted the same kind of attention. It could be that wind and solar were simpler to understand; they had fewer variables and therefore attracted many more eager entrepreneurs.

But I was fortunate that my partners were so "brainy" and found it most entertaining to spend their weekends reading about such things as: closed-loop and open-loop biomass; fiber balance; the differences between green and dry fuel; agricultural livestock waste nutrients; non-hazardous waste materials; mill and harvesting residues; pre-commercial thinning; slash-and-brush; municipal solid waste; gas-derived from bio-degradation of solid waste; recycled paper; orchard, vineyard, grain, legume, sugar, and other crop by-products. Whew!

I discussed the complexity of all this with Paul, and he explained to me that, by the time we would open the plant, we would need to understand how every single component works, as that is the only way to be sure the plant is being managed properly. And since so much of our future potential cash flow would be coming from these projects, it was only natural that we get it right.

Wow! And I thought the Series 7 was difficult. Back to school.

REAL PROMISE

Though it would take the next nine months to close these new deals, I felt calm and relaxed. I was filled with happy anticipation. In another month, we would go out to raise the equity, which would give us working capital for the next year and pay us our salaries while we pulled all this together. We would have to give up a significant amount of the upside to the people who would put up the capital for this project, but that is the cost of not having your own working capital. And we still owed the principal to our original "friends and family" investors plus their 20 percent per annum which would double their original investment in four years. But these projects looked so promising that we would be able to pay them all back and still have profit left over for ourselves on an ongoing basis.

We had finally arrived after taking many wrong turns. And we also still had the Georgia hydro project in the works and were slowly pushing forward the Ukraine hydro rehab.

We had the beginning of a nice company in renewable energy with a whole host of projects in the works that could give us a pretty good ongoing income source. It was an exciting time.

Spring of 2009 had arrived and all the trees were blooming in New York; the streets were redolent with the smell of the blossoms. I felt alive. It was a time for giving, renewal and rebirth. I felt optimistic for the first time in years. To help make ends meet in the meantime, I took on a consulting job with my old partner Vitaly Pruss. I was to help one of his clients in Lithuania make contacts in the energy field here in the US and introduce him to the US Department of Commerce people in Vilnius. I also took on a consulting job with Rabbi Yitzchok Dovid Grossman's organization, Migdal Ohr, in Israel. The extra income from both these jobs would help me pay down my credit card debt. It was a little humbling to have to take on part-time work like this, but I was fortunate that the Almighty had provided for me in this way.

At the same time, feeling needed had led me to feel reborn, in sync with the season around me. I felt like I was a dormant tree coming alive, in bloom again, a sapling which had weathered the harsh winter: the snow, cold and ice of a New York winter when all visible life dies and hides. But, all along and deep down, it was storing its energy to burst forth again in full vigor once the snow melted and the frigid air warmed up.

I'd had my own psychic winter. I'd fought off frost bite. Many of my inner limbs had almost succumbed to the cold and barren wasteland of near bankruptcy but, like the trees around me, I felt resurgence, the sap of life bubbling back to the surface and, with it, hope and optimism.

Tulips were blooming in my neighbor's garden (weeds in ours as we hadn't been able to afford a gardener). Everywhere I looked, I saw red, yellow, pink – the street was awash in color. I felt alive and thanked God for getting me through the Arctic wasteland and back to life.

28

Credit Card Blues

While I waited for the money to start pouring in, I had to do something to put bread on the table – literally. The consulting jobs I was involved in were good, but they were not generating the kind of income I needed to stay afloat.

I had stopped paying my mortgage seven months prior and I feared foreclosure. Besides that, I had no way of reducing my credit card debt, which stood at $350,000.

Yes, as I've already confessed, I had made a big mistake of living above my means (like most of America, I might say in my defense). And I had borrowed heavily against my personal assets to keep the business going. But I thought Doheny Global would rake it in fast, so I had stopped generating other kinds of income.

Yes, I had learned my lesson. God had brought me to my knees, and in the process, brought me back to working for the Jewish people.

My salvation came from America's Voices.

What was it?

America's Voices was the brainchild of my good friend Malcolm Hoenline, the executive vice president of the Conference of Presidents of Major American Jewish Organizations. Malcolm approached me with the desire to bring celebrities, bloggers, sports figures, radio and TV talk show hosts – and anyone with a platform reaching large numbers of people – on fact-finding trips to Israel, and thus to counter the lies spread by anti-Semites. I told him that his project sounded like it was tailor made for me. Organizing such trips was what I have done for so many years – albeit formerly aimed at fundraising for Jewish outreach. Two weeks later, I was hired and was back in the saddle working for a cause. (And getting a paycheck once again.)

Within days, I had my first mission planned and another in the works – featuring Joel David Moore, co-star of *Avatar*; Greg Germann of *Ally McBeal* fame; and Tyler Bensinger, lead writer of *Parenthood* – and I felt energized in a way that I hadn't felt in a long time. It was good to be doing something for someone other than myself, to take a break from thinking about money.

The path I have taken to get back here is such a strange one. I know that I have always said – and genuinely believed – that once I made it big, I would become a full-time philanthropist and work full-time as a volunteer for Jewish causes. But I never imagined it would take me this long to get there. At this juncture, I had not only *not* made it big, I'd also piled up a huge mountain of debt, and it was going to take at least three years (and most likely five) before I could start accumulating some serious dough. Hopefully, by the time I'd reach sixty years of age, I would be in a position to finally become that wealthy philanthropist I dreamed of becoming when I first left the non-profit world. But what was so strange to me was that God had other plans for me.

I didn't heed God's warnings which grew more and more intense. He was posting huge billboards on the highways of life for me and I still ignored them. Kirk Douglas once said to me, "Pain is God's megaphone to wake up a sleeping world," and it took a lot of emotional pain and angst to let God's message finally blast through my thick skull.

My wife had told me years before that I should be involved in doing something for Israel. As usual, I didn't listen to her or to God. I suppose He was saying, "Irwin, you idiot, don't stop living a meaningful life while you wait to get rich, so you can *then* lead a meaningful life!"

Truly, I should have known that from all the Torah I had studied over the years. For example, Jewish wisdom teaches that you should return to the right path one day before the day of your death, and since you can't know the day of our death, the message is clear: "Do it now! Don't put it off till tomorrow, or the next day or the day after!"

I had been putting it off for too many years now. And I had to wonder – if I had stayed immersed in working for the right causes the past five years, whether I'd be facing the severe financial hardship that I was faced with now.

HITTING BOTTOM

Seven months earlier, I thought I had hit bottom. But since then, I'd found out what bottom really meant – it was a much deeper pit than I thought. I always felt that I was a responsible person, but now I was confronted with the choice of paying my credit card bills or putting food on the table – literally. Naturally, I chose to put the food on the table. In addition to ignoring missives from the credit card companies, I stopped making mortgage payments also.

Thirty days later, the incessant calls from collection agencies started. At 8:01 AM, the phones all over the house would start ringing. They had their computers simultaneously call my home line, my home office line and my cellphone, and they continued calling until 8:59 PM. Thirteen hours of incessant calls. I simply couldn't answer the phone anymore, or I just had to take it off the hook.

I felt horrible about it and I called several close friends and rabbis to discuss. The answer was the same from everyone: American law allows you to stop paying if you are no longer able to – that's what bankruptcy is for. In Jewish law, we even have the Sabbatical Year every seven years, when all debts must be forgiven. We were never meant to become enslaved for life to our debts.

Nonetheless, I felt like a deadbeat. I called all the credit card companies back and humbly explained my situation. It was cathartic in some strange way to confess to them how I had come to be in this sad state. They were all very sympathetic. They all agreed to renegotiate the debt, but when I failed to meet the new terms, they inevitably sent my file off to a collection agency once again and the whole process resumed.

Having no savings left and no credit line available, I had to humble myself and again ask friends for loans. I have always thought of myself as a compassionate and sensitive human being, but my levels of empathy for those in my straits rose through the ceiling. There are hundreds of millions of people who live like this always, with little hope of ever changing their situation. I became convinced this was an important lesson that I needed to learn before I could be blessed with wealth. I've told myself that it has been good for me to experience this, as much as I hated it.

I also learned who my "real" friends were. My neighbor Doron Cohen, whom I have always admired and respected, answered my request for a loan immediately and said he would help. He let me know he believed in me and was always there for me. My friend Ira Greenstein did also, and he even apologized for taking two days to get back to me. Apologized? What a mensch! He even offered to help me find a job. My old buddies from Rodman & Renshaw – Michael Vasinkavich and Ed Rubin – called me to say, "You left Aish because of us, so we feel responsible. How can we help? Come in and see us, and we will write you a check."

Their responses reminded me about the importance of treating every human being with respect and feeling true empathy for their situation, to put yourself in their shoes. Being broke and being forced to ask others for loans made me pledge that when I was on my feet again, I would never forget the lessons I had learned and would always treat others who were less fortunate with great respect.

I appreciated that this was a lesson I needed to learn. But the truly fascinating aspect of all this was that while I waited to get rich, I was going back to work for a Jewish cause and felt once again that I was making a meaningful and powerful contribution to the world.

AND THE MONEY KEPT (NOT) ROLLING IN

At the end of June 2010, I was still waiting for the biomass project to come to fruition. I was not sure why it is that everything takes longer than planned – at least in business. Coffee in the microwave warms up fast, and Jiffy Pop popcorn seems to burn before you know it, but deals take longer than imagined – always.

My silent and never-failing partner, Rabbi Zilberman, had gathered a *minyan* to pray at the Western Wall (aka the Kotel) for my success; I felt I could count on him always. I could not imagine what would have happened if he had given up on me.

I thought about this as I boarded a flight to the Ukraine to explore some ways of making money there again, and the airplane gave me a metaphor for my current life situation. I was like a stunt pilot flying a Piper Cub with one engine, risking a mid-air stall with neither a switch to restart the engine nor a parachute. I was flying without any kind of fail-safe system.

My credit cards had always been that for me, but now I had none. I had never realized the comfort and security that a wallet full of plastic gave me. The US Mint would have me remember that "In God We Trust," but I trusted in a never-ending credit line.

I was an idolater in the full sense of the word – no different than those ancients who worshipped idols of stone or wood, but mine were plastic. And suddenly I was deprived of the protection they afforded. How was I supposed to travel to a foreign country without being able to whip out one of my cards to pay as I went along? What if my flight was cancelled and I had to rebook with a different airline? What if I needed to stay longer or move hotels?

I was away from home, and I felt exposed and vulnerable in a way I hadn't felt before. Ever! I found myself calculating every expense, secretly counting and recounting the cash I had with me. I had even collected spare change that lay gathering dust for years in a desk drawer – coins from various countries in Eastern Europe, plus some Euros and Swiss Francs – and now I went to the currency exchange window to see how much spending power this motley collection would generate in the Ukraine. Was it enough to buy me dinner?

It reminded me of when I used to count the pennies in the cookie jar as a kid to go buy a popsicle. Is this what an energy financier building his company is supposed to look like?

I felt like an idiot.

That said, I had no choice but to double down. Or, to put it another way, to go 110 percent in. I jumped, and now I was waiting for the parachute to open, or I'd hit the ground with a splat.

To prevent the second option, I decided to give God His due. I committed to spend as much time on my spirituality as I spent on my physicality. I mean, if I was going to exercise my body for an hour a day, then I had to give equal time to my soul. Some might think this was a strange equation – more like a Faustian bargain with the devil – but it made me feel less guilty about being consumed with my waistline, muscles and youthful appearance.

Yes, here is where I confess to my obsession with looking young. I have (as anyone who has read this far already knows) an obsessive kind of personality, but while I was struggling with debt and waiting, hoping and praying for one of my ventures to finally start making money, my obsession with my appearance reached a new high – or low (which would be closer to the truth).

Looking good made me feel good. I remember a time when a close friend of mine, Jon Medved (founder of Our Crowd and Vringo) told me at his IPO party (held at his penthouse overlooking the New York harbor): "You look so great! You just get younger and younger! How do you do it?"

I couldn't believe how good those words made me feel. But now that I recall that exchange, I can't help but be reminded of the words of the Carole King song, *You're so vain, you probably think this song is about you, don't you, don't you*? Yeah, I did think it was about me. I knew it was about me.

Okay, I will give myself a little credit here. Jon's words did make me feel great, but also, just as I was feeling great, I was feeling bothered that his words made me feel great. Why did I care so much about my looks? Why was I consumed by such superficial nonsense? Was I shallow? Had I lost my center?

Unfortunately – or fortunately – I heard, in my mind, a resounding "yes" in answer to all those questions.

THE GARDEN OF EMUNA

To combat my obsession with my physicality, I decided to devote time to my spirituality and, as the vehicle for that, I chose to re-read *The Garden of Emuna* by Rabbi Shalom Arush. And what was he telling me?

The desire for money shows a lack of *emuna* [trust in God]. Those who believe in Hashem, [i.e., God], know that the quality of their lives doesn't depend on the amount of money they have, but on the extent they acquire *emuna* and succeed in performing Hashem's will.

Prayer, charity and *teshuva*, [returning to God in repentance], are the only solutions to financial difficulties. If Hashem gives a person the tribulations of financial straits, then money won't solve that person's problems; he or she will only get a different and possibly worse set of tribulations.

Yikes!

I read those words over and over again. I examined them one by one, looking for their essence. I tried to chew them over, to taste them, to feel them, to absorb them into my inner core, to extract from them their meaning for me personally.

I felt like I was reading an alchemist's formula for changing base metal into gold – here he was revealing the secret of secrets, the path to eternal life. I wanted these words to fuse with my soul, but the more I read them, the more I struggled with them. I tried to tell myself that I had to be happy now, even though I was in debt up to my ears. I tried to tell myself that the quality of my life should not be dependent on wealth but on having a relationship with God. Yet, I still struggled. The words were simple words; they were easy to read and understand, but hard to make real.

If Hashem gives a person the tribulations of financial straits, then money won't solve that person's problems; he or she will only get different problems and possibly a worse set of tribulations.

Okay, yes, God had put me in this situation because it was good for me. And I have grown, haven't I? I have become more compassionate; I have become more sensitive to how most of America lives, one crisis away from insolvency. So many people out there think: "If I get a flat tire, how will I pay for the new tire? If my fridge breaks, how will I buy a new one? If I lose my job, will I lose my home?" And now I was one of them.

I told myself that I would never again squander my money like I used to. I would live simply. I would be grateful for all I had NOW. I would be happy NOW. I would not wait till I got rich.

But even as I told myself these things, a part of my brain knew that I was an addict – I would need another fix, not of drugs or alcohol, but of the finer things in life that only lots and lots of money can buy.

I had been mainlining the crack of materialism for so long that I was totally brainwashed. It had become part of my inner being. I needed a deep cleaning of my stained soul. I wish such a process existed – that you could go to a soul cleaner, like you go to a dry cleaner. Perhaps that's what the fires of hell are for – not to punish sinners but to scour their souls of all the scum they'd accumulated.

I knew that my soul was a mess; it needed one of those industrial-strength cleansing experiences. And that cleansing experience, Rabbi Arush's book told me, is *teshuva* – returning to God in repentance:

> *Teshuva* is the only way to end tribulations since there are no tribulations without transgression. As long as a person refrains from [returning to God in] *teshuva* – even with all the money in the world – he or she will suffer because of their outstanding and uncorrected transgressions.

Reading those words, I resolved to do just that. Yes, I knew that I would still be tortured by my inner demons – I'd still be worried about looking good, and still yearning for material things – but I was taking the first step in the right direction.

I realized that I had been riding a wagon that had gone down the same dirt path for so many years that it made deep ruts in the ground, and even if I changed wagons now, the new wagon would still fall into those same ruts. That's how mental habits work – even when you begin to see reality a new way, they are too hard to simply cancel. But I had an awareness of them now. I knew they were not healthy and I knew there was another reality, another way to view the world and another way to use my wealth (should I ever get it).

IN RETROSPECT

It is so strange the way God's hand guides the world and the players in it. When the subprime mortgage crisis hit in 2007, the financial giants – titans like Bear Stearns and Lehman Brothers – fell over like dominoes along with tens of thousands of other businesses worldwide.

Because that happened, our Odessa deal collapsed as well. But in retrospect, it was really God's blessing that we did not get that financing, because personal incomes fell swiftly as well, and high-net-worth buyers lost the inclination and – let's be honest – the ability to buy second homes on the Black Sea. If we'd secured that property, the value of the land would have dropped to a fraction of what we'd have paid for it, and we'd have had very few buyers for our fancy houses. And, worst of all, we'd have nothing to show for all our efforts. So, as much as I was devastated by the international real estate collapse and, in particular, our inability to close the Odessa deal, it really was a blessing in disguise.

We then spent a year working on figuring out what our business focus should be. My relationship with Ambassador Lasha Zhvania brought us to the Republic of Georgia, where we jumped into hydro power. Before you entered into any business, you needed to immerse yourself in it, learn from the experts, and go down the road a while before you knew for sure if a viable business model existed. You needed to know if you could get financing for it, if government regulations stood in your way (this was a special concern in the energy business), and if there was enough reward in relation to the risk involved. Without a good risk/reward profile, financing wouldn't be forthcoming, and you would end up giving away too much of the upside to your investors.

A year later, after tens of meetings in Tbilisi, countless phone conversations with World Bank officials, and after even forming a partnership with one of the leaders in hydro, it became clear that Georgia hydro didn't fit our business model and was not the path for us to take.

We then leveraged our relationships in energy, to start exploring biomass projects in Europe. Once again, we engaged experts and slowly became our own experts in the field, learning everything there was to know about this. We developed relationships throughout Europe and took trips to Latvia, Lithuania, Bosnia, Herzegovina, Bulgaria, Romania, Poland, Belarus and Ukraine to look for opportunities. In each case, we'd engaged local lawyers and accountants to learn the nuances of the particular country's tax systems and difficulties in doing business there.

All this took time and money. Our money. My money! Initially, I re-financed my home, and I did so over and over again as its value continued to increase and the credit card companies continued to throw at me new opportunities for taking on debt. I was supporting my share of the business through an ever-expanding credit line based on various debt instruments.

After some time, we realized that the biomass energy business model was doable but it was fraught with a lot of complexity, as energy production is highly regulated and a lot of the multi-national energy giants were already involved – same with wind and solar power. However, we did discover a niche which was very intriguing to us – the torrefaction of biomass.

Rather than creating a fuel and converting it to energy, and then selling that energy on the grid – in a similar way as with hydro, solar or wind power – with torrefaction, we would create a green fuel and then sell the fuel itself to a coal burning utility. We wouldn't be in the energy producing business, but the manufacturers of a green fuel which we could sell to those who did produce energy (such as coal-burning utilities which badly needed to cut down emissions). Since we would be creating green fuel and selling it to the utilities that would then create the energy, we would not be regulated in the same way that they were.

We slowly became experts in the process, reading everything that was published about it – and there was a lot because many universities had tinkered with experimental plants, but no one had launched a commercial grade, continuous-process plant anywhere in the world. But we did find one company which was currently involved in building such a plant, the first in Europe, so that validated our thinking. We flew over there to meet with them and put together our own expert team. We would be the first in the US to launch such a project.

Did I ask: "Why hasn't anyone else done this before?" No, because I was too excited by the prospects and already counting dollar signs, as I was prone to do.

29

How Biomass
Became Bio Mess

I opened the first e-mail of the morning to read great news! It was from our lawyer, Howard Margulies, who had been pressuring his contacts in the energy field to assist us in lining up power purchase agreements. He informed me that utility companies (and he named a few) had biomass teams "frantically" looking for projects.

Yes! The utility companies were reading the writing on the wall that they had to move away from dirty coal and find clean sources of energy, and that they had to do this quickly, or else face federal fines.

Next e-mail – more great news. This time from my doctor, Dr. Yakov Tendler, reporting on the results of my blood tests. Cholesterol total: 145! Awesome!

I quickly pulled out the file where I keep all my test scores from prior years to compare. (I am a little neurotic about this – anal might be a better adjective – I even started an Excel chart with the results of each test side-by-side, to contrast and compare.) The numbers from past years weren't nearly as good – hovering between 158 and 209 – so this was by far the lowest I have been in ten years. Now, I have to admit that ingesting 5 milligrams of Crestor, the cholesterol lowering medication, certainly helped, but also my diet and commitment to exercise played a significant factor.

The rest of my blood tests were all in the normal range, including my PSA result – only 0.06, whereas a higher number would indicate a possibility of prostate cancer, a top worry of every aging male along with thinning hair. But my hair was still coming in strong! No male-pattern baldness in evidence, and my weight and waistline were decreasing as well! I felt great – I was beating back death.

I know, we are all mortal and unrelentingly marching towards death. The minute we are all born, the countdown starts. Yet, we still try to fight it off, each in his own way, and somehow the lowering of my cholesterol, the absence of any serious PSA indicator, and great blood pressure (70/100) made me feel like I was winning the battle.

I'd awoken that morning at 4:45 AM, my new wake-up time. I had moved it up from 5 AM, thinking that another 15 minutes a day adds up to 105 minutes a week, 420 minutes a month, or 84 hours a year, which is more than three days a year of life. That is another way to beat back death, isn't it?

Continuing with my e-mail reading, I only saw more great news. A message from Paul – who, together with David and Scott Claymore, a specialist in tax law and partnership law, had been down South all week – informed me that their meetings over there had gone extremely well. They had looked at two projects – one in Missouri and one in Arkansas – and the latter seemed very promising.

The e-mail from Paul was followed up by a voice message from him, which I heard when I turned on my cellphone. Paul had called the previous night, but part of my new way of living life was turning off the cellphone early. In the past I had kept it on all the time and would even check it in the middle of the night, but I let go of that habit. I wanted to spend more time with my wife and girls. The night before, we had watched *American Idol* together, and even though I thought the show was silly and represented many things about competition I disliked, I valued the opportunity for all of us to do something together, no matter that it was around the TV. Times like these were so precious, and I wanted more family moments in my life.

Now, I listened to Paul's message which contained more details about what they'd found. The bottom line was that we were looking at tax-free financing and were hopeful of a power purchase agreement at 12-14 cents a kilowatt hour which, together with the renewable energy credits, made this project a homerun.

Absolutely superb. Excellent progress. The stars were aligning at last.

And yet, a part of me was afraid of getting too excited. Didn't I feel this way about Novosibirsk, Moldova, and Odessa also? I had learned a long time ago that business is tough and so many things can go wrong at any time and – no matter how hard you work – you really need God to help you. There is always too much that's out of your hands.

Although Paul was keeping me in the loop, it felt strange to be less involved in this project than in the prior ones where I did more of the heavy lifting. Apparently, God wanted to make it clear to me that when I do succeed, it will be all a gift from Him and not a direct result of my efforts.

After I prayed and worked-out, I joined Judy in the kitchen where she was opening some parcels of pictures which had arrived in the mail. They were 8x10s of the family taken at Passover, when we were all together in Israel. I looked at one of Judy, me and all our eight kids with their spouses and children, our grandchildren. I focused on each face, each smile, the gorgeous little outfits all the girls were wearing, and felt overwhelmed with happiness. I started tearing up. This was our progeny! What a stunningly beautiful bunch! I felt so rich, so fortunate, so blessed. Deals just didn't seem to matter at that moment. I was already a very rich man.

NEW BIOMASS LLC

In the end, it didn't happen in Missouri or Arkansas, but – a full two years later (!) – in Mississippi. In the process, Doheny Global became New Biomass LLC.

Why Mississippi? Because the US government under President Barack Obama had decided that 10 percent of energy had to come from renewable, so-called "green" sources by 2012 (and 25 percent by 2015). Mississippi had no wind power or solar power, but they needed to get this clean energy someplace to meet federal standards, so where? The answer was "forest biomass."

Yes, it wasn't the greatest thing for the environment. Yes, it meant chopping down more forests, but it was "green," right?

The contradictions did echo somewhere in my brain, but I managed to silence them.

After raising $42 million in financing, we planned to open our first torrefied wood plant located between the towns of Quitman and Hickory, Mississippi, where we would be manufacturing wood pellets (made from sawdust left over from lumber production or from soft, fast-growing trees such as pine) to be sold to different utilities. The goal was 125,000 tons of output annually, but initially we would only be able to produce about 25,000 tons. Hopefully by mid-summer 2011, after we shipped off our samples to the utilities who would be our customers, we would be off and running, and generating serious cash-flow from the operation.

I vividly recall the day when I saw photos of the final construction stages of our plant. I stared at them in wonder and shock. It was surreal. I looked at the gleaming steel piping, the bright red pipe fittings, the workmen in construction helmets, assembling the torrefaction reactor. We had purchased a 70,000 square-foot warehouse where the plant would be housed and, in the pictures, I could clearly see the wood-receiving equipment being assembled with the first torrefaction line being put in place. And, for the first time in five years, I allowed myself to start to believe again that this project was for real. It was finally happening!

The incredible day finally came – on June 21, 2011 – when I got an e-mail message from Paul that they had finally flipped the ON switch at the plant, and all three reactors were up and running and processing torrefied wood. This was the first attempt, and a test only, but finally the thing was actually working.

I sat looking at the e-mail in excitement, wonder, awe and pleasure, muttering under my breath, "Thank You God ... Thank You God ... Thank You God ..." over and over.

Of course, we weren't totally there yet. There were still a lot of things that we needed to make happen. We needed to keep the system running continuously and churning out product on a 24/7 basis. We needed to line up the financing in order to bring this plant up to its projected output of 125,000 tons output per year. Most importantly, we needed to deliver our product to the utilities, get them to pay for it and commit to long-term orders. Then we needed to find locations for future plants, do those deals, arrange the financing and get them built fast, while we still had the jump-start on this market.

Phew! Even if we had every confidence of bringing it off, I felt so many conflicting emotions. So many steps, so many obstacles, so much waiting. I felt like the kid in the back seat of his parents' car, embarking on the promised road trip and asking as the car left the driveway, "Are we there yet?" Except – I've been asking that question for so many years now!

Yet, gratitude to God managed to dominate. I felt strangely optimistic, even though I recognized that the road ahead was a long one. I know, I know – I should have been haunted by the memories of the prior failures in investment banking, but I suppose that I so badly needed this to go right that I could not let those – let's face it, more realistic – thoughts invade. I wanted to focus on having a nice income, paying off the bills, taking nice vacations, buying a nice car again, and helping all my kids prosper.

I forwarded Paul's e-mail to several family members to share in the excitement of the moment. I also sent it to several friends who had loaned me money over the prior three years. I had been worried that they thought of me as a deadbeat who'd never pay them back, and at last I could show them that this project was truly coming to fruition and soon I would make them whole.

"No man is an island..." John Donne wrote, and God clearly wanted me to learn how true this is. He wanted me to acquire humility by realizing that I do not exist alone and that I am dependent on others. There is no way that I could have survived without the generosity of my friends who graciously loaned me money when I was in desperate straits. Every time I would see those folks, I'd repeat my thanks to them and reaffirm that I planned to repay them – God willing – very soon.

As I sat there reading Paul's e-mail over and over, I felt that perhaps I was gaining some wisdom at last. More than ever, I was conscious of the fact that I take myself with me everywhere – I carry my anxiety or my sense of peace with me wherever I go. It is the "I" within me that creates my experience of my reality; it is not the external reality which creates my experience. Whatever happens – good or bad – I always have a choice as to how I view it.

That is the power of free will, the power of the mind to create our reality. What we choose to think, we feel. The feeling comes so quickly on the heels of the thought that we don't see the connection. Thinking something is like turning on a light switch and the light, the emotion, is instantly energized and flowing. It happens instantly.

My life could be collapsing but I can always choose how I look at it (as a teaching moment from God, for example) and that determines what I feel. I could be filthy rich, but if I am having thoughts of insecurity, worry and anxiety – where do I invest my money, what if I make a bad deal and end up broke, what if I get cancer, what if my kids aren't happy – then, no matter how rich I am, there will always be thoughts to make me unhappy and distract me.

I remembered all that while reading Paul's e-mail, which told me that my deal was really happening, and the news didn't knock me off center. I had grown a lot in the intervening time. Oh sure, I still wanted it; I don't deny that, but I also recognized that I needed to make my life meaningful TODAY, with or without money. My wife needed my love TODAY. She needed me to be present and connected NOW. My kids needed me NOW. I couldn't use the lack of money, the crappy economy, the pile of debt to say, "Hey, I will love you tomorrow." I couldn't put off being the best person I could be until I got rich.

God had given me this lot and that meant I had to satisfied with it. Say the sages in *Ethics of the Fathers*, "Who is wealthy? The one who is satisfied with his portion." Maybe it was because I had finally learned this lesson that God finally let success in the door.

While writing this, I looked out my window. It was 5:30 AM and the light was slowly filtering in. It had rained the night before and the grass and trees were a rich, lush, verdant green. A mist was rising from the ground, and I thought of the passage from the Book of Genesis: "There went up a mist from the earth, and it watered the whole face of the ground."

A mist was coming up from the earth, in the form of my experiences of the past few years. It had watered and continues to nourish my every moment.

I was pulled out of my reverie by hearing the basement door open. Sara Temima, my six-year-old granddaughter, had woken up early. She walked into my home office, her smile lighting up my heart. I felt so blessed, so full, so content. I needed nothing else to know – and feel down in my very bones – that life is good.

THE END OF A DREAM

Shortly after the Mississippi plant started up, I wrote to my editor, Uriela Sagiv:

> Well, we are up and running. We have contracts and are shipping product. I will start to see money by the end of the year, finally. It has been a long haul. We will be building three new plants in 2012 and then our goal is to build three plants a year and have ten plants open by 2015. If this succeeds as we hope, we will have a company that is valued at $500-600 million and my share is one-fifth. It will be a few years before I am super rich if it all succeeds, God willing, but I am having second thoughts about the book as is. I don't know if I want anyone to know how I became so rich ...

Famous last words ... except that we didn't build ten new plants or even three new plants, because the very first plant went bankrupt.

What happened?

My answer: God had a different plan, and I had more lessons to learn.

The plant never really got going after the initial start-up. Problems with production persisted – more and more problems which required more and more money to solve. Six months turned to eighteen months, which turned to thirty-six months. Every time we thought we had resolved one issue, another popped up. I was slowly giving up hope that this would ever happen.

For well over a decade, numerous academic institutions, governmental agencies and private industries had focused on torrefaction technology, with a goal of bringing it to viable commercial status. The hope was that upon commercialization, torrefaction would play a crucial role in transitioning our society to a circular economy, where carbon-containing materials would be recycled, lowering overall carbon emissions and combating climate change.

Torrefaction had long been envisioned as the next logical step in the production of fuel engineered from biomass. This was what our whole venture was based on and why we thought we were going to become super successful and super rich.

Countless press releases and announcements had heralded supposed torrefaction successes the world over, only to be followed by deafening silence – with the exception of occasional news reports of fires, explosions and failed ventures.

Many millions of dollars had been spent without a single example of large-scale, ongoing commercial success. I should have realized that this was a sign that maybe the process was more complex than we had ever imagined. Our investors, as well as those who invested in other torrefaction ventures had become disillusioned, and many potential customers had all but given up on the idea that torrefaction would ever be commercialized.

As we discovered, there were many problems with the actual process of torrefaction. I suppose there was a reason that no one else had managed to make this technology work.

The torrefaction process actually generates a high volume of very volatile gases and the ability to handle these gases creates a significant number of other problems. As well, torrefaction involves heating biomass to well beyond its auto-ignition temperature. If the torrefied biomass is exposed to air prior to cooldown, it will burst into flames, potentially causing catastrophic loss.

In all cases, process interruptions can and often do occur. A commercially viable plant must be capable of operating 24/7, without interruption, for months at a time. But achieving uninterrupted operations without effective handling of the torrefaction gases is not possible.

Another much simpler issue is that the torrefaction process ends up creating wood pellets that are very brittle, and when we loaded them into railroad cars or river barges for shipping, they crumbled under the weight of the other pellets and the load that arrived at its destination was torrefied dust instead of pellets that could be put into a furnace and burned efficiently.

That's the long and the short of it.

THE ELUSIVE BIG SCORE

One day, when things were falling apart, I was speaking to a friend of mine, the late Lewis Katz, about my many failed business ventures. (Lewis was a very successful entrepreneur with estimated net worth of $400 million who was sadly killed when his private jet crashed due to pilot error in 2014.)

Lewis was a very kind and generous man. He had accompanied me on one of my missions to Israel with his son Drew and a group of business leaders, and when I had run into financial trouble back in 2007, he had loaned me some money to help tide me over. He had a huge heart and was a very caring human being.

I was telling him about all of our escapades – Doheny Global, the Odessa planned community of 1,000 homes, Radar Films, the hydro-electric projects in Nepal, Georgia and Pakistan, and finally the torrefaction project. He looked at me and, with a wry smile, suggested that I shoot a little lower.

I was stunned. "What do you mean?" I asked. "I need to shoot for the stars. How else will I ever get rich like you? I am sure you didn't succeed by aiming low."

He then told me something which changed my life and my path. As Lewis was one of the wealthiest men I knew, I valued his insights and wisdom. He was also quiet about his wealth; he didn't flaunt it, and I respected his values.

He said that he never tried for a big score in business. He was happy to just get to first base. He never went to bat aiming to swing for the fences. He had started in business as a car-jockey, parking cars, and then became a manager of the parking lot, and then realized it was a good business, so he bought one parking lot and then another. He proceeded in small incremental steps. Based on his experiences with wealth, he suggested I try to just get to first base and then build slowly from there.

Perhaps he had identified my entire problem. I realized that there was a part of me that felt very entitled. I somehow did not think that the normal rules of life applied to me. On some level, I really expected that I should not have to work like everyone else and was entitled to become super rich. I really expected that each one of our ventures – no matter how risky and huge they were – would succeed. Why shouldn't they? But now I was reminded of the sage advice I had heard a while ago: that if it was so easy, everyone would be rich.

Like Lewis pointed out, I was swinging for the fences with every one of my business projects. Perhaps if I had started small and just looked to get to first base, I would now be looking at some middling level of success with which I could build a larger business. Instead, I really had nothing to show for all these years of efforts.

Lewis's words hit home in a deep and profound way.

30

What I Now Know

When I'd walked off a cliff in 2005 with no safety net, I did so with total confidence in my ability to make it and to make it big. At the time, I wasn't a twenty-five-year-old flying solo either, but a fifty-year-old with a large family, a large home with a huge mortgage, and a ton of obligations that came attached. And I was totally oblivious to the risks involved.

So here is where I pause to give some advice to those who haven't yet made my mistakes, in the hopes that you won't be as stupid as I was.

When investors choose a hedge fund or a money manager or a financial advisor, they want someone who will take some risks on their behalf, in order to increase their returns, but they also want to be sure that that this person understands what risk means.

To take a hike in a rain forest (with no understanding of the wildlife), or to rappel down a ravine in the desert (with no idea how often flash floods hit the area), or to go sailing in the Caribbean during hurricane season (with no weather radar) and doing any of that with a guide who is as ignorant as you are is simply foolish. Not just foolish – the more appropriate word would be idiotic. For all those activities you need a guide who is truly an expert in the field.

The same goes when it comes to investing – it is critical to know how much risk is involved, how much risk you are prepared to take on and – more than anything – to make sure that the person whom you trust with making those evaluations truly understands the variables. And, naturally, all that also applies to launching a new business.

Yet, I was totally oblivious. I was worse than oblivious because I thought I knew it all. I was self-delusional and I had no guide of any kind to correct my course. Failure was simply not in my vocabulary. It was not an option I considered as even a remote possibility. I sailed into the face of a squall, without even a rudimentary understanding of the dynamics involved.

As I sit here looking back on it today, I can't believe just how self-delusional I was. I had truly endangered my family's survival. I am not sure what my thinking was, or if I was even thinking at all. I tend to be impulsive, and I would jump into new situations without fully thinking through what the potential consequences might be.

But in the process, I learned a lot.

If a working guy came to me today and told me he was thinking of going off into business or finance, what would I tell him?

I would tell him a few things:

- o Stay at your current job until you have at least eighteen months of savings in the bank.
- o Cut your overhead down to the bare bones before you go out on your own. Take a good hard look at every one of your expenses and see if you can chop off 50 percent from them first.
- o Try and get a sense of the risk and sacrifice involved.
- o Discuss your plans with friends and family and make sure you are emotionally prepared for the roller coaster ride, not that anyone ever really is.
- o Decide if you could downgrade if you had to. Could you psychologically handle losing all your wealth and starting all

over? Could you psychologically handle losing your home to foreclosure?

o   Is your marriage or primary relationship strong and stable enough to handle the stress of you being an entrepreneur? How much does that matter to you?

o   Are you personally psychologically secure, stable, balanced and in touch with what really counts in your life, so that you won't lose your center when the going gets rough? (Trust me, it inevitably will.)

o   On the flip side, are you secure enough in knowing what really counts if and when you do become successful? Are you sure that if that happy day comes, you won't implode, get lost in rampant/destructive acquisition binges, leave your loyal and long-suffering wife for a trophy wife and lose everything which is really important to you – such as your family?

THE FRAUGHT PATH OF THE ENTREPRENEUR

The life of an entrepreneur, as I have learned the hard way, is fraught with risk at every turn. So far, I'd had only a minimal amount of success and a boatload of failure, but I've seen enough of the guys who had succeeded to know that success can be just as – if not more – dangerous.

Launching a new business takes time and money. It can take a year of throwing yourself into the venture in full intensity before you even know if you have a viable business model. I saw this happen with our hydro power venture in the Republic of Georgia, for example.

But you can go into something you know very well and have years of experience doing and you can spend a couple of years setting up the project, arranging the permits, the financing (like we did in Odessa), then you still have to remember that the markets can turn against you in unexpected ways.

There is absolutely nothing you can do to protect yourself against a non-standard deviation event like what occurred at the end of 2007.

I actually thought that we were hedging against what was predicted to be a real estate recession in the US by going into real estate development in Eastern Europe. But no one predicted a world-wide meltdown of the credit markets or what turned out to be a world-wide recession. The few people that did made huge bets on such an event occurring – see the movie *The Big Short* – were so in the minority that the risks they took made them several *billion* dollars. They were able to make that kind of money just because they were betting against the conventional wisdom.

So who knew?! I for sure didn't!

Just like everyone else (including financial titans), I was tossed on the rocky shores of the economic meltdown as world credit markets were torn asunder. Then, after exploring and dismissing hydro and other renewable energy opportunities, I thought I had found salvation in torrefaction.

Finding the path to success is very much like mining for gold nuggets. They look nothing like gold. You have to sift through the muck to see what you have, and not just toss it aside as another rock or clod of dirt. If you don't invest the time, you may miss the diamond in the rough and yet, at the same time, a lot more "diamonds" turn out to be just rocks.

After a while, I had become jaundiced and pessimistic and found it really hard to believe that anything would work out – EVER!

So, another piece of advice for the budding entrepreneur:

Don't ever stop believing in your ability to succeed. Don't give up. You will fall many, many times, but the only thing you can do is pick yourself up and keep moving forward.

In war, you must go on the offense or you will be overrun. Obliterated. Conquered. Killed. But it takes great courage to move forward under withering fire from the enemy. In business, the unrelenting fire is the sneers of those who have watched you fail over and over again, even if they don't show it to you; what you imagine they are thinking is even worse than what they are actually thinking. Your own ebbing lack of self-confidence that follows each false turn will wear you down, so don't let that happen.

Building a business of value will take a minimum of four to five years. As I said, it can take a year before you even know if you have a real "business," and then it can easily take several years to launch your first step, line up the seed capital and bring investors on board, only to start to scale up the business and deal with the thousands of obstacles that will occur in any venture.

THOSE WHO WENT DOWN IN FLAMES

Having said all of the above, I have to bring up some of those whom I admired – those who made it big and then went down in flames when they made the wrong investment choices. Each of their stories is a lesson in itself:

Remember Alex Mashinsky? I thought I had a deal with him in a $70 million roll-out of a limousine business. As I mentioned, I knew Alex from my fundraising days when he donated $250,000 to Aish HaTorah after his first company, Arbinet, went public. He was a brilliant innovator who had more than thirty patents to his credit.

Alex got into the crypto business, but his company, Celsius, blew up on him in one of the first crypto implosions. He went bankrupt and, last I heard, he was under investigation in several countries, as well as facing fraud charges in the US.

Another guy who was a big donor to Aish and many other Jewish causes was Vadim Rabinovitch. What happened to him?

Vadim invested in politics, the biggest gamble of them all. And he picked wrong.

God only knows where he is living now – maybe in Cyprus? – or how much control he has over his vast fortune. I read that the government of the Ukraine had placed him on a list of the top 100 people it labeled as traitors. He had his citizenship revoked and was exiled from the Ukraine for his support of the Russian invasion.

And then there was Ted Field – the producer of *The Texas Chainsaw Massacre* – and my once-upon-a-time potential savior, who had made the *Forbes* list of the 400 richest people on the planet. He has since been accused of being a "deadbeat movie producer" who ran a "Ponzi-like scheme." Last I heard, he was defending himself in court against misrepresentations he allegedly made when soliciting money for a remake of the Jean-Claude Van Damme film, *Kickboxer*.

Which brings me to the biggest crash and burn story I know of – that of Merv Adelson, the American television producer of *Knots Landing* and *Dallas* among scores of other famous TV series. At one time he had an estimated worth of $300 million and homes in Bel Air, Malibu and Aspen. But then he invested wrong – including in a number of Internet start-ups – and he lost it all.

"His life was like a movie script you wouldn't even believe — rags to riches to rags," Irwin Molasky, his friend and former business partner, told the *Los Angeles Times* when he died in 2015, a pauper living on the Santa Monica beach in an apartment smaller than one of his walk-in closets in his former life.

Read and weep. Read and learn.

When I looked at the lives of the many successful people I previously mentioned, I had to be thankful to God for having spared me such a spectacular rise and such a shameful demise – both "the thrill of victory and the agony of defeat."

And now I had to take my own advice, and – after ten years of my own financial ventures and disasters – to find a way forward.

THE WAY FORWARD

When did my path to salvation begin?

I think maybe when I read the 2015 bestseller, *The Road to Character*, by David Brooks, the conservative *New York Times* columnist.

In this book, Brooks draws a sharp distinction between what he calls the "resume virtues" (those things you want on your resume – the achievements and skills that bring success) and the "eulogy virtues" (the things that people say about you at your funeral). The latter are the character traits that make you the kind of person you are when you are not playing a role or wearing a mask, the good inner person that friends and family recognize as the real you.

Reading that, I realized that I had gotten caught up in building an outstanding collection of "resume virtues" at the expense of my "eulogy virtues." I had gone chasing after success and veered away from trying to be the good person I once was. And I felt sick to my stomach. How had I gone so far astray?

The moment of truth descended upon me on Wesley Hills Day.

We lived in a part of Monsey, New York, called Wesley Hills, which is really a little village in its own right. Once a year, the village put on a fair in the park, called Wesley Hills Day, with lots of attractions for the kids – clowns, a petting zoo, pony rides, cotton candy, ice cream – all free. My kids looked forward to it every summer. It was a fun day where everyone ran around, scarfing up all the free stuff they could get their hands on.

But one particular year I couldn't attend. I had somehow planned a business trip to Europe on Wesley Hills Day and my flight was in the afternoon, which meant I would miss all the family fun.

I remember my taxi passing the park and me looking out the window at Judy and the kids walking to the fair without me. And my heart broke. What had become of me? Why was I choosing business over family time?

In my fundraising days, I remember saying to the people I solicited that I had never heard of anyone on their deathbed regretting that they had not spent more time at the office. Just the opposite – all the high-flyers regretted not spending more time at home. And here I was missing a special family experience because I had chosen more time at the office.

I started to cry as the park was left in the rearview mirror and the taxi continued on to the highway. I felt anguish, guilt, sadness. I was not the person I wanted to be. I was not the person I had once envisioned I would become.

This was not the life I wanted to lead.

31
Therapy and Me

I had been so full of enthusiasm for every one of my deals. But in the end, nothing worked out. All my projects ended up either in bankruptcy or in just plain old failure.

As I beat myself up over it, I took some small (tiny) comfort in reading that, according to the US Small Business Administration, over 50 percent of new business ventures fail in the first year and 95 percent fail within the first five years. I wondered whether I would have embarked on this journey if I had known this when I first started out.

Truth be told, I would have. Why? Because I wouldn't have believed that such a thing could happen to me. I had an overblown sense of entitlement and was mired in egocentricity; I didn't let myself think – even for a moment – that the rules of stark reality, which apply to everyone else, applied to me. I was different. I never imagined that failure was ever an option.

But failure was definitely an option and I had failed.

When that finally dawned on me, I felt very depressed. The world just didn't seem fair. I was supposed to be rich. Instead, I was worse off than before I started on this quest for wealth and was struggling with a mountain of debt. I felt physically drained and emotionally depleted.

What had happened to all my dreams? I had expected so much of myself – and, indeed, had accomplished much – but the possibility of my ever being hugely wealthy had evaporated, and I felt like I had a lot of losses to mourn and a lot of baggage to unpack.

JUDY'S FORESIGHT

Some years before I hit that brick wall, my sensitive and brilliant wife Judy had the foresight to suggest I begin therapy of some kind. She saw that after so many defeats – even if I still had not given up and was counting on biomass to come through – I had burned out and was very depressed.

Judy had read *Lucky Man: A Memoir* by Michael J. Fox in which he recounts how Jungian psychotherapy helped him cope with the depression he experienced following the discovery that he had Parkinson's disease.

As she read this inspirational book, she began to think that if it worked for Michael, it might work for her husband. She shared the book with me and suggested that I seek out a Jungian analyst.

I have to say that, at this point, Judy was desperate. This was not how marriage was supposed to turn out. Unlike me, she didn't care about riches – her primary focus was the family. But she had to face the fact that, after thirty years of marriage, her idea of a loving relationship was gone. She had an unhappy husband, who had left a career as the respected fundraiser for a major Jewish organization to strike out on his own in business. Like the ever-loyal wife she was, she supported me in this as in all of my endeavors. But when I was emotionally absent because I was working for a Jewish cause, it was easier for her to justify her sacrifice. Now, I was doing it for selfish gain and I wasn't even succeeding at that, so it was much harder for her to swallow the many bitter pills that went along with it. She came to the conclusion that things had to change and she wasn't going to let up until it did.

When Judy suggested I try this type of analysis, I knew she had hit on something. And I agreed to follow up.

REBIRTH

It was the first day of spring – 78 degrees outside. I drove by a riotous flowering of brilliant pink blossoms and saw the sun piercing through them in a surreal way – rebirth was exploding. Only the blind or intoxicated could miss the experience. I have been both most days. I would drive by scenes like this and hardly notice. Where did I need to race to every day with my awareness so dulled and diverted? I was chasing phantoms lodged in my subconscious, pursuing dreams that come from somewhere outside myself, but I didn't know their origin. Yet they consumed me and took over my free will. It seemed as if aliens had hijacked my life and now drove my emotional engine and steered my ego.

I wondered where my unconscious motivations originated? Were they my own? Did they originate with my parents or even grandparents? With the society around me? With the very capitalist underpinnings of the United States, the country where I was born? Would they drive me to my death?

And is this why God told Abraham, "Go for yourself"? There was an implied message in those words: "Go for yourself, from your land, from your birthplace, from your father's house to the land that I will show you."

I knew there was an inner self – the soul – that I needed to tap into. I felt like it was trying to bubble up to the surface, but my frenetic activity wouldn't let it. What was I trying to avoid? What was I running from when I was running to the next deal? This constant nervous energy kept me from being present. No sooner was I here, than was I thinking that I must be there.

When I turned 57, I decided it was time to grow up. Since Judy so strongly recommended Jungian therapy, I decided to try it. I started by reading up on Carl Jung, the Swiss psychiatrist who founded analytical psychology. Initially a follower of Sigmund Freud, he embraced many of his mentor's ideas, but departed from others. Mainly, Freud read so much into the sexual drive, whereas Jung interpreted it as a spiritual drive.

When I found my Jungian analyst, Dr. Gary Trosclair, I was sold by his explanation online:

> The basic goal and attitude of Jungian analysis is to build an ongoing relationship with the unconscious. Rather than seeing it merely as the repository of repressed memories, Jung viewed the unconscious as a source of direction and healing. At the same time, this unconscious also contains our dark side, which is important to face directly and come to terms with. Jungian work is explicit in its respect for spirituality, the arts and the unconscious. Jung encouraged us to learn about human development by understanding mythology and religion. His followers have continued to develop these ideas, also using research from science and other schools of therapy.

THE JUNGIAN WAY

My first date with Dr. Trosclair was on March 6, 2012. I told him that I had a beautiful wife, eight beautiful children, many grandchildren, and that I had been moderately successful in business, had even gained fame with my books and projects, and yet I was miserable. I felt like I just could not go forward anymore – very little was giving me pleasure in life.

This confession unleashed a torrent of tears. I thought I would never stop sobbing. I had been holding on to so much disappointment, shame and despair. I berated myself for all the kids' birthday parties I'd missed because I was traveling so much or was just plain distracted. Plus, I felt a torrent of guilt over the lack of attention, compassion and caring I had shown Judy, because I was too caught up with striking it big. The reservoir of emotion surrounding all my failures in family relationships was bottomless and overwhelmed my capacity to contain it.

The past five years had beat me up, torn me down and left me feeling like road-kill. Worse than road-kill. Not even vultures wanted to pick me up. Perhaps the sanitation department would get around to me eventually. A disgusted garbage worker would sling my decomposed remains into the back of his truck and unload me at the county dump along with a heap of other detritus.

I had not been aware how bereft I had been feeling, how trampled by life, until I walked into that psychoanalyst's office.

I recall that on the third visit, Dr. Trosclair asked me if I felt good about anything in my life. Yes! I felt good that I had accomplished a lot – if only in that I had fathered eight beautiful children. They were all accomplishing important things in their lives. But I felt pain when I started to talk about my work. From 1982 to 1996, I did a lot of good. I impacted hundreds, if not thousands, of young adults. However, the past fifteen years had been a wasteland. I felt burned out, lost and empty.

He asked me if once I had been energetic and positive, if this helplessness that he sensed in me was something new. I didn't know how to answer. Did I once have youthful enthusiasm? Was I once optimistic? When was the last time I felt that way?

He also asked me if I had any recurring dreams or fantasies. There was one, which happened regularly:

I bump into the reservations manager on my last day in the hotel, as I am bringing my suitcase to the bus. I have not seen her, as she has been away. I feel elated to see her. I had met her six months ago. She is young and innocent. I feel badly that I had not seen her the whole trip. Kind, naïve, positive, upbeat, yet unaware of what life is about. My heart beats quicker. I look into her eyes. Soft, tender, kind, gentle. I want to sweep her off her feet, take her to my castle and protect her from any hurt. Keep her there in her innocent, unblemished form. She has not been scarred by rejection or defeat. It has not lain waste her soul. She needs me to build a protective fence around her, to save her from the vagaries of war, of failure, of hurt and pain. Let me protect her. She should not know tears.

As I discussed it with Dr. Trosclair, I realized that this message from my unconscious was speaking to me loud and clear. Of course, there was no real reservations manager in my life. This woman whom I didn't know represented the lost part of my soul, the part of me that has abandoned its hope, its naiveté, its sense of wonder, its belief that anything is possible.

The past five years had been punishing and, as a result, I had given up. There was a sense of maturity that comes with age, experience and wisdom, but one never wants to lose the innocence of youth. Even in old age that sense of wonder at the universe is a critical aspect of our selves which we must not give up. I saw that I had lost it, but my soul was wiser and was teaching me what I must reclaim.

SIX MONTHS LATER

After six months of therapy, I was just beginning to tap into my storehouse of pain.

What have I stored there? All the opportunities I lost. All the hurt I inflicted. All the mistakes I made. It was a bottomless pit of psychic debris – a black hole of sadness sucking everything into its vortex.

On each visit to my analyst's office, I dove into this pit of pain, angst, despair, hopelessness, hurt, guilt, confusion. Come out, come out, wherever you are – can Irwin come out to cry today?

One moment sunshine, calm seas, clear horizon; in the next instant, a typhoon. I felt buffeted by whirlwinds, cross currents, rip tides. From where did they come? It took just a word, a thought, a feeling and I was catapulted by yet another geyser of emotion that erupted from unknown depths.

I never knew what the trigger would be. I'd just lose control as my emotions would overwhelm me. They'd spew out wildly, uncontrollably, having been held in captivity for so long. I cried so hard, I thought at times that I would choke. My windpipe would close on me as I struggled to control the fury erupting from within. I'd gasp for air, panicked that I was suffocating.

I'd leave each session emotionally drained, totally exhausted, yet somehow feeling more whole. A part of my being which had been lost for years, covered with the debris of life, had been rediscovered.

Although after all the digging into my psyche, I'd emerged covered with dirt, caked with miners' mud, I felt cleansed. Each descent was a prelude to an ascent. The dirtier, the cleaner. The uglier, the prettier. The more pain, the more joy. The more pressure, the more release. The greater the conflict, the greater the resolution.

I had embarked on a journey of self-discovery, and now I felt in touch with my soul again. I felt it guiding me, pushing me forward. I knew not where it would take me, but I learned to trust its guiding light.

I never thought I would look forward to the insights and hidden mysteries that tears leave in their wake. Pain brings tears. But, as the tears disappear, in their place comes growth, resolution, peace and wholeness. It is as if the tears wash away the husk surrounding the inner core, and in that place a seed is found … and it blossoms.

A DIFFERENT APPROACH

I met with Dr. Trosclair for close to a year, and every session was pretty much the same – I'd say hello and then I'd start crying. I had been holding on to so much unhappiness.

But as much as I felt that this type of analysis had helped me – unlocked a lifetime of stored pain and opened me up to new growth – I thought it was time for therapy that was more interactive.

I had been advised that what would fit me best at this stage would be Gestalt therapy, which actively engages parts of one's psyche that are in conflict with each other. Gestalt therapists call it "chair work." You sit in a chair and imagine the sad or angry part of yourself sitting in a chair opposite, and you express your feelings toward it. Then you switch to the other chair and become that part. It is powerful transformative work and helps you dig deeply within.

My search for a new therapist led me to Neal Levy, who was trained in Gestalt therapy and who also practiced something I'd never heard of before called Core Energetics.

When I entered his office, I immediately spotted, piled in the corner, all sorts of props which intrigued me. He had boxing gloves, a punch blocker, a bolster which looked like an oversized rolling pin and plenty of cushions. I soon found out what these were for.

In practice, Core Energetics is the polar opposite of Jungian analysis. While Dr. Trosclair never left his chair, rarely showed emotion, and just listened while I talked, Neal got physically active.

For example, in one session, he told me that he sensed I was carrying a lot of anger just beneath the surface, but I was not in touch with it; instead, I was expressing it through hurtful behaviors toward my loved ones. He suggested I put on the boxing gloves and start punching as he held a blocker. I did it tentatively at first, but he urged me on. Within minutes I was boxing as hard as I could and yelling at the top of my lungs. This went on for about five minutes until my tears broke through, and I was screaming, crying and punching in anger.

The belief of Core Energetics is that we get ourselves into trouble because we learn to repress our emotions when we sense that they are not welcome. Our parents do the best job they can, but there are times when every child is a little too much for a stressed-out caregiver. I don't remember how this happened to me, but I imagine that when I got too rambunctious for my Mom or Dad, they may have yelled, "Calm down! Sit still! Stop moving!" Or when something happened that caused me to cry, they may have said, "Be tough. Grow up. Don't be such a baby." After hearing these kinds of comments repetitively, I must have learned not to allow myself to feel what I was feeling and eventually to lose touch with my emotions. But my blocked emotions didn't go away, they just get locked up inside my body.

One of the techniques I learned in Core Energetics was something called TRE, which stands for "Tension and Trauma Releasing Exercise." This technique was developed by Dr. David Berceli who observed, while serving as a missionary in war-torn Sudan, how differently adults and children reacted as bombs were falling. Everyone curled up into a ball, but the children trembled, whereas the adults just held their fear in. He realized that the adults had learned to block their natural stress-reducing mechanism, and they needed help recovering their God-given ability to release it.

I tried Dr. Berceli's exercise – which involved putting pressure on the psoas muscle, one of the body's most significant muscles overlying the spinal column – and the effect was profound. The exercise induced a tremor in my body which lasted about a half hour. As I trembled, tremendous amount of tension that I had stored up was released. I had the most amazing sense of energy streaming up and down my whole body. I felt alive, present, relaxed. The only way I know how it describe it is that it was a very spiritual experience.

These techniques opened up deep blockages within me. The years of suppressed anger, stress and tension finally burst through all my defenses and came pouring out. I was amazed at how much I had been holding in. No wonder I had little energy left. I was using all my life-force to hold everything in, so that I wouldn't explode. Through therapy, I rediscovered a part of myself that I had lost. Somehow, I felt more whole.

Judy and I also did couples therapy together with other therapists, with whom we earned the nickname "The Bickersons" because of our constant arguments. One session we began complaining about each other's inability to compromise. But they wouldn't allow us to focus on the content of the dispute; instead, they wanted us to feel the anger underneath the words. They suggested we each take the opposite end of a long thick rope and have a tug of war, in order to feel the underlying dynamic.

We each picked up our end of the rope, and I got ready to pull with all my might. Judy saw me and just dropped her end. To me it was a fight to the finish and I was going to win no matter what. But Judy just did not want to fight anymore. I learned that day the importance of the maxim, "Do I want to win? Or do I want to stay married?"

Another time, our therapists asked us to place ourselves in the room in relation to how we wanted to be with each other. Judy just left the room. This jolted me and made me realize that if I didn't change, I was going to lose her. I was going to end up living the rest of my life as a lonely, sad human being.

In my defense, I will say that I threw myself into therapy with all my being. Just the way I did most things over the top, so too I resolved to change myself from the ground up.

TWO YEARS LATER

After I had spent two full years in therapy, I remember a breakthrough moment.

We had dinner in front of the fireplace – Judy, Ilana (then twelve), Sara (then eighteen) and Sholom (then twenty). After dinner, I strummed a little on the guitar, which I had just begun to learn. Then Sara and Sholom started playing on their guitars, jamming and singing together. Sara's voice is high and pure, and as she sang, tears started to stream down my face. I got up from the couch and went and sat next to Judy on the floor. Emotions – all good – washed over me. I felt happy to be alive. I felt thankful for such a beautiful, spiritual family. I felt only love and gratitude. I leaned over and held Judy's hand and said to her, "This is just so beautiful. This is worth preserving. We are so lucky."

I felt so thankful to be alive and to have such a special family. Sara's voice touched me deeply. Her beauty and innocence and yearning for closeness to God could be felt as she sang different Shabbat songs. I got up and went into the living room to pray as the sun was setting, and I was moved to speak to God from the heart and to thank Him for such goodness in my life.

I thought that this is so much more valuable than going out and building another company. To be able to sit here and enjoy the beauty of a loving family is what I truly wanted. This was meaningful and permanent and so much more powerful than throwing myself into a new business. What for? To become rich? To become more power-ful? So people will say, "Wow, Irwin is so smart"? Not a chance.

In my Core Energetics therapy session earlier that day, I had to scream as I tried to shake the hold that money/success had on me. I had to hit to break the grip of its arms around my body and de-mand my life back: "Go away! Leave me alone! I want me!" But it was in the soft strumming of the guitar and the sweetness of my daugh-ter's voice that the shackles were finally released. In that beautiful, quiet moment, a deeper realization was born, one that I had strug-gled with in the intensity of the session.

I now knew that this was the real stuff. The choice was laid out clearly before me. It was a gift from God. I worked hard on getting clarity on that today. The lure of power, of money and of social ap-proval that goes along with wealth is very strong, but the impact of these few moments – when I was surrounded by my family with the fire crackling and my wife by my side – brought the two choices into stark contrast and there was no longer a battle over which choice was the obvious one.

In the past, when I would have such an insight, I would write it up and e-mail it to Judy. This time, I typed it, printed it and went up-stairs, lay down beside her on the bed and read it to her. Tears came again. I felt human. I felt love. I felt close. I enjoyed sharing my feel-ings with her, and it brought me closer to her and closer to the real stuff of life.

It truly was a special moment that I will always cherish. Some-thing clicked inside. I felt real. The warmth of love flowed, and the intimacy of feeling close to another human being warmed my soul.

32

A New Way of Being

The saying goes, "It's not over till the fat lady sings." Well, by the time the fat lady sang and the Mississippi biomass plant formally declared bankruptcy, I was in a decent place financially.

While my partners were on site for years, dealing with the myriad problems of the first-ever torrefaction plant in the US – problems which no mortal was able to solve and make a profit of any kind – I went back to doing ordinary business work. I had no choice; my overwhelming debt and my innate sense of responsibility demanded it. And that proved my salvation.

I took on several consulting jobs, but my best and most satisfying business connection came through the US Department of Commerce. While working on the Odessa project (which ultimately failed due to the worldwide crash of the mortgage market), I made a good impression on Richard Steffens, then the Commerce Department's envoy in the Ukraine. He asked me to co-lead a trade mission to the Republic of Georgia, and – when it came off well – our friendship was forged. Another trade mission to Belarus followed. By the time Rich became the senior commercial officer in the US Consulate in Montreal, we had done several such missions together.

Eventually, Rich brought me on board to assist him in running something called the Certified Trade Mission Program, which was set up to assist fund managers and, at the same time, to bring in foreign capital into the US.

The process is quite simple. Fund managers sign up (through TradeMissions.org) for a mission trip, which I organize. We fly to a foreign country where – through the US Embassy and the US Department of Commerce – we meet potential investors interested in US companies. Fund managers love this because raising capital for a new venture is one of the hardest things in the world. (I do not know anyone who wakes up in the morning, jumps out of bed and says, "Boy, I can't wait to make some cold calls today!") So, this program helps them meet new investors and raise venture capital (VC) from outside the US.

VC typically provides funding for new businesses that do not have access to stock markets and do not have enough cash flow to take on debt. This arrangement can be mutually beneficial because businesses get the capital that they need to bootstrap their operations, and investors gain equity in promising companies. Funding for new ideas and inventions is necessary to bring them to market, and VC is one of the most – if not *the* most – meaningful capital and wealth-building resource available.

Why would the US Department of Commerce want to get involved in helping entrepreneurs raise funds? Because VC plays a critical role in the US economy. For example, in recent decades, VC has generated more economic and employment growth in the US than any other investment sector. Annually, VC delivers an astonishing 21 percent of gross domestic product (GDP) in the form of VC-backed business revenues.

And what does this mean to Joe Public? For one, 7.5 million jobs a year. In 2020 alone, workers in those jobs earned $500 billion in wages and benefits and generated another $900 billion in GDP.

And – music to the ears of any government – these workers paid $141 billion in federal, state and local taxes.

Since I started with this program in 2012, I've organized 68 trade missions and brought over 750 US fund managers to 15 countries where they have met over 10,000 potential investors. In 2023, we went to Geneva, Zurich, London, Dubai, Riyadh, Hong Kong, Singapore, Mexico City, Toronto and Montreal. In each location, I've arranged for each fund manager to meet with anywhere from 35 to 110 potential investors in a "speed-dating" format.

I feel good that I'd helped entrepreneurs raise capital and hopefully avoid some of the disheartening experiences I've had in my career. It has been a meaningful way to give back and, in some small way, to build bridges of understanding among the nations by connecting people from different countries with each other.

I've always run these trade missions as Irwin Katsof and never mentioned to anyone that I was also a rabbi. I figured that would just be confusing to people and, in many parts of Europe, I was afraid of unnecessarily igniting an ugly anti-Semitic response. But a funny incident happened on a recent trip to Singapore when the Deputy Chief of Mission, Stephanie Syptak-Ramnath, who hosted the opening networking dinner at her residence, introduced me as Rabbi Katsof. I was immediately surrounded by the many Singaporeans asking to take photos with me as if I was a celebrity. To them I was! I did not realize that the Jewish people, "the People of the Book," are respected and even revered in Asia. Jews are seen as a holy people by many Hindus and Buddhists, and there is minimal anti-Semitism in the Far East. Much to my surprise, it actually helped me become even more effective, as I was suddenly a sought-after trade mission organizer.

These projects have covered my overhead, and while they've been nothing to get rich on, they allowed me to meet investors around the world and expand my network. Moreover, I got to help people, which I always enjoyed doing. And most importantly for me, I was doing something *good* by introducing investors to projects they might not have otherwise supported, but which the US government deemed would make the world a better place.

COMMITMENT TO ONGOING THERAPY

I was beginning to feel good about myself again. All those years of therapy had helped set me in that direction, but I also realized that working on myself is a lifetime undertaking. Maybe some people can spend two years in therapy and, after confronting some issues stemming from their upbringing or childhood traumas or whatever, they can simply move on. But I've come to realize that this does not describe me. So my goal became deepening my self-awareness and personal consciousness, and never to allow myself to slide down the slippery slope of my neuroses again.

Any form of therapy is hard work. A real slog. Because the ego is so resistant to change. As Rabbi Yisrael Salanter, the 19th-century founder of the Jewish ethical movement known as *mussar*, once said, "It is easier to learn the whole Talmud than to change just one character trait."

In *Ethics of the Fathers*, it is written, "Who is strong? The one who conquers his inclinations." Now, on one level, this could be referring to anyone who is able to control the physical, selfish desires of his body. (Can I learn to become a giver rather than a taker? Can I give a tenth of my earnings to charity rather than keeping it all for myself?) On a deeper level, I believe this is saying that real strength of character comes from being able to make deep changes in one's basic nature.

I had been struggling with that for years. I had put in solid time. I even took a Core Energetics' practitioner-training program where, in addition to the weekly therapy, I went to several retreats a year for four years, putting in an additional 800 hours of intense therapeutic work. Plus, I put in about 100 more hours training to become a teacher of TRE (Tension and Trauma Releasing Exercise). As a result, I certainly gained much greater self-awareness, but the struggle with my nature wasn't over. I felt as compulsive as ever. I needed to do more.

That realization led to a few new – and for me, surprising – places. First, I decided to pursue a Master's Degree in Transpersonal Psychology at Atlantic University. (Atlantic U is private, non-profit distance-learning institution based in Viriginia, and it is an arm of Edgar Cayce's Association for Research and Enlightenment.) Second, I decided to investigate how indigenous people practice the ancient art of accessing the subconscious via psychedelics.

The latter fascination began when I saw in the *Wall Street Journal* – a newspaper I have read daily for most of my adult life – a review of a book by the social anthropologist, Michael Pollan, *How to Change Your Mind: What the New Science of Psychedelics Teaches Us About Consciousness, Dying, Addiction, Depression, and Transcendence.*

I immediately ordered it on Amazon, but if one book on psychedelics was good, then weren't five books even better? I ordered every one I saw. Of course, that was just one indicator of my compulsivity.

Through therapy, I had come to recognize in myself an insatiable thirst for more and more – always. If I became interested in a new topic, one book on it was never enough; I had to buy a half-dozen. When I decided to become physically fit, a little jogging wasn't sufficient; I had to train to run a half-marathon. When I made money for the first time, having one car wasn't enough; I had to have three.

Dr. Gabor Maté, one of the world's foremost psychiatrists and experts on trauma and addiction, talks about this phenomenon in his book, *In the Realm of Hungry Ghosts* – one of the many I had to buy on trauma when I decided to master that topic.

I have a deep hole within me that I keep trying to fill up with things outside of me – whether it was being president of the Loyola U Student Association, or getting President Bill Clinton and Steven Spielberg to attend my banquet, or trying to make enough money so I could give away a million dollars. Why did every project have to be over the top? Why wasn't it enough for me to see a Core Energetics therapist once a week? Why did I have to enroll in a four-year program to become a Core Energetics practitioner, and then, on top of that, a teacher of TRE?

Dr. Maté's talks about the empty hole that so many of us feel at our core – a hole we try to fill up with work, or expensive toys, or serial relationships. All such behaviors have the same root cause – deep within, we feel a sense of emptiness and we either work to avoid it or try to fill it up with things or people.

One of my teachers at Core Energetics, Sam Cagnina, said that he sensed within me a little boy who kept trying to grab the silver spoon which somehow always evaded his grasp. He said this child was always wanting more, more and more! It is a behavioral trait that drives Judy a little crazy at times. When we are on one vacation, I am already planning the next one. She has repeatedly asked me to try to be present on *this* vacation and just to enjoy it without needing to plan the next one. Yet, it is difficult for me to do so, even if I am always working on it.

RESEARCHING PSYCHEDELICS

So, working on it, I devoured Michael Pollan's book over one weekend. It was fascinating and it opened me up to a whole new world of the use of plant-based medicine and psychedelics for mental health purposes. He talked a lot about how the use of such drugs could help people transcend themselves and see the world in totally new ways.

This was important to me. I had felt trapped for years in one mindset or another. Who was the real me? I needed to know. First, I was the student radical, and then the rabbi wanting to change the world, and after that the entrepreneur pursuing wealth and power. But will the real Irwin please stand up?! I really did not know, but I knew I wanted to find inner peace.

Of the different psychedelics described in the Michael Pollan's book, what attracted me most was one called "toad" or "bufo." This drug comes from a rare species of toad native to the Sonoran Desert, *bufo alvarius*, which produces a venom known as 5-MeO-DMT, a poison capable of killing a grown dog. "Toad/bufo" is also an extremely potent natural psychedelic – it is much more powerful than its cousin, the famous hallucinogenic DMT. It is very fast acting, as within seconds of inhaling the vapor, you are transported into an alternative state of consciousness which lasts anywhere from 30 to 45 minutes. It is known as the Mount Everest of psychedelics and, of course, if I was going to start anywhere, it had to be with *the* most intense and frightening!

Currently, "toad/bufo" is being scientifically studied in clinical research. In 2019, a study at Maastricht University in the Netherlands found that a single inhalation of 5-MeO-DMT resulted in the patients' enhanced satisfaction with life and decreased psychopathological symptoms, including depression, anxiety and stress – all of which were sustained for up to four weeks after the initial experience. Similar conclusions were drawn from research done at Johns Hopkins. The Center for Psychedelic Research, at Imperial College London, also looked into it and found patients reporting an ego-death experience which had a radical impact on the users, especially in the case of addiction.

After reading all that, I knew I had to try it. Shortly afterwards, I just happened to hear about John (not his real name), a doctor of pharmacology who administered "toad/bufo" in a controlled setting. When I met him, he told me that he used to work at one of the major NYC hospitals until he got sick and tired of constantly handing out Valium and Prozac to help heal his patients' unhappiness. Somewhere along his journey, he discovered psychedelics and began offering them to those who wanted to try them under medical supervision.

I called him and made an appointment for Judy and me, because we decided to do this together.

When we arrived, John greeted us dressed in a long white shirt, white pants, and a red bandana across his forehead. New Age music was playing in the background. There was a plate on a table where you could leave an offering. How much you gave was up to you.

I was quite nervous and he assured me that the most important thing to do was to surrender to the experience. Not to fight it, or it could be painful.

But surrender was not in my DNA.

Judy stood beside me, while he stood in front of me as he explained the process: I was to take three deep breaths and he would vaporize a small amount of the psychedelic extract and blow it into my mouth and nose, and I was simply to hold it in my lungs as long as I could, and then I was just to relax and allow myself to fall backwards; his assistant would be there to catch me and slowly lower me to the floor. Not that I would be able to stand even if I wanted to.

He then gave me two statements to read. Each consisted of declarations such us: "I accept that the joy I longed for is already in my life. I accept that the love I prayed for is already within me. I accept that the peace I asked for is already my reality." I read slowly, purposefully and with great intention. I knew this was serious.

As soon as he blew the vapor into my mouth and nose, I felt like I had been blasted out of a cannon at a billion miles an hour. I was holding on to the sides of the cannon with all my available strength, but in a second it also became clear to me that it would be impossible to hold on. Yet I did not want to let go. I thought that if I did, I would die. I felt a fear I had never felt before in my life as I tried with all my strength not to let go. My soul was at the edge of the earth's gravitational pull, and the string holding my soul to my body was about to snap.

And then – boom! – the string holding the two together broke and I was catapulted into the outer stratosphere. My ego disintegrated. Everything I knew as Irwin disappeared and I became energy. But it was not that I was aware of Irwin looking at Irwin, because now Irwin was pure energy, nothing more. I was a pure light floating in the heavens. Time and space no longer had meaning and I felt a profound sense of connection with the universe – at one with God. More than ever before, I understood what it meant to be truly accepted and unconditionally loved. I was finally home.

It was a state of bliss.

THE DEEPEST KNOWLEDGE

All we know as long as we are a soul in a body is an experience of duality. There is always "I and thou," as the brilliant Jewish philosopher Martin Buber posited. We are always aware of the "I" – that it is "I" speaking to another. The closest we can ever feel to being one with another is the act of sexual intercourse but, even then, we are aware of the duality of the experience. I am I, separate from you, and you are you.

Yet we all yearn for that sense of connection with God, with the Divine, with the Life Force beyond us and inside us, so that we can somehow transcend our painful separateness. From the moment of our birth, once our souls descend into our body, we feel separate from God. And something just doesn't feel right. We develop many strategies to help eliminate this sense of distance. Through repetition, these strategies become embedded in our personality and character. But this only distances us more from a connection with God, and we continue to strengthen the strategies in an effort to eliminate this distance and the angst that we feel. As a result, we develop a character armor which gets embedded on the molecular level. The effort we make so much of the time, if we are aware, is an effort to get back to a connection with God, but if we are not aware, it is spent running from the angst.

However, everything in this world is really here to teach us about our relationship with God. Our whole life is an effort to become one with God. That is what the *Shema* prayer is all about: "Hear O Israel, the Lord is our God, the Lord is One." Jews are required to say it three times a day – in the morning prayers, the evening prayers, and before going to sleep. It is supposed to be the last thing we say before we die. Why? So that we have one last chance to understand what it means to become one with God before our soul leaves the body.

The material world is a microcosm of the non-material world and is here to teach us how to relate to the Divine. Indeed, the fact that we feel separate from all other human beings and from all creation sets up an inner tension at the deepest level of our being that we spend our whole life running from. We avoid it in various ways like binge-watching TV, consuming food, acquiring material goods, and – at its worst – with compulsions and addictions to gambling, shopping, alcohol, drugs, porn, or the like. We are all running from the deep sense we have of being ultimately alone and separate on this globe, which is spinning at a speed of roughly 1,000 miles per hour.

At the beginning of creation, God said, "It's not good for man to be alone," and so he created Eve from Adam's rib. We are forever trying to connect with that other half of our being, but it is impossible for, ultimately, we *are* alone. We are born alone and we will die alone. But that yearning for oneness, which makes us look for a life partner, is really there to teach us to yearn for oneness with God.

The experience of "toad/bufo" gave me, for the first time, a sense of non-duality. I was one with God. I was pure energy. There was no longer any fear at my core. There was no separateness or aloneness that I needed to avoid by being a workaholic or striving for acceptance through success. My life was perfect as it was. I felt perfect as I was. I felt totally at peace.

After a short period – I was told it was about 25 minutes – I had an awareness of my arm. I touched my arm and hand with a sense of novelty. I had an arm, I had a hand, I had a body. I felt sensation beginnings to return to each limb. I felt a sense of wonder, amazement, pure joy. I now knew that I was a soul in a body, a spark of divinity. A breath of the Divine was enlivening my body. Just as it is written, "God created man in His image … and He blew into his nostrils the breath of life, and man became a living soul."

I looked out the window. I saw the sun slowly setting and felt the power of the Divine infusing nature. Duality had returned to my experiential world, but it was a duality that had just experienced God. I was reminded of the young man I had met in Kiev who had seen God – who had died and been reborn. But whereas he said he couldn't tell me anything about it, I could. I knew that I had been with the Divine. My ego had dissolved for a brief moment in time and I now knew God. The challenge would be to hold onto this knowledge.

I looked over at Judy. She was lying beside me. Her initial experience had been very rough as she fought the ego dissolution stage longer than I did. But as she started to come back into her body, she looked at me, and we both knew each other's souls in the most intimate way possible. Tears filled our eyes. Our hearts were open fully, and we felt intense love, trust, appreciation and respect for each other.

Anything that had happened before to keep us separate was gone and we felt as one. The pettiness of old hurts disintegrated. The need to be right or the winner no longer counted. We had a sense of knowing intensely that we were partners in this life and in eternity. We reached out to each other and took hold of each other's hands gently and stayed like that in silence. We were one with each other as we had both experienced oneness with God. We knew we would never be the same again.

THROUGH THE LOOKING GLASS

Maybe right now you are sitting there and thinking, "Whoa Irwin! Have you gone off the rails? Experimenting with psychedelics? Really?!"

In response, let me direct you to a *New York Times* article, dated October 17, 2019 and entitled, "Taking Ayahuasca When You're a Senior Citizen." That article begins by describing the experience of a venture capitalist – yes, a venture capitalist! – George Sarlo, age 74, with ayahuasca, a psychedelic brew made from a vine called *banisteriopsis caapi*, which is native to the Amazon and which has been used there for healing since time immemorial. The *New York Times* goes on to report on the growing popularity of psychedelic use among staid, conservative people, even those in their twilight years like Mr. Sarlo:

Ayahuasca tourism is thriving, with more and more people happy to fly thousands of miles to take part in weeklong ceremonies in Peruvian jungles, or to seek out more luxurious contexts, like a four-star resort that comes complete with masseuses, pools, and state of the art fitness centers. And, notably, ayahuasca's increasing popularity knows no age limits: many of those now showing interest are squarely in Mr. Sarlo's own demographic.

These seniors and many others who flock to retreats in Mexico, Costa Rica and Peru are only the latest group to discover the benefits of psychedelics. Researchers at top-tier medical schools like Harvard, Yale, Stanford, Mount Sinai and Johns Hopkins have been way ahead of them, judging by the number of articles on the subject appearing in the *New England Journal of Medicine* and *Nature*.

Indeed, psychedelics have become one of the hottest topics in mental health and at least one – ketamine (previously known as a "horse tranquilizer") – has won FDA approval for compassionate use in treating post-traumatic stress disorder (PTSD), obsessive-compulsive disorder (OCD) and treatment-resistant depression. Two other psychedelics – MDMA (commonly called "ecstasy") and psilocybin ("magic mushrooms") – are in line for approval as well.

According to another article in the *New York Times* – "The Psychedelic Revolution is Coming; Psychiatry May Never Be the Same," dated May 9, 2021 – "Psilocybin and MDMA are poised to be the hottest new therapeutics since Prozac. Universities want in, and so does Wall Street." The article reports that Johns Hopkins has founded a Center for Psychedelic and Consciousness Research, having invested $17 million in the project, and is studying the application of psilocybin for the treatment of depression and Alzheimer's. It quotes Dr. Roland R. Griffiths, the center's founding director: "We have to be careful not to overpromise, but these are fantastically interesting compounds with numerous possible uses."

Prince Harry, in his memoir *Spare*, speaks at length about his experiences with medically-supervised use of psychedelics to treat his trauma and depression brought on by the violent death of his mother, Princess Diana. He couldn't be more positive about the result, as he writes: "They didn't simply allow me to escape reality for a while, they let me *redefine* reality."

In a recent interview on the vlog headlined, *Out of the Shadows: Jewish Approach to Mental Health*, Dr. Jacob Freedman, a board-certified psychiatrist practicing in Massachusetts and Israel, stated that if asked to discuss the benefits of psychedelics ten years ago, he would have said, "You are crazy!" And even two years ago, he would have said "Absolutely not!" But since then, he has changed his mind because scientific research has shown that certain psychedelics can be life-saving. He stressed that their use needs to be supervised by qualified professionals, but their benefits can no longer be denied.

And I can testify to that.

Carl Jung famously said, "The first half of life is devoted to forming a healthy ego, the second half of life is going inward and letting go of it." My initial experience with "toad/bufo" showed me how good letting go of the ego was for me – even more, how much I needed to do this.

Was it a shortcut to oneness with God, who demands that the relationship with Him be won the hard way – by living a moral life, by being "holy"? Possibly. That is a question I have yet to answer for myself.

What I do know is that I did gain invaluable insights from my experience, though I recognize that my problems and my path to solving them are not for everyone and, for some, may be dangerous spiritually.

As for me, I felt I had learned one of the deepest and most important lessons of my life. Not the least of which was that God does guide my every step.

Conclusion:
Only the Best of Times

In October of 2019, Judy and I rented a house in Jerusalem to spend more time with our kids, seven of whom were living in Israel by then, along with eighteen of our grandkids. And when Covid hit six months later, we got stranded there. So, we decided to make it permanent – we became Israeli citizens. Our decision coincided with our fortieth wedding anniversary, which reminded me that, three thousand years ago, the Israelites wandered in the desert for forty years before settling in the Promised Land, and it had taken us that long too.

This led us to another decision – to buy a home in Jerusalem. Although we had scaled down our expenditures, I had made some money by investing in bitcoin, and we could afford something decent.

The interesting thing about investing in bitcoin is that I had no idea how it worked, but my son Jacob had become a Blockchain evangelist and urged me to go for it. So, I took a chance. In retrospect, I can see that the gambling streak was still active in me – the part that wanted to get rich quick and thought that I could beat the system. This time, I actually did do well. It's as if God saw I had learned the painful lessons I needed to learn and rewarded me at last.

My bitcoin returns allowed me to put a down payment on a home in a part of Jerusalem called French Hill, which adjoins the campus of Hebrew University on Mount Scopus. Homes there are a lot less expensive than where we had previously rented – Talbiyeh, the neighborhood that boasts the residences of the President of Israel as well as the Prime Minister – but we would be closer to where our daughters Batya, Sara and Ilana live with their families. Indeed, we'd be a five-minute walk from each of them and a five-minute drive from our son Sholom and his family

We found a small cottage, which we called our "midget cottage" as it was much smaller than anything we had ever lived in before. It had been built cheaply in the 1970s, so it was over fifty years old and tired, and it would require a lot of renovation. These took a year! (Don't ask me why – it's Israel.) But we moved in at last and are very happy to have scaled down.

A long time ago, my friend Lewis Katz advised me not to try for a home run in business, but to let myself be satisfied with getting onto first base. I am on first base with a variety of business ventures and am happy to let God decide if any of them will get me to second base.

In addition, I have various consulting deals going and I am running trade missions for the US Department of Commerce. I get a great deal of satisfaction from this and I feel that I am doing something good for the world by connecting investors and entrepreneurs worldwide and building bridges between many different nations.

In the future, I want to return to helping people grow spiritually and emotionally. Toward that goal, I've earned an MA degree from Atlantic University in Transpersonal Psychology, with a multi-faceted focus on dream interpretation, meditation, plant-based medicine, therapeutic breathwork, spiritual crisis intervention and spiritual mentorship. In addition, I have become certified as both a Core Energetics and a TRE practitioner. And, of course, I am still an ordained rabbi.

I think I have enough credentials, training and experience to establish a practice in a helping profession – to become a counselor or life coach. I do not see myself as a community rabbi, but I do want to help people discover their path to themselves and to a greater spirituality. I keep thinking about what God said to Abraham when He asked him to break new ground: "Go for *yourself*, from your land, from your birthplace, from your father's house, to a land that I will show you."

ME TODAY

Back in March of 2012, when I walked into a Jungian analyst's office for the first time, he asked me what brought me to him. I explained that I have a beautiful wife, amazing children and grandchildren, that I'd actually made some money for the first time in my life, and that I had all the toys and security I could want, and yet I was miserable.

For the next eleven years, I moved from Jungian analysis to Core Energetics to psychodrama, couples therapy, the Hoffman Process, meditation training, Enneagram workshops and plant-based medicine. For the past three years I have been working with an amazing and wise Hakomi therapist – who has a strong background in trauma and family therapy and who uses a mix of Eastern/Western techniques – as I have continued to cope with my inner turmoil.

There has always been a little voice inside of me telling me that I am not good enough, smart enough, successful enough, or rich enough, and that voice was driving me to accomplish the impossible, which just led me to feel more angst.

But not anymore! I am finally at peace with myself.

I realized this one day in July 2023, when my therapist asked me what I wanted to accomplish in that day's session.

When she had asked me this question in the past, I would routinely bring up my desire to work on one of my many issues – my regrets for all the lost years of chasing success and not being present for my wife and children, my disconnection from myself and distance from God, my sadness at all the lost opportunities in work and life, or my anxieties about aging and fears of becoming sick and infirm.

This day was different. When she asked me what I wanted to accomplish in this session, I said that I didn't really know. She followed up by asking what I was feeling, and I said that I felt content. When I heard those words come out of my mouth, I sat back in surprise.

Yes! I really do feel content with my life. I am happy just where I am. It is a new and strange sensation. For a change, nothing is lacking and nothing is wrong. It is so novel that I almost have trouble believing it. For so many years, the one constant in my life was feeling the knots in my stomach. I would wake up with them and go to bed with them. My life was a series of crises, going from deal to deal, disappointment to disappointment, living on the edge of one financial disaster or another, defaulting on credit cards and other debts. For many of those years, I had a closer relationship with my cellphone than with my wife.

I sat there in silence, trying to come to terms with this new sensation in my belly — not the usual ball of pressure, which I know to be anxiety, but a new sense of calm and quiet. I said, "I do not really know what to say, except that I feel at peace." In that moment I felt that, after all the hard work I have put in, I had become a different person, a better person, the person I always wanted to be.

Psychologist Stephen M. Johnson, the author of *Characterological Transformation: The Hard Work Miracle*, says that changing your character requires persistence, consistency and bravery, and when it happens, it is truly a miracle.

To stare in the mirror and say, "I don't like who I have become and I want to be different," is not for the faint of heart. But to really become different requires not only hard work but also the grace of God, and that is why it truly is "the hard work miracle."

I have been working toward that miracle for a number of years, and I'd committed to transform myself with all the power I could muster. It meant life or death to me. And I think that I was able to get there because of my particular strengths and weaknesses which actually boil down to the same thing. It is true what they say – that your greatest strength is also your greatest weakness. In my case, my aggressiveness and tenacity allowed me to accomplish much in life, but these very traits got me into trouble, because I couldn't walk away from a deal when I should have. More recently, these traits have served me well when I committed my heart and soul to personal transformation. As a result, I am a better person, a more loving husband and father, and more connected to my soul and to God.

That's not to imply that there are no issues in my life. I do have tons of responsibilities to live up to, but they don't cause me as much anxiety as before. The main difference is that nowadays I feel at peace – if not all the time, then a lot of the time and maybe even most of the time.

Being alive means that there will be stresses on the system – that is the way of our organism. The only time we flatline biologically or emotionally is if we are dead or on Thorazine. Being at peace does not mean I sit in a Buddha-like state of tranquility or that I don't feel any stress, anxiety, worry, fear, sadness or anger. What it means is that I can make space for the different emotions as they arise through the normal course of my day.

I have been able to build my personal vessel to be large enough that I can hold my feelings and allow them to be present without triggering in me an overreaction. In the past, when I felt distressing emotions, it was a call to action to repress them – to get busy, to find distractions, to project and reject – and that often resulted in frenetic and compulsive activity.

Through excellent therapeutic guidance and much hard work on my part, I have come to a place in life where I can now allow whatever emotion is there to be there and just to accept it, get to know it, with curiosity and self-love. Not *all* the time, but a lot of the time. And that is okay. I no longer need perfection. My best effort will suffice. I am loveable and good just the way I am! Doing the best that I can do is also okay. It is a journey. It is simply putting one foot in front of the other each day.

As I walk my new-found path, I have a sense that God is with me and everything is going to be okay. I am happy with my lot in life and I don't crave more.

There is a beautiful story told in the Book of Genesis about the meeting between Jacob and his brother Esau. It was a dramatic meeting, as the brothers had been estranged for many years, and Jacob feared that Esau still nursed his murderous rage over the blessing of the first-born which Jacob had usurped. So, Jacob hoped to soften up his angry brother by bringing an over-the-top gift of some 500 goats, sheep, camels, cows and donkeys. As it turned out, Esau welcomed him back with open arms and declined the gift, by saying: "I have *plenty* my brother … Let what is yours remain yours." To which Jacob replied, "Please accept my gift as it has been brought to you. God has been kind to me and I have *everything*." (Esau took it.)

The Talmudic sages comment on the choice of words used by Esau and Jacob, noting that they illustrate the difference in their characters. Esau said, "I have *plenty*," which implies, "Yes, I have a lot, but I still want more." But Jacob said, "I have *everything*," which implies, "I want nothing more."

Through a lot of hard personal work on myself, I have gotten to the point in my life's journey where I can honestly echo the words of Jacob:

"I have everything. I have what God wants me to have, and it is enough."

Acknowledgments

First of all, I must express my undying gratitude to my teacher and mentor, Rabbi Noah Weinberg of blessed memory, to whom I owe so much. He was a giant among men, a visionary, a true leader and an inspirational giant who connected me to my Jewish roots and helped me establish a relationship with God.

Next, my thanks go to my editor, Uriela Obst Sagiv. There really are no words to describe her talent. Over the ten years it took to produce this book, she motivated me, guided me, inspired me with her steady hand and skills. She put the many different stories of my life together and knit them into a whole. This book would not have been possible without her.

I also must thank my eight children – Batya, Aaron Yosef, Yakov, Simcha, Bracha, Sholom, Sara and Ilana – who have been the light of my life. For many years, as they were growing up, I was absent – busy trying to make a living, building many different organizations, and I deeply regret not being a greater part of their lives. I am working on making that up to them now. I love and respect each one of them and their amazing spouses, my children through marriage – Yoni, Rifka, Jenny, Chaya Rachel, Aviva, Mendel and Nosson.

I am also working on being present in the lives of my twenty-five amazing grandchildren, who have become my greatest joy in life. No words can describe the pleasure I get from just seeing them smile, watching them grow.

All of you – thank you for being there for me!

But my greatest thanks go to my wife Judy. She has stood by my side and supported me through forty-two years of marriage. Everything I have accomplished is because of her support, loyalty and strength. She has been both my rudder and anchor and kept me connected when I was drifting away. She brought into the world and raised our eight beautiful children and for that I am forever indebted to her. She is the matriarch of our family.

Judy – I love you now and forever!

About the Author

Irwin Katsof is the president of Trademissions.org, which – in cooperation with the US Department of Commerce – organizes trade missions to foreign countries for American alternative asset fund managers to help them seek out new sources of capital and, at the same time, do global good

Prior to becoming a businessman, Irwin was a rabbi and fundraiser for the Jewish outreach organization, Aish HaTorah. In addition to *Living Dangerously*, his memoir, he has written three books: *Powerful Prayers*, co-authored with Larry King; *How to Get Your Prayers Answered*; and *The Words Can Heal Handbook*.

Irwin holds a Master's Degree from Atlantic University in Transpersonal Psychology with a specialty in Applied Spirituality. He has eight children and twenty-five grandchildren and has been married to his wife, Judy, for forty-two years. He splits his time between Rockland County, New York and Jerusalem, Israel.

www.ingramcontent.com/pod-product-compliance
Lightning Source LLC
Chambersburg PA
CBHW060757120626
46557CB00001B/5